The Best

Of

SPORTS AFIELD

The Best

Of

SPORTS AFIELD

The Greatest
Outdoor Writing
of the 20th Century

EDITED BY JAY CASSELL
&
the Editors of
Sports Afield

The Atlantic Monthly Press
New York

Printed in the United States of America

DESIGN BY GARY GRETTER
Library of Congress Cataloging-in-Publication Data
The best of Sports afield: the greatest outdoor writing of the 20th century/
edited by Jay Cassell & the editors of Sports afield—1st ed.
p. cm.
ISBN 0-87113-644-9
1. Hunting. 2. Fishing. 3. Outdoor life. I. Cassell, Jay. II. Sports afield
SK33.B48 1996
799—dc20 96-20342

Acknowledgment is given to the following for use in the book: "My Old Kentucky Gobbler" copyright © 1972 used by permission of Douglas Harbour; "Ghost Trout" copyright © 1945 used by permission of Dr. William Halstead; "Deadliest Creature on Earth" copyright © 1970 used by permission of Mary Louise Scott; "The Saga of Veenie Holbrook" copyright © 1958 used by permission of Grace E. Janes; "North Umpqua Steelheads" copyright © 1935 used by permission of Dr. Loren Grey; "The Year the Brown Bear Went Mad" copyright © 1960 used by permission of Mrs. Gil Paust; "Horns of Gold" copyright © 1978 used by permission of Anna Jobson; "Annie Oakley Ruled the Traps" copyright © 1926, "A Duck Hunt with Clark Gable" copyright © 1939 and "Silver Cans" copyright © 1956 used by permission of Clara Robinson; "This Was My Alaska" copyright © 1977 used by permission of Joan Salvato Wulff; "Hunt the Old West (Part 1)" and "Hunt the Old West (Part 2)" copyright © 1960 used by permission of Bradford Angier; "Trail's End" copyright © 1933 and "Shift of the Wind" copyright © 1944 used by permission of Sigurd T. Olson and Robert K. Olson; "The Old Brown Mackinaw" copyright © 1956 used by permission of Ellen MacQuarrie Wilson; "$7,000,000 Adventure with Bears" copyright ©1969 used by permission of Ludo Wurfbain; "Hunting Is More Fun than Killing" copyright © 1949, renewed 1977 by Jean Bethell Gardner; "Upstream or Down?" copyright © 1949 used by permission of Franklin G. Wade, P.O.A.; "Breamers Stop at Nothing" copyright © 1950 used by permission of Havilah Babcock, Jr.; "Africa's Big Five" copyright © 1960 used by permission of Lorraine K. Keith by Theodore F. Keith.

Special thanks go to the following people, whose help was invaluable in the making of this book: Carol Cammero, Fred Kesting, Lorraine Loughran, Terry McDonell, Tom Paugh and Lamar Underwood.

To my son, James, and my daughter, Katherine: May they grow up
appreciating the outdoors, and all it has to offer.—J.C.

Atlantic Monthly Press
841 Broadway
New York, NY 10003

10 9 8 7 6 5 4 3 2 1

C O N T E N T S

THE STORY OF SPORTS AFIELD

This book is a celebration, a tribute to the greatest outdoor writing of the 20th Century. Picking the best stories from more than 100 years' worth of magazines was not easy. Each story, we decided, should teach, but also entertain. Each should put the reader into the writer's shoes (or waders). Each should be a sample of the writing of its day.

There are 50 stories in this collection, all examples of hunting, fishing and adventure prose at its finest, by authors whom readers of *Sports Afield* will recognize: Jimmy Robinson (1926); Zane Grey (1935); Nash Buckingham (1945); Erle Stanley Gardner (1949); Elmer Keith (1960); Russell Annabel (1969); Red Smith (1972); Thomas McIntyre (1981); Thomas McGuane (1995); and more.

Credit for these stories must not go just to the great writers who wrote them, but also to the editors of *Sports Afield*, for without their judgment, none of them would have been published in the first place. To put these articles into perspective, then, to see how they were originally chosen, and how, taken together, they form the foundation for the magazine you see on the newsstand today, let's look at the story of *Sports Afield*. It's a magazine that has influenced the lives of outdoorsmen throughout the 20th Century...

The oldest outdoor publication in North America, *Sports Afield* was founded in 1887 by Claude King. The first issue, in January of 1888, was eight pages long and printed on newspaper stock, out of Denver, Colorado.

The "Journal for Gentlemen" promised, in King's words, "To be devoted to hunting, fishing, rifle and trap shooting, the breeding of thorough-bred dogs, cycling and kindred sports . . ." The subscription price was $1.50 per year, with single copies selling for 15 cents.

A few years later, King expounded on his philosophy: "*Sports Afield*—has an ambition above that of simply entertaining and amusing the public; it wants to help propagate the true spirit of gentle sportsmanship, to encourage indulgence in outdoor recreations and to assist in the dissemination of knowledge regarding natural history, photography, firearms and kindred subjects."

Before the decade was out, *Sports Afield* had expanded and moved its operations to Chicago. The magazine grew quickly, with some issues running 96 pages. It soon became not only a voice of the West, but a spokesman for hunters, fishermen, campers and shooters across the U.S. Other magazines—including some current competitors—entered the market, but *Sports Afield*'s commitment to strong, intelligent outdoor writing separated it from the pack.

By 1927, when King stepped down as editor and turned the reins over to Joe Godfrey, *SA* was in full stride. Zane Grey started writing for the magazine, as did Jimmy Robinson, beginning a 60-year association with the publication. In 1930, Ivan B. Romig and his associates took over *Sports Afield*, combined it with a smaller publication—*Trails of the Northwoods*—and moved the offices to Minneapolis. A string of editors worked the helm of *Sports Afield*, which struggled during the Depression years to stay afloat. It did, and by 1934 the magazine was in the black.

Long before conservation issues became politically correct, *SA* was speaking out, trying to make the public aware of environmental concerns. Its credo: "We believe in sane conservation, will oppose pollution, and stand for the enforcement of our game laws."

More quality writers appeared toward the end of the 1930s; Gordon MacQuarrie and Archibald Rutledge were just two of many headliners. Many followed through on the conservation theme. The circulation rose to 250,000, and the magazine topped the 100-page mark. Nash Buckingham started writing during World War II, a time when citizens looked to *Sports Afield* as an escape from the trying times—and when, overseas, GIs read the magazine to remind them of home.

In 1945 Ted Kesting, an associate editor on *Country Gentleman* magazine, was hired as editorial director and brought from Philadelphia to Minneapolis. His assignment was to expand and modernize the venerable *Sports Afield*. At 26 years of age he was the youngest editor of a major national publication in the U.S.

Kesting soon discovered there was a sameness to all of the major outdoor magazines: many topics were similar each month, photos were poor, good writers rare. To set *Sports Afield* apart, Kesting signed up more solid writers. One he brought on board was angling editor Jason Lucas, whose writings about bass fishing became legendary. Another was mystery writer Erle Stanley Gardner, who became known for his articles defending gun owners and hunters' rights. By October 1948 *Time* magazine reported that "*Sports Afield* has become the biggest of all outdoor monthlies. Last week it put to bed a November issue that would go to 800,000 customers, a record for its 61 years. Colorful as a hatband full of flies, it was filled with picture stories and crackling adventure stuff. . . ."

In 1953 the publishing giant Hearst Magazines tendered an offer to Walter Taylor, the publisher. It wanted the best magazine in the expanding outdoor field and offered to buy it, providing Kesting and his staff came along. The sale was made, and *Sports Afield* moved its offices to New York City.

Meanwhile, the magazine continued to grow, attracting such writers as Col. Townsend Whelen, Jack Denton Scott and Russell Annabel. Circulation hit the 1,100,000 mark in 1961. By the late 1960s Homer Circle, Tom Paugh and Zack Taylor had joined the ranks. The cover price jumped from 35 to 50 cents a copy.

In 1970 Kesting announced he was stepping down after 25 years as editor and named Lamar Underwood as his replacement. Under Underwood's guidance, the likes of Gene Hill, Nick Lyons, Vance Bourjaily and John Madson all appeared in the periodical's pages. The Almanac came into existence in 1972 and was an immediate hit with readers.

Eventually, Underwood moved on, to be replaced by saltwater editor Tom Paugh. The Paugh years saw major redesigns, plus a downsizing in circulation as the magazine adjusted to the competitive times. Grits Gresham, Thomas McIntyre, Ted Kerasote and Anthony Acerrano all brought their expertise to the magazine, which continued to publish not only exciting adventure stories mixed with well-informed how-to-do-it pieces, but to comment on conservation issues as well.

As Paugh stated in his *Adventures in Editing* column in October 1987, the issue that commemorated the 100th anniversary of the founding of the magazine, "You have our promise to bring to you each month the best of what the world of hunting and fishing has to offer." Paugh kept that vow until his retirement in 1994, when a new editor and publisher, Terry McDonell, came from *Esquire* magazine and devoted himself to leading *Sports Afield* into its second century. To keep the magazine at the forefront of sporting literature, McDonell has brought in such writers as Thomas McGuane, Guy de la Valdéne and Ian Frazier.

Ultimately, what is at the heart of any successful magazine is people; and in this, *Sports Afield* has no equal. Throughout the years, the magazine has always had a staff devoted to the outdoors, to hunting, fishing and camping, and to the preservation of those sports for future generations. Hence this book . . . more than 100 years in the making. We have searched through all the back issues, and have tried to cover as many subjects as possible—although, of course, it is impossible to cover 108 years in one book. Some of your favorite authors also may be missing. Archibald Rutledge and Jason Lucas are two standouts whose works couldn't be shoehorned in. You'll have to wait until Volume II for them; but don't worry, you'll see them eventually. The sports covered in the magazine—duck hunting, deer hunting, bass and trout fishing—are so evocative, so popular, that they will always elicit good writing. And we plan to be here, to publish those stories for you.—*JAY CASSELL*

Hunting

Africa, Alaska and Canada are the settings for many of the best hunting stories to appear in the magazine. (Don't miss BUFF, by Thomas McIntyre, 1981; and HORNS OF GOLD, by John Jobson, 1978). But when you read the stories that take place in less exotic settings (duck hunting in SHIFT OF THE WIND, Sig Olson, 1944; HUNT THE OLD WEST, Col. Townsend Whelen, 1960; upland birds in IN FIELDS NEAR HOME, Vance Bourjaily, 1970), you'll realize how good we've got it in our own backyards.

••• *A naturalist and environmentalist, Sig Olson wrote of hunting in his early years as dean of Ely Junior College. He eventually went on to write such classic books as* THE SINGING WILDERNESS *and* REFLECTIONS FROM THE NORTH COUNTRY, *and became famous for, among other things, protecting the Boundary Waters Canoe Area in Minnesota. Here, he writes of a whitetail buck—a swamp buck—surviving hunting season. Olson was 34 when he wrote this.*
—OCTOBER 1933 •••

TRAIL'S END by Sig Olson

It was early morning in the northern wilderness, one of those rare breathless mornings, that come only in November, and though it was not yet light enough to see, the birds were stirring. A covey of partridge whirred up from their cozy burrows in the snow and lit in the top of a white birch, where they feasted noisily upon the frozen brown buds. The rolling tattoo of a downy woodpecker, also looking for his breakfast, reverberated again and again through the timber.

They were not the only ones astir however, for far down the trail leading from the Tamarack Swamp to Kennedy Lake browsed a big buck. He worked his way leisurely along, stopping now and then to scratch away the fresh snow and nibble daintily the still tender green things underneath. A large buck he was, even as deer run, and as smooth and sleek as good feeding could make him. His horns, almost too large, were queerly shaped, for instead of being rounded as in other deer, they were broad and palmate, the horns of a true swamp buck.

The eastern skyline was just beginning to tint with lavender as he reached the summit of the ridge overlooking the lake. He stopped for his usual morning survey of the landscape below him. For some reason, ever since his spike-buck days, he had always stopped there to look the country over before working down to water. He did not know that for countless generations before him, in the days when the pine timber stood tall and gloomy round the shores of the lake, other swamp bucks had also stopped, to scent the wind and listen, before going down to drink.

As he stood on the crest of the ridge, his gaze took in the long reaches of dark blue water far below him; the ice rimmed shores with long white windfalls reaching like frozen fingers out into the shallows, and the mottled green and gray of the brush covered slopes. His attention was finally centered on a little log cabin tucked away on the opposite shore in a clump of second growth spruce and balsam. Straight above it rose a thin wreath of pale blue smoke, almost as blue as the clear morning air. The metallic chuck, chuck of an axe ringing on a dry log came clearly across the water, and a breath of air brought to him strange odors that somehow filled him with a vague misgiving.

He was fascinated by the cabin and could not take his gaze from it. On other mornings, it had seemed as much a part of the shoreline as the trees themselves, but now it was different. A flood of almost forgotten memories surged back to him, of days long ago, when similar odors and sounds had brought with them a danger far greater than that of any natural enemy. He rubbed the top of a low hazel bush and stamped his forefeet nervously, undecided what to do. Then, in a flash, the full realization came to him. He understood the meaning of it all. This was the season of the year when man was no longer his friend, and it was not safe to be seen in the logging roads or in the open clearings near the log houses. He sniffed the air keenly a moment longer, to be sure, then snorted loudly as if to warn all the wilderness folk of their danger, and bounded back up the trail the way he had come.

Not until he had regained the heavy protecting timber of the Tamarack Swamp, north of Kennedy Lake, did he feel safe. What he had seen, made him once again the wary old buck who had lived by his cunning and strength through many a hunting season. Although he was safe for the time being, he was too experienced not to know, that before many days had passed, the Tamarack Swamp would no longer be a haven of refuge.

As he worked deeper into the heavy moss hung timber, he stopped frequently to look into the shadows. The trail here was knee-deep in moss and criss-crossed by a labyrinth of narrow rabbit runways. Soon his search was rewarded, for a sleek yearling doe met him at a place where two trails crossed. After nosing each other tenderly, by way of recognition, they began feeding together on the tender shoots of blueberries and still green tufts of swamp grass underneath the protecting blanket of snow.

All that morning they fed leisurely and when the sun was high in the heavens, they worked cautiously over to the edge of the swamp. Here was a warm sunny opening hedged in by huge windfalls grown over with a dense tangle of blackberry vines. They often came here for their afternoon sunning, as the ice-encrusted ovals in the snow attested. Leaping a big windfall that guarded the entrance to the opening, they carefully examined the ground, then picked their beds close together. There they rested contentedly with the warm sun shining upon them, little thinking that soon their peace would be broken.

The snow had fallen early that autumn and good feed had been scarce everywhere, except in the depths of the Tamarack Swamp, where the protecting timber had sheltered the grass and small green things. The plague had killed off most of the rabbits, and the few which survived were already forced to feed upon the bark of the poplar. The heavy crust, forming suddenly the night after the first heavy snow, had imprisoned countless partridge and grouse in their tunnels. As a result, small game was scarce and the wolves were lean and gaunt, although it was yet hardly winter. The stark famine months ahead gave promise of nothing but starvation and death, and the weird discordant music of the wolf pack had sounded almost every night since the last full moon.

The swamp buck and his doe had not as yet felt the pinch of hunger, but instinct told them to keep close to the shelter of the Tamarack Swamp, so except for the morning strolls of the buck to the shore of Kennedy Lake, they had seldom ventured far from the timber. They had often heard the wolf pack, but always so far away that there was little danger as long as they stayed under cover.

Several days had passed since the buck had been to the shore of Kennedy Lake. As yet the silence of the swamp had been unbroken except for the crunching of their own hoofs through the icy crust on the trails, and the buck was beginning to wonder if there was really anything to fear. Then one day, as they were again leisurely working their way over to the sunning place in the clearing, they were startled by the strange noises far toward the east end of the swamp. They stopped, every nerve on edge. At times they could hear them quite plainly, then again they would be so faint as to be almost indistinguishable from the other sounds of the forest.

The two deer were not much concerned at first. After satisfying themselves that there was no real danger, they started again down the trail toward the clearing. They could still hear the noises occasionally, but could not tell whether they were coming closer or going further away.

Then just as they neared the edge of the swamp, the sound of heavy footsteps seemed suddenly to grow louder and more distinct. Once more they stopped and stood with heads high, ears pricked up, listening intently. This time they were thoroughly alarmed. Closer and closer came the racket. Now they could hear distinctly the crunching of snow and the crackling of twigs, and then the whole east end of the timber seemed to be fairly alive with tumult, and the air reeked with danger.

The buck ran in a circle, sniffing keenly. The same scent that had come to him from the cabin, now rankled heavily in the air, and he knew the time had come to leave the shelter of the Tamarack Swamp. He hesitated, however, not knowing which way to turn. Back and forth he ran, stopping now and then to paw the ground, or to blow the air through his nostrils with the sharp whistling noise that all deer use when in danger.

A branch cracked sharply close at hand, and the scent came doubly strong from the east. With a wild snort the buck wheeled and led the way toward the western end of the swamp followed closely by the doe. Their only hope lay in reaching a heavy belt of green hemlock timber which they knew was separated from the western end of the Tamarack Swamp by a broad stretch of barren, burned-over slashing. As they neared the edge of the swamp they stopped, dreading to leave its protection. From where they stood they could see the dark wall of timber half a mile away. A brushy gully ran diagonally toward it across the open slashing, offering some protection, but the hills on either side were as stark and bare as an open field.

Again came the crack and crunch, now so close that the very air burned with danger. It was time to go. They bounded out of the timber, their white flags waving defiance, and were soon in the brush gully, going like the wind. Just as they sailed over a windfall, the buck caught a glimpse of something moving on a big black pine stump on top of the ridge to their right. Then the quiet was shattered by a succession of rending crashes and strange singing and whining sounds filled the air above them.

Again and again came the crashes. Suddenly the little doe stopped dead in her tracks. She gave a frightened baa-aa-a of pain and terror as the blood burst in a stream from a jagged wound in her throat. The buck stopped and ran back to where she stood, head down and swaying unsteadily. He watched her a moment, then, growing nervous, started down the trail again. The doe tried bravely to follow, but fell half way across a windfall too high for her to clear. Again the buck stopped and watched her anxiously. The snow by the windfall was soon stained bright red with blood, and the head of the little doe sank lower and lower in spite of her brave efforts to hold it up.

Hurriedly the buck looked about him. Several black figures were coming rapidly down the ridge. He nosed his doe gently, but this time she did not move. Raising his head he looked toward the approaching figures. Danger was close, but he could not leave his mate.

A spurt of smoke came from one of the figures, followed by another crash. This time the buck felt a blow so sharp that it made him stumble. Staggering to his feet, he plunged blindly down the gully. His flag was down, the sure sign of a wounded deer. Again and again came the crashes and the air above him whined and sang as the leaden pellets searched for their mark. The bark flew from a birch tree close by, spattering him with fragments. In spite of his wound, he ran swiftly and was soon out of range in the protecting green timber. He knew that he would not be tracked for at least an hour, as his pursuers would wait for him to lie down and stiffen.

He was bleeding badly from a long red scar cutting across his flank, and his back trail was sprinkled with tiny red dots. Where he stopped to rest and listen, little puddles of blood would form that quickly turned bluish black in the snow. For two hours he ran steadily, and then was so weakened by loss of blood that at last he was forced to lie down.

After a short rest, he staggered to his feet, stiffened badly. The bed he had melted in the snow was stained dark red from his bleeding flank. The cold, however, had contracted the wound and had stopped the bleeding a little. He limped painfully down the trail, not caring much which direction it led. Every step was torture. Once when crossing a small gully, he stumbled and fell on his wounded leg. It rested him to lie there, and it was all he could do to force himself on.

While crossing a ridge, the wind bore the man scent strongly to him, and he knew that now he was being trailed. Once, he heard the brush crack behind him, and was so startled that the wound was jerked open and the bleeding started afresh. He watched his back trail nervously, expecting to see his pursuer at any moment and hear again the rending crash that would mean death.

He grew steadily weaker and knew that unless night came soon, he would be overtaken. He had to rest more often now, and when he did move it was to stagger aimlessly down the trail, stumbling on roots and stubs. It was much easier now to walk around the windfalls, than to try to jump over as he had always done before.

The shadows were growing longer and longer, and in the hollows it was already getting dusk. If he could last until nightfall he would be safe. But the man scent was getting still stronger, and he realized at last that speed alone could not save him. Strategy was the only course. If his pursuer could be thrown off the trail, only long enough to delay him half an hour, darkness would be upon the wilderness and he could rest.

So waiting until the trail ran down onto a steep ravine filled with brush and windfalls, the buck suddenly turned and walked back on his own trail as far as he dared. It was the old trick of back tracking that deer have used for ages to elude their pursuers. Then stopping suddenly, he jumped as far to the side as his strength would permit, landing with all four feet tightly bunched together in the very center of a scrubby hazel bush. From there, he worked his way slowly into a patch of scrub spruce and lay down exhausted under an old windfall. Weakened as he was from loss of blood and from the throbbing pain in his flank, it was all he could do to keep his eyes riveted on his back trail, and his ears strained for the rustling and crunching that he feared would come, unless darkness came first.

It seemed that he had barely lain down, when without warning, the brush cracked sharply, and not 100 yards away appeared a black figure. The buck was petrified with terror. His ruse had failed. He shrank as far down as he could in the grass under the windfall and his eyes almost burst from their sockets. Frantically he thought of leaving his hiding place, but knew that would only invite death. The figure came closer and closer, bending low over the trail and peering keenly into the spruce thicket ahead. In the fading light the buck was well hidden by the windfall, but the blood spattered trail led straight to his hiding place. Discovery seemed certain.

The figure picked its way still nearer. It was now within 30 feet of the windfall. The buck watched, hardly daring to breathe. Then, in order to get a better view into the thicket, the hunter started to climb a snow covered stump close by. Suddenly, losing his balance, he slipped and plunged backwards into the snow. The buck saw his chance. Gathering all his remaining strength, he dashed out of his cover and was soon hidden in the thick growth of spruce.

It was almost dark now and he knew that as far as the hunter was concerned, he was safe. Circling slowly around, he soon found a sheltered hiding place in a dense clump of spruce where he could rest and allow his wound to heal.

Night came swiftly, bringing with it protection and peace. The stars came out one by one, and a full November moon climbed into the sky, flooding the snowy wilderness with its radiance.

Several hours had passed since the buck had lain down to rest in the spruce thicket. The moon was now riding high in the heavens and in the open places it was almost as light as day. Although well hidden, he dozed fitfully, waking at times with a start, thinking that again he was being trailed. He would then lie and listen, with nerves strained to the breaking point, for any sounds of the wild that might mean danger. An owl hooted over in a clump of timber, and the new forming ice on the shores of Kennedy Lake, half a mile away, rumbled ominously. Then he heard a long quavering call, so faint and far away that it almost blended with the whispering of the wind. The coarse hair on his shoulders bristled as he recognized the hunting call of the age-old enemy of his kind. It was answered again and again. The wolf pack was gathering, and for the first time in his life, the buck knew fear. In the shelter of the Tamarack Swamp there had been little danger, and even if he had been driven to the open, his strength and speed would have carried him far from harm. Now, sorely wounded and far from shelter, he would have hardly a fighting chance should the pack pick up his trail.

They were now running in full cry, having struck a trail in the direction of the big swamp far to the west. To the buck, the weird music was as a song of death. Circling and circling, for a time they seemed to draw no nearer. As yet he was not sure whether it was his own blood bespattered trail that they were unraveling, or that of some other one of his kind. Then, suddenly, the cries grew in fierceness and volume and sounded much closer than before. He listened spellbound as he finally realized the truth it was his own trail they were following. The fiendish chorus grew steadily louder and more venomous, and now had a new note of triumph in it that boded ill for whatever came in its way.

He could wait no longer and sprang to his feet. To his dismay, he was so stiffened and sore, that he could hardly take a step. Forcing himself on, he hobbled painfully through the poplar brush and clumps of timber in the direction of the lake. Small windfalls made him stumble, and having to walk around hummocks and hollows made progress slow and difficult. How he longed for his old strength and endurance. About two-thirds of the distance to the lake had been covered and already occasional glimpses of water appeared between the openings.

Suddenly the cries of the pack burst out in redoubled fury behind him, and the buck knew they had found his warm blood-stained bed. Plunging blindly on, he used every ounce of strength and energy that he had left, for now the end was only a matter of minutes. The water was his only hope, for by reaching that he would at least escape being torn to shreds by the teeth of the pack. He could hear them coming swiftly down the ridge behind him and every strange shadow he mistook for one of the gliding forms of his pursuers. They were now so close that he could hear their snarls and yapping. Then a movement caught his eye in the checkered moonlight. A long gray shape had slipped out of the darkness and was easily keeping pace with him. Another form crept in silently on the other side and both ran like phantoms with no apparent effort. He was terror stricken, but kept on desperately. Other ghost-like shapes filtered in from the timber, but still they did not close. The water was just ahead. They would wait till he broke from the brush that lined the shore. With a crash, he burst through the last fringe of alders and charged forward. As he did so, a huge gray form shot out of the shadows and launched itself at his throat. He saw the movement in time and caught the full force of the blow on his horns. A wild toss and the snarling shape splashed into the ice rimmed shallows. At the same instant the two that had been running along side closed, one for his throat and the other for his hamstrings. The first he hit a stunning blow with his sharp front hoof, but as he did so the teeth of the other fastened on the tendon of his hind leg. A frantic leap loosened his hold and the buck half plunged and half slid over the ice into the waters of Kennedy Lake. Then the rest of the pack tore down to the beach with a deafening babble of snarls and howls, expecting to find their quarry down or at bay. When they realized that they had been outwitted, their anger was hideous and the air was rent with howls and yaps.

The cold water seemed to put new life into the buck and each stroke was stronger than the one before. Nevertheless, it was a long hard swim, and before he was half way across the benumbing cold had begun to tell. He fought on stubbornly, his breath coming in short, choking sobs and finally, after what seemed ages, touched the hard sandy bottom of the other shore. Dragging himself painfully out, he lay down exhausted in the snow. All sense of feeling had left his tortured body, but the steady lap, lap of the waves against the tinkling shore ice soothed him into sleep.

When he awoke, the sun was high in the heavens. For a long time he lay as in a stupor, too weak and sorely stiffened to move. Then with a mighty effort he struggled to his feet, and stood motionless, bracing himself unsteadily. Slowly his strength returned and leaving his bed, he picked his way carefully along the beach, until he struck the trail, down which he had so often come to drink. He followed it to the summit of the ridge overlooking the lake.

The dark blue waters sparkled in the sun, and the rolling spruce covered ridges were green as they had always been. Nothing had really changed, yet never again would it be the same. He was a stranger in the land of his birth, a lonely fugitive where once he had roamed at will, his only choice to leave forever the ancient range of his breed. For a time he wavered torn between his emotions, then finally turned to go. Suddenly an overwhelming desire possessed him, to visit again the place where last he had seen his mate. He worked slowly down the trail to the old Tamarack Swamp and did not stop until he came to the old meeting place deep in the shadows where the two trails crossed. For a long time he did not move, then turned and headed into the north to a new wilderness far from the old, a land as yet untouched, the range of the Moose and Caribou.

◆◆◆ Olson, who passed away in 1982 at the age of 83, hunted ducks well into his 70s. In this classic story, he writes of taking a chance on the weather—and reveals the inner feelings that most hunters share.—DECEMBER 1944 ◆◆◆

SHIFT OF THE WIND

by Sig Olson

My mind was made up. I would work all day Saturday and might even go to church on Sunday morning. The more I thought about it, the more indecisive and masterful I became. My old gypsy ways were over. I was to see that there was infinitely more satisfaction in getting a host of long-neglected jobs out of the way than in heading for the rice beds to what I knew would be just another fiasco as far as ducks were concerned. I felt virtuous and substantial. This weekend I'd stay home.

But as the days passed and Friday night was only a matter of hours away, a strange excitement filled my being. I had a feeling that something unusual was going to happen and I was never one to take my hunches lightly. There was, I began to sense, just the barest ghost of a chance that the wind might shift for perhaps an hour, just long enough to make them uneasy. One shot would be enough, one last flock careening over the decoys.

Another thing, it was getting late. October was getting well along and though the weather wasn't ripe, it was the time of year when anything might happen and wouldn't it be criminal to be caught with a shovel in one's hand or pushing a wheelbarrow with the flight coming down? And this I knew, too, that when the ducks did come, they would come with a rush. All they needed was a jittery temperature and a shift of the breeze to send them hurtling down out of the north.

And though the days for a month had been warm, I knew the snow soon would be flying and then it would be all over, portages covered with yellowing leaves, the rice beds blue and gold. There was just a chance something might happen and it wouldn't hurt to take a little swing around to look things over. If there was nothing doing, I would turn right around and come back, finish that perennial bed, the storm windows and the other things that had been waiting all fall.

"Thought you were staying home this weekend," queried Elizabeth, as she watched me stack the tools. "You know there isn't a chance of a flight this weekend any more than last. The weather report says there will be no change and you know yourself the barometer is steady."

I tried to explain that I had been having a feeling that most barometers couldn't register, a sort of hunch that something might happen which would redeem the past barren month, that to play safe I'd decided to look things over once more, a sort of final reconnaissance, so to speak.

Two hours later, I was in my old blind looking at the same old duckless skyline, watching the slowly drifting haze of forest smoke and a coppery sun working its way over the northern Minnesota wild rice beds. A lone mallard took to the air far down shore, winged its way leisurely toward the horizon. I followed its slow, almost tired flight until it was a mere speck drifting over the trees. For a moment it disappeared and then I saw it again, now steadily holding one position. Suddenly, I realized that it was larger, that it had changed the direction of flight and was coming toward me.

The bird was dropping fast toward the rice bed it had left, then rose once more high above the trees; another low flying circle close to the water and then to my delighted eyes there were two heading swiftly toward my blind. No chance of that pair decoying to a bunch of bluebills off a point. They were looking for some quiet, shallow bay down the lake. There was just a chance, however, that they might come within range.

I slipped off my safety, got set—no use even trying to call that pair—a chance for a double if they were close—hold dead on and pull ahead. Another few seconds and they would be in range. Big birds they were and slow, heavy with the rice they'd been feeding on all fall; not too much of a lead. One was slightly ahead. I held to the point of its bill, followed through and fired, turned quickly and caught the second as it was climbing for the clouds. Both birds were falling now, fell almost together in twin water spouts in the midst of the decoys.

In a moment I had them back in the blind, a greenhead and his mate, laid them close beside me where I could watch the changing colors of their plumage and where I could feel them once in a while just to know my luck had changed. We would have them for Sunday dinner stuffed with wild rice, some cranberries and all the trimmings, concrete evidence of my excellent judgment. I was almost happy as I stood there congratulating myself, almost forgot that my good fortune wasn't due to a shifting of the wind or a change of weather; almost forgot that what I really hoped would happen, that the flight of northern bluebills would somehow get underway, seemed no nearer to materialization.

A raven wheeled high in the still smoky blue, circling, floating on the light breeze. One wing, I noticed, had lost a feather. It was a rather ragged looking pinion and the bird seemed to favor that side more than the other.

The great bird swung toward me, spiraled sharply downward and lit in a pine tree back of the blind. Then and there it proceeded to tell the world what it thought and watched me with a mind, I was sure, to the potential carrion it hoped I might become. While watching the raven and marveling at the superb scratchiness of its voice, I suddenly became conscious of a difference in the behavior of the blocks. For hours they had bobbed steadily, sedately, never changing position; but now they were bouncing around frantically, pulling their anchor string, getting together in peculiar and undignified formations; all that, in spite of the fact there had been no apparent change of wind. I had been so busy visiting with the raven that I had failed to notice what was going on, but now I watched the sky, the decoys and the water with new excitement.

Long experience had taught me that decoys can be as good barometers of weather change as the waves themselves. Now they were riding quietly for the first time since I came and the water was dead calm. Then a long series of riffles started out from shore and the rice bent and swayed beyond the decoys, swayed toward the south in a distinct breeze from the hills behind me. In half an hour the air began to clear as the wind out of the north steadied and I knew my hunch had been correct. At least for the moment, things were different.

If it would only hold, the ducks back in the innumerable pot holes and beaver flowages would get restless and begin to move. I watched those new riffles and prayed. If they stayed, my weekends of waiting would not have been in vain, my sacrifice of the perennials would be more than justified and everything else answered for.

The sky began to darken with real clouds, not smoke this time, and the shores changed from their old sunny gray and red to a somber dullness. The coppery sun disappeared entirely and the air grew appreciably colder. If I were a mallard or even a bluebill, I thought excitedly, and saw what was in the wind, I would pick right up, no matter where I happened to be, and streak straight for the south.

But the mallards did not share my excitement, or the bluebills, and two long hours went by before anything happened. Then came a swift hurricane of wings that almost took my breath away, one closely packed, lonesome bunch of bluebills streaking it down the channel with the speed that only miles of flying can give. Far out of range, the flock bore steadily for the west end of the rice bed with a surety of purpose that bespoke no interest in me, the decoys, or the wonderful stand of rice along my side of the shore. I watched desperately as they grew smaller and smaller, faded at last against the rocks and trees of the far end of the lake. Then, for a panicky moment, I thought I had lost them entirely, that drifting patch of black dots soaring for a moment into the blue only to fuse an instant later with the haze. Then, miracle of miracles, the dots suddenly grew more distinct again, swung swiftly into the wind and came once more down the center of the channel, this time directly toward my point. I crouched, got under cover, prayed with all my soul once more. This was the moment, this the realization of the hunch I had had all week. All I asked was one short chance.

They were getting larger, swinging toward shore, would surely be in range if they held their present course. Still too high, but as they went over I called steadily, seductively, saw them hesitate, then veer. They had heard and were coming over. This time it would be different.

I shifted my stance, parted the brush in front of me, braced myself in good shooting position, got set.

They were swinging in now, a matter of seconds and they would be in range. Perennials, storm windows, fertilizer and shrubbery, what piddling, mediocre stuff. This was worth dying for.

My safety was off, a new shell in the chamber. A split second and they were in—over the decoys—pandemonium—whistling wings—outstretched necks—tails and feet braced for the landing—consternation as I rose.

"Pick your bird and hold dead on; don't shoot at the bunch; always pick a single." The old admonitions flashed into mind. I drew hastily on a big black and white drake, fired and watched with joy as he crumpled neatly and lit. Turning, I drew speedily on another quartering away, saw him skate on the water, bounce with his momentum. And they were gone as swiftly as they had come.

But what was that? A lone single had separated himself from the flock and was tearing back along the shoreline as though possessed. He was coming high, just at the limit of range, would pass right over my point, a perfect overhead shot. Once again, I held at the end of a bill boring into space, this time with a feeling that I could not miss, followed an instant and at the extremity of the angle swept just ahead and fired. At the report, he folded his wings, did a somersault, dove for the rice bed, struck in a funnel of spray. It was the sort of shot one remembers all winter long and I yelled for the sheer joy that was mine. That alone was worth the whole season of waiting, days of standing around with nothing to while away the hours but the chickadees and whiskey jacks, the long empty days with not a wing moving. This was more than compensation, it was double proof that my judgment was infallible.

Pushing the canoe out into the rice, I picked up my ducks almost reverently, two drakes and a hen, all well feathered and plump, the first of the northerns. Back on shore, I hung them carefully in the crotch of an aspen, hung my two mallards just below, admired them to my heart's content. No ordinary birds those, each one a thrilling shot, a story in itself.

I watched the horizon an hour longer, but not another duck swung into view. The shifting of the wind had unsettled one lone flock or perhaps it was just my luck. In any case, the rest of the bluebills knew and to prove that contention, the sun came out once more and the clouds evaporated into the same old hazy sky I had known for a month. Gradually, the wind shifted back to its accustomed corner in the southwest and the flight was over.

Tomorrow, I reflected, was Sunday. Chances were that after this lone heaven-sent flurry, nothing would stir for another week. I decided to pick up my outfit, my five beautiful ducks, and go home. In the morning, I thought righteously, I would go to church as a substantial citizen should. I might even get up early and attack that perennial bed or take off the screens. Here was a chance to redeem myself in the eyes of the world.

As I paddled down the lake that afternoon, my mind was at peace and I was happy, happy with the knowledge that I was doing right and that all was well. But at the portage I did an unforgivable thing for a man who has made up his mind. I turned to have one last look at the rice beds against the sunset, stood there athrill with their beauty, watching and wondering. Suddenly against the rosy sky was a long V of black dots and the peace that was mine a moment before vanished swiftly. There must have been 100 and they were settling into the rice near the blind I had left. And there were more, flock after flock in silhouette against the sky. The rice was alive with wings. These ducks, I knew, were riding in ahead of a storm. The flight was on.

For a long time I stood without moving, watched the incoming flocks until it grew too dark to see, wondering what to do. And then I knew, for after all I had promised no one but myself. Almost stealthily, I cached the decoys where I could find them easily in the dark of the morning, threw on the canoe, plodded up the portage toward home.

••• *Mystery writer Erle Stanley Gardner, best known for the Perry Mason series, wrote for* SPORTS AFIELD *from 1949 into the mid-1960s. The following piece, and a four-part series on the perils of gun registration called* THE LAW THAT LEAKED *(1950), established Gardner as a defender of sportsmen's rights.*—OCTOBER 1949 •••

HUNTING IS MORE FUN THAN KILLING
by Erle Stanley Gardner

Hunting is the way Nature intended man to keep healthy, keen and mentally alert. No one ever developed ulcers by hunting. Hunting is a remedy, a tonic and a sport. It's Nature. I've tried hunting with rifle, shotgun, bow and arrow, and camera.

Now as far as enjoyment is concerned, I think that hunting is a lot more fun than killing, but, if you take away the ability to kill, you automatically take away most of the fun of hunting.

I get a lot of pleasure out of hunting with a camera, but to me it doesn't compare with the thrill of stalking with a weapon. In my own case, the feeling of relative impotence I have when I hunt with a bow and arrow is more than offset by the fact that the handicap of the weapon greatly increases the pleasure of the *hunting*.

In certain parts of this country, it is no trick at all for a fairly good hunter to get within 150 yards of big game. Of course you can shoot at that distance with a bow and arrow, but since you can't control your shot, it's not fair to you and it's not fair to the game.

I have hunted with men who could come pretty close to putting an arrow into big game at 70 yards. There are very, very few of them in the United States who can do that. It takes infinite work on the practice range.

In my own case I want to have big game at less than 40 yards if I'm hunting with a bow and arrow, and if I'm hunting small game I want to get within 15 to 20 yards.

There is nothing which can quite compare with the thrill of being within 150 yards of a wary deer and then spending half an hour trying to cut that distance down to 40 yards. It's something a person has to experience in order to appreciate.

However, I, personally and as a matter of individual preference, am about to quit hunting big game with bow and arrow. I don't have the time to keep in sufficient practice to feel that I have a right to loose an arrow at big game.

I have killed deer, elk and wild hogs with bow and arrow. I have killed all sorts of small game, such as rabbit, fox and game birds, with bow and arrow.

In the hands of an expert, the bow is a very deadly weapon. In the hands of a novice, the bow is an instrument of cruelty.

I will now say the same thing about a gun.

I think a hunter owes it to himself and owes it to the game to make himself as proficient as possible in the art of hunting. And that's entirely different from skill in shooting, although no man should consider himself a good hunter unless he's also a good shot. Unfortunately, too few people realize the obligation which is imposed upon them to make themselves as expert as possible in the sport of hunting.

A year or so ago, I had a very good, clean bow shot at an elk at about 40 yards. It was in deep forest, and in broken country. I had to make a snap estimate of the range. I loosed an arrow and the line of that arrow was exactly where I wanted it to go. It was headed directly back of the shoulder, but, as the arrow approached the game, I realized I had misjudged the range just enough so that the shaft was going to be a few inches high.

I wounded that elk. It was the first big game I had ever badly wounded and failed to kill with an arrow.

In this case, the guides felt the elk would recover. I wasn't so sure. We trailed it all afternoon until it quit bleeding and joined another herd. It was not a happy afternoon.

But let's get back to hunting.

How much do we actually know about hunting?

When I first took up rifle hunting, I could get close enough to deer so that I could connect with my .30-30. I thought that made me a great hunter. Then I took up bow and arrow shooting and found I didn't know anything about hunting.

The same was true of rabbits. I used to hunt rabbits with rifle and with shotgun. I thought I knew a lot about rabbit hunting. I didn't know anything.

There is this much to be said for hunting with a bow and arrow. It will teach a sportsman more about hunting in two seasons than he will have learned in all of his lifetime up to that point.

Very few people really know anything at all about stalking. It is, of course, an art in itself. When the gun hunter thinks he is walking quietly, he is actually thinking in terms of his weapon. If his weapon is efficient at 150 or 200 yards, he only needs to walk quietly enough to get within that distance of wary game. But when a hunter has a weapon which requires him to get within 40 yards of game he begins to learn a great deal about stalking.

An interesting adventure which happened two years ago will serve to illustrate my point.

I was hunting with bow and arrow in the Primitive Area of Idaho, and had worked my way along the ridges a mile or so above our camp. We were camped on a creek about two miles from its intersection with the Middle Fork of the Salmon River. To the south of our camp was a long slope covered with big patches of heavy brush which stretched up to the divide. South of that divide the slope dropped very abruptly down to the Middle Fork and was completely barren of cover.

Working back toward camp after combing the ridges, I was stalking down the slope following the edge of a patch of brush when I started playing tag with a nice four-point buck. He had heard me but still didn't know exactly where I was, or exactly what I was, and he was trying to get a good look at me. At the same time, I was trying to get a good look at him. We played tag for some seconds, and then I finally spotted him, working his way along through the brush with his ears twitching, his nostrils testing the wind. He was about 110 yards away. That was farther than I wanted to shoot, so I tried to get closer. He had worked around so the ground between us was heavy brush, and I couldn't proceed quietly and swiftly at the same time. In fact it was almost impossible to even proceed quietly.

He got sight of me, saw that I was a man, and started buck-jumping up the hill. Then he slowed to a trot, looked back over his shoulder a few times, settled down into a long, swinging stride and went right straight up the hill. Just before he came to the top he looked back and deliberately lied to me.

That is, he gave a snort of alarm and started making terrific buck-jumps again. He went over the top of that hill in a cloud of dust as though he were headed for the southern part of the state and didn't have too much time to get there.

Knowing that the south side of the hill was completely devoid of cover, and having by that time learned how deer will deliberately lie to a hunter on the theory that all's fair in love and war, I decided that in all probability the deer had put on all of those buck-jumps for my especial benefit. I realized he might actually have dashed over the crest of the hill at a dead run, then stopped, intending to turn and quietly walk up to the nearest place where the brush offered concealment. Then he intended to sneak right back into the same patch of brush.

Despite my weariness, I hurried 300 or 400 yards over to the west while the deer was over the ridge and therefore unable to see me, then proceeded to reclimb the ridge, working my way up a draw, puffing, blowing and scrambling, heedless of rolling pebbles, making the best time I could—but it was a steep ridge and it took me some 20 minutes to get to the top and work my way over to the other side.

Then I did exactly what I felt the deer must have done. I sneaked along the bare side of the ridge until I came to a point even with the protruding tongue of heavy brush which marked the edge of the brush patch. Then I pussyfooted up over the top.

I wish I had had a camera with me then, and had had the time to use it.

The buck was standing about 50 yards below me anxiously watching the downhill side of the brush patch in order to see if I had been completely taken in and given him up, or whether I was going to come back looking for him. The fact that I seemed to have completely disappeared bothered him. He knew that in the time which had elapsed I should have either gone on down the slope, having marked the deer off as a hopeless chance, or I should be working my way up toward him. The fact that he had lost me bothered him.

He was standing like a statue, just back of the edge of the brush, looking over it, studying the hillside intently, ears cocked forward, every muscle tensed for swift, decisive action.

Now the bow is a weapon which is entirely different from a rifle. Just my head was protruding over the ridge. A rifle would have slipped into position nicely and Mr. Buck would have dropped in his tracks before he knew what hit him. But with my weapon it was necessary to raise the bow and draw back the arrow in order to get a shot. When the tip of that bow came protruding up against the sky line it gave just enough motion (or perhaps the sun may have flashed from the polished surface of the bow) so that the deer got one startled glimpse of my head and shoulders and the top of the drawn bow silhouetted against the sky line.

I don't know what the world record is for a standing jump made by a buck deer over a brush patch on a steep downhill, but whatever it is that buck holds it.

By that time he decided he had gone quite far enough with the game of tag. He felt it would be the part of strategy to get completely out of the country. Apparently he made a good job of it.

Now in my rifle hunting days, it would never have occurred to me that the deer was deliberately lying to me when he changed his pace and went galloping over the top of the ridge with every apparent indication of heading for the southern part of the state.

And there I have to admit that I owe something to the bow and arrow I would never have had otherwise. That stalk up the hill and the pleasure of having outwitted the buck, even though only temporarily, was more fun than the actual killing of a dozen bucks. In fact if I had been hunting with the rifle I would have bagged him when he was 110 yards away looking for me in the brush, and thought I'd done a fairly good job.

And while I'm on the subject of deer stalking, don't ever forget that after game has seen the hunter, and then loses sight of him, it's all but impossible to make a good stalk.

I've been amused listening to novices who tell about seeing a deer watching them. They walk toward him "in plain sight" while he "just stands there." Then the hunter finds the concealment of a little gully or the cut bank of a stream, and starts making a stalk, carried out with every precaution—only to find the deer isn't there when the hunter slowly raises himself on his hands.

Of course the deer isn't there—not in our western country anyway. When the hunter got out of sight, so did the deer.

If the hunter had pretended he hadn't seen the deer he might have stood some chance, even if a slim one.

A year or so ago I was working my way up a deep draw over on Santa Rosa Island, off California. Two deer jumped up ahead of me and ran headlong around the bend of the canyon ahead of me.

I promptly backtracked around the point below me, climbed the canyon and worked the ridge. After some 300 yards, I cautiously looked over the crest.

There were the two deer standing behind a brush patch some 150 yards away, and were they talking!

They stamped their feet with impatience, looked at each other and very plainly said, "Now where the devil did he go? He's had plenty of time to get around that point. Where is he?"

I couldn't get any closer so I sat there for some 10 minutes, enjoying the spectacle. Then they fidgeted themselves into an ecstasy of fear and started running.

During the days when I hunted rabbits with guns, I don't think I was ever able to make a stalk on a rabbit when he was concealed in the shade of a patch of sagebrush, so that I saw the rabbit before he saw me.

After I took up bow and arrow shooting, I was able to do it on numerous occasions. When that happens, quite frequently the rabbit, feeling he has lost the advantage of concealment, will simply freeze in position. If he feels the hunter hasn't seen him, he will frequently dash into explosive flight for the shelter of the next clump of brush, and will be pretty certain to get there before there is time to get set for a shot.

The trouble with archery today is that it has grown too fast.

Some 25 years ago those of us who hunted with bow and arrow were a relatively few people who loved hunting more than killing. It was a fairly proficient group of hunters. (I was always a relatively poor bow and arrow shot and unhesitatingly put myself near the bottom of the list—but some of these men were marvelous woodsmen.)

For the most part, we didn't hunt big game. We did lots of small game shooting, however, and we did quite a bit of what came to be known as "stump hunting."

That is one great advantage of the bow and arrow. It is a sociable weapon. Archers returning from a deer hunt can have a lot of amusement by saying, "Suppose that stump over there on the hill was a deer." The archer takes a blunt arrow from his quiver and proceeds to show his companions just what he would do if the stump actually were a deer. Then his companions show him what they would do. Then there is a general discussion about range, trajectory and cast. Arrows are retrieved and someone else will pick a suitable stump for the next shot. Miles and hours dissolve in genial adventure.

Archers who went hunting deer in those days were qualified to hunt deer. They had served a long apprenticeship in hunting small game with bow and arrow. They were proficient as hunters and as archers.

Then came the vast influx of newcomers to the ranks. Sympathetic legislators advanced the seasons, or opened territory to bow and arrow hunting which was not available to rifle hunters. This naturally attracted people who wanted to hunt deer that "weren't so darned wild."

The result has been that too many archers who haven't served their proper apprenticeship are out shooting arrows at deer, particularly in the midwestern country where second-growth timber and abandoned roads give a man a chance to have a fairly close shot without being too proficient as a hunter.

Out in the western districts we never bothered about the amateur archers, because a man who wasn't a woodsman simply couldn't get a decent shot at a deer with a bow and arrow.

In my own case, in view of what happened with that wounded elk, I'm toying with the idea of a new technique.

I am going to take my rifle, and I am going to hunt just as I would if I were armed with a bow and arrow. I am going to pass up all shots at more than 50 yards and then when I pull the trigger I am going to make it a point to see that the animal drops in its tracks, killed quickly, cleanly and mercifully. In that way I hope to get as much thrill out of stalking big game with a rifle as I did with a bow.

And, incidentally, I hope that every state game commission provides a field test for bow and arrow applicants for big game hunting licenses, and refuses to grant a big game license until the archer has demonstrated his ability to handle his weapon with sufficient skill to prove that he's really entitled to hunt big game.

The idea of letting anyone who can pick up a bow and a quiver of arrows go out and shoot big game is preposterous. Incidentally, it's just as preposterous to let anyone who can buy a rifle hunt big game. I'd like to do the same thing with rifle hunters, but I realize that's virtually out of the question.

However, I do know that archers are now at the point where they're hurting themselves by the avalanche of numbers. It takes more than a bow and a quiver of arrows to make an archer.

As far as that's concerned, it takes more than a weapon to make a hunter.

Hunting is a marvelous recreation, but when you go blundering along through the forest with a gun on your shoulder or a bow in your hand, you aren't hunting. You may think you're hunting, but you're not.

The photographs which accompany this article were all taken on actual hunting trips during open season, in hunting territory and under hunting conditions. Virtually all of them were taken with a small camera which I could carry in a little case at my belt. The lens was of short focal length and therefore the image of the game was exceedingly small.

But some of the pictures of wild rabbits caught off first base, so to speak, give some indication of the fun of stalking. And the story of those Wyoming deer (shown in the photos) is an adventure in itself.

And I think most sportsmen will agree with me that it's more fun to hunt than to kill. But unless the hunter has a death-dealing weapon, he isn't really hunting.

He's just walking around.

••• The author of 13 books, Robinson was present during the first discussions on a national duck stamp in 1932 and helped formulate the concept for Ducks Unlimited. Nothing ever swayed his love for duck hunting; silver cans only heightened it.—NOVEMBER 1956 *•••*

SILVER CANS
by Jimmy Robinson

All morning the deep, booming, late October wind hurtled out of the North. Sweeping down the long reach of Lake Manitoba, it gathered speed enough to bend double the vast canebrakes of our Delta Marsh. We were glad to be inside, safe from the turmoil, but our comfort was short-lived.

An unearthly medley of rattling and sputtering, climaxed by a terrible screech of brakes, rose above the thundering voice of the storm. Then it ended as suddenly as it began. Even the wind seemed still by comparison with the human juggernaut that burst through the door of our hunting shack. Walt Bush even dropped his gin rummy hand to stare at the intruder.

It was Rod Ducharme, a giant, black-thatched French-Canadian from nearby St. Ambroise.

"Chemmy, da seelver cans are here!" He had never learned to pronounce "Jimmy" like other people.

I had been getting ready to gin and this eruption threw me completely off my stride. "Will you drop dead?"

To Rod the game of gin was so much Greek. He probably never even heard me.

"Yah, da seelver cans, Cheemy!" he bellowed. "De're here, ya betcha! In da mornin', by golly, we go get 'em, huh?"

I grinned, snatched a quick look at Bush's sour puss (he had been losing steadily), then I wiped the grin off and turned to Rod.

"What's here? I'm sleeping in the morning."

"Seelver cans, Cheemy, I tol' ya about dem. Ya said t' be sure t' let ya know if dey come or ya break my neck. I comer here fast as my truck go."

How Rod expected me to break his neck, set atop a 6-foot 3-inch frame carrying 280 pounds, I wouldn't know. But he seemed impressed. His skill as a Delta Marsh duck guide was as proverbial as his feats of strength, and they were legendary. Once, when my car was stuck in a heavy rain on a delta dirt road, Rod and another native had merely carried it to solid footing.

"You call that wreck a truck?" I said. "Sounds more like a wagonload of loose bolts. And the only silver cans I know of are on the dump behind the St. Ambroise general store."

But I knew what he meant—perfectly.

The year before, Rod had written me after we closed the duck camp. He told of being out on the marsh as it was freezing up and all other ducks were long gone. He saw some big flights coming in from the lake. They were cans—the biggest canvasbacks Rod had ever seen, and the whitest. They flashed in the sun like silver—"seelver cans."

I had at once put in a long-distance call to Bert Cartwright, chief naturalist for Ducks Unlimited at Winnipeg: "What do you know about overgrown canvasbacks that come into the Delta Marsh a week or two after most of the other ducks have gone?"

Bert had heard of them. He believed these outsize cans composed a flight from the most northerly part of the breeding range. Up there the long hours of daylight permitted them to develop more completely in body size and plumage. But few people had seen them. They came only after the big bays were making ice and the hunters had put their guns away. They stayed but briefly, then arrowed eastward for Chesapeake Bay.

"All right," I said to Rod. "Tomorrow it is—if I can get Bush away from this gin rummy game."

Walt was skeptical. "Never heard of such flights before. I don't think they exist. But you'd have to break my leg to keep me off that marsh tomorrow."

At 4 the next morning Walt, Frank Lavalle and I were at Rod's house in St. Ambroise, 30 miles around the marsh to the east. A hearty breakfast of pancakes and home-smoked bacon awaited us.

"We take da truck t' da marsh," Rod announced. "Can't affort t' break down an' lose time gettin' dere dis mornin'."

I shuddered. Here was the world's most sublime optimism. What made this big meatball think his truck would hold together long enough to get us to the marsh?

Five minutes later we were careening madly along in "da truck," charging through an ice-slicked trail of matted cattails and cane. My fine breakfast was back in my mouth, my teeth were rattling and I was bouncing like a dowager on her first bronc ride. The morning was jet black and I couldn't see Walt, but at intervals I could hear low moans escape him.

Rod had two boats cached at the end of a narrow channel that extended inland from Cadham's Bay. They were frozen solid in ice. He and Frank went to work with axes.

We shivered in temperatures a few degrees below freezing as we waited. The north wind, raw and biting, was still with us, but instead of roaring as it did the day before, it was only muttering. This should be a good day for "da seelver cans."

We pushed the boats out onto the channel ice, then settled them through the crust, and Rod, in the lead boat with Frank, started belaboring the ice with a bludgeon of an oar made from a 2 by 6 plank. Hercules, in all his 12 labors, never worked so hard. We made progress. Before I knew it, open water gleamed ahead through the now lightening gloom. While we were still in the ice, Bush changed to Rod's boat, Frank to mine.

We had almost a mile of open water to cross, straight into the bite of the north wind. Our destination was a group of small islands near the northwest shore of the bay. The silver cans could be rafted there, in the lee.

Dawn came as we were making the traverse, and the first ducks began to appear. A few goldeneyes, two or three tight little bunches of bluebills. There were no canvasbacks. The sky was clearing as the north wind pushed the overcast rapidly before it. Though I had on 1/4-inch long-johns, by the time we made the island my teeth were chattering like a telegraph key and I was bemoaning the ill-starred day I first met Rod Ducharme. That Jonah, with parka off and hands bare, had worked up a nice sweat.

He assigned Frank and me to a small island with a nice growth of bulrushes and moved on to select another shooting stand. The islands curved away to the southwest and Rod headed in this direction, almost downwind. Soon he and Walt were out of sight behind another island.

Forty yards from our blind, Frank tossed out canvasback decoys—big, white-backed blocks for late-season shooting. He mixed a few 'bill stools with them. Then we pulled rushes around us, and I snuggled into a sack of hay with which Rod, in one of his lucid moments, had equipped the boat. The wind couldn't reach us here, and, as the red ball of sun began to crawl above the wide marsh, blood started moving in my veins again.

Still no cans. A few bluebills darted in and one flight of goldeneyes swept past. I thought nostalgically of some canvasback shoots I had known . . .

Now, the canvasback is the king of ducks in the old hunter's book, and an epicure's delight in the bargain. He is the hardest of them all to hit as he hurtles hell-bent across the sky. The big bulls remind you of a jet fighter with their bullet heads and sharp, small swept-back wings. Those wings claw air at such a furious clip that they send the big flat bodies racing along faster than any other duck.

They are straight-away speedsters made for a big track, and they never flare or dodge.

One of the wariest of ducks and usually suspicious of decoys, once he has made up his mind, the canvasback just bores right in like a dive bomber on a pin-point mission. His reliance always is on his speed, and he is apt to get so close before you can let off a shot that he makes your 12-gauge pattern look like a rifle slug. When he comes tearing over you—quail-high at 70 miles-an-hour air speed (often 100 in relation to you on the ground!)—you can take a bow if you drop him.

Somebody fetched me a clobber on the back, hard, and I heard Frank's voice shouting. "Cans, Jimmy! Silver cans. North. A big flight heading this way. Wake up, Jimmy! Get set."

I swiveled for a look behind me. A big flock was bearing down, riding the north wind like the tail of a comet. They were over us and past before I could reach for my gun. Then they zoomed up and wide, circled well out and parked in open water. Were they Rod's silver cans? I began scratching in the hay for my glasses.

"They were silver cans," Frank assured me. "I thought they'd never come. I thought they'd probably left the marsh. If you hadn't slept so sound I would have said to leave this spot an hour ago. Now I think we're all right. More goin' to come." He kept his eyes on the northern sky over Lake Manitoba. The flight had come from there. I began tossing Rod's blasted hay overboard and at last found my glasses.

"They're comin'!" Frank said.

I saw a small cloud of dark specs which materialized almost instantly into a flock of cans—big ones—and they were heading straight for our blocks. They swept past, a long-shot high, and their great bodies flashed bright silver in the sun as I caught the quick whistle of their blurred wings. What music!

A few birds dipped a trifle, then they were over the bay. Frank gave them a *brrr, brrr* and five silver cans sliced off in a tight bank. We hunched and tried to wish them in. Straightened out now, they came plummeting wide open to the blocks. I watched, mouth open. It was a sight to remember. Silver cans . . . big ones!

Somehow I got on the lead bird and pulled. It dropped, close in. Frank got it and handed it to me. I took it reverently. It was easily the biggest duck I had ever shot. And so white. I thought of Rod's description, flashing "seelver."

"More comin'!" Frank warned, and I hunched down. Three bunches were swooping in. They whooshed past and a dozen birds turned back to Frank's call. I took two big bulls and so did Frank. He marked where they drifted into the rushes.

They kept coming now, a dozen, five, three. They began to peel off regularly to the decoys, diving incredibly fast. We took only the biggest bulls.

"Never have I seen anything like this," Frank said. Nor had I. When he counted out our limit we just sat there watching them in utter fascination. Several flocks were still slashing through the sky.

"Haven't heard no shootin' from Walt and Rod," Frank said, as we picked up the decoys. Now that I thought of it, I hadn't either. Could these two characters have missed the flight lane? We headed in the direction Rod had taken. The north wind was still blowing, tireless and raw.

Moving around a point, we beheld Walt. He was perched on a muskrat house swinging his arms to keep warm. Decoys were riding in front of his vacant blind, off to the left of the rat house. At intervals his arms would raise above his head and he would turn his face up to the heavens as if in supplication. It was positively mystifying.

As we got closer, I could make out a rapid-fire mumbling, then I was able to recognize a few phrases like "that no good" . . . "that bug-brain" . . . "that addlepated son of a . . . " This was not like Bush, who is the most mild-mannered of men.

"Is something wrong?" I asked soothingly as we came up. "Where's Rod?"

That did it. Walt seemed to explode like a balloon of bubble gum. "Don't ever mention that name to me again!" he roared. "I'm going to leave him here for crow bait! That's all he's good for."

He stopped to get a new grip on his vocabulary. "I've been sitting here on this anthill of a muskrat house for hours . . . and that pea-brain's got my gun. He went away with it! I practically had to comb those silver cans out of my hair. I had to watch 'em playing in my decoys."

Another pause. "And what is he doing? Shooting silver cans all by himself. That's what he's doing. I heard a gun blasting all morning off in his direction to the south. I tell you it's more than a man can stand. Give me a gun. I'm going after that goatherder!"

I pushed quickly away from the rat house before Walt could climb aboard. My mind visualized a dozen possible contingencies—all bad. Here was a dilemma that had to be solved at once, without gunfire, and I was sure it would be much better if Bush was still enthroned on his muskrat pile when I came up with the doomed Rod. By this time, I reasoned, the rat house must be practically like home to Walt anyway. I closed my ears to his heart-rending cries.

I took an oar with Frank and we humped it downwind. Not far beyond Bush's throne a considerable expanse of open water appeared, with more islands on the far side. At another turn around an island we saw a second figure on a rat house, also hysterically waving its arms.

"What goes on?" I groaned to Frank. "What is this strange affinity for Manitoba rat houses?"

It was Rod . . . who else?

"Start talking," I said as we edged into him. "You're in danger of having your hide shot as full of holes as a flour sieve."

Rod swallowed hard and rolled his eyes. His face wore a pitiful, pleading expression.

"Cheemy," he choked. "Cheemy, what have I deed? . . . Poor Walter . . . poor Walter! He want t' shoot dose beeg, seelver cans so bad!"

His agony was almost contagious. I think I felt a twinge of sorrow for him.

"I didn't mean it, Cheemy. Ya talk t' Walter. I am as eenocent as da new born babe. All at once, da oar she was gone . . . like dat! What could I do—sweem?"

Eventually we got his story. He had set Walt on a rat house while he put out decoys. In the process one of his oars had slipped unnoticed from the boat and drifted out of sight. It was then he had discovered, to his total dismay, that he had Walt's gun. He had tried desperately with one oar to buck the north wind back across that stretch of open water, but it was no use. All he had been able to do was wait for the wind to die or for Frank and me to come. He had spent an anguished morning.

As he crouched dejectedly on his own rat house, screened by rushes, the big, silver cans had begun pitching into his blocks. It had come to be more than any mortal could endure. So he had taken an occasional shot as the morning wore on.

Rod pointed in his boat. Ten big silver cans lay there.

We tied his boat behind ours, and he and Frank pulled against the wind toward Bush's rat house. As we came up, Rod suddenly stowed his oar and became extremely busy with the decoys, untangling anchor lines. I looked for Walt's gun and couldn't find it. There was only one place it could be . . . under the boat's hay pile. If bad came to worse, Rod figured to have time to start swimming, anyway.

By now Walt had taken in the situation and greeted us, honest, with a grin. He was still balanced safely, with the sure feet of long acquaintance, upon his mud pinnacle. But he must have had a bad moment when the good-hearted Rod raised his eyes for the first time and said:

"Ya look all in, Walter. I got a whole limit o' seelver cans. Why don't ya take dem and den ya won't have t' stay and shoot any more?"

••• *Col. Townsend Whelen (1877–1961) was commissioned into the army by President Theodore Roosevelt. He was an expert in arms (he devised the 35 Whelen cartridge), hunting and camping, and was on the* SPORTS AFIELD *staff for many years. Near the end of his career, he wrote of hunting when the West was young.—*APRIL 1960 •••

HUNT THE OLD WEST
by Col. Townsend Whelen

Owing to a number of circumstances it has been impossible for me to hunt in our western mountains for a number of years. When an opportunity to visit them came again recently, I found conditions relative to hunting much changed. The fine old mountains were still there, as magnificent as ever, but no longer exactly primitive. That is, they were all well known and accurately mapped. No longer does the visiting sportsman have to find his own way through them, often cutting his trails. No longer does he have to find for himself the localities where the game he sought was plentiful. No longer does he have to plan a long expedition and supply his own equipment. The demand for more and more hunting in these regions and the limited holidays that busy sportsmen are able to afford have changed all this. A system of guides and outfitters has grown up. The outfitter now supplies the hunter with everything he needs, except his personal effects, and transports him quickly into the best game districts by pack train, where he can get his trophies and meat in the least time, usually 10 days or two weeks. Now the sportsman has only to be able to ride a horse and shoot. It was very different in my day; it occurred to me that it might be interesting to record how a successful trip was pulled off in the Old West of my younger days.

• • •

When I was hunting in British Columbia in 1906 there came into my camp one evening the old hunter and trapper William Manson. Around the fire that evening he told me of a wonderful new hunting country that his brother had just discovered. His brother had been prospecting in the Upper Finlay River region of British Columbia, and not finding "colors" to his satisfaction decided to return to his home on the lower Fraser River. He built a raft and floated down the Finlay to the Peace, and down that river to the canyon. There he started overland—with a pack on his back—along the eastern edge of the Rockies to Yellowhead Pass and then to the source of the Fraser, floating down it to his home. All the long way down the eastern slope of the Rockies, four or five days after he left the Peace, he passed through a most wonderful game country. Moose, caribou, sheep, goats and bears were more plentiful than he had ever seen them before. And the country was entirely uninhabited and primitive.

This account fired my desires and I longed to hunt in the area, but of course that was then impossible for me. Even to get on the edge of it was several hundred miles from the nearest railroad, and it would take a far longer leave than the Army was then granting.

But during World War I the Canadian National Railway tracks were put through Yellowhead Pass and the country became more accessible. I corresponded with the railway about it and was advised to contact a young man, Stanley Clark, who had just taken up a horse ranch at the eastern entrance to Yellowhead Pass. Stanley informed me that it was evidently a wonderful game country, that the southern portion of it had just been made into a national forest and roughly mapped. He had an idea that there would be a demand for his horses for Government exploring parties and sportsmen, and he indicated he would like to know more of it. So we cooked up an expedition into the area. I obtained a 2 1/2-month Army leave, and in August 1922 met him at Entrance at his ranch.

Our arrangements were that he would furnish the two saddle and four pack horses we figured we would need, with saddle equipment for them, and a canvas Indian tepee. I would furnish all the rest of the camp equipment (which I had) and the grub. I had my .30-06 sporting Springfield rifle with Lyman sights, and I took along a similar rifle for Stanley. He had a little .22 Stevens pistol with 10-inch barrel which proved very useful for grouse. I made arrangements with the Western Cartridge Company to test a new .30-06 cartridge which was just introduced, loaded with a 180-grain, open-point, boattail bullet and having a muzzle velocity of 2727 fps. I bought the grub supply at the little trading post at Entrance, the usual stake of those days—flour, baking powder, oatmeal, cornmeal, dried beans, bacon, dried prunes, apricots and loganberries, canned butter, several cans of strawberry and blackberry jam, sugar, salt, pepper and a sack of potatoes and onions. That was a different menu from the elaborate assortments that sportsmen demand today, but adequate for those who are assured of killing sufficient meat.

So we started out, just the two of us with our six horses—not a deluxe outfit, but we figured it would do. Ahead of us to the northwest loomed the high snowcapped wall of the Rockies and unknown adventures. The Smoky River drains the eastern slope of the Rockies, from its source near Mount Robson until it flows northeast into the Peace. The country to the east of the Smoky was in the newly created Forest Reserve, which was fairly well known and had been hunted a little, and Stanley figured that we had better hurry through it and get into the more primitive and less-known country across the Smoky.

So for the first eight days we traveled up the Rock and down the Sulpher rivers to the Smoky. All this was perfectly glorious country: fairly wide valleys, open and carpeted with low willow brush. From the valley bottoms the pine-spruce and aspen-clad hills arose, and just back of them were the high, rough, multicolored and snowcapped mountains. There was a rough trail over to the Smoky, an elaboration of old game trails, but in places it petered out and we had some stretches of rough going.

We saw little game the first eight days, and did not stop to hunt. On several occasions we saw white spots high up on the rocky mountainsides, and when we put our binoculars on them they turned out to be goats. And one early morning when I poked my nose out of the tepee a bull moose was trotting along the hillside across the little creek. Soon we were seeing lots of game of all kinds high up around timberline as we went along.

Don't get the idea that this was all just the delightful horseback ride that most modern sportsmen now enjoy going into hunting country, with guides, horse wranglers and cooks. We rose at the first streak of dawn. One of us, chosen by lot, started out to find and drive in the horses which would be grazing anywhere from nearby to two miles from camp. Half of them were hobbled, and all had bells, so they were usually not too hard to find and drive in. Meantime the other fellow would be cooking breakfast and taking down the tepee. Breakfast over, we would saddle and pack the horses, which took us about an hour of hard work. Then we started off on the day's journey, one of us riding ahead to pick out the trail or the easiest way through thick and rough stuff, and the other bringing up the rear and driving the four pack horses along. We would ride on, examining and noting the country, and looking for game signs, until about 2 or 3 o'clock, when we would camp at the first place that afforded good water, horse feed and dry firewood. Usually at such places we would find tepee poles stacked up against a tree. The country we were in used to be a favorite hunting ground for the Indians until the nearby plains began to be settled and they moved down where they could be closer to the trading posts. But the Indians left their tepee poles stacked up, much to our advantage, for it takes some time and labor to cut and trim the 11 poles needed to erect a tepee. However, we did not often pitch the tepee on these one-night stands. It was so much easier just to smooth off a spot near the campfire, lay down a pack cover and a couple of horse blankets and top it off with a sleeping bag.

After we had made camp each night and turned the horses loose to graze, one of us would start supper, and if there was time the other would start out with the little pistol and a fishline to try to get grouse or trout, usually with satisfactory results. We turned in as soon as it got dark because we had no illumination other than the campfire and candles.

The Sulphur River flows west, and then makes an abrupt turn to the north to join the Smoky River 15 miles below. At the turn we continued straight west, climbing a high range that divides the two valleys through what is known as Kvass Pass, named after Freddie Kvass who trapped this region and once brought back a fabulous winter's catch of fur that sold for $2000!

From this high pass we tumbled and scrambled down the steeply avalanched bottom of a small creek valley to the Smoky River, reaching it close to the mouth of its tributary, the Muddy River. The Smoky, a swift mountain river some 75 yards wide and chalk-colored from the limestone country where it rises, has four tributaries draining the mountains to the west: the Jack Pine, the Muddy, the Sheep and the Porcupine. All of these were roughly indicated on the map we had. This was the fabulous game country that Manson had told me about many years before. Little was known about it, although we learned later that several hunting parties had entered it but left no record. Several years previously Miss Mary L. Jobe had passed through it on her way to try to climb Mount Kitchi, a high peak across the Continental Divide.

Fording the Smoky we got pretty wet, for the river was almost over the horses' backs and very swift, so we camped one day on its west bank to dry out.

Leaving the Smoky, we started up the high range beyond just south of the valley of the Muddy River, a small stream that was not muddy at all. At 4 o'clock we camped at timberline. Ahead of us were the mountains that constitute the main range of the Rockies; magnificent ranges of high peaks, most of them snowcapped. The view was so glorious that we pitched our tepee wide open, like a lean-to, with the fire in front so we could enjoy the view. Next morning I started out for my first real day of hunting. Stanley had some repair work to do on saddles and equipment, and he said he would start out himself as soon as the chore was done. Our anticipation ran high.

To the west two peaks reared up, with a big basin in between that had high cliffs on either side. But slide rock at the head of the basin offered good prospects of a way out. I headed toward it, striding swiftly through a grassy meadow, not expecting to see anything there, when suddenly, coming over a slight rise in the ground, I came right on a big white billy goat grazing in a slight depression. I was taken entirely unawares. In fact, I thought I had a clear view of everything for 400 or 500 yards around, not having noted the depression. The goat was also surprised, and we just stood and stared at each other for some seconds. Then he turned and trotted out of sight before I could collect myself. The next time I saw him he was beyond sure range and headed for the cliffs to the south side of the basin.

Continuing up the basin, I climbed the slide-rock at its head. Looking down while plodding up, I saw numerous shale fossils.

From the top of the slide at the head of the basin I could look over countless miles of high mountains, piled up, peak after peak. On the grassy side of one, about three miles away, I saw what appeared to be four animals that were not moving. Putting my 8X binocular on them, I still could not tell if they were sheep or caribou. Anyway, they were too far off to be included in that day's plans. Then I looked off to my left, and there was that goat lying asleep on the cliff some 500 yards away. From my slide-rock saddle a steep ridge ran over to the goat cliffs. It was an ugly-looking route, snow-covered with a cornice of snow on the right side overhanging a vertical precipice, and awfully steep on the left, but I decided to try it. With my heart in my throat most of the time, I finally got across to the cliff, the configuration of which was such that I was able to approach within about 150 yards of the goat unseen. At my shot, high up through the shoulders, the animal simply wilted, and I gingerly continued my climb along the cliff to it. It was a splendid big billy with nine-inch horns, and

I had my first trophy. I dressed it out, skinned it, packed the head and skin in my rucksack, and rolled the carcass over the cliff. It went down with three enormous bounds and landed where we picked it up the following day with a pack horse.

Leaving our camp we headed north along the main range of the Rockies, forded the Muddy, and went up a canyon to a little beaver dam were we made our next camp. From that camp we both went out to hunt and prospect. I climbed the range to the north, saw nothing except some old sheep sign and trails, but while looking back at the range on the south side of the Muddy, I could just make out some sort of animal on a grassy slope above timberline. I studied it for a long time. It moved its location three times in two hours, but each time stopped at one small spot. Most likely, I thought, a grizzly digging out ground squirrels. I told Stanley about it that night, and we decided to put packs on our backs, go over there and make a spike camp and see what we could find. It was too rough for the pack train. We camped that evening alongside the Muddy, but about eight miles above where we had previously forded it. Next morning we could see that a heavy snowstorm was raging above on the range where I had seen what I thought was the bear. No use to go up there that day, so Stanley started down the Muddy and I up it to hunt. Then things began to happen for me. First of all, I nearly collided with a young bull moose. We were only about 10 yards apart when we discovered each other. We both froze, and remained so for possibly two minutes, when the bull turned its head away and slowly walked out of sight. It was quite evident that these animals here had never seen a human being before.

Going on half a mile I saw through the pines two moose trotting ahead of me. I could not see if either was a trophy bull, so I trotted fast ahead. Both moose dropped over the bank down into the Muddy bottom out of sight, and just at that instant I heard a lot of galloping up on the mountainside to the right where the timber was much more open, and never before have I seen such a sight. The whole mountainside seemed to be milling with caribou. There seemed to be at least 25 in the herd. As I watched, one magnificent big antlered bull detached himself from the herd, ran down the hill and stood on the cutbank, apparently looking down at the two moose. I lost no time in slamming one of the new Western bullets into its chest. It toppled sideways against a big moss-covered rock and lay still, and I had my second trophy, the finest bull caribou I have ever shot. What great good luck! The trophy now hangs on the wall of the Hearth Room at my summer home *Someday* in Vermont. We had a little disappointment the next day, however. The bull had evidently been rutting hard, and we just could not swallow the meat, but we were living all right on the small trout we caught in the Muddy. The old billy shot five days before proved too tough for both of us. Finally, we saved only the fat.

The third day there were signs of its clearing on the range above where I thought I had seen a bear, so we started up. Arriving at timberline, everything was snow-covered and in a fog. We could not see 100 yards, but soon we did come on fair-sized bear tracks in the snow. We tried to follow them, but they just wandered back and forth everywhere—a grizzly hunting ground squirrels. So we decided to go downwind east along the range, keeping 100 yards apart so as to have the greatest visibility. We had gone about half a mile when the fog began to lift. Now we could see 200 yards, and there stood the bear. I shot instantly. The bear let out a big bawl, put its head down between its legs and rolled down the mountainside until it was out of sight in the fog. I raced down after it, Stanley following after me. In about 300 yards I found it, stone-dead, a medium-size female in the finest fur. The bullet had entered just behind the chest cavity, had made a five-inch hole on the opposite side, and some of the bears entrails were wrapped about it like a belt. Not much excitement to killing that grizzly. It was all over too soon. We dressed and skinned it and packed the skin, skull and all the meat we could carry down to our fly camp, and the next day over to our horse camp in the canyon, beside the beaver dam. So I had my third trophy, and all the luck. Stan had not yet had a shot. So it goes. But his luck was to come later. That bear was lucky for us also, because its meat was perfectly delicious. We ate every bit of it we could carry back.

I must not fail to record that climbing back out of the valley of the Muddy to our horse camp was just downright hard work up a very steep, mossy slope. We were burdened with two fine trophies and a lot of meat. But the recompense came late that afternoon as we topped the last summit and looked down at our camp pitched alongside the beaver dam. The sun was just setting and the valley had literally turned to gold. The whole atmosphere was thick golden, as golden as the fog had been white up where the bear was shot. I stopped in my tracks and just sat down and gazed. Stanley sat down also, saying, "The Lord is in His holy temple, let all keep silence before Him."

·   ·   ·

We were two contented young hunters in this beaver-dam camp in the little-known Rockies of Alberta during the fall of 1922. Stretched on frames around us, drying, were the skins of our grizzly, goat and caribou, and we feasted on the liver and ribs of the bear for several days while the skins were drying. Whisky-jacks were all around us, begging for tidbits of meat. It was a typical old-time western hunters' camp scene. After we had completed the job, we continued north, climbing the high range that divides the Muddy from the Sheep Creek drainage.

That night we camped on Sheep Creek beside the camp of an Indian hunter. Stanley knew him, and was told by him that if we went down Sheep Creek for about two miles we would come to a smaller creek flowing into it from the north. The Indian said that he remembered as a boy hunting up that creek with his father, and that here were lots of sheep up there. So of course two days later found us camped at the head of that creek, and it was indeed sheep country.

The grassy meadows above timberline were criss-crossed almost everywhere with the telltale sheep trails. We hunted that country the next day together. We did not glimpse any of the sheep, but we did have several adventures. Going along a ridge we flushed (that is the right word) a nanny goat and its kid. Again I was struck with the fact that these animals had never seen a human being before, for that nanny and kid just sedately walked along that ridge about 50 yards ahead of us.

While we were following them, Stanley looked down the slope to the right, and there were three caribou, a very fair bull, a cow and a calf lying down. We at once left the confiding nanny and kid and started to stalk the caribou. Halfway down the ridge the three animals sprang to their feet and started on a rapid trot along the opposite slope. We could distinctly hear their anklebones clicking. They went about half a mile, circled, came back exactly where they had been before and again lay down. I told Stanley that I had often read of these inexplicable scares of caribou, and their coming back to the same place after their mad run.

Anyhow, we continued our stalk on them, got to within about 150 yards, beyond which there was no more cover, and Stanley took a shot at the bull, and missed it. We felt pretty sad as we wandered back to camp, but that was not the last of it. Just as we were about to lay down our rifles and brew a pot of tea and take it easy, Stanley looked up the ridge, and there stood that bull caribou looking down at us. This time Stanley did not miss, and the bull practically rolled into camp.

The next day we hunted across the divide separating this creek from another flowing east. Here, too, sheep trails criss-crossed all the pastures lying just below the rocks and snow. Looking down into a valley we saw a fair-size bull moose striding along, grunting every few steps, evidently on the trail of a cow. Then we saw nothing until a little past noon when I was in the lead. Striding up a slope and keeping eyes skinned on the skyline, I saw the head and shoulders of a sheep. Instantly, I crouched down, and together we crept to the crest. There, in a hollow below us, not 200 yards away, was a band of 23 ewes and lambs. Some were grazing. Some lying. The lambs were playing around. Two of the ewes were a dirty white all over, almost like Dall sheep. We just lay there and watched them for a long time. As the sun moved around and cast its shadow they all moved to stay in the sunlight, feeding uphill. It was delightful to see them so close, unaware of any danger. After a while we backed up and left them, circling around to escape giving them our wind. Several hours later we turned back, not having seen any more game except for many marmots. Then on the way campward we suddenly saw some sheep coming ahead of us. At once we both crouched down and froze, and three ewes and two lambs came on at a walk and passed not more than 50 yards below, looking directly at us several times but evidently thinking we were only rocks.

This was apparently a ewe range. We hunted another day but could not find the rams. We thought they must be farther up Sheep Creek, so we went back to that stream and started up it. We traveled for three days, stopping a day at each camp to hunt the mountains to the north and south, but saw no indication of game of any kind and no sheep trails. This was evidently one of those localities that game never frequents, and a sportsman hunting it only would think the country held no game. Of course, one of the advantages of hunting today with a guide who knows the country is that the sportsman does not waste time in unprofitable country such as this.

So we turned around and retraced our trail of the the last three days to where we had first struck Sheep Creek, and then continued down the creek—hard going with no semblance of a trail. Late that afternoon, Stanley rode ahead, picking a route, while I followed, driving our four pack horses. I saw Stanley hold up his horse, throw his hand in the air, then beckon me to come on. Jumping off my horse and pulling my rifle from it scabbard, I ran up to him. He pointed down the creek which was plainly visible from where we stood. There, standing knee-deep in the creek, was a fine bull moose with a good head. "Want him?" Stanley asked. "Yes," I said and started to sit down for the shot. "You've got to kill him quick. If he gets in those thick jack pines across the creek we will never see him again," Stanley said. I held just at the top of his back above the chest and eased off the shot. The bull sank down into the water. "Don't kill him so quickly," Stanley yelled, "we will have one hell of a time getting him out of there!"

We rode down to the bull, out into the creek, put our lariats around the bull's horns and without much trouble snaked him out onto the bank. Then we made camp right there, and proceeded to examine our prize. It was a big bull with a nice 48-inch head, a good trophy. We stayed there the next day, for we had our hands full butchering the bull, cutting the meat up into portions that would pack on our horses, and cleaning the scalp and skull. The scalp needed several days to dry, so we decided to remain longer and scout that lower Sheep Creek country.

Next morning, Stanley crossed the creek to examine the country to the south, while I climbed directly north up the range. Getting up to timberline, I saw a goat ahead near the crest, and decide to stalk as close as I could for a photograph. Getting closer, I saw there was a big boulder behind which I could approach fairly close. I reached the boulder without alarming the goat, and peeped over. As I raised my head slowly, a pair of goat horns appeared just the other side of the boulder. I lowered my head, got out my camera in a hurry, set the focus for 10 feet, raised and snapped—and I had a peach of a close-up of that goat. Of course, that alarmed the goat, and it trotted off and joined the first goat I had seen, about 100 yards ahead in the rocks. Those two goats stood there and looked at me. No chance whatever of getting closer for another picture.

So I left them and went on to the crest of the range to see what lay beyond. Here the crest was snow-covered, so I lay down and crept forward slowly so as not to expose myself on the skyline. Then I reached the crest where I could begin to look down. Holy smoke! I was on a snow cornice, and right below me was a great void. Very slowly, I crawled back to safety, then traversed several hundred yards to the left where there were some rocks from which the country ahead could be safely viewed. From there a big valley lay below, terminating to the left on a rock-rimmed basin. Getting out my binocular, I examined them. There were nine goats, including two kids. Two were standing knee-deep in the little stream that issued from the basin, just soaking their hoofs I guess. I was not particularly interested in them, for of course I already had my goat trophy and we were not in need of meat.

So I started to examine the mountainside across the valley, and in a few minutes saw three animals in the field of the glasses, and then a little beyond two more. I could see they were sheep all right, but could not tell if they were rams or ewes until one crossed a patch of snow that silhouetted big curling horns. Rams at last after many days of hard hunting around timberline! I watched them for some time. They were just grazing quietly. They were so far off it was not possible to stalk them that day, so I decided to leave them and return the next day with Stanley.

On the way back I had a bit of an adventure. I was very thirsty and lay down at the first little creek I came to for a drink. As I did so I heard something thumping a little tree, and then something trotting. I turned over and looked to where the sound came from, and there came a small bull moose. He trotted right up to me, almost above me. His nose was almost above my feet. I was frightened and covered him with the muzzle of my rifle. Then I yelled at him. You never saw such a surprised animal in your life. He almost tumbled over backward, and trotted off, grunting at every step. Evidently he thought I was a cow.

Before daylight the next morning Stanley and I were on our way to the ram pasture. Yes, they were still there, but much farther to the left on the hillside toward the basin, and the goats were still in the basin. As we watched and planned a stalk, the goats climbed upward toward the sheep. The sheep evidently did not like this intrusion, and they too moved upward, and finally walked up to the top of the rocks above the head of the basin and lay down, probably for their midday nap.

That was the signal we had been waiting for. We moved away from them and out of sight on our ridge, descended into the valley to the right, and then started to climb the mountainside where they had been previously feeding, which was out of sight from where they were lying. That was an awful climb. The dirt and grass stood just as steep as it possibly could. We would climb 100 steps, then sit down and get our breath. After a time we got to the top, soaked to the skin, although it was freezing. We peeped over. Yes, the sheep were still there lying down. We moved along the ridge, keeping just below the crest so the sheep could not see us. It was about a mile to them. Every few hundred yards we would look again to be sure they were not moving. The crest here was composed of little pinnacles of rock, with slide-rock in between each. The rams were lying on the slide-rock between two pinnacles. We could just see the curl of two horns, but dared not try to get closer, so we lay there for the time being. In about 15 minutes the animals began to get up, and then we could see them clearly, five big mature rams. They started to move, and we waited to see if they would continue in a line which would bring them about 100 yards directly below us on the slide.

We were ready. I put the sling of my rifle on my arm and got into a steady prone position. Stanley moved beside me and did the same. On came the rams at a slow walk. The leading ram was a magnificent animal with a complete curl. I bet his horns would have gone well over 40 inches! But in those days rams' horns were not judged by the length of the curl, but by the circumference of the horns at the base, and the second and third rams seemed to have much more massive horns. I whispered to Stanley that I would take the second ram, and he said he would take the third. When these two rams got about 100 yards directly below us I fired at mine, and Stanley followed instantly with his shot.

Then a funny thing happened. All five rams stopped instantly in their tracks. The two we fired at did not move a particle. It was utterly impossible that we should have missed. It was a dead-easy shot, only 100 yards, and we were both in steady prone positions with gunslings on our arms. We could hardly believe our eyes. I imagine about five seconds expired. We were both about to shoot again, when our two rams slowly toppled over, just exactly as if they were toy sheep and someone had slowly pushed them over with his finger. We watched them roll over and over down the slide and out of sight. We dreaded for fear they would ruin their horns, and jumped up and started to leap down the slide after them. Then another funny thing happened. The two of us ran directly past the three remaining rams which just stood there and watched us. It appeared as if there was a ram not 20 feet on either side as I ran through them. These rams had never seen a man before. We were in a virgin game field.

Those rams rolled about 300 yards down the slide and landed within a few feet of each other. My, how big they seemed! They must have weighed at least 250 pounds apiece. The horns were not injured in the slightest. Stanley and I stood over them, shook hands and congratulated ourselves. After a time we started to look around. Wow! The rams had rolled almost into the bunch of goats, and there was one big billy close by. Stanley lost no time in collecting him and had his goat trophy. I shall never forget that day.

We gutted all three animals where they lay. It was now getting late. It would be dark in an hour. No place to spend the night; no wood and no shelter, so we decided to try to make our base camp that night and come back on the morrow with the horses.

We got to the top of the ridge where I had first seen the sheep the day before, and could look down into the Sheep Creek valley and see just about where our camp lay below as the light was going out of the sky. We took a sight on a peculiarly shaped peak on the range opposite which was directly in line with our camp and started down. Fifteen minutes later even that peak blotted out, and we had to steer just by my memory of that mountain slope. (I had already been over it three times). As soon as we got down into the timber we cut 10-foot poles and used them to feel ahead.

It was one o'clock in the morning before we got to the creek, and we struck it within 100 yards of our tepee. A pretty good job of dead reckoning in the dark. Stanley lit a candle. I started to make a fire. He was busy in a pannier, and pulled out a parcel wrapped in brown paper. He opened it. It was a fresh head of cabbage. "I've been keeping this hidden for the night we got our rams," he said. So an hour later we sat down in the cheerful light of the fire in the tepee to a delicious supper of creamed fresh cabbage.

The next day we returned and retrieved our trophies.

There is little more to tell. It was late in October, time to turn back if we did not want to be caught in a deep snow that might close the passes over the high range between the Smoky and Athabaska. It took us 12 days to reach the railroad. The fourth day we ran completely out of store grub and from then on lived on meat straight. The night after we crossed the highest pass we had 18 inches of snow. We were just in time. It made going rather hard because we had to break a trail on foot for our horses, and of course it wiped out all vestiges of the old trails. Down in the valley of the Athabaska there was no snow at all. We were welcomed back, for we brought four horse loads of fine meat.

Our little "expedition" had been most successful. We had seen some most beautiful country, had looked behind the ranges, and had put a new hunting country on the map. Besides this I had five fine trophies which along with others now adorn the walls of the Hearth Room at my summer home, *Someday*. The ram had the place of honor above the fireplace.

*••• Cowboy, bronc buster, hunting guide, plus one of the country's most knowledgeable experts on big-bore calibers, Elmer Keith was a legend in his time. The designer of the 41 and 44 Magnum revolvers, plus the 333 O.K.H. rifle, Keith wrote for all the major outdoor magazines —often about hunting in Africa.—*HUNTING ANNUAL 1960 •••

AFRICA'S BIG FIVE
by Elmer Keith

Africa has more dangerous game than any other continent. Elephant, rhino, buffalo, lion and leopard constitute the so-called big five. Opinions vary greatly, even among the members of the East African Professional Hunters Association, as to which of these species is the most dangerous. During two weeks spent in Nairobi and Arusha, I met and conversed with most of the 17 White Hunters who comprise the field staff of White Hunters, Ltd., as well as many famous hunters from other safari outfitters, lone hunters and game rangers. In endeavoring to find out which species each individual considered the most dangerous, I listened to many firsthand accounts of fatalities, maulings and close calls with each of the Big Five. All agreed that the conditions under which the game was hunted had every bearing on which species could be more dangerous.

After many years' correspondence with famous African hunters, I spent 40 days in the bush with John Lawrence of White Hunters, Ltd. While many individual African hunters work solely on their favorite species, these professional White Hunters work on all species, usually having out on safari clients who want all the Big Five. They hunt 10 months of every year, and practically all of them have had close calls or have been mauled or tossed at one time or another. John Lawrence has had a wide and varied experience in 12 years as a White Hunter. He also told me what to expect of these species under different conditions. My own very limited experience in taking the Big Five corroborated his statements 100 per cent. All were unanimous in their opinion, that, under certain conditions, any of the Big Five could be deadly dangerous. All were big-bore men, and I failed to find a single small-bore advocate among the entire lot.

Most of them agreed that a .375 Magnum with scope sight and backed up with a 12-bore shotgun loaded with SSG buckshot were the proper tools for leopards; all were unanimous in their recommendations for the other four species, nothing smaller than the .400 Jeffery, .404 and .416 Magnums, the .424 O.K.H. or .425 Westley Richards and ranging upward to the .577 double rifle. Some preferred the magazine capacity of the big-bore bolt-actions, but most of these men preferred the double hammerless cordite rifle. All agreed the .458 Winchester was an excellent cartridge for the larger species. All advocated soft-nose for lions and leopards, and some for the first barrel or first shot on buffalo, but all agreed on the solid full-jacketed slugs for elephants and rhinos and most of them thought these slugs would serve for the buffalo as well.

Let us take up each species in turn so you can better form your own opinion as the most dangerous of the Big Five.

◆ ◆ ◆

Though I do not feel competent to judge, I would place Old Jumbo on top of the list of big game and also as the most dangerous. When hunting elephants you are up against an intelligence not found in any other animal. Tembo lives to a very old age, probably considerably greater than the average span of man, and he learns as he lives. Good tuskers are nearly always lone bulls that have left the herds, but they have the bad habit of nearly always having from one to three askaris with them. These are younger bulls who have taken up with the old chap you are after. They will feed downwind of the old bull you want. They are usually short-tempered and on the lookout for any possible danger to their patriarchal friend. Sometimes you find two or more great bulls together, as we did on our first elephant stalk, but one of them had half of one tusk broken off and a third of the other. His mate carried a good 100 pounds of ivory on the right side, and I wanted to take him at 40 yards with my .476. When he did not turn around after an hour, we found he had no tusk on the left side at all, so we passed him up. My next elephant stalk was typical of what can be expected. Lawrence and two of our boys had to work through a big herd of cows and calves after they had obliterated the tracks of the four bulls we had trailed for 16 miles. Those cows were disturbed and on the prod for some reason, possibly a strange bull in the herd. However, the old slick-heeled boy that made 22-inch tracks had three askaris with him. Two were very large bulls also, but packed small young ivory, and the fourth was a smaller young bull. On account of the three askari bulls turned head-to-tail a few yards behind the old boy I wanted, I had to shoot him through the heart so he would run off and in so doing take those three askaris with him.

John told me to take the heart shot in such a case, and I gave this elephant both barrels of the .476 Westley Richards through the heart, one after the other. He went about 150 yards before falling, but as expected and desired, the three young bulls not only followed him but kept on going. In elephant hunting the danger comes not from the great tusker you are after, as a rule, but either from askari bulls who have taken on the job of protecting him or from some peevish cow in a herd.

Elephants usually water in the night, then trek as far back into the bush as possible for anywhere from six to 20 miles before they stop. The older and wiser the tusker, the farther he will go before stopping to feed or rest up in the heat of the day. His trail may cross and intermingle with other herds of cows and they may ultimately keep fairly close together. You may get the wind right and make a good stalk on the bull, only to find a young askari bull or an old cow looking right down your collar from the cover of some bush. Such animals will often charge on sight.

In waiting up for elephants in the native shambas, you have the advantage, but when you trail them into dense bush the advantage is on their side of the fence, so to speak.

Every member of a troop or herd of elephants should be located before opening hostilities, especially in heavy forest or dense thorn bush, else you may have an old cow or askari bull tap you on the shoulder and ask, "Aren't you the gink who just bumped off grandpa?" Lone bulls in open country or open bush are comparatively easy, and you can work in with the wind in your face and take the brain shot; but in dense thorn or heavy forest, especially when in full leaf, it is a far different proposition. My friend Boyd Williams was within six feet of a grand old bull, but could see only patches of hide and could not determine where a vital part was, and was charged by a young askari and had to kill him. Of course the old bull slipped away.

The elephant's sense of smell is second to none in this world. Its hearing and vision are fair; its ability to move quietly is remarkable. A mouse makes far more noise running over dry leafy ground than does an elephant, as I had occasion to notice last fall when a wounded bull charged us upwind. We ran back out of the wind and he stopped. We never heard another sound from him, but a mouse made plenty of noise running over the dry leaves, while that large elephant slipped away after losing our scent with never a sound. For all of his great bulk, an elephant's gray hide seems to blend with the thorn and bush and he can do a good job of hiding with very little cover. Of course when a troop stampedes, it is pandemonium and plenty of noise, but an elephant can also slip away as silently as any white-tailed deer.

An elephant's anatomy is different from that of any other animal. After studying the skulls a good bit, I marveled that one could reach the brain at all, even with heavy rifles and solids. The frontal shot presents a target about three by five inches. Hit him between the eyes or a trifle higher, depending on the range. The side shot offers by far the best target. The slug should be placed on a line between eye and ear hole and about an inch forward of the true ear hole. Don't be misled by the wrinkle above the ear hole, for it is far too high to hit the melon-shaped brain. This, for a square broadside shot. If you are to the rear of broadside, then the slug must of course be placed farther to the rear of the ear hole. If forward, from right angles, then it must enter farther forward. The heart is located right between the forelegs and about 18 to 24 inches up from the bottom of the chest. The chest slopes sharply upward from the belly, so the best heart shot is obtained just slightly to rear of the square broadside. Aim on the wrinkle or fold in the skin behind the shoulder. The lungs are higher up, but do not extend back under the ribs as far as on all other game. A heart or lung shot should never be administered behind the rear edge of the ear when it lies back along his side.

Though my friend Gerrit Forbes, who hunted three trips with W.D.M. Bell in the old days, once killed a good bull at 200 yards with his .577, Old Tembo should be taken only at very close range. I shot mine at 40 yards, which Lawrence said was very long range on an elephant. Most professionals such as Bob Foster and John Taylor prefer to work in close—15 to 25 yards is about right—then carefully place that vital first shot and the job is done if they go for the brain. Bob Foster once made a very long run on elephants, each dropped by a single brain shot. He uses a pair of double .470s. Bob Foster, like Forbes and Taylor, is however a very experienced elephant hunter. If the novice is nervous he should, if he has a heavy rifle, go for the heart shot as it is a much bigger target if the animal is turned right. John Lawrence said he usually had his clients shoot the first barrel for the heart, preferably at 15 to 20 yards, then fire the second barrel as quickly as possible, which they usually land higher in the lungs. John uses a matched pair of .416 Rigbys and is very fast in their operation. He said as he grew older he would probably go to a .500 three-inch double express. Norman Read told me he preferred to take his elephant at just 12 yards.

Frontal shots from very heavy rifles, .458 Winchester, .465, .470 and upward will usually stop or turn an elephant if they land very close to the brain, but smaller rifles will have no effect at all on him if they miss the brain. If given the heart or lung shot, you can expect him to run anywhere from 50 yards to a quarter of a mile before going down. If given a head shot and you miss the brain and he does not go down, your chances of ever seeing that elephant again are very slim. Lawrence cautioned me, in case we ever trailed up a wounded bull, that I should then shoot only for the brain, as a wounded elephant will turn on you from a heart shot and kill you. If unwounded and given the same shot, an elephant will simply lurch into a 25 mph run in the direction he is turned, acting the same as most other game would; but if already wounded and trailed up, then he knows you are after him and will turn on the shot instantly and charge. No matter if you have to wait an hour or two to get the exact shot you wish, it is time well spent. Professional elephant hunters live to ripe old age, only if they are very careful of that vital first shot. Know exactly where your rifle shoots for elevation at the ranges you will employ it. If you get close to a wounded bull and he comes for you and you are too close for the frontal brain shot, then bat him in the center of the chest right where the windpipe enters the chest. A solid placed in the bottom of the head if you are almost under him can also range upward into the brain if it misses all the heavy molars; but he is liable to get you with trunk or tusks in falling, or his momentum may carry him over you unless you have room to dodge. A man was killed in the section I hunted by a wounded cow, which charged the two hunters. The man was armed with a .470. He hit a tree with his first shot and misplaced his second slug. His partner's .375 Magnum had little effect on the cow until she had crushed his partner. An elephant carries the trunk curled up under its chin in charging and can slam it out with pile-driver force once he gets in reach of you. This trunk also is then in the way of a frontal chest shot and the brain is the best chance left. Remember, a wounded elephant can trail you like a hound dog with his keen snorkel and will lead you into very dense bush, then circle downwind of his trail and waylay you just as will a wounded grizzly or brown bear.

In the wet season a sack of dry ashes is excellent for testing the wind, and in the dry season, which was the time I hunted, a handful of dust is excellent. Or you can use the age-old method of wetting a finger and holding it up. "Make haste slowly" is a good axiom when hunting elephants. If you are nervous in the slightest, it is then best to wait until you are calm and cool, before attempting the shot. If I am ever again lucky enough to get back to Africa I will put in most of my time on the elephant, for I consider it the world's grandest big game. My greater disappointment on my first trip was that a spine injury prevented me from taking another elephant with that old maestro, Bob Foster of White Hunters, Ltd.

♦ ♦ ♦

Buffaloes, or as the natives call them *M'Bogo*, in Swahili, are probably the roughest customers in Africa, or the world for that matter, if wounded. More White Hunters placed the buffalo on top of the list of dangerous game, than any other of the Big Five. If not wounded, buffaloes are seldom dangerous. They are usually found in small groups of two or three old bulls or small family groups. In the dense bush and on the plains and in some swamps they often run to very large herds. Some of my friends have encountered herds of several hundred each. Even when surprised in dense tall grass, or thorn, as we had happen on two occasions, buffaloes will usually clear out if you give them a chance. Only previously wounded beasts are apt to charge unprovoked.

Wound a buffalo, however, and he becomes a devil incarnate. He will lead you to a good ambush and then wait up for you downwind, where he can get the jump on you. Once he starts his charge, nothing will stop him but death. You can break a shoulder and slow him down, but he will keep right on coming until you kill him. He will select his hideout with care and will wait for hours on end for you to follow up his trail. If possible to circle downwind and hide, he will do so and then jump you from behind after you have passed his hideout.

I have read many accounts of hunters being charged by a whole herd of buffalo. To my notion, these instances are not charges at all. Buffaloes, like young domestic cattle, are often very curious and a herd will often come right up to a hunter if they have not been hunted and face him, with necks outstretched and noses searching for his scent. They are then just curious, and it is not a charge in any sense of the word. The old bulls may be in the lead and others may jostle and crowd forward to see for themselves what this strange creature is, but they are then not charging at all. Usually if the hunter stands his ground they will soon satisfy their curiosity, wheel and run off. Their gait is a fast, yet peculiar, lumbering gallop that will cover ground at about 30 mph at full speed.

The danger in buffalo hunting comes from the odd animal some native may have wounded and failed to follow up. These beasts usually live alone and are vicious. They will also usually hang out in dense cover where they can hide and way-lay the hunter. Biltong hunters and native poachers often wound buffalo and let them get away, with little effort being made to finish the job. These animals then become the most dangerous on earth, for you never know when one will be encountered. My friend Ed Helm killed a very fine old bull who had a native arrowhead imbedded in back of a shoulder in a very large festering wound. Evidently the poison employed had been stale and it had not killed the bull. Ed put him down with one shot and finished the job.

The type of country hunted has every bearing on the danger involved. If it is nice open bush, then little trouble will be encountered if that first shot is placed right. But if it is very tall high grass, as where we hunted in the swamp at the lower end of Lake Manyarra, then anything can happen. The one bull we jumped there was at just a few feet range, probably five paces away, and he came up out of the mud with a grunt and stood facing us for two minutes, the while he shook his head and grunted at us and John proceeded to cuss him out. Finally with a shake of his head he swapped ends and ran. Had he been a wounded bull, we would have been hard pressed to down him before he was on us.

He can soak up an unbelievable amount of heavy slugs and still keep coming, unless spine or brain is hit. Hunters told me of one bull absorbing 11 .375 Weatherby Magnums plus a handful of .470s before he went down for the count. Nearly every hunter who has worked long on buffalo has had some close calls, and all have seen buffalo take a lot of hammering if that first shot was not placed just right. Heavy slugs that would often stop or turn an elephant or rhino only infuriate further a wounded buffalo. Although he is a powerful, stocky animal, resembling somewhat a black Angus bull in shape, his legs are longer and he is ever so much faster. A buffalo also is very cunning and uses his head in planning his attack. Unlike with an elephant, you can kill one bull out of a herd and the others will run off. If you shoot and wound him he will likely leave the herd and select a hiding place to lie in wait for you, but his companions will go on about their business.

While an elephant herd may attack if provoked or with young calves, a buffalo herd will usually run off if given a little time to satisfy its inquisitive nature. A wounded animal however is something else, and no more determined adversary can be found on this green earth. Hunters have been treed and the wounded buff stayed with them sometimes all day and night until he died or some help came along to kill him. When you set out for a buffalo, remember it is you or him when you start hostilities, so it's imperative that you stalk to certain killing range if at all possible and then make absolutely sure your first shot is a killing hit.

John Lawrence says he has had to turn down many fine buffalo heads because they could not get close enough for his clients to be sure of a killing shot. He said he would not let the average client shoot at over 50 yards. Buffaloes water regularly and once located can often be approached as they come and go to water. During the heat of the day they usually shade up in some swamp, deep brushy donga or dense forest. The good heads are usually on the old solitary bulls that have been whipped out of the herd, though sometimes magnificent heads will be found in a herd. Often two or three old bulls will roam around together, probably from the desire for companionship and mutual protection against the lion, their only enemy except man.

The brain is hard to hit on a buffalo. His head goes up as soon as he spots you and the point of aim should be the end of the nose for a brain shot. The buffalo does not lower his head in a charge until ready to toss you, so frontal shots should go down the nasal passage. The heavy horn bosses will often break up or turn a heavy slug, although I have seen heads that had been killed with a forehead brain shot just under the horn bosses. Usually when taking a charging buffalo, it is well to break a shoulder and slow him down. A heart shot will eventually kill him but won't do it soon enough to save the hunter. If a broadside shot is offered, then the center of the shoulder in line with the spine is the most killing shot you can administer. The brain can also be reached from the rear if the animal is quartering away and you hit him at the base of the neck in line with the brain behind the horns.

The last two shots I fired in Africa were from my .476 Westley Richards at a big buffalo bull. He was a lone bull feeding off to one side of a big herd. Broadside on at 63 yards I took him square through the heart with a 520-grain solid, and the effect was exactly the same as if he had been hit with an electric goad. He simply jumped into a 30 mph run. Pulling the big rifle down out of recoil, I swung my sight under his chin and swung with him as he ran and gave him the second barrel. That struck him square in center of shoulder and broke both shoulder and spine. The bull's chin hit the grass, his front legs folded back under him, while his hindquarters stayed up in the air. He sledded along for 30 feet on his chin in this position before hitting heavy rocks and stopping his slide. I consider the buffalo next to the elephant as top African game. A good buffalo head is something to be proud of.

◆ ◆ ◆

Of all the curious-shaped game of Africa, the rhino exists today just as he did back in prehistoric times. He is a hangover from the Pleistocene at least. Two species exist in Africa and three in Asia. Of the two African species the black rhino is still legally shot, but the white or square-mouthed rhino is now fully protected. The black species, actually he is not black but gray, is the more vicious.

Rhinos will fight hell out of anything or anybody at any time, even their own kind. Their senses of smell and hearing are very acute but their eyesight is very poor. Ordinarily if not hunted they are stupid beasts and easily accounted for, but in a country where they have been continuously hunted for their horn and hide, they can be very very hard to come by. The horn is worth about $12 a pound in Africa, and I have heard it was worth as much at $20 an ounce in India as an aphrodisiac. Continuous poaching for the horns has now driven the rhino back into the very thickest thorn scrub in many sections of Tanganyika and other provinces. The rhino waters in the early evening and then treks back into the thickest thorn he can find, usually on some rocky hills. He lives on the twigs of bitter thorn and other plants. The dung is deposited in one place, usually near some tree or stump or fallen log, then he kicks it all over the place with his feet. He is almost always accompanied by his retinue of tiny tick birds, who not only pick the ticks out of the wrinkles in his heavy hide, but also flutter up above him and give him instant warning of any danger. The rhino is the source of much of their food and they take damn good care of him.

He is as unpredictable as a March wind. He may charge any sound at once, or he may stand perfectly still and try to locate the danger and then barge away in the opposite direction, with head held high and his little pig tail sticking up over his back. He crashes through the heaviest thorn with the greatest ease, just like a huge hog. He will weigh two or three tons and can run 30 mph. John Lawrence had one chase him up a bush road. John was driving the safari jeep car, and the rhino was fast enough to catch up and ram a horn through one of the spare tires carried on the rear end of the jeep.

We trailed rhinos into the thickest thorn several days, and always the wind would change, or the rhino would circle downwind of us, or he would hear the thorns scraping on our shirts. Then he would depart in a hurry, giving us not even a glance at his gray hide. On some occasions we made successful stalks only to find nice long-horned cows with tiny calves and of course turned them down as they are illegal with young calves. When you have to get down on hands and knees, or travel stooped over to get under the thorn, then the rhino has every advantage and I found him hard to approach under such circumstances.

Usually rhinos are encountered when hunting other game and offer no problem except to find one with a good horn. The White Hunters consider them stupid beasts and place them at the bottom of the list of the Big Five, but I notice they are also very careful to keep a heavy rifle loaded with solids in their hands when in dense thorn inhabited by rhinos. The beast's utter stupidity is what makes him dangerous, for he is just as apt to charge any sound as to run, and in dense thorn, where you cannot dodge, or run, he has the advantage. Get into a heavy thorn thicket with several of the beasts around you, and you can get in a tight spot very easily. A rhino can be dodged but not outrun. In a charge the horns cover the frontal part of the brain so it's best to break a shoulder, which will usually turn him off his course and then give you a side shot which should go through shoulder into spine. Unlike a buffalo, he is easily turned. He will make false or bluffing charges, but the hunter never knows when he starts one whether it is a bluff, or will be carried through. In spite of considerable protection, poachers still take a lot of rhinos.

A young bull rhino was the only one of the Big Five to give me a charge, and I broke that up at its outset with a 520-grain .476 slug in the end of the nose, right under the horn. The heavy slug shattered all the upper jaw teeth on the right side, and doubt very much if that rhino could see after the first slug hit him. He simply stood on his head and rooted his way toward us. When he did get up on his front feet and I shot for his left shoulder, he again fell on his nose from the effects of the first slug, and my second slug raked his ribs, kidneys and lodged in the right ham. Lawrence then took him on while I reloaded, and put his first .416 410-grain slug in the flat of right shoulder behind the bone but raking back to the left flank. This shot brought him up on his feet and running, but also turned him away from us and he ran right out in the open. John caught him again through the tops of the boss ribs over shoulders. By then I was reloaded and hit him square in the right shoulder and the slug went on through the spine killing him instantly.

A rhino comes fast, and waiting too long while he took movies of a charging rhino cost Charlie Cottar his life. He had killed hundreds of them, one with a small prospector's pick that he drove down through the animal's spine as it charged past him. Yet in the end a stupid rhino accounted for this grand old hunter.

◆ ◆ ◆

The African lion is considered the King of Beasts, and certainly is a most magnificent old gentleman. Many experienced professional hunters place him on top of the danger list. Where lions are much hunted they will make every effort to escape unnoticed, and usually do a very good job of it. In Kenya and Tanganyika it is unlawful to shoot them by artificial light, except in the case of a man-eater. Lions are like the leopard, nocturnal. They make their kill, eat their fill and then like to lie up in the shade during the heat of the day. To get a good-maned lion today takes some doing, unless you are very lucky. Most of these are killed at the end of the rainy season in the thorn bush country. This, because the lion is a dirty feeder. He gets blood and offal all over his big face and mane, then the hot sun dries and cakes it there. When he barges through the thorn his great ruff is torn out and scrubbed away, until a lion at the end of the dry season in thorn bush country usually has only a short ruff left of his once-magnificent mane. Many writers claim that the lioness does the killing. I did not find this to be so at all times, for we once found where two lions had killed a young rhino and the rhino's horns were still covered with long blonde lion mane.

Pairs of big lions kill not only young rhinos and elephants but buffaloes as well. These buffalo-killers are usually very fine large specimens. My old buffalo had huge scars on back and shoulders and the ears were ripped, showing plainly a lion had been on him at one time. I also saw a huge bull giraffe, with one ear chewed off and was completely sans a fly-chaser from a lion. My sable bull also had his tail chewed off and was completely sans a fly-chaser. The game ranger at Manyoni told me there had been found three dead calf elephants in the last two years that were killed by lions and also dead lions killed by elephants. One baby elephant had been killed by a lioness, and the lioness was found pressed down into the earth until it was perfectly level. The cow elephant had caught the lioness and simply stamped her right down into the ground.

Usually, lions travel in small prides or families, but some prides number upward of a dozen animals. Usually one old male is the boss and he may have one to three lionesses and their cubs with him. My old lion had three lionesses with him and one of them had three small spotted cubs with her. A young maned lion was also included in the pride. We jumped another pride the day I killed my buffalo. It consisted of a young maned lion, a lioness and four grown cubs.

Lions are best hunted by baiting. You hang up a bait and tie it securely with heavy ropes, then slip up to the bait each morning at day light with suitable cover and with the wind in your favor. If you are lucky you may, in time, get a shot at the King of Beasts. We ran lion baits for 16 days before getting a shot at the old man. We had seen a lioness on the bait the previous morning and could hear the rest of the pride feeding on the rhino hams in the bush, so we simply slipped away and got them another zebra. The next morning we had lions all over the place, and they were so full that they slept a bit late and we had our lion. John Lawrence knows his lions and knows how to hunt them. The lion is grand game, and should be so treated. Only adequate rifles should be used on him, and that first shot should never be fired until you are certain of making a killing or crippling hit.

Lions are often located by the buzzards. If you investigate, any time you see a cloud of buzzards circling, you will usually find a lion kill and can then put out additional baits in that section and have an excellent chance of getting your lion. We found several kills but most were too old to do us any good. We sat up one whole afternoon on the rhino kill only to be eaten by tsetse flies, and I am convinced the lions watched us from farther up that ridge. We found their tracks the next day and trailed them several miles until we lost their spoor. Lawrence has trailed up a good many lions, and after a good rain on suitable ground they are not hard to track. We trailed up one but jumped him in a heavy low bush, and all I saw was the bushes jump three times and heard his short grating roar as he took off. John saw him for one jump and said he was a magnificent full-maned lion. Although we put out a bait for him at once and waited for the buzzards to come to the bait and thus attract the lion, no birds showed. I am convinced the native poachers had poisoned them in that section, for we found very few buzzards there.

Most White Hunters insist on their clients using only heavy rifles on lions. John Lawrence told me he would be very unhappy if I used my small rifle on lion, a .333 O.K.H. throwing a 300-grain bullet at 2,400 feet, and told me to use the .476 which I did. I planted the 520-grain soft-nose right through his heart at 100 yards as he lay stretched out on the ground. Even then he was able to jump to his feet, give one short coughing roar, swap ends, make three more jumps into the bush, and one after entering it, before he hit thorn so thick he could not get through and died there. In spite of all his experience with lions, John told me they still made his hair rise when one turned loose a full-throated roar at the start of a charge. A lion comes very fast, and there is nothing above his eyes but hair. Aim should always be below the white spot on the chin of a charging lion, for his teeth will often break up or deflect a slug. Most fatalities on lions are the result of the hunter shooting too soon and not letting the beast get close enough to make certain of his shot. If a magazine rifle is used, then one should feed them to him from the start; if a big double is the gun, then I should favor waiting until the lion was 50 yards away for the first shot and make it good, then follow with the second barrel. A lion roars to unnerve the hunter and get him rattled. Lawrence told me a lion often emits one coughing roar after another during the charge. Best procedure is to kill him the first shot if possible, and then if you do sustain a charge, take your time and break it up with the next shot if possible.

In some sections the local native warriors all have lion headdresses, and for this reason good-maned lions are very scarce there. Once the natives ring a lion and close in on him there can be but one ending. He may kill or maul a native or two, but they will make a pincushion out of him with their long spears. There is not much danger in a sportsman killing a lion over a bait when backed up by a competent White Hunter, if he makes sure of his first shot. If he muffs that first shot and lets a wounded lion get into high grass, or heavy bush, then there is every possibility of someone getting mauled. Usually the White Hunter then takes on the job and orders his client to stay out in the open. The lion is a gentleman, and even when wounded and lying in heavy cover, he will nearly always warn the hunter by one of his roars before he charges. He may bluff at times, but when he makes up his mind to come, then he comes like a bat out of hell, and to the finish, either your life or his, depending on how well you shoot.

The natives in many sections have the habit of burying their dead by simply carrying them out of the boma and leaving them for the hyenas to eat. In the morning the deceased is gone as completely as if he had never been there. Sometimes old lions, long past their prime and unable to catch their own game, will drive the hyenas off such a feast and get started eating the body. They will then become man-eaters. Others who have been wounded by man and can no longer kill their own game will sooner or later kill a native, and having found how easy it is, will continue and become man-eaters. Man-eaters still account for a great many natives each year in Africa, and although the game department trails and kills every one it hears of, a new crop occurs every so often. Russell Douglas of Tanganyika Tours had a lioness tree his natives last year and it stayed right in camp until they killed her, in the light of the car headlights. Of all dangerous game, I believe the man-eating lion or leopard or the man-eating tiger of India to be the worst. Being nocturnal they kill their man of a night, when they have every advantage. They also have no fear of man and become very cunning in their attacks. My vote goes to the man-eater as the most dangerous game in the world.

◆ ◆ ◆

Although small in stature, the leopard is classed as one of the Big Five of African dangerous game, and deservedly so. My friend Gerrit Forbes always claimed the leopard should be called the Prince of Beasts. He is a beautiful animal, perhaps one of the most beautiful of all the feline tribe. He is wise and cunning, nocturnal in his habits, and wears one of the best camouflage suits of all African game. Like our Chinese pheasant he can hide perfectly in any cover, or almost no cover at all. He will fight man, beast or devil at any time. Though he will slink away and hide if he gets a chance as a rule, don't underestimate him, for he is not afraid of you. Leopards, or *chui* as the natives call them, have a prodigious strength and will kill and carry a buck that is much larger and heavier than themselves up a tree and hang it over a limb by its horns. Then they will stay with that kill until it is eaten up. A leopard will attack unprovoked at times when you approach his kill, and at other times he will jump you for pure cussedness. If wounded, the spotted devil will hide in the best cover he can find and you will never see him as a rule until he jumps you. They are fast as chain lightning. If in heavy cover, you will get no chance to raise your gun. Best procedure when a wounded leopard jumps for you is to poke the gun at him like a spear and shoot at the same time. Lawrence told me to use this procedure when we drove into the high grass where my leopard had run after I shot him.

I had taken the heart out of this leopard, so we found him dead. We had waited for the boys to hear the shot and bring up the jeep and by that time it was dark so we loaded both shotguns with buck and drove into the grass where the last savage growls had come from the leopard. I for one was very glad to find him dead in the headlamps of the jeep. Our trackers knew the score and each had armed himself with a panga and sat in the backseat ready to chop the leopard off either Lawrence or myself if he landed on us.

One morning as John Lawrence and I approached a lion bait we had hung in a thorn tree, a big tom leopard came out of the tree right over our heads, so to speak, and landed with a grating growl right in front of us. I swung my .476 Westley on him instantly and would have killed him, had not John yelled, "Don't shoot!" John said had either of us been alone and walked under that tree, the spotted cat would probably have landed on his back. The leopard had appropriated our lion bait and of course considered it his own meat, so was very nasty in his remarks as he left. Once a leopard attacks, he will not quit and is just as persistent as a weasel; he will either kill or be killed before the fray ends. A leopard usually grabs a man with teeth and front paws, trying to find the throat with his teeth, the while he doubles up and kicks with those terrible hind claws and tries to disembowel his adversary. Although a man has a better chance of surviving a leopard mauling than a lion mauling until his hunting companions can help him, he is very certain to be in a sad state when it is over.

The best possible insurance against a leopard mauling is to shoot only when you can be absolutely certain of making a killing hit. If you hit him too far back or don't center a vital organ and he gets into the grass or bush, then someone is certain to get hurt when you come up with him. Shotguns loaded with buck are far better weapons for following up a wounded leopard than a rifle. Remember, a wounded leopard will seldom disclose his hiding place until you come in certain reach of him. Then he will come like a flash and be on you instantly. He is so very fast, you will see only a spotted blur and be very lucky to get off even a shot, let alone hit the beast vitally. The above are some of the reasons why the leopard is considered by many very experienced White Hunters to be the most dangerous of all African big game.

Leopards are on the increase, at least in Tanganyika, where I hunted and any hunter should have no trouble getting a leopard by baiting one. I saw three in broad daylight and could have killed all of them easily after I had killed my own spotted cat. The special 500 shilling license and one only to a hunter offers the leopards enough protection so that they will be with us for a long time.

Of a night we heard them several times and they emit a sort of coughing, grating growl. The sound carries for a considerable distance on a still night. My leopard let out a grating growl every jump after I shot him through the heart in the bait tree and as he ran for the tall grass, then he stopped and growled for some time in one spot. His savage growl is like nothing else I ever heard and resembles the noise of forcing a circular saw through a hard, knotty log. He leaves no doubt in your mind as to his savage intentions if he gets in reach of you. A leopard is so incredibly fast he often catches monkeys and baboons. Dogs are his special dish. A dog has no chance with him at all if alone, and even in packs some of the dogs are bound to get killed when they close with a leopard. Though only half the size of a big jaguar, *chui* has as much stark courage as any animal on earth and is just as fast as anything that breathes. He is generally rather smaller than the American cougar or mountain lion and has small feet, but even a small leopard is 10 times more dangerous than any cougar. A very big tom leopard would run about eight feet in length, tip to tip, and weigh around 200 pounds, but the average would probably be nearer 6 1/2 feet in length and 125 pounds.

Any good rifle such as the .30-06 upward is plenty gun for a leopard, but the slug must be placed in a vital area. Tanganyika law however makes it mandatory that you use nothing less than a .375 caliber rifle in power, on lions, and a .400 on elephants, buffaloes, rhinos and hippos. It is a very good law. The leopard is not hard to penetrate and you need a soft-point or hollow-point that will expand very easily, so maximum damage is done on passing through the animal. As John Lawrence once remarked to me. "It's better to have a big hole through a leopard's hide, than a lot of holes in your own."

••• A retired engineer living in Louisiana, Van Rex Boyett spent a good deal of time bear and sheep hunting in Alaska and Canada in the 1950s and 1960s. The following, totally true article is the only one he ever sold to a major national magazine; we're glad it was SPORTS AFIELD.—DECEMBER 1962 *•••*

JACK'S LAST HUNT
by Van Rex Boyett

Both men and horses bowed their heads as our pack string pushed endlessly on into the teeth of the driving snowstorm. It was one of those miserable camp moving days that will never be forgotten. Snow fell down our necks, our hands were raw and bleeding, we were saddle weary and half frozen. Our only thought was reaching the next campsite before night fall.

This was the fourth of October 1959, and winter was setting in. It was the last hunt of the season, and its windup seemed none too soon. My hunting partner, Jimmie Walker, and I were returning from the source of the Prairie River in northern British Columbia. We were headed downriver after hunting the great Stone rams, whose realm is that fantastic upended world of dying glaciers situated north of the Prophet and Muskwa rivers—but that's another story! Jack Powell, brother of the well-known outfitter, Gary Powell, was our guide. The rest of the party included Luther West, an assistant guide, and our cook, Fred Klatt, one of the few real old-timers left in the north country.

Ahead, Jack reined up. The pack horses stopped in turn, as they took up the slack in the string. Jack leaned sideways in the saddle and peered through the slant-ing flakes, then climbed off his horse and looked intently. A moment later he turned and motioned for Jimmie and me to ride on up. There, meandering across the trail, were enormous grizzly tracks headed toward the horse carcass on the river bar. Almost a month earlier we had passed the dead horse and reckoned then that a griz-zly was sure to be working it by the time we came back.

Since Jimmie wanted a grizzly on this trip more than anything else, it was quickly decided that he and Jack should ride ahead and try to catch the grizzly at the kill, while the rest of us took the pack string on to make camp. They hurriedly broke off the trail, as little time remained before dark.

With this change of events, it seemed only a short while before we made camp and had coffee bubbling in the cook tent. As I sat steaming by the cherry-red stove, with the misery of the day ebbing away, I realized anew how discomforts and hard-ships of the north country cause one to appreciate such commonplace things as shelter, fire and coffee.

Jack and Jimmie had to detour three or four miles to the east, then approach the kill upriver, in order to reach the only possible vantage point having an unobstructed view. They tied their horses about a half mile away and made the final approach on foot. Wind and falling snow muffled their steps as they moved along, but the wind was at their backs—all wrong! Having no other choice, they eased through the small spruce along the river bank, then climbed the bluff and looked into the gulch.

The dead horse lay on a narrow sand bar about 120 yards away. While the griz-zly was not in sight, it was certainly obvious that he had been there. The horse was about half eaten, and driftwood had been piled up on the remains in typical grizzly fashion. Snow was tracked and torn up all around, and a well-used trail led from the carcass up the cutbank into thick spruce bordering its edge. Maybe the bear had gotten their scent and slipped into the protective timber, or maybe he was just lying concealed, watching his find.

A grizzly working a kill will usually bed up close by and watch it, eating inter-mittently until nothing remains. Sometimes this may take a week or 10 days. During the period of watching, anything that happens to blunder on the scene is almost certain to be attacked—even birds.

Jack carefully searched for the bed with glasses, but failed to locate it. However, with the poor visibility, it could easily have been overlooked. Between then and dark no living thing appeared, so they backed off and headed for the horses.

We had a celebration in the cook tent that night. Fred did justice to sheep backstrap, and we spun bear yarns with abandon. Everybody chipped in his version of the certain finale. The chances were 10 to 1 of catching the old boy at his busi-ness within the next day or so. In fact he was about as good as skinned right then. I needled Jimmie about making a one-shot kill—to keep the taxidermist from hav-ing to sew up too many buttonholes. We all laughed and cajoled, as choice barbs flew in all directions. It's too bad that camp wit, like a good joke, has the habit of being so soon forgotten and seldom recorded. Later we fell asleep to the gritty rattle of fine snow hitting the tent and to the sporadic jangle of horse bells, peculiar to hobbled horses pawing for grass under the snow.

The next morning Jack and Jimmie were back at the river by daylight. The grizzly had fed and was gone. They checked again along about midmorning, then after dinner and again just before dark, but with the wind whipping their scent upriver, they had little expectation of seeing the bear.

The following day started out the same—more night feeding, wind still wrong, and no bear. However, late that afternoon, perhaps a half hour after taking up the vigil, the wind died. Everything became as still as death. Presently a timber wolf emerged from the dark spruces and slunk out onto the sand bar. He watched the timber for several minutes, circled the carcass and cautiously started to feed. Then it happened!

Without a sound and almost too quickly to follow, the big grizzly came down the cutbank and made a vicious pass at the thief. The alert wolf nimbly leaped aside and backed off, watching at a respectable distance while his old enemy took possession of the kill. With another feint and a snarl at the wolf, the grizzly pulled the driftwood and debris off the carcass, climbed aboard and began feeding.

Jimmie rested his .30-06 across a low spruce limb which had been previously trimmed for the purpose. Then came Jack's only admonition, "Watch it, Jim; don't shoot too high. There's a lot of hair on his back."

The grizzly was broadside, as Jimmie settled the crosshairs on what looked to be his shoulder blade and fired. At the crack of the rifle the wolf whirled and vanished. The bear was knocked completely off the horse and lay on his back, feet kicking the air. Jimmie covered him almost a minute until the kicking subsided and stopped, then decided there was no use punching any more holes. It looked so convincing that Jack didn't insist on shooting again, as his better judgment dictated.

"Good boy, Jim, you got him with one shot!" Jack shouted, pounding his back. Both men jumped to their feet and happily exchanged congratulations.

Glancing back, Jack gasped in disbelief, "Shoot again, Jim! Shoot!"

The grizzly, now back on his feet, was lumbering toward the timber at a rolling gait. Jimmie whipped up the rifle and hastily fired two more offhand shots without any apparent effect. As the bear cleared the cutbank and disappeared into the spruce, he gave no evidence of being hurt. Both men stood dumbfounded at the realization of what had happened—then cursed their stupidity when speech returned. No shooting light remained, so they headed for camp in utter dejection.

Irrespective of the field of endeavor, it is common for all men to try to salvage victory out of defeat, so here; in lieu of a celebration in the cook tent that night, everybody was dead serious, considering what steps to take to turn the tables. Possibly the grizzly was dead with a fatal lung or heart shot, or maybe he had only been stunned with a high hump shot—so went the varied speculation until bedtime. A follow-up in the morning would soon tell, and everyone agreed it would be grim business.

After breakfast Fred decided he would go along. His excuse was to chop wood and build up a fire while the skinning took place, and to help carry the hide back, since they would be traveling on foot. I suggested that maybe I should also go along as backing gun, but Jimmie declined this offer. He wanted to make the kill alone, and felt that if the job should need finishing, the firepower of his automatic rifle was more than ample.

Jack, as is the custom with British Columbia guides, carried no gun. This I have never understood. A rifle had been standard hardware with Alaskan guides of my experience.

"Say, Jack," I questioned, "just what do you do when a grizzly comes charging out of a thicket?"

He grinned and came right back, "Well, Rex, we trust our hunters, but just in case, we always push the dude out front, then run like hell!" We all laughed, and this took the edge off the situation.

Luther and I watched the procession start out upriver. Old Fred bringing up the rear with gunny sacks tied around his feet and legs, and with the camp axe over his shoulder.

The grizzly's trail wound through the thickest cover he could find. Near the river the trail was well blooded, and where it passed between close trees, blood and fatty tissue had rubbed off on both sides, indicating that he was shot through. Rather than follow directly on the trail, Jack traveled off to first one side, then the other. He carefully detoured around thick places of concealment and picked up the trail beyond, where it could be seen for some distance. With every few steps, it was necessary to stop and survey what lay ahead. This was a slow and dangerous undertaking, calling on a man's keenest senses. Jimmie followed several steps behind, gun in readiness and his finger on the safety. Fred no longer carried the axe on his shoulder. After a nerve-racking half mile, they all knew the grizzly was not dead.

Presently wolf tracks joined those of the bear, and soon the first bed was located, but it had long since been vacated, the reason plainly written in the snow. The wolf had followed the grizzly to his bed, knowing he was wounded, then had begun harassing his old enemy. Snow and brush were torn up in all directions where the infuriated grizzly had tried to catch his circling tormentor. The fighting started his wound bleeding again. Apparently he finally gave up fighting and tried to get away, only to have the wolf follow and continue the fiendish harassment. Every 100 yards or so another skirmish had taken place; it had been a wicked, all-night affair.

Jack rightly figured that, as long as the wolf tracks stayed with the grizzly, there was little reason to continue tracking with their original caution. Certainly they could not approach dangerously close to the bear without the wolf breaking off the engagement.

It was in and out of brush and timber tangles for four or five miles, then the tracks became fresher. Soon afterwards the wolf trail turned off. Seeing this, Jack resumed the slow and careful procedure. When little balls of snow could be detected crumbling down into the tracks, he know they were right behind the bear. The trail led downwind, and Jack also knew the grizzly's radar snout kept their position constantly pinpointed. It was a tense and deadly game, which would eventually lead to a showdown.

Jack noticed that the bear always walked, and refused to run or to climb—

maybe it was because he was too badly hurt—or maybe it had to do with the contempt which he held for his persistent antagonists.

Finally the trail turned down a ravine and headed for the river about a half mile away. Jack knew immediately that the grizzly meant to put the river between him and his pursuers, rather than stand and fight. Urging Jimmie to hurry, he broke into a dead run toward the river. As they pushed through the last screening brush, they knew they were too late—far across the opposite river bar, the grizzly was entering the timber. He had succeeded in breaking off the game without a showdown, and without discredit to either contestant.

The river was running ice, far too dangerous to try wading and continuing the chase. For the second day in a row, the hunters turned toward camp, exhausted and beaten

The situation looked awfully gloomy that night. There was only one more day left to hunt. Another snowstorm, threatening all afternoon, finally let go. All our horses had wandered off down the valley, no telling where. Strategy now turned to continuing the chase tomorrow on horseback, if the horses could be located in time, and if the swirling snow didn't pile up overnight and obliterate the trail.

As is sometimes the case when hunting talk dies down, the conversation drifted around to everyone's life history. I recall Jack telling how he had been shot through the lungs in World War II. He then told of the tough days he'd had as a boy in this part of the country, and finally about the ranch he had carved out of the bush down on the Peace River; and how since the ranch was now demanding so much of his time, he expected this would be his last hunt as a professional guide.

Long before daylight the next morning Luther took off to hunt the horses. Fred was down at the river, breaking shore ice to get coffee water. Jimmie was still in the sack, and Jack and I sat warming by the stove, discussing the plans for the day.

Speaking in a reflective mood, as if talking to the stove, Jack began, "I think we had better forget the grizzly and go after a moose today. Not enough fresh snow last night to wipe out his trail, but I don't think he's hurt too badly. However, it's up to Jim, whatever he wants to do."

"Jack," I countered, "if you go after him on horses, you're sure to overtake him, since he won't run, and he won't climb. Now just one of two things can happen—either you will catch him crossing the river or an open ravine, or else he will turn on you."

He grinned and answered, "That's why I think it's a good day to go after moose."

At breakfast, Jimmie's undaunted hopes that today would be the day settled the question. Before long Luther got back with the horses. Today would tell the tale!

A half mile from where he crossed the river, the grizzly bedded up. At the approach of the horses he moved out, and it was here they again picked up his fresh trail. Just as on the day before, he traveled downwind through thick cover. Always he was just ahead, but he refused to run.

Jack never relaxed his caution, skirting the dense cover, carefully surveying what lay ahead each time before moving up. Finally the trail turned up along a side canyon—the bear was going to climb!

Just below timberline, the excitement of the chase mounted. The bear should break into the open any minute now. However, the trail turned toward the canyon, paralleling timberline. Knowing what the grizzly had in mind, they urged the horses forward to intercept and cut off an escape back toward the river. But at the canyon rim the trail turned back down along its very edge—the old devil had already slipped by.

There was still a slim chance for a crossing shot at one of several open side ravines a little way below. In the next desperate moment of abandon they forged directly down the bear's trail which entered a snow-laden spruce thicket. In the middle of the thicket Jack felt a breath of wind in his face! Suddenly he realized the bear had just executed a complete semi-circle and was no longer relying on his sense of smell. This, together with the thick cover, bespoke of an ambush, and a cold, spine-tingling chill came over him. Immediately he started to rein up, but the action came too late!

In a lightning flash the grizzly was on the horse. Buck squealed in terror and pitched wildly, sending his rider sprawling. Turning from the horse, the grizzly pounced on Jack like a cat. Before he could throw up an arm in defense, a vicious swipe caught his head, half stunning him and ripping the scalp off the left side of his skull. Through reflex action, Jack balled up, trying to protect his face and neck with his arms. For the next few seconds, as the grizzly alternately batted and shook him, Jack tried to play dead. This, however, became unbearable, as the long fangs crunched the bone in his shoulder and left arm.

"Shoot, Jim! Shoot! Shoot the S.O.B.!" he screamed in agony. But no shot came! Again he screamed, as the grizzly bit through his heavy mackinaw into his ribs and side—still no shot came!

In the moment of truth before certain disaster, a man's thought oft times race over many unrelated things—so with Jack's "This is it! What a way to die! Home! Bernice and the kids! The life insurance just paid up!"

Shock now dulled the intense pain, as the grizzly held him down, methodically gnawing away at his left thigh. Jack saw the canyon rim only 10 feet away—it would be better to die going over than being eaten alive. Summoning more strength than he possessed, he suddenly fought for his life. With his free leg he landed a vicious kick on the grizzly's snout. In pain and frothing rage the bear turned loose momentarily and grabbed another hold with viselike jaws, but in the precious second of freedom Jack gained a foot or two toward the cliff. By a furious flurry of kicking and clawing he reached the cliff edge a foot at a time, and pulled himself over, literally dragging the bear with him to the brink.

Releasing his leg grip to get better leverage, the grizzly caught Jack's foot and started pulling back up. Jack fought back desperately to maintain his suspended head-down position, kicking furiously and digging his fingers into rock crevices.

Then a miraculous thing happened—his ankle-high moosehide moccasin pulled off, along with his overshoe and wool sock. In pulling free, the bear's fangs ripped his foot open. Down he went tumbling and smashing into the rock projection some 50 feet below the rim. It withstood his impact and he clung there trembling, safe for the moment from death above and below.

Using one hand he pushed his dangling scalp back and wiped the blood out of his eyes. Above, the grizzly stood watching, his mouth dripping foamy saliva, but seeing his prey in an inaccessible position, he turned and disappeared. Jack waited several minutes to see whether the bear would return. Then without realizing his own condition, he tried to climb back to see what had befallen Jim. Unable to reach the top he began the precarious descent down the cliff face to the canyon floor far below him.

Jimmie was about 40 feet behind when the attack occurred; however, the spruce was so thick that he could only hear what was going on. He shucked his mittens and tried vainly to get his rifle out of the tight saddle scabbard before dismounting, but his frightened horse reared and plunged wildly, making it impossible. When he tried to dismount, the terrified horse dragged him through the thicket, almost breaking away with the gun. Finally he got the horse snubbed enough to yank out the rifle, only to have him break free the next instant.

By now, calls for help and sounds of the scuffle had ceased—everything was perfectly quiet. Jimmie slipped back through the thicket, rifle ready, expecting the grizzly to pounce out on him from any side. Presently he got a glimpse, as the bear left the scene—then in overwhelming panic, he dashed forward, backing up to a high boulder at the cliff edge, and stood covering the thicket with his rifle. There was no sign of Jack. The bloody snow was so torn up that it told nothing. Jimmie, in his shaken state of mind, reasoned that Jack had been killed and dragged off, and that he alone was left with the grizzly. To try to get away through the timber with the grizzly lurking there for his next victim was a terrifying thought, so he climbed over the rim and began descending the cliff face, around a projection from the point where Jack had gone down.

At the bottom of the canyon Jimmie suddenly rounded a bend and ran headlong into Jack. He was so shaken, he threw up the rifle and covered him until he recognized what he saw. To each man, it was almost as if the other had returned to life.

Finding no broken bones, and after tying a shirt around Jack's head to stop the flow of blood, the two men headed down the canyon for camp—15 miles away. Jack, reeling from the loss of blood, hobbled along as best he could, with only a wool sock on his torn foot.

The trek back to camp became one ordeal after another. The canyon walls pinched in to ice-glazed waterfalls, necessitating extremely hazardous climbs where a slip would end it all. At the mouth of the canyon they saw where the grizzly had just crossed the trail ahead of them, and they lived in constant fear of another attack, until after they crossed the river. Wading the river, a chance which had to be taken, almost ended in disaster. Running slush ice rushed past in the swift current and nearly swept them off their feet as they clung to each other. Their wet clothes soon froze to their legs and became as lead. Repeatedly, Jack fought back waves of unconsciousness. On and on he went, now completely insensitive to pain. They had to reach camp!

Late that afternoon Jimmie played completely out, saying that he could go no further, and they must stop and build a fire and wait for help. But Jack sternly refused and kept stumbling on—he knew that he might not survive a night in his condition with temperatures dropping to a dangerous 15° below.

Long after dark we heard a shot some distance from camp, then a few minutes later two more shots. When we went out with the gasoline lantern, we could see two pitiful figures, approaching on foot through the snow. The shots had been intended as the distress signal, but the rifle had jammed on the first round—how lucky the gun was not called on during the attack.

We heated pan after pan of water and dressed Jack's wounds as best we could, while details of the encounter were unfolded. I almost passed out pulling spruce needles and matted hair from between his scalp and skull with sharpened match stems, while he sat stoically on a panyard without wincing. There was no way to determine the extent of internal injuries—we could only hope they were not too serious. Neither man's feet were frozen, only because they had kept moving. The rest of the night we stoked the stove and kept Jack doped with aspirin.

There were three saddle horses left. It was still a day's travel on to Gary's main camp at Blue Lake, where our bush pilot was scheduled to rendezvous the next afternoon. But unless a break came in the weather, the plane would never get through, and even if it should, we were fearful that Blue Lake might have already frozen over. In that event it would require five more days horseback to get Jack from there to the Alaska Highway.

Bush pilots of the North are masters at their trade, and have to be to survive. I shall never forget my anxiety on take-off, when the pontoons cleared water less than 50 feet from the rim ice. An hour later Jack and I were back in Fort Nelson, where he got penicillin shots and was sewn together, 25 stitches in the head alone. It was found that no vital organs had been pierced by the bear's fangs.

Jack and I flew on down to Fort St. John together, in order that he could receive further medical attention. News of the encounter traveled fast. At the airport one of his friends came up with an open grin and jibed, "What happened, Jack; did the dude out-run you this time?"

Last year Jack wrote that he had decided that the ranch could still get along without him for several months around hunting season. Since then it has, and probably will for many more. Undoubtedly, the grizzly still roams that wild region, a more truculent customer than ever. But for years to come, Jack, like Captain Ahab in Moby Dick, will always be on the lookout—for a giant silvertip with a scar on his hump.

••• *The author of 12 books, including* THE UNNATURAL ENEMY, *Vance Bourjaily has written for many magazines, including* THE NEW YORKER, ESQUIRE *and* SPORTS AFIELD. *Though he no longer lives in his beloved Iowa, many of his outdoor experiences took place there, in fields near Homestead.*—OCTOBER 1970 •••

IN FIELDS NEAR HOME
by Vance Bourjaily

Any autumn. Every autumn, so long as my luck holds and my health, and if I win the race. The race is a long slow one that has been going on since I started to hunt again. The race is between my real competence at hunting gradually developing, and, gradually fading, the force of the fantasies which have sustained me while the skills are still weak. If the fantasies fade before the competence is really mine, I am lost as a hunter because I cannot enjoy disgust. I will have to stop, after all, and look for something else.

So I shan't write of any autumn, or every autumn, but of last autumn, the most recent and the most skilled. And not of any day, but a particular day, when things went really well.

7:45   No clock need wake me.

7:55   While I am pulling on my socks, taking simple-minded satisfaction in how clean my feet are from last night's bath, relishing the feel against them of heavy, close-knit wool, fluffed and warmed and freshly washed, the phone rings downstairs. I go down to answer it, stocking-footed and springy-soled, but I am not wondering particularly who the caller is. I am still thinking about clean feet and socks. Even 20 years after infantry training, I can remember what it is like to walk too far with wet lint, cold dirt, and calluses between the flesh and the matted stocking sole, and what it is like to long for the sight of one's own unfamiliar feet and for the opportunity to make them comfortable and unrepulsive.

It is Mr. Burton on the phone.

"Hello?"

"Yeah. Hi, Mr. Burton."

"Say, I've got some news. I called a farmer friend of mine, up north of Waterloo last night. He says there're lots of birds, his place hasn't been hunted for a week."

"Uh-huh."

"I thought we'd go up there instead."

Mr. Burton is a man in his late 50s whom I've known for two or three years. He took me duck hunting once, to a privately leased place, where we did quite well. I took him pheasant hunting in return, and he has a great admiration for my dog Moon. He wants his nephew to see Moon work. The kid has a day off from school today.

But: "The boy can't go after all," Mr. Burton says. "His mother won't let him. But say, I thought we might pick up Cary Johnson—you know him don't you? The attorney. He wants to go. We'll use his car."

Boy, I can see it. It's what my wife calls the drive-around. Mr. Burton will drive to my house; he will have coffee. We will drive to Johnson's house. We will have coffee while Johnson changes to different boots—it's colder than he expected. Johnson will meet a friend who doesn't want to hold us fellows up, but sure would like to go if we're sure there's room. We will have coffee at the drugstore while Johnson's friend goes home, to check with his wife and change. It will be very hot in the drugstore in hunting clothes; the friend will phone and say he can't go after all. Now nothing will be holding us up but the decision to change back to my car, because Johnson's afraid my dog's toenails will rip his seat covers. Off for Waterloo, two hours away (only an hour and a half if Mr. Burton knew exactly how to find the farm). The farmer will have given us up and gone to town. Now that we're here, though, we will drive into town to the feed store, and . . .

"Hell, Mr. Burton," I say. "I'm afraid I can't go along."

"Sure you can. We have a date, don't we?"

"I'll be glad . . ."

"Look, I know you'll like Johnson. That's real hunting up there—I'll bet you five right now we all get limits."

I will not allow myself to think up an excuse. "I'm sorry," I say. "I'll be glad to take you out around here." I even emphasize you a little to exclude Johnson, whoever he is.

"I pretty much promised my farmer friend . . . Oh, look now, is it a matter of having to be back or something?"

"I'm sorry."

"Well, I told him we'd come to Waterloo. There are some things I have to take up to him."

Not being among the things Mr. Burton has to take to his farmer friend, nor my dog either, I continue to decline. Hot damn. Boy, boy, boy. A day to myself.

Ten months a year I'm a social coward, but it's hard to bully me in hunting season, especially with clean socks on.

8:05   Shaving: Unnecessary. Shaving for fun, with a brand new blade.

Thinking: Mr. Burton, sir, if your hunting is good, and you

get a limit of three birds, in two hours 2
& it takes two hours driving to get there 2
& an hour of messing around on arrival 1
& an hour for lunch 1
& two hours to get back and run people home . . . . <u>2</u>
                                                                                                        8

you will call it a good hunt, though the likelihood is, since you are no better shot than I, that other men will have shot one or more of your three birds. There is a shoot-as-shoot-can aspect to group hunts; it's assumed that all limits are combined, and it would be considered quite boorish to suggest that one would somehow like to shoot one's own birds.

Thinking: suppose I spend the same eight hours hunting, and it takes me all that time to get three pheasants. In my eccentric mind, that would be four times as good a hunt, since I would be outdoors four times as long. And be spared all that goddamn conversation.

Chortling at the face behind the lather: pleasant fellow, aren't you?

Thinking: God I like to hunt near home. The known covert, the familiar trail. And in my own way, and at my own pace, and giving no directions, nor considering any other man's. Someday I'll own the fields behind my house, and there'll be nothing but a door between me and the game—pick up a gun, call a dog, slip out. They'll know where I've gone.

Thinking as I see the naked face, with no lather to hide behind now: I'll take Mr. Burton soon. Pretty nice man. I'll find him birds, too, and stand aside while he shoots, as I did for Jake, and Grannum, and that short guy, whatever his name was, looked so good. Moon and I raised three birds for him, one after another, all in nice range, before he hit one. Damn. That's all right. I don't mind taking people. It's a privilege to go out with a wise hunter; a pleasure to go out with one of equal skill, if he's a friend; and a happy enough responsibility to take an inexperienced one sometimes. Eight or 10 pheasants given away like that this season? Why not? I've got 12 already myself, more than in any season before and this one's barely 10 days old. And for the first time, missed fewer than I've hit.

Eggs?

8:15   Sure! Eggs! Three of them! Fried in that olive oil, so they puff up. With lemon juice. Tabasco. Good. Peppery country sausage, and a stack of toast. Yes, hungry. Moon comes in.

"Hey, boy. Care to go?"

Wags.

"Wouldn't you just rather stay home today and rest up?"

Wags, grins.

"Yeah, wag. If you knew what I said you'd bite me."

Wags, stretches, rubs against me.

"You'd better have some breakfast, too." I go to the refrigerator. Moon is a big dog, a Weimaraner, and he gets a pound of hamburger mornings when he's going to be working. I scoop out cold ground meat from its paper carton, and pat it between my hands into a ball. I roll it across the floor, under his dignified nose. This is a silly game we play; he follows it with his eyes, then pounces as if it really were a ball, trapping it with a paw. My wife, coming in from the yard, catches us.

"Having a game of ball," I say.

"What is it you're always telling the children about not making the same joke twice?"

"Moon thinks it's funny."

"Moon's a very patient dog. I see you're planning to work again today."

I smile. I know this lady. "I really should write letters," I say.

"They can wait, can't they?" She smiles. She likes me to go hunting. She's still not really convinced that I enjoy it—when we were first married I liked cities—but if I do enjoy it, then certainly I must go.

Yes, letters can wait. Let them ripen a few more days. It's autumn. Maybe some of them will perish in the frost if I leave them another week or two—hell, even the oldest ones are barely a month old.

8:45   I never have to tell Moon to get in the car. He's on his hind legs, with his paws on the window, before I reach it. As I get in, start the car, and warm it up, an image comes into my mind of a certain hayfield. It's nice the way this happens; no reasoning, no weighing of one place to start against another. As if the image were projected directly by the precise feel of a certain temperature, a certain wind strength—from sensation to picture without intervening thought. As we drive, I can see just how much the hay should be waving in the wind, just how the shorter grass along the highway will look, going from white to wet as the frost melts off—for suddenly the sun's quite bright.

8:55   I stop, and look at the hayfield, and if sensation projected an image of it into my mind, now it's as if my mind could project this same image, expanded, onto a landscape. The hay is waving, just that much. The frost is starting to melt.

"Whoa, Moon. Stay."

I have three more minutes to think it over. Pheasant hunting starts at nine.

"Moonie. Quiet, boy."

He is quivering, whining, throwing his weight against the door.

I think they'll be in the hay itself—tall grass, really, not a seeded crop; anyway, not in this shorter stuff that grows in the first 100 yards or so along the road. Right?

8:58   Well. Yeah. Whoa.

The season's made its turn at last. Heavy frost every morning now. No more mosquitoes, flies. Cold enough so that it feels good to move, not so cold that I'll need gloves: perfect. No more grasshoppers, either. A sacrifice, in a way—pheasants that feed on hoppers, in open fields, are wilder and taste better than the ones that hang around corn.

The season's made its turn in another sense—the long progression of openings is over: Rabbits, squirrels, September 15. Geese, October 5. Ducks, snipe, October 27. Quail, November 3. Pheasants, November 10. That was 10 days ago. Finally, everything that's ever legal may be hunted. The closings haven't started yet. Amplitude. Best time of the year. Whoa.

8:59   Whoa! Now it's me quivering, whining, but I needn't throw my weight against the door—open it. I step out, making Moon stay. I uncase the gun, look at it with love, throw the case in the car; load. Breathe cold air. Good. Look around. Fine.

"Come on, Moonie. Nine o'clock."

9:00   I start on the most direct line through the short grass, toward the tall, not paying much attention to Moon, who must relieve himself. I think this is as much a matter of nervous tension as it is of regularity.

"Come on, Moon," I call, keeping to my line. "This way, boy."

He thinks he's got a scent back here, in the short grass; barely enough for a pheasant to hide in, and much too thin for cold-day cover.

"Come, Moon. Hyeahp."

It must be an old scent. But he disregards me. His stub of a tail begins to go as he angles off, about 30 yards from where I am; his body lowers just a little and he's moving quickly. I am ignorant in many things about hunting, but there's one thing I know after eight years with this dog, if you bother to hunt with a dog at all, believe what he tells you. Go where he says the bird is, not where you think it ought to be.

I move that way, going pretty quickly myself, still convinced it's an old foot-trail he's following, and he stops in a half-point, his head sinking down while his nose stays up, so that the gray neck is almost in a shallow S-curve.

A cock, going straight up, high, high, high. My gun goes up with him and is firm against my shoulder as he reaches the top of his leap. He seems to hang there as I fire, and he drops perfectly, two or three yards from where Moon waits.

"Good dog. Good boy, Moon," I say as he picks the heavy bird up in his mouth and brings it to me. "Moonie, that was perfect." The bird is thoroughly dead, but I open my pocket knife, press the blade into the roof of its mouth so that it will bleed properly. Check the spurs—they're stubby and almost rounded at the tip. This year's pheasant, probably. Young. Tender. Simply perfect.

Like a book pheasant, I think, and how seldom it happens. In the books, pheasants are said to rise straight up as this one did, going for altitude first, then pausing in the air to swing downwind. The books are quite wrong; most pheasants

I see take straight off, without a jump, low and skimming, curving if they rise much, and never hanging at all. I wonder about evolution: among pheasant generations in this open country, did the ones who went towering into the air and hung like kites get killed off disproportionately? While the skulkers and skimmers and curvers survived, to transmit crafty genes?

"Old-fashioned pheasant, are you? You just set a record for me. I never dreamed I'd have a bird so early in the day." I check my watch.

9:15   The device I was so hopeful of is not working out too well. It is a leather holder which slides onto the belt, and has a set of rawhide loops. As I was supposed to, I have hooked the pheasant's legs into a loop, but he swings against my own leg at the knee. Maybe the thing was meant for taller men.

"Moon. This way. Come around, boy." I feel pretty strongly that we should hunt the edge.

The dangling bird is brushing grass tops. Maybe next time I should bring my trout creel, which is oversized, having been made by optimistic Italians. No half-dozen trout would much more than cover the bottom, but three cock pheasants might lie nicely in the willow, their tails extending backwards through the crack between lid and body, the rigidity of the thing protecting them as a game bag doesn't.

"Moon. Come back here. Come around." He hasn't settled down for the day. Old as he is, he still takes a wild run, first thing.

I'm pretty well settled, myself (it's that bird bumping against my leg). Now Moon does come back into the area I want him in, the edge between high grass and low; there's a distinction between following your dog when he's got something and trusting him to weigh odds. I know odds better, and here is one of those things that will be a cliché of hunting in a few years, since the game-management men are telling it to one another now and it's started filtering into outdoor magazines: the odds are that most game will be near the edge of cover, not in the center of it. The phrase for this is "edge factor."

"Haven't you heard of the edge factor?" I yell at Moon. "Get out along the edge here, boy." And in a few steps he has a scent again. When he's got the tail factor going, the odds change, and I follow him, almost trotting to keep up, as he works from edge to center, back toward edge, after what must be a running bird. He slows a little, but doesn't stop; the scent is hot, but apparently the bird is still moving. Moon stops, points, holds. I walk as fast as I can, am in range—and Moon starts again. He is in a crouch now, creeping forward in his point. The unseen bird must be shifting; he is starting to run again, for Moon moves out of the point and starts to lope; I move, fast as I can and still stay collected enough to shoot—gun held in both hands out in front of me—exhilarated to see the wonderful mixture of exuberance and certainty with which Moon goes. To make such big happy moves, and none of them a false one, is something only the most extraordinary human athletes can do, after years of training—it comes naturally to almost any dog. And that pheasant out there in front of us—how he can go! Turn and twist through the tangle of stems, never showing himself, moving away from Moon's speed and my calculations. But we've got him—I think we do—Moon slows, points. Sometimes we win in a run down—usually not—usually the pheasant picks the right time, well out and away, to flush out of range—but this one stopped. Yes. Moon's holding again. I'm in range. I move up, beside the rigid dog. Past him. WHIRR-PT. The gun rises, checks itself, and I yell at Moon, who is ready to bound forward:

"Hen!"

Away she goes, and away goes Moon, and I yell: "Whoa. Hen, hen," but it doesn't stop him. He's pursuing, as if he could get up enough speed to rise into the air after her. "Whoa." It doesn't stop him. WHIRRUPFT. That stops him. Stops me too. A second hen. WHIRRUPFT. WHIRRUPFT. Two more. And another, that makes five who were sitting tight. And then, way out, far from this little group, through which he must have passed, and far from us, I see the cock, which is almost certainly the bird we were chasing (hens don't run like that), fly up silently, without a cackle, and glide away, across the road and out of sight.

9:30 "There's got to be another," I say to Moon. A man I know informed me quite vehemently a week ago that one ought never to talk to a dog in the field except to give commands; distracts him, the man said, keeps him too close. Tell you what, man: you run your dogs your way, and I'll run my dog mine. Okay?

We approach a fence, where the hayfield ends; the ground is clear for 20 feet before the fence line. Critical place. If birds have been moving ahead of us, and are reluctant to fly, this is where they'll hide. They won't run into the open. And just as I put this card in the calculator, one goes up, CUK CUK CUK, bursting past Moon full speed and low, putting the dog between me and him so that, while my gun is ready, I can't shoot immediately; he rises only enough to clear the fence, sweeping left between two bushes as I fire, and I see the pellets agitate the leaves of the right-hand bush, and know I shot behind him.

Moon, in the immemorial way of bird dogs, looks back at me with what bird hunters who miss have immemorially taken for reproach.

We turn along the edge paralleling the fence. He may not have been the only one we chased down here—Moon is hunting, working from fence to edge, very deliberate. Me to. I wouldn't like to miss again. Moon swerves to the fence row, tries some likely brush. Nope. Lopes back to the edge, lopes along it. Point. Very stiff. Very sudden. Ten yards, straight ahead.

This is a beautifully awkward point, Moon's body curved into it, shoulders down, rear up, head almost looking back at me; this one really caught him. As now we'll catch the pheasant? So close. Dog so steady. I have the impression Moon's looking a bird straight in the eye. I move slowly. No need for speed, no reason to risk being off balance. Let's be so deliberate, so cool, so easy. The gun is ready to come up—I never have the feeling that I myself bring it up. Don't be off balance. He'll go now. Now. Nope—when he does, I try to tell myself, don't shoot too fast, let the bird get out a little, but I'm not really that good and confident in my shooting. Thanks be for brush loads. Ought to have them in both barrels for this situation. Will I have to kick the pheasant out? I am within two steps of Moon, who hasn't stirred except for the twitching of his shoulder and haunch muscles, when the creature bolts. Out he comes, under Moon's nose, and virtually between my legs if I didn't jump aside—a rabbit, tearing for the fence row. I could recover and shoot, it's an easy shot, but not today; I smile, relax, and sweat flows. I am not that desperate for game yet.

I yell "Whoa" at Moon, and for some dog's reason he obeys this time. I should punish him, now; for pointing fur? But it's my fault—sometimes, being a one-dog man, I shoot fur over him, though I recognize it as a genuine error in bird-dog handling. But with the long bond of hunting and mutual training between us (for Moon trained me no less than I did him), my taking a rabbit over him from time to time—or a mongoose, or a kangaroo—is not going to change things between us.

In any case, my wife's never especially pleased to see me bring a rabbit home, though the kids and I like to eat them. I pat Moon, who whoaed for the rabbit. "Whoa, big babe," I say softly. "Whoasie-posner, whoa-daboodle-dog, big sweet posner baby dog . . ." I am rubbing his back.

10:40 Step out of the car, look around, work it out: the birds slept late this morning, because of the wind and frost, and may therefore be feeding late. If so, they're in the field itself, which lies beyond two fallow fields. They roost here in this heavy cover, fly out to the corn—early on nice mornings; later, if I'm correct, on a day like this. When they're done feeding, they go to what game experts call loafing cover—relatively thin cover, near the feeding place, and stay in it till the second feeding in the afternoon; after which they'll be back here where they started, to roost again.

The wind is on my left cheek, as Moon and I go through the roosting cover, so I angle right. This will bring us to where we can turn and cross the popcorn field, walking straight into the wind. This will not only be better for Moon, for obvious reasons, but will also be better for shooting; birds in open rows, hearing us coming, can sail away out of range very fast with the wind behind them. If it blows towards me, they'll either be lifted high, going into the wind, or curve off to one side or the other.

The ragweed, as we come up close to it and Moon pauses before choosing a spot at which to plunge in, is eight feet high—thick, dry, brittle, gray-stemmed stuff which pops and crackles as he breaks into it. I move a few feet along the edge of the draw, shifting my position as I hear him working through, to stay as well in range of where he is as possible. I am calmly certain there's a bird in there, even that it's a cock. I think he moved in ahead of us as we were coming up the field, felt safe when he saw us apparently about to pass by, and doesn't want to leave the dense overhead protection now.

But he must. Moon will send him up in a moment, perhaps out the far side where the range will be extreme. It will be a long shot, if that happens, and Moon is now at the far edge, is turning along it, when I hear the cackle of the cock rising. For a moment I don't know where, can't see him, and by the time I do he's going out to my right, almost back towards me, having doubled away from the dog. Out he comes, already in full flight and low, with the wind behind him for speed. And yet I was so well set for this, for anything, that it all seems easy—to pivot, mounting the gun as I do, find it against my cheek and the bird big and solid at the end of the barrel, swing, taking my time, and shoot. The bird checks, fights air, and tumbles, and in my sense of perfection I make an error: I am so sure he's perfectly hit that I do not take the second shot, before he falls in some waist-high weeds. I mark the place by keeping my eye on a particular weed, a little taller than the others, and walk slowly, straight towards it, not letting my eye move away, confident he'll be lying right by it. Moon, working the ragweed, would neither see the rise nor mark the fall and he comes bounding out to me now, coming to the sound of the shot. I reach the spot first, so very carefully marked, and there's no bird there.

Hunters make errors; dogs correct them. While I am still standing there, irritated with myself for not having shot twice, Moon is circling me, casting, inhaling those great snuffs, finding the ground scent. He begins to work a straight line, checks as I follow him, starts again in a slightly different direction; I must trust him, absolutely, and I do. I remind myself that once he trailed a crippled bird more than half a mile in the direction opposite from that in which I had actually seen the bird start off. I kept trying to get him to go the other way, but he wouldn't; and he found the pheasant. It was by the edge of a dirt road, so that Max Morgan and I could clock the distance afterwards by car speedometer.

Our present bird is no such problem. Forty feet from where the empty shell waves gently back and forth on top of the weed, Moon hesitates, points. Then, and I do not know how he knows that this particular immobile pheasant will not fly (unless it's the smell of fresh blood), Moon lunges. His head darts into matted weeds, fights spurs for a moment, tosses the big bird once so that he can take it by the back, lifts it; and he comes to me proudly, trotting, head as high as he can hold it.

11:00 Iowa hunters are obsessed with corn. If there are no birds in the cornfields, they consider the situation hopeless. This may come from the fact that most of them hunt in drives—a number of men spread out in line, going along abreast through standing corn, with others blocking the end of the field. My experience, for I avoid that kind of hunt every chance I get, is quite different; I rarely find pheasants in cornfields, except along the edges. More than half of those I shoot, I find away from corn, in wild cover, and sometimes the crops show that the bird has not been eating grain at all but getting along on wilder seeds.

But as I start to hunt the popcorn field, something happens that shows why driving often works out. We start into the wind, as planned, moving down the field the long way, and way down at the other end a farm dog sees us. He starts towards us, intending to investigate Moon, I suppose. I see him come towards the field; I see him enter it, trotting our way, and the wind carries the sound of his barking. And then I see—the length of a football field away, reacting to the farm dog—pheasants go up; not two or three, but a flock, 12 or 14, and another and another and another, cocks and hens, flying off in all directions, sailing down wind and out of sight. Drivers and blockers would have had fast shooting with that bunch—but suppose I'd got up? Well, this gun only shoots twice. And, well again, boy. Three's the limit, dunghead. And you've got two already.

11:30   Two birds before lunch? I ought to limit out, I ought to limit out soon. And stop looking for pheasants, spend the afternoon on something else. Take Moon home to rest, maybe, and know that the wind's going down and the sun's getting hot, go into the woods for squirrels, something I like but never get around to.

Let's get the other one. Where?

We are walking back to the car, the shortest way, no reason to go through the popcorn field after what happened. Where? And I think of a pretty place, not far away.

11:45   Yes, it's pretty. Got a bird here last year, missed a couple, too, why haven't I been here this season? It's a puzzle, and the solution, as I stop the car once more, is a pleasure: I know a lot of pretty places near home, 20 or 30 of them, all quite distinct, and have gotten or missed birds at all of them, one season or another.

There are no pheasants this time, only signs of pheasant; roosting places, full of droppings. Some fresh enough so that they were dropped this morning. A place for the next windy morning; I put that idea in a safe place, and move back, after Moon—he's pretty excited with all the bird scent, but not violently; it's not that fresh—towards the fence along the soybean field. We turn from the creek, and go along the fence line, 20 or 30 feet out, towards an eight-acre patch of woods where I have often seen deer, and if I were a real reasoner or a real instinct man, not something in between, what happens would not find me unprepared. Moon goes into a majestically rigid point, foreleg raised, tail out straight, aimed at low bushes in the fence row. I hardly ever see him point so rigidly without first showing the signs he gives while the quarry is still shifting. I move in rather casually, suspecting a hen, but if it's a cock rather confident, after my last great shot, and there suddenly comes at me, buzzing angrily, a swarm of —pheasants? Too small—

hornets? Sparrow? Quail! drilling right at me, the air full of them, whirring, swerving to both sides.

Much too late, surprised, confused—abashed, for this is classic quail cover—I flounder around, face back the way I came, and pop off a pair of harmless shots, more in valediction than in hope of hitting. Turn back to look at Moon, and up comes a straggler, whirring all by himself, also past me. There are no easy shots on quail, but I could have him, I think, if both barrels weren't empty. He's so close that I can see the white on neck and face, and know him for a male. Jock though I am, at least I mark him down, relieved that he doesn't cross the creek.

Moon works straight to the spot where I marked the straggler, and sure enough he flushes, not giving the dog a chance to point, flushes high and I snap-shoot and he falls. Moon bounds after him and stops on the way, almost pitching forward, like a car when its brakes lock. Another bird. Ready. I hope I have my down bird marked. Careful. *Whirr*—I damn near stepped on him, and back he goes behind me. I swing 180 degrees, and as he angles away have him over the end of the barrel. As I fire, it seems almost accidental that I should be on him so readily, but it's not of course—it's the one kind of shot that never misses, the unplanned, reflexive shot, when conditioning has already operated before self-consciousness could start up. This quail falls in the soft maple seedlings, in a place I won't forget, but the first one may be hard.

He's not. I find him without difficulty, seeing him on the ground at just about the same time that Moon finds him too. Happy to have him, I bring Moon back to the soft maple seedlings, but we do not find the second bird.

12:30 Lunch is black coffee in the thermos, an apple and an orange, and the sight of two quail and two pheasants, lying in a neat row on the car floor. I had planned to go home for lunch; and it wouldn't take so very much time; but I would talk with my family, of course, and whatever it is this noon that they're concerned with, I would be concerned with. And that would break the spell, as an apple and an orange will not.

12:45 Also

1:45   and, I'm afraid

2:45   these hours repeat one another, and at the end of them I have: two pheasants, as before; two quail; and an afterthought.

The afterthought shouldn't have run through my mind, in the irritable state that it was in.

The only shots I took were at domestic pigeons, going by fast and far up, considered a nuisance around here; I missed both times. But what made me irritable were all the mourning doves.

There are doves all over the place in Iowa, in every covert that I hunt—according to the last Audubon Society spring census at Des Moines, doves were more common even than robins and meadow larks. In my three hard hours of barren pheasant hunting, I could have had shots at 20 or 25 doves (a game bird in 30 states, a game bird throughout the history of the world), and may not try them. Shooting doves is against the law in Iowa. The harvesting of our enormous surplus (for nine out of 10 will die before they're a year old anyway) is left to cats and owls and—because the dove ranges get so crowded—germs.

Leaving the half-picked cornfield, I jump yet another pair of doves, throw up my gun and track them making a pretended double, though I doubt that it would work.

Three hours of seeing doves, and no pheasants, has made me pettish, and perhaps I am beginning to tire.

A rabbit jumps out behind the dog, unseen by Moon but not by me. At first I assume that I want to let him go, as I did the earlier one; then he becomes the afterthought: company, dinner—so you won't let me shoot doves, eh rabbit? He's dead before he can reach cover.

3:00   Now I have only an hour left to get my final bird, for pheasant hunting ends at four. This is a symbolic bird: a good hunter gets his limit. At noon it seemed almost sure I would; suddenly it's doubtful.

I sit in the car, one hand on Moon who is lying on the seat beside me. We've reached the time of the day when he rests when he can.

3:10   On my way to someplace else, I suddenly brake the car.

"Hey, did you see that?" I am talking to Moon again. He has a paw over his nose, and of course saw nothing. I look over him, eagerly, out the window and down into a big marsh we were about to pass by. We were on our way to the place I'd thought of, an old windbreak of evergreens near an abandoned farmhouse site, surrounded by overgrown pasture, and not too far from corn. It's an ace-in-the-hole kind of place for evening shooting, for the pheasants come in there early to roost; I've used it sparingly, shown it to no one.

Going there would be our best chance to fill out, I think, but look: "Damn, Moon, snipe. Snipe, boy, I'm sure of it."

On the big marsh, shore birds are rising up and setting down, not in little squadrons like killdeer—which are shore birds about the same size, and very common—but a bird here, a bird there. Becoming instantly invisible when they land, too, and so not among the wading shore birds. I get out the glasses and step out of the car, telling Moon to stay. I catch one of the birds in the lenses, and the silhouette is unmistakable—the long, comic beak, the swept-back wings.

"You are snipe," I say, addressing—well, them, I suppose. "Where've you boys been?"

Two more whiz in and out of the image, too quickly to follow, two more of my favorite of all game birds. Habitat changes around here so much from year to year, with the great fluctuations in water level from the dam, that this marsh, which was full of snipe three years ago, has shown none at all so far this year. What snipe hunting I've found has been in temporarily puddled fields, after rains, and in a smaller marsh.

"I thought you'd never come," I say. "Moon!" I open the car door. "Moon, let's go." My heartiness is a little false, for snipe are my favorite bird, not Moon's. He'll flush them, if he must, but apparently they're distasteful to him, and when I manage to shoot one, he generally refuses even to pick it up, much less retrieve it for me.

Manage to shoot one? Last year, on the first day I hunted snipe, I shot 16 shells before I hit my first. That third pheasant can wait there in the hole with the other aces.

Remembering the 16 straight misses, I stuff my pockets with shells—brush loads still for the first shot but, with splendid consistency, high-brass 7 1/2s for the second, full-choke shot. I won't use them on a big bird, like a pheasant; I will on a tiny bird, like a snipe. The snipe goes fast, and by the second shot you need all the range you can get.

I should have hip boots now. Go back and get them? Nuts. Get muddy.

Down we go, Moon with a certain silly enthusiasm for the muskrats he smells and may suppose are now to be our quarry. I see that the marsh water is shallow, but the mud under it is always deep—thigh-deep in some places; the only way to go into it is from hummock to hummock of marsh grass. Actually, I will stay out of it if I can, and so I turn along the edge, Moon hunting out in front. A snipe rises over the marsh at my right, too far to shoot at, scolding us anyway: *scaip, scaip*. Then two more, which let the dog get by them, going up between me and Moon—a chance for a double, in a highly theoretical way. I shoot and miss at the one on the left as he twists low along the edge. He rises, just after the shot, going up in a tight turn, and I shoot again, swinging up with him, and miss again.

At my first shot, the other snipe—the one I didn't shoot at—dove, as if hit. But I know he wasn't; I've seen the trick before. I know about where he went in, and I decide not to bother with Moon, who is chasing around in the mud, trying to convince himself that I knocked down a pheasant or something decent like that.

I wade in myself, mud to ankles, mud to calves, up to the tops of the low boots I'm wearing; no bird? What the hell, mud over the boot tops, and I finally climb a hummock. This puts up my diving snipe, 10 yards further out and scolding, but the hummocks are spaced too far apart in this part of the swamp so there's no point shooting. I couldn't recover him and I doubt that Moon would. I let him rise, twist, swoop upwards, and I stand as still as I can, balanced on the little mound of grass; I know a trick myself. It works; at the top of his climb the snipe turns and comes streaking back, 40 yards up, directly overhead. I throw up the gun for the fast overhead shot, and miss.

I splash back to the edge and muck along. A snipe goes up, almost at my feet, and his first swerve coincides with my snap shot—a kind of luck that almost seems like skill. Moon, bounding back, has seen the bird fall and runs to it—smells it, curls his lip and slinks away. He turns his head to watch me bend to pick it up, and as I do, leaps back and tries to take it from me.

"Moondog," I say, addressing him severely by his full name. "I'm not your child to punish. I like this bird. Now stop it."

We start along again, come to the corner where the marsh dies out, and turn. Moon stops, sight-pointing in a half-hearted way, and a snipe goes up in front of him. This one curves towards some high weeds; I fire and miss, but stay on him as he suddenly straightens and goes winging straight out, rising very little. He is a good 40 yards away by now, but he tumbles when I fire, and falls on open ground. It takes very little to kill a snipe. I pace the distance, going to him, and watch Moon, for Moon picks this one up. Then, when I call to him to bring it, he gradually, perhaps sulkily, lowers his head and spits it out again. He strolls off as if there were nothing there. I scold him as I come up, but not very hard; he looks abashed, and makes a small show of hunting dead in a bare spot about 10 yards from where we both know the snipe is lying. I pick up the bird, and tell Moon that he is probably the worst dog that ever lived, but not in an unkind voice for I wouldn't want to hurt his feelings.

This a pleasanter area we are crossing now: firm mud, patches of swamp weeds, frequent puddles. Moon, loping around aimlessly, blunders into a group of five or six snipe at the far side of a puddle, and I put trying to get a double out of my mind; I try to take my time; pick out an individual, follow him as he glides toward some high reeds and drop him.

Now we go along, towards the back of the marsh, shooting and missing, hitting just twice. One shot in particular pleases me: a snipe quite high, in full flight coming towards me. I shoot, remembering a phrase I once read: "A shotgun is a paint brush." I paint the snipe blue, to match the sky, starting my brush stroke just behind him, painting evenly along his body, completing the stroke about three lengths in front where I fire, and follow through. This is a classic shot, a memorable one, so much so that there are just two others I can put with it—one on a faraway pheasant last year, one on a high teal in Chile. The sky is all blue now, for the snipe is painted out of it and falls, almost into my hand.

It is just 3:55.

There is magic in this. The end of the legal pheasant hunting day is four o'clock.

4:00   Just after the pheasant, I kill another snipe, the sixth. He is along the stream, too, and so I follow it, awed at the thought that I might even get a limit of these. But on the next chance, not a hard one, I think too hard, and miss the first shot, as he twists, and the rising one as well.

We leave the watercourse for a tiny marsh, go back to it (or a branch) through government fields I've never crossed before, by strange potholes and unfamiliar willow stands. We flush a woodcock, cousin to the snipe, but shooting him is not permitted here. We turn away in a new direction—snipe and woodcock favor different sorts of cover. And sometime along in there, I walk up two snipe, shoot one very fast, and miss a perplexing but not impossible shot at the other, as he spirals up.

"There he goes," I think. "My limit bird." He flies into the east, where the sky is getting dark; clouds have come to the western horizon and the sun is gone for the day, behind them.

5:03   In this remnant of perfect habitat, the sky is empty. It is five minutes till sunset, but it is dusk already, when my last snipe does go up, I hear him before

I see him. I crouch down, close to the ground, trying to expand the area of light against which he will show up, and he appears now, winging for the upper sky; but I cannot decide to shoot, shouldering my gun in that awkward position. And in another second it is too late, really too late, and I feel as if the last hunter in the world has let the last snipe go without a try.

I straighten up reluctantly, unload gun, and wonder where I am. Suddenly I am tired, melancholy, and very hungry. I know about which way to go, and start along, calling Moon, only half lost dragging a little. The hunting is over and home an hour away.

I think of quail hunting in Louisiana, when we crouched, straining for shots at the final covey, as I did just now for the final snipe.

I find a little road I recognize, start on it the wrong way, correct myself and turn back along it. A touch of late sun shows now, through a rift, enough to cast a pale shadow in front of me—man with gun—on the sand road.

♦ ♦ ♦

We were on an evening march, in some loose company formation, outside of training camp. We were boys.

I watched our shadows along the tall clay bank at the side of the road. We were too tired to talk, even garrulous Bobby Hirt, who went AWOL later and spent two years, so we heard, in military prison. He was a boy. We all were. But the helmeted shadows, with packs and guns in silhouette, were the shadows of soldiers—faceless, menacing, expendable. No one shadow different from the other. I could not tell you, for after training we dispersed, going out as infantry replacements, which of those boys, whose misery and defiance and occasional good times I shared for 17 unforgotten weeks, actually were expended. Several, of course, since statistics show what they do of infantry replacements. Statistics are the representation of shadows by numbers.

♦ ♦ ♦

My shadow on the sand road is of a different kind. I have come a little way in 19 years, whatever the world has done. I am alone, in a solitary place, as I wish to be, accountable only as I am willing to be held so, therefore no man's statistic. Melancholy for the moment, but only because I am weary, and coming to the end of this day which, full of remembering, will be itself remembered.

Moon is beside me, tired now too, throwing his own pale dog-shadow ahead. And the hunter-shadow with him, the pheasant hanging from the hunter's belt, sniper bulging in the jacket—the image teases me. It is not the soldiers, but some other memory. An image, failing because the sun is failing, the rift closing very slowly. An image of. A hunter like. A dream? Not a dream, but the ghost of a dream, my old, hunter-and-his-dog-at-dusk dream. And the sun goes down, and the ghost with it, and the car is in sight which will carry us home.

••• Born in Texas in 1920, Dave Harbour wrote his first article for Sports Afield *in 1945 while serving as a pilot in the Air Corps. He spent 23 years in the service; during that time he produced many articles and books on the outdoors. His specialty was the wild turkey, whose comeback he helped promote across the U.S. When Harbour died in 1988, he did so in the woods, admiring a turkey he had just shot, while on assignment for the magazine. This story shows how difficult it is to outsmart an old gobbler.—*APRIL 1972 •••

MY OLD KENTUCKY GOBBLER
by Dave Harbour

There was no moon, but the faint outline of tall hardwood against a skyful of twinkling stars guided me along the ridgetop. I stumbled over an occasional log, and brush clawed at my thick trousers and snake-proof boots. I hurried, moving faster and faster toward the knoll I had to occupy by the first crack of dawn, and not one second later.

When I reached the knoll, I collapsed on a decaying log and waited for my breathing and heartbeat to return to normal. The inky air was still and cold, touched by the subtle perfume of pine and dogwood blossoms. The deep silence about me was interrupted only by the soft, monotonous notes of a lonesome whip-poorwill telling its mate that spring had come.

I eased three magnum 6s into my old Remington 12-gauge and felt for my call to make sure it was in its proper place in my left pocket. Then that exhilarating wait for dawn and all its promise began. To this old gobbler hunter, these golden pre-dawn moments alone make every spring turkey hunt worthwhile. As the new day is slowly born, great bronze birds go into full strut before your unbelieving eyes and shatter the woods with their thundering gobbles . . . and you wait for a new tom, the biggest you've ever dueled, to challenge you. This morning was no different from hundreds of other golden pre-dawn mornings, except that it was unfolding in Kentucky's wild and beautiful Land Between the Lakes, where I had never hunted gobblers before.

And dawn came in the same miraculous way. Beginning in the East, the stars were replaced with a sweep of slowly expanding grays and silvers. Hazy silhouettes turned into great oaks, birch and maple trees wearing crowns of spring buds and tiny new leaves. The sky pinkened, and white dogwoods and green pines sprang out of the darkness. A melody of bird song began, then crescendoed to almost deafening proportions.

The gobble rang out on schedule, well ahead of sunup, but it was not the loud booming gobble I had expected. Instead of roosting in a hollow close to the ridge I was on (as I had predicted he would the evening before), I could tell by the faintness of his rattle that the old bird was in a hollow to my right and several ridges over. My only course of action was to head straight for him with all possible speed. There was still a chance that I could reach his vicinity before he quit gobbling and before one of the other 200 hunters who had checked into the area that morning would beat me to him.

Twenty minutes and three steep ridges later, I paused to get my breath and listen. It was in another ideal listening spot, on a long high ridge sparsely studded with ancient hardwoods holding up a sky now on fire with the first rays of the new sun. Before me, three small finger ridges jutted down into a deep and heavily timbered hollow. Across the hollow, on the side of the next high ridge, I could make out an old field covered with tall grass and tangles of briars and brush . . . a perfect magnet for nesting hens, and therefore, for gobblers.

GIL-OBBLE-OBBLE! GIL-OBBLE-OBBLE! The king of the forest was now announcing his supremacy from near the bottom of the brushy hollow ahead and directly down the finger ridge from my position. I eased down the side of the little ridge some 200 yards and chose a calling spot behind the roots of a big oak that had been upended by a windstorm. My calling position could not have been more promising. I was completely shielded by the big mass of roots, yet I could see through them. And the ridge between my position and that of the love-crazed tom was almost barren of brush and trees—the kind of open terrain that a wary old gobbler invariably uses to approach a coy and stubborn hen.

I waited a few moments, placed my gun within reach and chalked my old box. Then I queried the tom with three soft yelps. He came back with a double gobble that shook me to the soles of my feet! He hadn't had a hen, and he was ready for one! But he was also cautious. Instead of running straight to me, like many toms will when they answer that first call with a double gobble, this wise old bird remained just out of sight in the hollow below. He gobbled again and again, coaxing me to come to him.

I played the waiting game for 20 minutes. Then I cradled the box in my hands to muffle my next series of yelps and to make the old tom think I was working away from him. Very softly I scratched out a *Ke-oke, ke-oke*, which in turkey language means "Good-bye lover, it could have been great."

The old tom roared back with a passionate gobble. And then I saw him top the ridge below in full strut. His great black and chestnut tail was fanned wide. His mammoth wings dropped to the ground. Tints of green, golds and purples sparkled from the broad blackness of his ruffed breast, and his long beard, thick as a man's wrist, dropped almost to the ground. *Vtt-vrrr-oo-mm-i* came the sound of the booming strut. Then another *Gil-obble-obble! Gil-obble-obble!*

An opera like this, played on a remote forest stage in the soft light of a new sun, is almost more than a man can bear. How he wishes that this magic moment could last forever. And, in a sense it does, for it will be re-lived 100 times in 100 places: in the wait for dawn in other spring woods, over tall cool drinks on summer evenings, and in the quietness of nights when men dream instead of sleep.

The old tom was in no hurry, but he moved slowly up the ridge toward me, stopping every few minutes to strut and gobble. Through the tangle of roots, I watched him come. He closed to 100 yards, then 80. My safety had long been off, and I was watching him come over the barrel of my 12.

Suddenly, the old gobbler switched from full strut to a posture of alarm. His long neck stretched high and he stood as still as a black stump. A second later he exploded into the air, topped the big hardwoods and sailed across the hollow toward the old field beyond. I heard the crunch of dry leaves on the main ridge above . . . and saw another hunter sneaking toward me.

When the young man, expertly camouflaged from head to toe, moved close to my position, I stood up and said, "Hello." He put his finger to his lips, signaling me to be quiet, then tip-toed over. "There's a big gobbler gobbling just down there below!" he whispered.

I told the youngster what had happened. He apologized and we talked turkey for a few minutes, then parted. I used the rest of the morning to become more familiar with the range of this big gobbler.

I focused my search in the vicinity of the long ridge with the old field across the hollow. I found a few hen and gobbler tracks in that area, and a couple of high knolls close to the field which would make promising listening spots for future hunts. I computed a compass course to this area from the nearest road on my map for future use, then another back to my car. I reached the check station a few minutes before the 11:00 checkout deadline.

The spine-tingling sight of that big gobbler had already made my long trip from Leesburg, Florida to Kentucky's Land Between the Lakes worthwhile. I had left my outdoor writing tasks and had arrived for the six-day season on the afternoon before, April 14. This had given me a few pre-hunt hours to scout the woods, to find gobbler scratchings and tracks and to select the listening point I had first heard the old gobbler from on opening morning of the season.

I made this trip to Kentucky last spring for two primary reasons: I had long wanted to take a Land Between the Lakes gobbler because this is the only area where an original flock of our Kentucky turkeys, the largest of our eastern wild turkeys, exists today. According to Bob Smith, TVA biologist and turkey expert, this area has never been stocked with a transplanted bird, and the colony there is entirely of pure, native blood. Second, I had already been lucky enough to take fairly easy gobblers in Florida and Alabama that spring, and I was looking for the challenge of a really difficult hunt. And no gobbler hunt in the U.S. is more difficult than that which is held each spring in Land Between the Lakes. Permits are not limited, about 1000 hunters usually check in during each of these six-day hunts . . . and they have never killed more than 12 gobblers during any one spring season.

Land Between the Lakes is one of the most scenic wild areas in the East. It is a 170,000-acre isthmus, completely uninhabited, magnificently wooded with mature forests, and lying between Kentucky Lake and Lake Barkley, along the Kentucky-Tennessee border. It is managed by the TVA as a public recreational area, and abounds with whitetail and fallow deer, as well as its modest but growing population of wild turkeys. It is beautiful country.

Kentucky Dam Village State Park, near the little town of Gilbertsville, is less than a 30-minute drive from Land Between the Lakes' north entrance check station. For this reason, I had made arrangements to bunk in a cabin there during my gobbler hunt. I returned to the cabin, grabbed lunch and an hour's sleep, left my gun, then headed back for a more thorough study of the hunting area.

I decided to scout new territory with the hope of finding more sign and an alternate hunting spot. On a dim road crossing a remote hollow, I had the good fortune to run into two other wild-eyed gobbler chasers. Harold Knight, who owns a barber shop in Cadiz, Kentucky, and Dave Hale, a farmer from nearby Gracey, were intimately familiar with every inch of turkey range in Land Between the Lakes. Both had taken big gobblers during two of the last four spring hunts. These congenial young men appraised me for a few minutes, then took me in like a long-lost friend. They briefed me on the most promising areas to scout and showed me an amazing new turkey call that Harold had developed.

I collect turkey calls, and thought I had seen them all, but Harold Knight's invention was radically different from any I had ever seen. It is the only diaphragm-type call I have ever run into which anyone can use effectively with little or no practice. This patented call (which I understand will hit the market shortly) is a small tube with a rubber diaphragm over one end. By blowing against the rubber diaphragm, even a novice caller can produce a perfect hen yelp, soft or loud, and with a little practice, he can produce realistic clucks, putts, whines, ke-ke runs and even gobbles! I conned Harold out of one of his calls, and then and there staked my future gobbler-hunting success on its effectiveness.

When we separated that afternoon, Harold and Dave had circled several turkey areas on my Land Between the Lakes map which I had obtained, along with my hunt permit, by writing the TVA Information Office at Golden Pond, Kentucky. We agreed to scout and hunt separately but to meet at the check station to compare notes after each morning's hunt.

For the second morning, my alarm buzzed at 2:30. By 3:30, I had polished off a quick breakfast and had reported at the check station. When it began to get light a little after 4:00 a.m., I was on the same finger ridge where I had last seen the old tom the previous morning. Again it was quiet, still and cold—a perfect morning for gobbling. But not a bird sounded off in my area. I called from many likely spots through the rest of the morning, but got no results. I was back scouting more new territory by midafternoon and remained until black dark, but failed to hear a bird or find significant sign.

The third day was a disappointing duplication of the second, except that I worked the ridges and hollows around the old field and discovered enough fresh sign to convince me that hens were indeed nesting in there, and that at least one old gobbler, probably the one I had worked the first day, was still using the area. Harold and Dave had heard gobblers both days but had also failed to score.

The last three days of the hunt didn't begin until April 22, giving me four days of needed rest and the chance to wrestle with Kentucky Lake's slab-sided croppies. I fished with Dick Douglas and Bill Jones out of Cedar Knob Resort, Benton, Kentucky and had a great time. I heartily recommend this bonus fishing fun to any turkey hunter who visits the Land Between the Lakes area.

On April 22, torrents of rain poured down during the entire day. All morning I shivered under a pine on one of the knolls near the old field, hoping that the rain would stop, but I was rewarded only with a bad cold. The next morning, however, was another perfect gobbling morning, clear, crisp and still.

Well before dawn, I was perched on a comfortable stump in the center of a fallen treetop. I was on a high knoll adjacent to the old field which I knew birds were using. From my well-shielded position, I could hear any gobbler which might come from either of the two big hollows on both sides of the field and I knew when light came my gun would command the only open clearing in the area, one between the thick grass and brush in the field and the thick forest which bordered it. I had studied turkey country long enough to know that this little clearing was a likely fly-down spot for any gobbler which might be roosting near it, and a likely strutting area for any gobbler in that general area to head for. This hunting area was also promising because it was two miles from the nearest road; therefore, competition from other hunters would be unlikely.

That familiar parade of old gobblers passed by. Light and bird song finally came and I waited for that booming gobble which I fully expected to hear at any moment. Just before sunup, a dim and distant gobble echoed far to the north. But I remained in my comfortable hiding spot, knowing there had to be at least one good gobbler in my immediate vicinity.

The new sun now blazed through the big hardwoods and still no sound from my gobbler. I decided to make the first advance. Cupping Harold Knight's magic tube in my hands, I queried the forest with a series of four soft, inquisitive yelps. But only a distant crow answered: I remained in my strategic position for another 15 minutes, then yelped again. I couldn't help marvel at the realism of the mellow notes this new call produced. If there was indeed a gobbler around, he should already be in the treetop with me!

Another 15 minutes passed and I had almost given up. If there was a tom in the area, I decided that he already had a harem of hens or had been spooked off his roost by some other wandering hunter in one of the bottoms below.

It was then that I made the most unforgivable mistake a gobbler caller can make. I left my gun on the ground and stood up to stretch. The forest exploded behind me. The crash of breaking limbs was almost deafening. Instead of picking up my gun, I turned to watch the big buck leap away. But the buck was a monster gobbler propelling his great body straight up through the tangle of brush and trees! I stood there hypnotized, with a foot-long beard inching upwards not 10 yards from my face. The vertical speed of the great bronze blur slowly increased, like a big rocket leaving the launch pad. Even when the big tom leveled off above the high treetops, he would still have been an easy shot . . . if I had had my gun!

I sat back down on the stump and the full impact of my monstrous misfortune gradually permeated my shocked brain. I had called the sneaky old tom to within a few yards of my position. If he had gobbled one time he would have been easy meat. If I had waited a few seconds longer before standing, I would have seen him. If I had picked up my gun before I stood up, he would have been a sure target. Even if I had picked up my gun when I heard the explosion behind me, I still could have killed him. I concluded that someone up there just didn't want me to kill a Land Between the Lakes gobbler.

That afternoon, I joined in one last strategy session with Harold and Dave. Both smiled knowingly when I told them about muffing my big opportunity. "None of us turkey chasers will ever get good enough not to be whipped by wary old gobblers," Harold consoled. "And that's exactly the reason we keep right on chasing them."

The next morning would be it. Either we would score then or go home empty-handed. Dave had located an old bird which gobbled its head off that morning. It came to his call, but hung up just out of gun range over a ridge. Dave didn't think he had spooked the old tom, and that was the bird he intended to make his last gamble on.

Harold had located a remote hollow that morning where three birds were gobbling at daylight. He thought he had called one of them up well after sunup, but the bird approached in thick brush and he couldn't positively identify it as a gobbler, and, of course, he let it go. Harold was certain that none of these old toms had been spooked and he encouraged me to try for one of them the next morning. We got out our maps and Harold laid out two courses from the nearest road to the two main ridgetops on each side of the hollow. Harold selected the ridgetop that he would occupy at dawn, and strongly recommended that I head for the other. Since I had spooked the old tom out of my favorite area that morning, Harold's plan seemed to make a lot of sense. I told him that I would probably be there.

For the first night of my long hunt, I hit the sack feeling completely defeated. I had only one morning left to outwit a wary gobbler on the toughest ground I had ever dueled on. I had only two dawn listening points to choose from, and neither was very promising. If I went to the area Harold had suggested, I would be severely handicapped by not being familiar with the terrain. If I went to my old listening spot, the gobbler I had spooked the morning before would probably be roosting a mile away. Once more, I set the alarm for 2:30 and passed out.

By the time I left the check station that final morning, it was almost four o'clock. I decided to gamble on the new ridge Harold had suggested and headed for our pre-selected parking area. About half way there, I passed the familiar jeep trail that led toward my old hunting spot. I couldn't keep my foot from slamming down on the brake pedal. I pulled into the trail, then started to back out again. After all, I had decided that Harold's new spot would offer me the greatest promise. But a voice inside me commanded, "Go on down your old trail." And I did. I parked the Bronco in the same old spot and made the same long pre-dawn journey to my stump in the fallen treetop overlooking the small clearing. Only this time I was 10 minutes later than usual, and dawn came so quickly there was no time to watch that parade of old gobblers go by in the dying darkness. I sat on the stump almost without hope, and thinking only of how I had spooked the big gobbler from this very spot the morning before.

One last time I watched the magic of a Kentucky forest slowly materialize. It was another crisp silver dawn and the eastern sky was now streaked with pink. A mighty gobble rang out, so near me that I could hardly believe it was real! The old tom was roosting on a steep ridge side not 200 yards below the little clearing my gun commanded!

No turkey hunter deserved a second opportunity like this but it was real . . . and it was mine. If the old gobbler had been roosting a bit further away, I would have been utterly confident of a kill. I would have waited until he flew down from the roost, then eased him in with a series of sexy hen yelps which I could reproduce perfectly with my new call. But he was so close, my best course of action was to attempt to make him fly directly to the clearing. This called for the soft clucks of a sleepy hen that had just sailed to the ground, and I had not practiced these difficult clucks with the new call.

I eased the little tube to my lips and cupped it tightly in my hands. Somehow, I managed to emit a reasonable facsimile of three very soft and sleepy clucks. A few seconds later, I heard the churning of great wings. The big gobbler sailed down in the center of the little clearing, exactly as I knew he would. My gun was on him when he landed, and from that moment on he was mine. From my well-hidden position, I watched him ruffle his mass of multi-colored feathers and stretch one big wing. His thick beard almost dragged the ground. Then his sky-blue head raised high as he stretched his long warty neck. His beady eyes burned straight into mine, and I fired, holding a few inches high.

The old monster crumbled as the charge of 6s slapped his head and upper neck. Slowly, I walked over to him and absorbed the full magnificence of the moment. It was not yet sunup, yet the most memorable experience of this old turkey hunter's life had already unfolded in the splendor of those wild Kentucky hills. I carried my trophy to the nearest limb to see if he met the most rigid criterion set for trophy toms by most old turkey chasers. He did, indeed, hang from the limb by his long sharp spurs! I flung the big bird over my shoulder and headed for the Bronco and check station.

Harold and Dave had not scored, but they were almost as exuberant at my good fortune as I was. On the check station scales, my old tom weighed 22 1/2 pounds, the heaviest gobbler I have ever taken. His thick beard measured 10 inches even. He was one of eight toms killed last spring in Land Between the Lakes. The other seven were killed by native Kentuckians.

When I headed back to Florida, I said good-bye to Harold and Dave and remarked one more time, "This was my greatest gobbler hunt . . . I don't know how I could have been so lucky!" Dave was kind enough to reply, "It wasn't all luck. You worked harder than any of the rest of us, and it was that new call of Harold's that lured the old bird in." Harold added, "And don't forget that voice that told you to turn into your old trail when you had planned to hunt with me. With all that help, how could you have missed?"

••• John Madson, who passed away in 1995 at age 72, wrote his first magazine article for TRUE in the 1950s. After that he wrote for publications such as SPORTS AFIELD, AUDUBON and SMITHSONIAN. His most popular book, THE TALL GRASS PRAIRIE, came out in 1982. He didn't go afield as much as he wanted.—JANUARY 1974 •••

GOING OUT MORE by John Madson

Some years ago, our state conservation department paid for a special survey of hunters and what made them tick. About the only thing I can remember about it is how it related men's ages to their hunting efforts.

The average young hunter started out in his mid-teens, gunning up a storm. His hunting effort rose until he was in his early 20s, and then it fell off. Of course it fell off. Chasing girls is a full-time project if it's done right—and doesn't leave much time for other sport.

Then, when he was in his late 20s, his hunting effort began to pick up again. The result of cabin fever, if we read the sign right. Our young hunter had married and settled down now, the honeymoon was over, and Sugar Pie was on the nest and beginning to talk about house painting. It was time to dust off the old smokepole and head for the boondocks. From then on, hunting effort continued to climb through the hunter's 30s, leveling off in his 40s and declining slowly from then on as the old boy grew thick of waist and heavy of foot.

That's how it's been with me. Today, pushing the half-century mark, I'm shocked to see how little hunting I'm doing each fall and winter. I've been going out less, and I don't like it.

I'm still sound of wind and limb and can hoof it all day through grouse covers and along the chukar-partridge slopes. My shooting may be better than ever; what I've lost in reflexes and vision has been made up for in judgment and repression of buck fever. Today I'm probably as cool on a covey rise as I'll ever be.

However, in the past few years much of my game hunting has been replaced with other types of hunting.

The family has needed more money for college tuitions and the second car. There has been growing responsibility at work. In a dozen ways, my hunting time and energy have been diverted into other channels—and none are as much fun as the old ones. So, last fall marked the beginning of a personal revolt. There'll be some changes made. I'll be going out more.

My old highs will never be reached again, I'm sure. I'll never have another 80-mallard season, or a 50-bird pheasant year. But I'm gonna do better than I have been doing!

Going out less has been the result of a decline in my free time, not a decline in my free spirit. Under the grizzled fur on this bosom thumps the heart of a stripling nimrod. Last fall before my first squirrel hunt of the season, I slept fitfully, walking in the night and seeing scope reticles in the darkness. And that was only a squirrel hunt, mind you! Before a deer hunt or a grouse hunt—especially ones that I've traveled for—I hardly sleep at all. No, the old fever is still there. Give me a whiff of Hoppe's No. 9. and I'm hot to trot. It's the old freedom that's almost gone. I'm not really sure why. But I am sure that I haven't changed my mind about hunting itself.

I've been a hunter too long, both amateur and professional, to be driven from the field by slob hunters, intensified land use, antihunting sentiment or any decline of "free" hunting. Such things have existed ever since I can remember, and in my files are prophecies of doom from hunting magazines 40 years old. When it comes to hunting, I'm a realist. I'm no Pollyanna, smiling through tears and offering the world my cookie. But I'm no Chicken Little, either, running about and crying that the sky is falling. Hunting has been around for a long time. It will be around for a long time to come, and it will continue to offer the hunter as much as he's willing to search and work for.

The rising number of slob hunters may cramp my style, but they won't keep me at home. I've learned that the best way to avoid them is to simply avoid opening days, highly touted game areas and the easy going. I hunt later now, and more on the rough edges of the main action. This doesn't mean that my chances of finding game are greatly diminished; they may even be enhanced. I hunt better when I'm not crowded; being less hurried and not angry, I'm more inclined to hunt well. There still are special places I can find that will be mine—personal little corners of prime country that I've bought and paid for. Not with money, but by investing things that the slob hunter is rarely willing to spend. I learned long ago that good hunting is never free. It must always be paid for in some currency—maybe time, or effort or even money. Perhaps it involves all three. But it's there if the hunter is willing to foot the bill. If there's one guy who really gravels me, it's the freeloader who expects prime hunting at no cost of any kind. (If you need a definition of the slob hunter, that's a good one.)

I don't stay home because game habitat is shrinking, or because more hunters are gunning less land. There's still plenty of hunting to be had. On one weekend of Iowa pheasant hunting last fall, we asked eight different farmers for hunting privileges. We were turned down only once and on four of the other seven farms we were the only hunters who had been there. A couple of years ago we spent three days hunting ruffed grouse and never saw another hunter. Within 20 miles of my home I have hunting privileges on at least four farms, and in the past two years I haven't seen any other hunters on those places after quail, squirrels, rabbits or deer.

Nor does the current antihunting surge bother me. I understand my motives for hunting far better than my critics understand theirs—and I believe that my motives are more valid. Criticism of my sport might deter me if I had any real respect for antihunters. But as a professional wildlifer with 35 years of hunting mileage, I just can't generate any real respect for my critics. The militant antihunters whom I have met lack real credentials, not just as hunters but as outdoorsmen. I'll listen to any antihunter who wears out a pair of field boots in two years—but I know none who do. The antihunters I've known are dabblers, and fair-weather outdoorsmen at best. Holding no respect for them, I am unmoved by their lack of respect for me. Having my lifestyle attacked by Alice Herrington or Cleveland Amory is like being run over by a baby buggy.

If I am hunting less, it isn't because I feel that the act of hunting degrades me or the creatures that are hunted. For me, the first measure of hunting isn't whether it is civilized, or conforms to suburban morality, but whether or not it jeopardizes the things that we hunt. If we hunt well, no game species is jeopardized. If we hunt badly, which is to say unethically or in ignorance, the species can be jeopardized and that is unforgivable. We must hunt so as to jeopardize no living species and in ways that shame neither hunter nor hunted.

I've known men who have hung up their guns, feeling that wildlife has enough problems without being hunted in the bargain. However, I feel a different sympathy for the animals—a sort of kinship that comes from sharing the same problems. As an elk or a bobwhite is endangered by habitat deterioration, so am I. But I know myself and the animals well enough to understand that my act of hunting makes little real difference. As those creatures are besieged by a pitiless technology, I know that they need me—the hunter. About all we have is each other. I wouldn't care to live in a world with no wild creatures or wild places left—and I suspect that the hunted animals may not be able to live without me either. If my interest in hunting wanes and I hang up my gun, who will succor the wild creatures in the only ways that they really feel—by defending the little scraps of life range still left to them? As a hunter, I may be the only one that the wild creatures really have; and those wild creatures—biological indicators of the sort of quality environment that makes my life worth living—are all that I really have.

So my diminished hunting activity is not a sign of sentimental concern for wildlife. If I hunt less, it's not out of sympathy for the hunted; nor is it because I feel that I'm taking undue advantage of noble animals. If I'm sure of anything, it's this: That the act of ethical hunting is not an act of disrespect for an animal. Rather, it is a testimonial to that animal and what it stands for. It is a most genuine declaration of value. I do not hunt for the joy of killing but for the joy of living, and for the inexpressible pleasure of mingling my life, however briefly, with that of a wild creature that I respect, admire and value. Then, too, I have a hunch that my act of hunting pays infinitely more respect to a game animal than if I stayed home and watched that animal perform on a television special.

Long ago, I learned that my hunting is not just for meat, or horns or recognition. It is a search for what hunting can give me, an effort to win once again that flash of insight that I've had a few times: That swift, sure intuition of how ancient hunters felt and what real hunting—honest-to-God real hunting— is all about. It is a timeless effort to close that magic circle of man, wildness and animal. Maybe, someday, I'll no longer have to go hunting to close that magic circle—but the day has not yet come.

What this adds up to, and what I miss most, is the freedom in hunting. Hunting is one of the last genuine personal adventures of modern man. Just as game animals are the truest indicators of quality natural environment, so hunting is the truest indicator of quality natural freedom.

I once read of a noted physician who visited a northern deer camp for the first time. He wasn't a hunter, and it was all new to him. He stood by the cabin door one evening, watching some hunters dress deer while their buddies offered the ribald advice that you'll hear in a happy deer camp when the meat pole is full. Standing there, listening to the good laughter and the easy talk, the doctor turned to his host with a look of sudden understanding and said: "Why, these men are *free*!"

That's it. The real hunter is probably as free as it's possible for modern man to be in the teeming technocracy of ours. Not because he sheds civilized codes and restraints when he goes into the woods, becoming an animal, but because he can project himself out of and beyond himself and be wholly absorbed in a quieter, deeper and older world.

Another question I've asked myself: If I'm hunting less than I did, is it because I've found better outdoor things to do?

I try to savor every quality outdoor experience that I can. I canoe wild rivers, camp on desert islands in the southern sea, pack deep into remote wilderness by horse and foot and those are all splendid things to do. My travels take me to some far, fair places. Come the fall season, however, and the time for squirrels and .22s, I feel the old itch again. The feeling doesn't fade with the years; it deepens. And no amount of canoeing, hiking, exploring or fishing can really substitute for hunting.

It has occurred to me, of course, that I'd be better off not hunting. There's a lot to be said for staying at home in the fall. The nonhunter isn't likely to suffer charley horses, weariness, pain, hunger, cold, frustration, sleeplessness and those weekends away from home. His autumns are bland and peaceful. He doesn't neglect his family or drive his body beyond sensible limits, or invest money and time in costly equipment and travel. He takes autumn as it comes—a rich, mellow season whose keenest thrill is weekend football. By comparison, the real hunter is a flaky intransigent who starts coming unglued at the first turning leaf. To him autumn isn't just another time of year—it's the reason why the rest of the year exists.

A while back, I asked an old friend in Arkansas's Boston Mountains if he planned any fall smallmouth fishing up on the Big Piney.

Pat considered this, and said:

"Aw, I reckon not. Come October, I start waitin' on the birds."

"Pat, you know October is the best time to fish for smallmouths," I said.

"Sure it is," he replied, "and you know how I like to ketch them brown bass. But come fall, I'm obliged to wait on birds."

"But your quail season doesn't come in until early December."

"Which ain't my fault," Pat said thoughtfully. "Neither is bein' what I am. You know, I wouldn't go to hell to shoot a quail, but I'd mess around the edge until I fell in."

For men like that, the long wait until hunting season is like the long night before opening day. They are restless, tossing and turning and waiting for first light—or autumn. Their lives would be more placid and serene without hunting. But then, the churchyards are filled with serene, placid men who did not hunt.

It all adds up to this, an ancient Roman inscription in a ruined forum near Timgad, Algeria: "To bathe, to talk, to laugh, to hunt—this is to live."

Bathing I've been getting a lot of. But with no more hunting than I've had lately, I don't have much to talk or laugh about. That's done with. Next season I'll be going out more, going out home again.

••• *John Jobson was a pillar of this magazine for 27 years, until his death in 1979. He was camping editor for 16 years, and hunting editor after that. A pal of Jack O'Connor, he wrote about hunting across North America; many of his stories had a self-deprecating, ironic tone, some of which comes out in this tale.*—JANUARY 1978 •••

HORNS OF GOLD
by John Jobson

Our laden Beaver bush plane came in fast, landing loonlike on a shimmering, tiny lake. The Yukon mountains towering above held at that time the richest Dall sheep pastures in North America. That's what I had come for and I eagerly helped unload the plane.

Happily free of his outsize load, the pilot taxied to the far end of the sparkling tarn, turned and leaned on the throttle, causing the airframe to quiver and the powerful radial engine to roar. Almost at once the pontoons bit the water, the faithful ship lifted breathtakingly free at beachline, its floats brushing a stand of far-north spruce. The wings triumphantly waggled "so long" and we breathed again.

"Well," sighed the Old Outfitter, biting his lower lip, "we're here." And so we were, for 45 days. Talking that pilot into risking his aircraft in my behalf was the final hurdle in an incredible accumulation of frustrations afflicting me at one point with colitis, an onset of shingles, and incipient pulsating cheek-twitch. A sucker for nostalgia, I had foolishly approached a partially business transaction from the romantic view, and it had taken some overdue luck to salvage the operation.

Since boyhood, I'd yearned to collect a trophy Dall ram. That king with golden, full-circle, flare-tipped crown and glittering ermine coat. A huge, blocky, thick-necked roman-nose specimen. A 43- or 44-incher, I told myself. Not to best the other guy at all. Because for decades I'd loved the animal, and I wanted one of my own, to have and to cherish through the years. Seeing his noble head on my den wall would make my existence fuller. Rich and fulfilled.

A 43-inch Dall ram has never been anything deliberately to plan, go for and acquire. It was a lot easier then than now, but with old wise rams, lots can go wrong. Logistics should be coldly calculating. A combination of expert counsel, experience, ability and benign fortune thrown in. You cannot guarantee yourself that initial planning and subsequent tactical execution will put you and that one ram at the same place at the same time.

I was acquainted with North American sheep and had bagged several desert rams, two bighorn and one fair Stone. The game was sort of turning out, you might say, that I was working north to the one I wanted most. I'd been north—had even seen Dalls and Fannin from the highway. I could have harvested an average white ram, but didn't. It came one day that things seemed to jell, as they do if you're lucky. And I went after my Dall monarch with my heart, not my head.

Not only did I want to hunt the most likely sheep pastures available then, I wanted the all-time classic white-ram guide. Back in the late 1920s and early 1930s my father had raved about one colorful, spectacularly successful guide, famous in articles and books. Dad's regard and enthusiasm for him was permanently conta-gious. I never forgot the name, or that Dad had said if he hunted Dall sheep, his ideal, perfect arrangement would be to have this man as his guide.

My little sister Jeanne, who lived in Washington, D.C., got me Xerox copies of old outdoor-magazine articles on this fellow from about World War I up till 1928. I went at them like a lady bug after an aphid, and my enthusiasm fanned anew to Bessemer-furnace temperature. The Old Outfitter was still alive. He would be the frosting on the dream-hunt cake. His letters were lucid, logical and brimming with promise. The fact that he had no recent references I chose to ignore, feeling that belaboring this gauche detail was akin to asking Bette Davis to make a screen test for a TV cameo appearance.

Expert Yukon hunter-sportsmen insisted he'd been over the hill since V8s replaced the Model A. My wife worried. "Why don't you get someone more up-to-date? Younger? Recommended?"

I explained it would mean ever so much to me to get my big ram with him. "He's old," I soothed, "but big rams are best found with a wise head, not fast feet."

Along the Alaska Highway, we heard disturbing rumors that the Old Outfitter was a has-been. Too many hills, too much grog, the frost of too many winters on his shoulders, we heard. On the scene with mounting apprehension, we went into the game department to pay respects and purchase a license (alien). The Director of Fish and Game, a kind gentleman named Jeff Bidlake, asked me who my outfitter was. I told him. He threw up his hands.

"Oh my, Mr. Jobson," he shook his head. "He has no outfitter's license. We haven't renewed it. He has horses left all right, and some gear, but with his drinking problem . . . he disappears, you see. He has kept clients cooling their heels for two weeks, here in town, while he recovers from a bender. Has no credit, no supplies. He's in some minor difficulty with the police. He's insulting to clients. And we have had it up to here with complaints."

My wife and I looked at each other. No Elmer Sizzle super-salesman I, and it's questionable if that would have worked with Mr. Bidlake anyway. But he kindly listened to my earnest plea; and he took my ambition, inherited from Dad, seriously. We called the editor of *Sports Afield*, who told him I was a pillar of honest young manhood and that he would guarantee responsibility for any untoward cost to the Yukon government that this impending fiasco might bring about. I talked with the police and a couple of merchants. Mr. Bidlake told me to send the Old Outfitter in to him, with money. They had a terse, crystal-clear, mostly one-sided conversation while I strode the hall like an expectant father. The Old Outfitter had license and supplies.

My next chore was to buddy up to the highly independent bush pilot, who would no longer fly the outfitter or his clients. "You'll regret it," he told me.

These preparations took longer than it takes to tell—several days, in truth. But sober and with a bit of scratch, the Old Outfitter was a goin' outfit—a backwoods organizational genius, a T. R. Roosevelt of decisive action. He had dispatched two guides, two wranglers and upward of 35 horses to our rendezvous, where the bush plane landed on the beautiful little lake. Tents were up, caches were built, a dining table had been constructed from aromatic spruce. Kitchen shelves groaned with ample supplies, and sweet-scented blue woodsmoke spiraled lazily from the three camp stovepipes. Our homey sleeping tent had been pitched right over fresh grizzly tracks.

The Old Outfitter was in his element. A side glance and the hired help jumped. That camp was run like an admiral's flagship. I could see straightaway that this man was on top of his job, and I also could understand why, when pinned down in town, he might drink to excess and be crotchety. "This is our main base camp," he told us. "Out of here we'll hunt grizzly and moose. But first"—his eyes twinkled—"you want to see if the old has-been can get you up to a 45-inch ram, eh?" He expertly rolled a cigarette. His touch was sure. "Tomorrow we'll take horses and climb these mountains into sheep country. Prob'ly camp up there 10 days or more."

The young guide who led the pack train on the ascent the next morning had quite a sense of humor. His saddle horse slipped on some treacherously loose rock and they both came hurtling past us, a juggernaut of flailing hooves, ricocheting stones and divots. He stood, gave his clothing a token brushing, cupped his hands and yelled, "Don't go *that* way!"

On top we soon came to a lively broad valley, and for miles we followed its greenhouse-lush floor. Regal Osborn caribou bulls were finely etched against opalescent pastel skies. A familiar place for them, in the insect-discouraging wind. At least seven monstrous *Alecs gigas* bull moose, here and there, were feeding in the three-foot-tall yellowish dwarf willow and red ground-cover birch which mottled the mountainsides in delicate patterns. The moose's immensely long legs made them stand out as plain and tall as if they'd been on a clipped lawn. They looked *black*, and their huge antlers were being scraped of velvet, leaving alternate bloody and pure-white patches. The light colors would be bark-stained brown before long. Two mama grizzlies with cubs and one ponderous boar, unknown to one another, were busily plucking the hillside for succulent roots and juicy rodents. It was Shangri-la.

My wife turned and spoke. "Have you ever seen such an amount of game?" The Old Outfitter, ahead of Ann, turned with a speculative look. He did not approve of talk on the trail, even though this game to him was merely incidental. He was a *ram* guide.

We made a wilderness camp at the head of a draw right at the timberline, so that we'd have firewood for the sheepherder stoves used for cooking and heating. There were several comfortable tents, half the size of those at the main camp, thousands of feet below. We had a willing, hardworking crew. It was a happy camp, a camp with the smell of success.

Out of here the Old Outfitter took me on horseback into proven sheep pastures, undulating sweeps of seemingly limitless country beneath somber skies, reminding me of the moors in Wuthering Heights. Instead of heather, it was covered with a curly short grass much like buffalo grass of the Montana high plains. We'd ride out for two, three and four hours and glass for rams. We saw a multitude of sheep, and one day in a snow squall, the O.O. pointed out 40-odd ewes, lambs and young rams grazing near some boulders.

"For practice," he smirked, "I'll stalk you into the center of that bunch of sheep. Follow me and do as I say."

A little over a half-hour, by gum, there we were, too, with puzzled sheep all around us.

This was, if not a truly hard life, at least tedious. Riding out for up to four hours, hunting for seven or eight hours with another interminable ride in darkness, was making us hollow-eyed from lack of sleep and giving us irritable nerves and testy digestion. We saw mature rams in pairs and threes, and singles, that hovered around 40 inches

"You won't settle for anything less than 44 inches, eh," the Old Outfitter mused in an approving tone. He didn't wait for me to answer. "Tomorrow you and me'll take a really light mountain outfit and go to a spot I know. I had a German count there in 1920, but I don't take hardly anyone there, ever."

Leading a pair of packhorses, we rode up and out for what was our longest day so far. We had an old two-man "silk" tent, spartan supplies, little bundles of dry firewood and a diminutive stove made with a jackknife from a five-gallon oil tin. Our Hillary-type camp was alpine, more moss and lichens than grass. We saw no rams at all. Every sign was a year old. Fogs came up that billowed in like the London ones of Sherlock Holmes.

Twice we lost our camp, and never-ceasing howling wind swept vicious particles of icelike snow against us. Our faces were bombarded until they were hamburger raw, and I felt like screaming for the wind to stop. Supplies dwindled to chocolate candy, tea and tobacco.

One day we were standing with our backs to the wind, the loyal saddle horses hunched miserably. "This," said the O.O., "isn't time to be huntin' sheep. If we had any brains, especially you, Jobson, we'd hotfoot it back to timberline camp." I asked him to give it one more day. He beat his gloved hands together and shook his head mournfully.

Next afternoon the wind died and we crossed a great basin and came to a hitherto concealed ravine too steep to ride. We slipped and slid to a roaring alpine creek, waded it, got a grip on ourselves, and heroically clambered up the opposite wall.

At the top, the Old Outfitter peeked over and almost had a stroke. He motioned me to his side. "Take off your hat and take a look," he whispered.

It is facetiously said that the only way to tell the size of trophy horns or antlers is to shoot the beast and put a steel tape on him. This may be true if trophies are on the edge of being good, flirting with the lowest third in the record book. It's never true with exceptionally huge trophies. An outstanding one bellows like a bullhorn that it's one in thousands. There is no mistaking it.

I was looking into an Old Men's convention, the ram equivalent of London's Boodle Club on St. James's. Seven magnificent monsters—immense, blocky as bighorns, with huge horns circling and then flaring out, out, way out with unbroomed tips. Each, a trophy hunter's Grail.

Binoculars confirmed our estimate. "The biggest, third from left, will go an easy 47," the Old Outfitter murmured. "Maybe 48. All are record-book, but go for him. There's not one there less than 43 or 44."

Drenched in perspiration, I was trembling, breathing heavily—gasping really —from a combination of things. The arduous climb, the lack of decent food and the sight of those awesome rams was enough in itself to prostrate. Like others of certain strain of English descent, in emergency I'm inclined to act cool, nervousness coming after the event. But now I wondered. "Get a grip on yourself," I thought. "Remember, Dad is watching you. You've hit woodchucks much farther off than those rams. Be calm. It'll soon be over." I checked the rifle to see if a cartridge was in the chamber. I wiped the lenses of the scope. I took the tape off the muzzle.

"That's right," the outfitter counseled, in perfect control. "Rest. Lay on your back 'til you get your wind."

My hands still trembled with fatigue. At that split-second the fan was hit. Another giant ram, a lookout, strolled unconcernedly from behind a little rise, on his way to join the others, possibly for his relief, when he casually glanced in our direction, did a Pangborn double-take, came down with his legs making a buzzsaw blur. Intuitively the other seven were galloping all-out. The biggest ram was covered by two others, but a good one, probably 45 inches, was coming up behind, and the Old Outfitter, nearly out of his mind, wildly raged, "Second from last! Second from last! Now last! *Shoot shoot shoot . . . !*"

I had some low-growth in front of the scope, so I leaped to my feet. But I could not for the life of me find that damned reticle. It was a split spider-web with an infinitesimal tiny black dot. Great for California ground squirrels, but not for Yukon rams going like Arabian steeds. The third shot and that 45-inch ram rolled like a Western movie horse on the end of a flying-W snare.

"HOORAY!" cried the Old Outfitter.

At this point my .270 with Mauser action jammed. The ram got groggily to his feet, ran toward us, saw his mistake, turned and took off after the others, who by now were laboring along in dreadful difficulty. But they kept going and, in spite of some staggering and their alarmingly heaving sides, they made good time. You'd never have guessed these were granddaddies.

"Hell!" the Old Outfitter bitterly stormed. "You hit that one's *horns!* Of all the . . ." A sob escaped him.

I ran over the crest a bit, sat, got a good steady position, and fired my last two rounds. Each a heartbreaking miss. Spare ammunition was on the horses, by now 400 yards behind us. The noise had spooked them. The rams disappeared at last. They dipped over a crest, a thousand yards from us. My brief moment of truth had come and gone and I'd failed. The rams had won. I doubt if a matador in Madrid's bull ring who had missed his thrust and gotten gored in full view of thousands of *aficionados* would have felt worse.

And the Old Outfitter. He'd done his part, as Dad said he would, and more. He was silent, gazing blankly, in shock.

I cleared my throat, "Well," I attempted, "another day, eh."

"Those rams are *gone,*" he growled. "Country too rough to ride to."

"Well, maybe next year then."

He shook his head, punishing himself and me. "This is their last season. Too old. A bad winter's coming. They'll never make it. Many wolves around. I never in my life seen that many record rams together at once. That was a once-in-a-life-time."

"Well," I said. "I guess we better go."

◆◆◆ *Grits Gresham has written for* SPORTS AFIELD *for 35 years, the past 20 as its shooting editor. An accomplished hunter who has traveled the globe, he has written seven books, and has hosted a variety of TV shows, including* THE AMERICAN SPORTSMAN. *This article on hunting the king of beasts is one of his favorites.*—APRIL 1979 ◆◆◆

LIONS OF THE KALAHARI *by Grits Gresham*

With a palms-up gesture of the right hand, without breaking stride, Dumelo indicated that he had lost the trail. With a flick of that same hand he instructed Galabeso to search to the right. It wasn't necessary to send the "volunteer" to the left—he was already headed that way.

For three hours the pattern had been the same. The three Tswana trackers had followed the huge pug marks of a lion at a very fast walk, almost a trot. It was a pace that guaranteed that the "lost trail" routine would take place periodically, but the incredible eyes and instincts of the Africans ensured that the tracks would be found again with no lost motion.

Teamwork! The man on point at the time kept all of us aware, using a series of expressive hand signals which were unmistakable. That upturned palm—"I lost it"; the casual gesture with the index finger—"He went this way"; that flick of the hand right or left—"You guys check over there"; a low whistle—"I've found it."

Since the trackers were completely unarmed, it was imperative that we who were maintain the pace, keeping close on their heels. Ian Manning did so without effort. I managed, but with greater and greater difficulty as the broiling sun and sand—and the miles—took their toll.

Then the three trackers stopped, whispering among themselves, pointing down at the tracks. Ian listened, then joined in, and finally translated for my benefit.

"They think the tracks are old. Dumelo thinks we should just give it up, and so does the volunteer. Galabeso isn't sure, but he thinks the tracks were made today."

Kalahari! Some words are magic to hunters, and especially to outdoorsmen with even a passing familiarity with Africa. Kalahari is such a word.

This vast area, frequently called the Kalahari Desert, covers a major portion of the southern part of Botswana and sprawls over into South Africa. It is the last stronghold of the Bushmen, those strange, interesting and peaceful people who are renowned for coping with that arid land. And arid it is, with virtually no surface water except for the boreholes—wells—drilled by the government.

Kalahari. It's also a major stronghold of the African lion, and one of the few places where this magnificent cat can be hunted by tracking rather than over bait. In most places in their range, baiting a lion, or leopard, is the only practical way of hunting, as was true for tiger and is for jaguar. But it is undeniable that the prospect of hunting the king on foot, in his element, by following his pug marks, held for me a particular fascination.

"It's all set. We go into camp in Botswana on October 29, and you'll be hunting with Ian Manning." When that call came from Paul Merzig, the Chicago-based co-honcho of International Sportsmen's Adventures (ISA), it immediately became fete day on my sweltering Louisiana bayou. Nothing is really like the excitement of the hunt itself, but the anticipation of and planning for an unusual adventure come in a close second.

What rifle?

That's usually the first thought that pops into my mind when a big-game hunt is in the offing, and it was especially true in this case. When shot over bait, or when the cat is undisturbed under any other conditions, the choice of caliber isn't particularly critical for lion. But friends who had been there told me that when tracking a lion the odds of finding him in a disturbed state were quite good. And rather good that he would be in a very disturbed state, and very close.

I had just received a sample of a Colt Sauer in a .375 Holland & Holland, a new caliber in that rifle, and that became my choice. Off it went to Larry Kelly in Michigan to have it Mag-na-ported, and a call went out to Don Gobel at Weaver for a low-power variable scope.

"Would the middle of September be too late?" Don came right back. "By then I can get a production model of our new Steel-Lite scope shipped to your home right away."

That V4.5 arrived right on schedule and by the time my departure date rolled around several boxes of ammo had been run through the Colt. I sighted it to shoot a couple of inches high at 100 yards, using the 270-grain Remington Core-Lokt soft points and got excellent groups. Checking with a 300-grain solid at the same range brought a surprise. The Winchester Super Speed grouped eight inches lower. It isn't unusual for different bullet weights to shoot to different points of impact, of course, but this much difference was unusual, and something to keep in mind.

The flight from New York to Johannesburg, via Amsterdam, on KLM's superb big planes, was long and tiring. That was expected—seven hours from New York to Amsterdam; eight hours from Amsterdam to Nairobi; and 3 1/2 hours from Nairobi to Joburg; but the food and service were excellent. From Johannesburg we flew Air Botswana to Gaberone, the capital of that country, a one-hour flight in a Viscount prop plane manned by South African Airways personnel, and discovered that ours was the first plane to land in Gaberone in two weeks. The airport had been closed for runway repairs, which we didn't know until checking in for the flight. Lucky.

In Gaberone we immediately transferred our luggage to a chartered Aero Commander, and flew in an easterly direction for almost two hours to a settlement called Tshane. The landing there was not without excitement. It was the pilot's first trip to that strip, and from the co-pilot's seat, as we made the final approach, I got the distinct feeling that the two of us were looking at different airstrips. What made it more interesting was that I couldn't see the one he had committed for.

An ex-RAF pilot, he got us down safely, but on a short auxiliary strip which looked more like a gravel pit. He hadn't seen the main strip, a few hundred yards away along the edge of the Tshane pan—a dry lake bed. Ten minutes later an amazed Ian Manning drove up from the main strip, where he had been waiting.

From Tshane to our hunting camp was another 3 1/2 hours, a long, hot, swaying ride in the four-wheel-drive Toyota over a sand road. The route took us through the village of Kang, only 45 minutes from our camp.

Ian's hunting camp was something between an elaborate spike camp and semipermanent safari camp. There were three sleeping tents and a mess tent, plus small enclosures for the outdoor toilet and shower—a five-gallon can fitted with a shower head, hoisted high over a limb with a rope.

It was quite a comfortable situation for a new operation, and this one was new. This was an inaugural hunt in a recent affiliation between ISA and Ian's company—Wildlife Management, Botswana; and this was a new concession area for Ian. Except for a short hunt he had made there two months earlier, it's doubtful that the area had ever been hunted by others than local natives.

Born in South Africa of British ancestry, Ian has had years of hunting experience in Zambia, Rhodesia and Botswana, as well as in South Africa. Much of it was in game cropping and control. Following his studies in South Africa, he went to Nova Scotia to study wildlife management.

"My real interest," he told me as we rode for hours looking for lion sign, "is in total utilization of the wildlife resource. The primary purpose of my company is just what the name says—wildlife management. Safari hunting is just one aspect of that utilization."

Our hunting party, in addition to me, consisted of fellow outdoor writer Dave

Petzal; Norbert Leroy, a Belgian who flew Spitfires for the RAF in World War II now living in New York, and who is affiliated with KLM Royal Dutch Airlines; and Tom Thornber, director of advertising and public relations for Colt Firearms. Also along was Paul Merzig of ISA.

Ian's help in the guiding chores came in the economy-sized package of one Anton Wienand. This giant of a man—a conservative 250 pounds—was a delight to camp and hunt with. He is a veteran of safari operations in Zambia and Rhodesia.

Ian's concession is 65,000 acres in size, and includes a quarantine block amounting to half of that. Cattle being moved from the major cattle-growing area in the west to a huge meat-processing operation just east of our area (the largest such slaughtering facility in Africa), are held in quarantine for a period as a precaution against hoof-and-mouth disease. The five-strand, smooth wire fences which enclose this area, however, present a tragic problem for some game species, notably hartebeest. Hartebeest seldom try to jump the fences, and try to get through just by running into them a full speed. It's amazing that most do eventually get through, usually after being bounced back a few times, but too many become entangled in the wire and die a slow, painful death.

"The quarantine area and the adjacent ranch," Ian explained as we drove the borders looking for spoor, "have the highest game populations in this area of Botswana. The habitat is better, and then there are the boreholes drilled by the government for the cattle. Water is always an attraction in arid terrain. Lions are attracted to this area by the game—hartebeest, wildebeest, gemsbok, dicker, steenbok, springbok, and also by the cattle."

A good lion taken by tracking was my primary goal, and the pattern of Ian's operation toward that end was simple. We were awakened each morning at 4:45 and by daylight were cruising the borders and crisscrossing the interior of his concession, searching for lion tracks. Some days we returned to camp about noon for lunch, but were always back in the bush from mid afternoon until dark.

"Patience is what you must have to hunt lion here," the lean and tough Manning explained. "Once you find a fresh track you have an excellent chance of getting a shot eventually."

After four full days we had still seen no lion track, but those long days were far from uneventful. In that time I shot several hartebeest, one good head for a trophy, another for camp meat, and several which were tangled in the fences and had to be dispatched. And I did get a magnificent male gemsbok, the largest member of the oryx family, whose massive horns measured 39 1/2 inches in length.

But no lion tracks.

"Lions are killing cattle and horses, and would you please come and kill them."

That, liberally translated, was the message which awaited us in camp the night of that fourth day. It was from the tribal chief in the village of Kang, and it created a wave of excitement among all of us.

On the next morning, day five, we were in Kang by 8 A.M. We first visited the tribal chief, C. P. Seipone, and then located the game scout who is the sole representative of the Botswana Game Department in this portion of the country. He did not know whose cattle had been killed, but would go with us to try to find out, and go with us to kill the lion. The prospect of a lion hunt, in fact, triggered tremendous interest among the natives. The foreman of a ranch near our camp insisted that he come along to help. Another man in the village of Kang volunteered, and eventually became "the volunteer" in our tracking party.

After making the rounds of several bomas around Kang, and going to the nearby pan where most of the cattle are watered, we still failed to pin down any definitive information as to the whereabouts of the marauding lions. All we got was a general suggestion as to the area, so Ian elected to head that way.

The day was particularly hot, but we continued to search. At exactly 1 P.M. there was a rap on the cab of the Toyota, and when Ian braked to a stop "the foreman" bailed off the top and ran back down the trail. He had spotted the faint impression of a lion track, and in seconds he, the volunteer and our regular trackers—Dumelo and Galabeso—were following the trail out across the veldt.

"It's a big male," Ian grinned. "Let's take a swig of water and go."

We made quite a procession. The four trackers were out front, followed by Ian and then me. Dave and Paul were just behind, as spectators and cameramen, and the game scout brought up the rear.

The scout was not a good representative for his department or his country. He wanted us to follow the lion in the vehicle and was obviously unhappy when we insisted that we wanted to hunt on foot. He would wait for us in the vehicle. But he changed his mind after we had gone several hundred yards and hurried to catch up.

After the first half hour he decided to return to the vehicle but first drank half of the water Galabeso was carrying for all of us. Now we were eight.

For the first mile or so the trail was a gentle incline which led to the rim of a large pan, a circular depression perhaps half a mile across. The hard baked bottom of the pan held no tracks, so we fanned out in an effort to pick up the trail on the far side. Again, it was "the foreman" who found it. The lion had been headed directly south, but it was on the far western edge of the pan that we found his tracks. They circled the huge dry lake bed and again swung southward.

We were already one hour from the vehicle, and Ian made the point that it was apt to be much, much more before either of two events occurred; we overtook the lion, or nightfall overtook us. The decision was made that Dave and Paul would return to the Toyota and bring it along over our trail. The foreman would track for them.

And then there were five.

From the point of our brief strategy conference, which took perhaps two minutes, the pace of our leaned-down hunting party picked up. The race was on.

A peculiar situation was developing. Game was abundant where we first found the lion's spoor, with herds of hartebeest, springbok and gemsbok in evidence. It was especially so around the pan, but now the big cat was moving from that land of plenty into areas which seemed virtually devoid of prey species. Not only were we seeing no animals, but we were finding no fresh sign.

We moved rapidly, and there was no energy or inclination, nor much necessity for conversation. Fully loaded with three of the fat .375 cartridges in the clip magazine and one in the chamber as was the case from the time we left the vehicle, the Colt Sauer weighed 9 pounds 12 ounces. Anticipating that the trek might be strenuous for lungs and legs unaccustomed to Kalahari conditions, I had stripped to the essentials: rifle and spare ammo. No cameras. No binoculars.

As the hours and miles passed, there was ample time for reflection. As is so often true, I found it necessary now and then to put things into perspective. "You are in the Kalahari area of Botswana, Gresham, not the scrub thickets of south Texas. The animal you're tracking isn't a cottontail, or even a whitetail. It's a big male lion that will probably weigh 400 to 500 pounds, and which has no problem killing a Cape buffalo with one swipe. Less problem with killing a tracker with one bite. A cat that can cover 100 yards in about four seconds. And, more important, that can move 20 yards in less than a second."

Ian's words of a few nights before, in that soft British accent, around the crackling campfire against a backdrop of the inimitable African sunset, came back. "There's no question but that this is the most dangerous kind of lion hunting, but it spoils you for any other method."

There was a moment of silence, then he added, "The client mustn't depend upon his professional hunter for protection."

Consistent with the actions of most predators, our lion stayed in the thickest cover along his general route, steadily eastward. Most of the terrain was fairly open, but other portions were dense enough to cover a pride of lions within 10 yards. It was in these stretches that Ian shifted his rifle from over the shoulder to port arms, and I followed suit.

"You must keep in mind," more of Ian's words came to mind, "that the tactics of lion tracking are geared to irritate him into making a stand. It's a case of pushing him until he won't be pushed any more."

I tried to keep just a step behind Ian's long strides, ready to move alongside in an emergency so both of us would have a full field of fire, but after three hours he must have noticed that I was lagging. A few words from him to Dumelo, in that universal patois through which the peoples of southern Africa converse, slowed the pace just a bit. I was grateful.

Then, to continue or not, that became the question.

Ian shushed the trackers, whose "conference" over our course of action was getting a bit noisy, and walked around a bit. While he was making his decision, I had come to mine. With as much equity as we invested in this big fellow, I was for staying until the end. Sleep where dark found us, and pick up the trail in the morning.

"It isn't all that old," Ian led me over to a print which was protected from the wind. "This was made sometime today. Let's keep moving."

It was 4 P.M. when he motioned the trackers to continue and grunted something to them that brought grins. I was too busy keeping up to find out what he said.

Less than 100 yards farther the bobbing, weaving, rolling gaits of the three Tswanas became stop action. It was instant freeze, and fatigue evaporated in that electric atmosphere. The lion had made a kill, and the three had come upon it suddenly as they rounded a dense thorn tree. Like gazelles poised for flight, they froze in place, eyes searching the surrounding thickets. Ian and I moved up quickly.

The kill was a porcupine, which had been eaten completely except for the quills and the intestines.

"Not more than an hour or two ago," Ian murmured softly, checking the carcass but constantly alert toward our perimeters. "Maybe he'll slow down now."

If he did, it wasn't obvious to me, but adrenaline had replaced tiredness, and I floated along in the wake of my front four. But an artificial high can't be maintained indefinitely, and after another hour the legs were beginning to lose that spring once more. The shadows, suddenly, were long, and the breeze on the back of my neck turned cool. I knew in little more than an hour it would be dark and cold.

Despite my vow to keep my attention focused entirely on the lion, my mind had wandered to thoughts of day, night and temperatures. Then the panorama exploded. Although it appeared to me in slow motion, the three trackers simply peeled off in a sunburst of action, passing Ian and me in a blur. The volunteer circled left, Dumelo right and Galabeso retreated to within touching distance. I stepped to Ian's right, and both of us had rifles to shoulders.

I could see nothing. There was a dense thicket immediately to our right. Just in front, from where the trackers had burst into flight, was a big thorn tree surrounded by low shrubs and tall grass. Beyond it, an opening, and then more thickets. The trackers must have seen the lion. Was it running? Where?

Then Ian's whisper came through. Galabeso had finally told him that they had almost walked into the lion. He was in the thicket at the base of the tree.

We could see fur through the grass, but even through my scope there was no definition. Was he asleep, or was he crouched—ready to rid himself of the annoyance of the past four hours? While I kept the rifle trained, Ian lowered his to use binoculars. Nothing. We moved a bit closer for a better look but then moved back again when Ian realized just how close we were.

"I'll try to make him stand up," Ian whispered, eyes never leaving the lion. "But be ready."

He rapped on the rifle stock with his knuckles. The fur twitched, and so did my blood pressure. But then nothing. Ian whistled. Nothing.

"Too risky," he eased closer. "If he's asleep he may jump up running, and you won't have much of a shot. Too near dark to have a wounded lion. If he's not asleep,

I don't want to provoke him into coming this way. We're just too close. If you can ever make sure which way he's lying, better shoot."

Then the lion rolled, his huge paws and legs describing an incredible arc up over the grass. I fastened my eyes on the light belly patch between the front legs as it almost disappeared down into the grass again. I took two steps forward, to clear the limb of a bush, and touched it off.

The lion stayed down, and the two additional shots I added proved unnecessary. We waited 10 more minutes, as insurance, before covering the 17-yard distance.

The trackers were jubilant, and there would be more of the same in Kang when cattlemen there got the news, but when I finally stooped down by the lion there came that twinge of regret that most hunters experience. It was an old male, hide scarred from countless battles, and in his neck were half a dozen quills from his encounter with the porcupine.

Tony Dyer's words, from his great book, *Classic African Animals: The Big Five*, Winchester Press, came back to me: "Once one of the great cats has had to resort to trying to live on porcupine, it is doomed. This otherwise helpless, slow moving animal can inflict dreadful suffering even on the most skillful lion."

And more . . . "Then he will become thinner and thinner, until the patient, knowing hyenas close in and he perishes as he has lived, by the rule of the fang.

"There are many human critics of the fact that man kills lions. Let them stop and think awhile of the alternatives. How else can a lion die, except in the jaws of the ever-ready hyena?"

The hyenas wouldn't get this one.

As we rolled into camp two hours later, the trackers advertising our success with song, Ian added the right touch: "It's a fine trophy, and well-earned." He raised his voice a bit over the music and grinned. "I'm glad he decided to stop. It would have been a cold night out."

◆◆◆ *Currently the hunting editor of* SPORTS AFIELD, *and residing in Sheridan, Wyoming, Thomas McIntyre has been writing for the magazine since 1979. Here he writes of his first visit to Africa, a continent that shaped his life before he ever set foot upon it.*—JUNE 1981 ◆◆◆

BUFF by Thomas McIntyre

They saw the buffalo after killing the elephant. The professional hunter switched off the engine and eased out of the battered olive Land Rover, carrying his binoculars. His client got out on the other side without making any noise, and one of the trackers, without needing to be told, handed his 300 down to him. The client fed the 200-grain Noslers into the magazine, put the 220-grain solid into the chamber and locked the bolt as the professional hunter glassed the buffs.

It was nearly sunset, and already in the back of the Land Rover lay the heavy curves of ivory, darkened and checked by decades of life, the roots bloodied now like a pulled tooth. They had found the old bull elephant under a bright acacia late in the afternoon, having tracked him all day on foot. He was being guarded by two younger bulls, his askaris; and when the client made the brainshot, red dust puffing off the side of the elephant's head, and the old bull dropped, the young ones got between and tried to push him back onto his feet, blocking any finishing rounds. But the bullet had actually just missed the bull's brain, lodging instead in the honeycomb of bone in the top of his skull. As he came to he regained his feet, and they had to chase him almost a mile, firing on the run, until he went down for good. By then it was too late to butcher out the dark-red flesh, so they left that task until the next morning when they would return with a band of local villagers and carry out everything edible, even marrow in the bones. They took only the tusks that afternoon. Still, when they finally reached the Land Rover again they were very tired, pleased with themselves, and ready only for a long drink back in camp.

So when on the way to that drink the professional hunter spotted a bachelor herd of Cape buffalo (with two exceptionally fine bulls in it), it was all a bit much, actually. But he motioned *his client to come around behind the Land Rover to his side, and crouching they worked behind the low cover toward the* mbogos.

The first rule they give you about dangerous game is to get as close as you possibly can before firing—then get another 100 yards closer. When the professional felt they had complied with this stricture, to the extent that they could clearly see the yellow-billed oxpeckers hanging beneath the bull's flicking ears and feeding on ticks, he got his client into kneeling position and told him to take the one turned sideways to them: put the solid into his shoulder, then pour on the Noslers. That was when the client noticed that the professional was backing him up with a pair of 8X German binoculars instead of his customary 470 Nitro Express double rifle, but the professional just shrugged and said, "You should be able to handle this all right by yourself."

Taking a breath, the client hit the buffalo in the shoulder with the solid and staggered him. The bull turned to face them, and the client put two quick Noslers into the heaving chest, aiming right below the chin. The buffalo collapsed. As the client reloaded, the second fine bull remained where he was, confused and belligerent, and the professional hunter urged his client to take him too, oh my yes, him too. This bull turned also after the first solid slammed into his shoulder and lifted his head toward them, his scenting nose held high. Looking a wounded Cape buffalo in his discomfitingly intelligent eyes is something like looking down the barrel of a loaded 45 in the hands of a mean drunk. That is the time when you have to be exceptionally mindful, however, of what you are doing out there in Africa and make your shots count—particularly when your professional hunter, who is backing you up with a pair of 8X German binoculars, leans over and whispers calmly, "Look: he's going to come for us."

Another careful breath and the client placed two more bullets neatly into the bull's chest beneath his raised chin, just the way he had on the first one, except this bull did not go down. That left the client with one round in his rifle, and as he was about to squeeze it off he wondered if there would be any time left afterward for him either to reload or make a run for it. But for now there was this enraged buffalo that had to be gotten onto the ground somehow. All the client could be really concerned about was holding his rifle steady until the sear broke and the cartridge fired and the bullet sped toward the bull—but just before the rifle fired its last round the buffalo lurched forward and fell with a bellow, stretching his black muzzle out in the dirt. Then he was silent.

Standing up slowly, the client and the professional hunter moved cautiously toward the downed buffalo (the rest of the small herd now fled) to find them both dead. Only then, in the dwindling light did they see that one of the first bull's horns, the horn that was turned away from them when the client first shot, had been broken away in recent combat and a splintered stump was all that remained. He had been a magnificent bull at one time, but at least the second bull's horns were perfect, beautifully matched sweeps of polished black horn, almost 50 inches across the spread. And there glittered a burnished half-inch steel ball bearing buried in the horn boss covering the bull's head like a gladiator's helmet. The ball bearing had once served as a musketball fired out of an ancient muzzleloader. Whoever the native hunter who fired it was, he must have had one overpowering lust for buffalo meat, and for buffalo hunting. What became of him after he shot and missed with his quixotic weapon at a ludicrously close range is probably best not speculated upon, however.

• • •

When I first heard that story I was a boy of 9 or 10. It was told by a gentleman of my acquaintance (a man who taught me how to hunt then, and with whom I have had the pleasure of hunting ever since), who had experienced it on a safari to Tanzania 20 years ago. Like most hunting tales, it has been twice and three times told since, yet unlike some others it has aged rather well and never grown tedious with the tellings. Every time I hear it, and see the massive head on the wall with the steel ball shining out of the horn, it explains something, mysteriously, of why a person could get daffy about hunting Cape buffalo. And, mystery or not, its power as a legend sent me off to East Africa once to hunt buffalo myself.

Black, sparsely haired, nearly a ton in weight, some five feet high at the shoulder, as smart and mean as a muleskinner's whip, and with a set of immense but elegant ebony horns which sweep down then up and a little back, like something drawn with a French curve, to points sharp enough to kill a black-maned lion with one blow—horns which can measure almost five feet across the outside spread—the African Cape buffalo is, along with the Indian water buffalo and the Spanish fighting bull, one of the three great wild cattle in the world today. Of these three, though, the water buffalo has now been largely domesticated, although a few animals transplanted to Australia and South America have reverted to the untamed state. The fighting *toro*'s wildness is the product of over 2000 years of men having restricted his breeding to keep the aurochs' blood still running through his veins. The Cape buffalo alone has had no dealings with men, other than of the most terminal kind.

With his ferocious temper, treacherous intelligence, and stern indifference to the shocking power of all but the most outlandishly large-caliber rifles, the Cape buffalo is routinely touted as the most dangerous member of the African Big Five (which also includes the lion, leopard, rhino and elephant). Whether he is or not all depends, as does almost everything under the sun, on what you mean. He is certainly not as sure to charge as a rhino or as quick as the carnivorous cats. And in the words of Grits Gresham, "Nobody ever got *wounded* by an elephant." But the buff is quick enough, and when he makes up his mind to charge, especially when wounded, there is no animal more obdurately bent on finishing a fight. In open flat country he may present no serious threat to a hunter properly armed, but you seldom encounter him in baseball-diamond surroundings. More often, he'll be in a swampy thicket or a dense forest. He is clever enough to go to cover and fierce enough to come out of it.

The best measure of the Cape buffalo's rank as a big-game animal may simply be the kind of esteem professional hunters hold him in. It is a curious fact of the sporting life that tall, strapping, red-faced chaps who make their livings trailing the dangerous game all come in time to be downright maudlin about which animals they feel right about hunting. Most first lose their taste for hunting the big cats, so that while they will usually do their best to get a client his one and only lion, their hearts will not be entirely in it: the predatory cats in their appetites for meat and sleep and sex are simply too close to us for comfort. Then there is the rhino, the hulking, agile, dumb, blind, sad, funny, savage, magnificent Pleistocene rhino who every day is getting hammered just that much closer to the Big Jump we term extinction—under present conditions only a raving sociopath could feel good about destroying one specimen of that fleeting arrangement of molecules we term rhino.

Out of the Big Five, then, that leaves only the elephant and the Cape buffalo to feel at all right about hunting, and to my knowledge hardly any real professional hunter, unless he has lost interest in hunting altogether, ever totally loses his taste for giving chase to these two. There is no easy way to hunt elephant and Cape buffalo—you must be able to walk for miles on end, know how to follow animal sign well, and be prepared to kill an animal who can just as readily kill you—and this makes them the two greatest challenges for taking good trophy animals, and the two most satisfying. Something about hunting them gets into a hunter's blood and stays. To offer one further bit of testimony on behalf of the buff, consider if you will the widely known piece of jungle lore that the favorite sport of elephants is *chasing* herds of Cape buffalo around the bush, and the buff's position as one of the world's great big-game animals seems secure.

Which is why I wanted to hunt buff and went to do so in the southwestern corner of Kenya (still open to hunting then) near Lake Victoria, in the Chepalungu Forest on top of the Soit Ololol Escarpment and above the Great Rift Valley, to arguably the loveliest green spot in all Masailand, and one which I dearly hated—to begin with, anyway.

To find buffalo there we had to put on cheap canvas tennis shoes (because they were the only things that would dry overnight) and slog every day into the dim wet forest (filled with butterflies and cobras, birds and barking bushbucks, gray waterbucks and giant forest hogs, rhino, elephant and buffalo), penetrating a wall of limbs and vines and deep-green leaves woven as tight as a Panama hat, and through which one could see no more than 10 feet in any direction. On going in, the advice given me by my professional hunter, John Fletcher of the late lamented Ker, Downey & Selby Safaris, Ltd., was that, in the event of my stumbling onto a sleeping buffalo (as well I might), I should shoot the animal dead on the spot and ask questions later. It took only a momentary lack of resolve at such a juncture, he assured me, to give a buffalo ample opportunity to spring up and winnow you right down. And that was the root cause of my hating this beautiful African land: It scared the hell out of me, and I hated being scared.

As we hunted the buffalo, though, a change began to come over me. We had had unheard-of luck on cats at the outset of the safari, so that at dawn on my fifth morning of hunting in Africa, while concealed in a blind constructed out of cut brush, I had taken a very fine leopard as he came to feed on the hanging bait—the cat toppling from the tree as a long yellow flame sprouted from the muzzle of my 300. And on the evening of the same day, we had incredibly gotten up on an extremely large lion, *simba mkubwa sana* in the words of the trackers, crouched in long grass which shaded his tawny hide to a lime tone, and I had broken his back with my 375, establishing what may very well have been some sort of one-day East African record for cats. So when our hangovers subsided two days later, we moved off from that more southern country near Kilimanjaro to Block 60 above the escarpment, assuming we would quickly take a good buffalo (a bull with a spread over 40-inches wide—literally 45 or better, with 50 inches a life's ambition—along with a full, tightly fitted boss), then move on again to the greater-kudu country we had, until the cats, not hoped to have time to reach.

Instead of a good buffalo in short order, however, we had to go into the forest every day for two weeks, first glassing the open country futilely at daybreak, then following into the cover the tracks the buffalo left when they had moved back in before dawn, their night's feeding done. In that forest, where the light sifted down as if into deep water, we picked our way for two weeks over rotting timber and through mud wallows, unseen animals leaping away from us on all sides, creeping forward until we could hear low grunts, then the sudden flutter of oxpeckers (more euphoniously known as tickbirds) flaring up from the backs of the buffalo they were preening, and then the flutter of alarmed Cape buffalo flaring up as well, snorting, crashing so wildly away (yet also unseen) through the dark forest that the soggy ground quivered, and the trees were tossed about as if in a wind storm, and the report of wood being splintered by horns could be heard for hundreds of yards through the forest. That was the sound a breeding herd of cows, calves and young bulls made as they fled; but other times there would be the flutter of oxpeckers and no crashing afterward, only a silence that the booming of my heart seemed to fill, and we knew we were onto a herd of bulls, wise old animals who were at that moment slipping carefully away from us, moving off with inbred stealth, or maybe stealthily circling back to trample us into the dirt! For much of those two weeks, then, I saw things in that forest through a glaze of fear as ornate as the rose window in a medieval French cathedral.

I discovered, however, that you can tolerate fear roaring like a train through your head and clamping like a limpet to your heart for just so long; and sometime during those two weeks I ceased to be utterly terrified by the black forms in the forest, and instead became excited by them, by the chance of encountering them, by the possibility that my life was actually on the line in there: my heart still boomed, but for a far different reason now. What was going on in that forest, I saw, was a highly charged game of skill: if you played it wrong, you might be killed; but if you played it just right, you got to do it over again. No more than that. But when something like that gets into your blood, the rest of life comes to lack something you never knew it was supposed to have before.

Then one evening we chased a breeding herd in and out of the forest for hours, jumping it and driving it ahead of us, trying to get a good look at one of the bulls in it. Finally we circled ahead of the buffalo into a clearing of chest-high grass where they had to cross in front of us. We hunkered down in the grass and watched them as they came out. The bull appeared at last, but he was only a young seed bull, big bodied but not good in the horns. As we watched him pass by, a tremendous cow buffalo, the herd matriarch, walked out, maybe 60 yards from us, and halted. Then she turned and stared directly our way.

If she feels her calf or her herd is threatened, the cow buffalo is probably as deadly an animal as there is; and at that moment I thought that was just the most wonderful piece of information in the world to have. It meant she might charge, and, may God forgive me, I *wanted* her to. Very much.

"All right," John Fletcher whispered, his William G. Evans 500 Nitro Express carried across his body like a laborer's shovel, "we'll stand now, and she'll run off. Or she'll charge us."

So we stood up, John Fletcher, me, and the trackers behind us, and the buffalo cow did not budge. We could see her thinking, weighing the odds, her nostrils twitching. John Fletcher and I brought our rifles up at the same time without a word and took aim: as soon as she started forward I knew I was going to throw a 375 into the center of her chest, exactly where my crosshairs were, and if she kept coming I would throw in another after that, but I would not run. As the seconds passed, I felt more and more that, for perhaps one of the few times in my life, I was behaving correctly, no fear clouding my vision now.

Then the cow snorted and spun away from us, following the herd, her calculations having come up on the negative side for her. I took my finger off the trigger, then, and carefully reset the safety. And all the trackers came up and clapped me on the back, smiling their nervous African smiles, as if to say, *You did well*. I was glad we hadn't had to kill the cow after all.

Yet, when at first light on our fourteenth day of buffalo hunting we reached the edge of a small dewy field and spotted three bulls feeding in it 100 yards away, I did not kill my first Cape buffalo at all well. Though he was the smallest-bodied buffalo of the three, old and almost hairless, his horns swept out nearly 45 inches, much farther than those of the other two, and when I fired—low, near his heart, but not near enough—he began to trot in a slow circle as the two younger bulls came past us at an oblique angle, just visible in the edge of my scope. I shot him again and again, anywhere, and again, and John Fletcher fired once, and at last the bull went down and I had to finish him on the ground. There was still, I had to admit, after the bull lay dead and all my ammunition was gone, enough fear left in me to prevent my behaving in a completely correct manner.

We went on hunting Cape buffalo after that right up to my last day on safari—John Fletcher looking for an even better trophy for me, and me looking to make up for the first kill, hoping there was still time. On the last morning of hunting we flushed a bushbuck. I had only the briefest second to make one of the toughest running shots I have ever tried and took the sturdy little antelope through the heart as he stretched into top speed. Suddenly I was very anxious to try another buffalo before leaving Africa.

We found the herd that evening when John and I and my nonhunting friend William Cullen were out alone, the trackers back helping break camp. The buffalo had been drifting in and out of the forest all that gray highland afternoon with us behind them, a bull's cloven print, as big as a relish tray, standing out from all the others. It seemed that we had lost them for good until a small boy, no older than four or five, wearing a rough-cotton toga and carrying a smooth stick, appeared startlingly out of the bush before us and asked in Masai if we would like to kill a buffalo.

The child led us along a forest trail to the edge of the trees, where he pointed across an open glade to the bull. The Cape buffalo bull, his tight boss doming high above his head, stood in the herd of 10 or 15 other animals in the nearing dark, only a few yards from heavy cover—in which, in no more than half-a-dozen running steps, he could be completely concealed. John Fletcher, for one, was something more than slightly aware of this. He remembered too well how I had killed my first bull, and though he'd said nothing, he knew how much the buffalo had spooked me. If I wounded this bull now and he made it into the forest with the light going, and the second rule they give you for dangerous game being that you follow all wounded animals in . . . well . . . John Fletcher looked at me carefully. There was no denying it was a good bull, though, and the trackers and camp staff would want some more meat to take home, and there was still a little light, and—*and oh bloody hell!*

I glanced at him, then back at the buffalo. I was, at that moment, as all right as I was ever going to get. This was where it counted; this was what it was all about; this was exactly what I'd come here for. It was in my blood now, only John Fletcher might not know that. I told him.

"Where," I whispered, easing the 375's safety off, "do you want me to shoot him, John?"

John Fletcher stared at me even harder then, but this time he whispered only, "There, in the shoulder."

You can see where a Cape buffalo's shoulder socket is under his hide, and if you travel through his body from there you will reach his spine where it dips down from his humped back to become his neck. That was where I laid my crosshairs and when the 270-grain Nosler hit him there it broke his shoulder and shattered his spine. Suddenly the bull was down, his muzzle stretched out along the short grass and the buffalos bellowing death song (what the professionals call "music" when they hear it coming from a wounded bull laid up in cover, because it means he's done for) coming from his throat. The rest of the herd wheeled on us then, their eyes clear and wide and most uncattlelike, the smell of the bull's blood in their nostrils. I finished the bull with one more round to the neck, and the herd was gone, vanishing as quickly as that bull could have vanished had my nerve not held and I had not behaved correctly.

That last night in camp, while the African staffed jerked long strips of buffalo meat over the campfire to carry back to their wives and children, John Fletcher, William Cullen and I sat in the dining tent and ate hot oxtail soup and slices of steaming boiled buffalo tongue and drank too much champagne and brandy, and laughed too loud too. We finished breaking camp at dawn the next morning and returned to Nairobi.

It seems I may have gone on at too great a length here already, but I wish I could go on even further to tell you all the other Cape buffalo stories I know, like the time John Fletcher was guiding a famous Mexican *torero* who meant to kill a bull buffalo with his curved steel sword—brought with him from Mexico for just that purpose—and what made him change his mind. Or how when you awoke in the middle of the night, needing to seek relief, and stepped outside your canvas tent, you might make out, just there on that little rise at the edge of camp, the silhouettes of feeding buffalo against the cold stars. Or how one of the many herds we chased out of the forest and across the green country led us into a spectacular cloudburst, and the storm wind began to swirl around so that our scent was swept in front of the 50 or 60 funereal-black animals and turned them back *on* us, and as they started forward I asked John Fletcher what we did now, and he said lightly, "Actually, we might try shooting down the lead buffalo and climbing onto its back."

But what I wish most of all is that I were back in those African highlands I grew to love, hunting the Cape buffalo I grew to love too—probably still scared, but only enough to make me sense my true heart curled inside my chest and beating, telling me of what I am capable.

••• *A native of Massachusetts, Steven Mulak has been duck hunting since his boyhood. He wrote many stories about waterfowling for the magazine in the 1980s, and has done two books:* BROWN FEATHERS *(1985) and* POINTING DOGS MADE EASY *(1995).* WAX AND WANE *was one of his first* SPORTS AFIELD *stories.*—DECEMBER 1982 •••

WAX AND WANE
by Steven Mulak

At times the waterfowl season seems shorter than its allotted number of days . . . times when the entire season can be compressed into a single day on the marshes:

• • •

5:40 A.M. The silence is overpowering. Andromeda and Pegasus shine boldly in the October sky overhead, and although the first hint of dawn shows in the east, the starlight is still reflected brightly in the water. I continue to glance upward in amazement. Crystal-clear dawns are not normally associated with promising waterfowling . . . except today. This morning we'll have fine shooting at unwary natives, and weather won't be a factor. It's opening day, and the hunting won't be as good until a month from now when the first winter storms push the migrants down from the Maritimes.

I finish securing the boat, then put the overhanging grape tangles over the gunnels. Probing ahead with an oar, I feel my way along the riverbank. There is a fallen tree in the dark water that I ease my way through, one half-step at a time, being careful not to rip my waders.

My father extends his hand and helps me up the bank. He has set up our folding stools behind some low sumac five yards back from the edge. He works the stickiness out of the action of his automatic, and I test out my call with a few tentative clucks and quacks. Then we settle down to the quiet business of waiting. I check my watch, not because I suspect that it is near shooting time, but because the first symptoms of the opening day butterflies have begun. If they ever stop, so will I. Things will brighten up early under the clear sky, and I'll check my watch a dozen more times during the next half-hour. Our conversation takes place in low tones.

"Is the boat okay?"

"I tied it under some overhanging vines."

"Coffee?"

"Sure." At this time of day, coffee is something felt as much as tasted, and it feels good. I rest the rim of my cup against my bottom lip blowing through the swirling steam as I stare out at my decoy spread.

"The rig looks good," my father whispers.

I nod a thanks. The silhouettes of the teal and mallard decoys are still dark and colorless, but they do look good. Daylight will reveal a fresh paint job on each bird; rich browns, and grays, crisp blacks, pure whites, iridescent greens. A season of use will eventually wash and scuff the colors, and they'll never seem so fresh as right now. All is new today: The guns show no signs of rust, my father's Father's Day waders wear no patches, and even the brass heads showing in the shell box are shiny.

The sky grows lighter, and patches of fog begin to accumulate over the water. Across the river several birches dressed in autumn amber emerge from the dark background of the woodland. When I can definitely see the color on the head of the nearest decoy, I check my watch and find that the season officially began more than a minute ago. I take a deep breath and flex my shoulder blades. Next to me, my father pulls back the bolt of his gun a half-inch, knowing full well there is a shell in the chamber but taking comfort from just seeing it there. Nervous preliminaries.

We wait.

"Okay . . ." I've seen them.

There is no need to say more. My father eases forward, crouching, and slowly turns to face the direction my eyes indicate.

The flock of ducks is silhouetted against the brightening dawn. The birds move quickly, and seem to be showing off their maneuvering skills. Teal. We lose them momentarily when they pass in front of the dark background, but they break the sky again much closer to us. There is no doubting their intentions; they come straight for the rig, skimming over the wisps of fog on the river.

The safety on my father's gun clicks off.

♦ ♦ ♦

7:50 A.M. I've never seen a whitecap on the swamp creek before, but there's no denying it now. Close behind it is another and farther out several more waves have their tops blown back upon themselves. Our eight decoys occupy half of the small triangle of calm water in the shallow lee of a broken-down black willow. If it were winter, this would be called a blizzard instead of a typical November storm.

We had brought enough decoys to lure the entire Atlantic Flyway, but thankfully we'd come to our senses in the gale winds before dawn and had put out only a handful. Chasing down storm-dragged decoys is no fun, especially when the ducks are flying, and on a day like this a waterfowler needs little more than to simply be near some sheltered water.

The season has waxed full. The migrants are in, as attested to by the variety of birds that have attempted to join our eight black duck decoys behind the willow. The only redhead I've ever seen in this state lies on the sacks of extra decoys behind us. My eyes keep wandering to the drake, as if in disbelief. Shooting in the gale is difficult, but we are getting plenty of practice. A small flock of mallards, flying low with the wind behind them, swings around the willow. When they see the calm water they turn outward, climbing into the wind as they look over the rig. Two hens peel away from the group, heading farther downriver, but the rest sideslip toward us, their formation scattered. Heading into the strong wind, the birds are actually flying sideways and backwards as they approach. The shot is confusing at best, and we both miss. In the gale, the mallard have only to think about flaring and they are instantly out of shotgun range. No second shots are possible.

We grin foolishly at each other and reload. There is more luck than skill involved in this sort of shooting, and misses need no excuse. We hunker back down into the rushes. The wind begins to spit tiny bits of ice along with the sparse raindrops.

I've read descriptions comparing the sound to rippling canvas, but those are from a time when duck hunters were full-time watermen on whom a strain-burst sail left a lasting impression. To me, the five buffleheads sound like an F4 accelerating close overhead after a bombing run. As with the watermen, the sound leaves a lasting impression. The buffs pass behind us, braking with an alarming din as they swing across the wind to come in lightly in the rough water beyond the rig. All five are drakes. They sit on the water rather than in it, seemingly inflated imitations. Their crisp coloration and blue bills do little to dispel the impression.

We watch them intently as they swim into the rig. My partner cups a hand to his mouth and leans toward me to be heard above the wind. "This doesn't sound too macho, but they're really cute."

I nod. They are

"What now?" he asks.

I glance out again at the little black and white ducks. They have fluffed out their feathers and are resting at the rear of our rig. "Let's wait for more mallards."

He grins, and nods in agreement.

• • •

11:25 A.M. We watch the hovering insect land on the knee of my waders. "A mosquito . . . amazing!"

My brother shakes his head. "This is crazy. November duck hunting is supposed to look like a Chet Reneson watercolor."

Late November brings an abundance of waterfowl to coastal New England, even as the inland migration begins to wane. Dawn brought fast shooting, but the tide has left us stranded on the sunny salt marsh for at least another hour. We wait, talking the talk of idle hunters everywhere: tomorrow's Patriot game in Foxboro, stories of our mutual father, speculations about where the ducks are and how well we'd be doing if we were there with them.

Then, because we have not paid attention for a sufficient number of minutes, a single black duck appears over the decoys. He is a rich brown loam color in the sunlight. Without announcement I stand and pump two quick shots at the bird and although he sags noticeably he does not fall. Instead he flies a straight line out onto the salt flats, losing altitude as if the load of shot had not so much injured him as weighed him down.

We stand, shading our eyes. Although we never actually see the duck fall, when he finally sinks from view we assume he's down. My brother estimated the distance: "He's weynafug out there."

I nod. "Probably farther."

After a moment's thought, he brightens and turns to me, his hand on my shoulder. "Well, for once I'm glad you saw him first," he grins. Overeagerness has its accompanying penance. Although it had been his turn to shoot, I am the one with the hike across the marsh in front of me.

I am halfway across the shallow tidal river when my brother whistles *bob-white*. I freeze, waiting, then hear his single gunshot and see two buffleheads flare off. A third is at the center of a ring of ripples just outside the decoy spread. He floats on his back with one blue foot idly paddling the air. The damsel of fate who controls the fortunes of wildfowlers must be a sadistic old biddie. She keeps score, and extracts penalties for specific transgressions; cripple a duck and pay by watching your brother cleanly kill a bird it would have been your turn to take. She's the same one who sends the mallards in when you're picking up the decoys after a fruitless morning.

My brother waves to me. "Hurry back!" There is more than the necessary amount of glee in his voice.

The muck on the far bank of the creek is exceptionally sticky. This must be part of my penance, too. Waders should come equipped with handles just above the heels; I'm always afraid I'll puncture them by pulling too hard to get out of the mud.

Up on the flats, the summertime expanse of waving grass has been turned into a stubblefield. The tides and winds of autumn sweep over the marsh and carry off the deciduous plant tops, leaving only short stems that are devoid of all resiliency. I crunch along through the brittle stubble, leaping the smaller cuts as best I can in my cumbersome waders and taking the long way around the wider channels through the marsh.

The salt flats are dotted with ponds at high tide, but they drain out with the ebb, leaving empty mud holes that contain nothing more than a puddle or two. My black is in the weeds at the edge of one such drained salt pond, and he springs into flight at my approach. He gives only the slightest indication that he is an injured bird. My shooting, never anything to brag about, is poorer than usual today. I fire once too quickly, then concentrate and center him with the second shot. The bird falls into the mud, but immediately rights himself and runs for the far weedy edge, waddling like some target duck in a shooting gallery. The pellets of my third shot strike all around him, but to complete the shooting gallery simile he rolls over and then pops back up again to resume his escape. I fumble in my pocket and take out another shell in time to load and fire again, but the results are the same. A walking duck, of course, is not nearly as vulnerable a target as a bird in flight, and my shots have evidently not penetrated the armor of his folded wings.

As the bird runs, so do I, trying all the while to keep the gun loaded and retain my footing on the slippery mud bank. At last I succeed in falling. When I look up, the bird has made it into the weeds. Unfortunately, to get there I must navigate around several cuts in the marsh. I arrive at the spot, but am no longer sure I know where it is. Weeds and cuts have a sameness to them, especially when viewed from a different angle. Davy Crockett ponders the problem for a moment and decides to look for tracks. They are easy to find in the soft mud. There is blood among the webbed footprints.

But the surface is harder in the weeds and the telltale tracks vanish. I look for feathers or blood or any other signs of the duck, but there are none to be found. I search farther in. The bird has been hit four times. He cannot be all that healthy, and he must be hiding nearby. I look farther up the cut, then into the next one. Protected from the winds and tide, the dead marsh grass around the drained pond is still knee high. It isn't all that thick, but a black duck has the perfect camouflage for this stuff.

Ten minutes pass, then 15. I look back at my brother. His estimate of the distance was accurate. The duck is going to die before morning. It seems a waste. Before I give up, I return and look again at the duckprints leading into the tall weeds. It seems hopeless, but I give Davy Crockett one last hearing. Squatting down like a golfer looking over a putt, the perspective is different. There, as obvious as a finger mark on newly brushed suede, is my own trail through the marsh grass—and that of the duck.

The hidden path ends, eight feet into the weeds. I stare at the lump of mud for a long moment before I can see the mottled khaki bill and the shape of the bird's head hunched into his breast feathers.

At times like this, looking a live cripple straight in the eye, I wish more than anything else that I had shot slightly better . . . or slightly worse.

◆ ◆ ◆

3:15 P.M. The dull, yellow-gray afternoon sky is typical of New England winter days; there is no warmth, brightness or shadow from the thin sunlight. It is as if the December sun has all it can manage to simply illuminate the landscape. In the peculiar silence that precedes a snowfall, each sound is magnified and thrown back at us from the woodline bordering the swamp. The new ice on the marsh will hold no weight today and it breaks noisily, but the cold is such that within a week all but the swiftest flowing waters will be frozen solid. Inland waterfowling is in its last waning days.

We've towed our boat through the ice and now we hide it in some flooded alders next to a springhole of open water. The crescent of brush accommodates the boat as if it had been planted with that purpose in mind. In the springhole I arrange a late-season rig of blacks, scuffed and in need of repainting, with a pair of baldpates thrown in for color.

With the solstice just two weeks away, sunset will come early. There is little more than two hours of daylight left. We settle in and begin waiting. My shins hurt from being repeatedly kicked by the shelf ice on the way in. In my pocket, the latest in my extensive collection of handwarmers has quit working. In that respect it is little different from all the others I have owned.

The quiet of the marsh is complete. The insects that buzzed and hummed a backdrop through the warmer months are silent now, and there are no birds to be heard save the occasional distant cawing of a crow. No breeze stirs the few remaining leaves. My partner feels the silence too, for he barely speaks above a whisper. "I saw a few flying out of here this morning . . . no reason to think they shouldn't be coming back to feed this afternoon."

"That'd be nice," I speak quietly as well. "You know, just once I'd like to be able to know ahead of time that we were going to have a gangbuster's day. That way we could shoot selectively and not have the feeling that the first hen to show up might be the only thing we'd see."

"This might be it, with the snow coming in and things freezing up all over." He ponders his own statement for a moment, then smiles inwardly. "Could be . . ."

We have made no agreement, but minutes later neither of us makes a move when a pair of hen mallards circles the rig and then eases in among the decoys. Conversation stops. We don't want to scare off the volunteers in our decoy regiment. The pair wanders along the icy edge of our springhole, muttering duckily as they feed.

Minutes later my partner nudges me and nods toward a talll pine we have been using as a reference point. I search the sky and finally notice a flock coming down the marsh, much higher than my eyes had been focused. They pass in front of us, perhaps 15 birds altogether. Several lighter ducks are mixed in with the blacks. I sweet talk to them with the call, but the only answers I get are from the visitors in our decoys. The flock makes the circuit of our end of the swamp; down into the frozen corner, around the meadow behind us, then back to our pocket of open water. They are low enough on the second pass for me to identify at least two as drake mallards.

Out in the black water, the decoys are the only color in the gray December landscape. The iridescent-green face and wing patches of the two baldpates seem especially gaudy among the washed-out tones of the marsh. The two

Suzies continue to feed 60 yards from the boat, paddling about and clucking softly. When one of them rears back and stretches her wings, I know the flock is ours.

The birds circle behind us for the fourth time. My ears follow the sound of air through their wings, and my eyeballs strain at the tops of their sockets. The birds appear below the brim of my downtilted hat, banking on their final approach.

Next to me, my partner takes a deep breath.

With capped wings and extended feet, the flock begins its flip-flopping descent; dark bodies, white wing linings, iridescent speculums against the dull winter sky.

We shoulder our guns together, eyes skyward . . .

◆ ◆ ◆

5:50 P.M. Coming back with the drone of the motor filing my ears, I wonder why the night is thought of as black. The sky and water are shades of cobalt and purple and ultramarine, and the passing shoreline is shadowed in tones of indigo. Some of the sky's colors blend and change and darken even as I watch, but nowhere is there a color I can label as black. The water mysteriously continues to hold the twilight glow even though the sky and landscape grow darker. Over the darkening treetops the Dipper is at its low winter point, nearly touching the horizon. The first stars of Cygnus the Swan shine in the west above the lavender that was sunset.

Mine is the only boat returning. There are no other gunners out on this last day of the season. Even the bats and snipe that kept me amused on other earlier evenings are absent, having headed for warmer climates. The season, which began with teal and native wood ducks, then waxed full during the inland and coastal migrations, and finally brought in the late redlegs in its waning days, has ended. Blacks will be the native ducks for the next few months. For some reason known only to themselves, they choose to remain on what little water stays open through the bitter New England winter. Two of their number lie on the decoy sacks in the bow. They are impressive trophies on the wing, but right now look for all the world like a couple of sopping-wet cats. Nothing is rattier looking than a dead duck that has spent a few hours in the bilge of a boat.

The reprieve from the cold that came with picking up and sacking the decoys is fading. I jam my hands deeper into the pockets of my parka, then finally hug them into my armpits and use my knee to steer the boat through the blue evening.

The work of hauling the boat onto the trailer goes quickly. I carry the gas can and motor to the back of the truck, then use a hand lantern to check for things that might have been forgotten in the shadows. My fingers are so numb that I cannot push the switch to shut off the light. Normally I am eager to be out of my waders and on my way toward home and supper. But I linger on this last night of the season. I toss the lantern into the cab and reach in and shut off the headlights and engine. In spite of my cold feet and fingers, I walk back to the edge of the river. One last time before the season slips completely into the past. I want to listen to the silence and see again the stars reflected in the quiet water.

••• *A. R. H. Bulu Imam, a professional hunter from Hazaribagh, India (in the state of Bihar, bordering Bangladesh), wrote about his experiences hunting rogue elephants and man-eating leopards and tigers in the 1980s. His straightforward style is gripping, and spares no detail.*—MAY 1985 •••

THE BANKA LEOPARDS by A. R. H. Bulu Imam

It was summer 1968. Mangar Ram had finished rocking his little grandson to sleep, and he laid the emaciated infant on the caked mud floor. His dwelling was the last hut in Piparia village in northeastern India. It stood at the end of a row of similar shanties along the dusty bullock-cart track that ran west toward the highway to Bhagalpur, half a dozen miles away. As the track ran out of the village at the other end, it meandered among lantana bushes until it merged into a number of footpaths.

Inside the hut, Mangar's wife cooked dinner. The weak glow of the smoking oil lamp cast a long, bright blade of light across the infant's forehead. Mangar Ram stood gazing at his grandson. He looked just like his father, Mangar's son. Both of the baby's parents were now dead. They were killed about two weeks earlier by a man-eating leopard only yards from Mangar's hut and almost at this very hour. Mangar and his wife had accepted it as yet another cruel act of fate.

Suddenly Mangar heard a horrible scream from his wife. He turned toward the sound with a numbed curiosity; his wife's once supple frame was being held in the jaws of a huge leopard.

The satanic creature stood looking at him an instant, its green eyes ablaze in the glow of the charcoal embers. Mangar shrieked involuntarily and wrenched free of his trauma and shock. Then he shrieked once more, for the last gasps of his dying wife came to his ears. As he shouted he grabbed a still-smoldering log from the fire and rushed at the animal. Dropping its burden, it disappeared as suddenly as it had come. Mangar fell on his knees beside the lifeless body and with his fingers tried to stop the blood gushing from his wife's throat. He turned his gaze toward the sleeping child. It was gone. His sorrow could now become absolute.

A few days later, I arrived at Camp Banka, near Mangar's home village. The Banka division of the Bhagalpur district in the eastern India state of Bihar has been notorious for harboring man-eating leopards. (They were recorded as far back as the last century.) Our men had preceded us and had started setting up the tents under the direction of Sanjhalu, the head shikari. A great woodsman, he has guided some to the world's most famous sportsmen. My father "Teetee" Imam (a well-known tiger hunter) and I were returning to Banka after a lapse of some years, but here, in this timeless land, things remained pretty much the same as during our last visit.

Killings reached a peak during the hot summer months. Only thorn bushes and lantana covered the area. There is hardly any game here, and only rarely will the odd pig or *kaker* be taken. Sloth bears and hyenas are plentiful, but neither are food for leopards. The big cats have to find an alternative. Since the villages contain few livestock or dogs, the only thing left is human beings.

In April the sickly sweet *mehua* blossoms ripen and start to fall. They are gathered by villagers to produce a coarse flour and a strong wine. Summer fires snap and crackle in the tinder-dry brush. Whatever little livestock the villagers possess is herded to watering places along the nearby Ganges River. Prowling the narrow village roads by night and stalking the *mehua*-gatherers at dawn, the leopards hunt. The fierce heat forces the villagers out of their baked mud huts at night to sleep under the cool of the stars and the man-eaters are provided with easier prey. Killings naturally increase.

Getting down from my Jeep, I strolled over to the small group huddled by the roadside. Mangar Ram—a thin, tall man—walked up to me. He told me about the pattern of recent kills, most of which had occurred during the night. It wasn't long before I had started to work out beats with Sanjhalu and my father. We had about two dozen goats tethered as bait, encompassing an area of some 250 square miles. Within a few days, the first animal was killed by a leopard. In this region, every leopard was a marked animal since it was either a man-eater or a potential one. I had a *machan* (blind) built and set up. At dusk a pack of hyenas arrived at the kill and started feeding. Rubbing a cartridge between my hands, I threw it down among them. They bolted immediately after receiving the human scent. Unfortunately, a leopard never appeared. The next morning we received news that three of our bait animals had been killed by hyenas during the night. Accordingly, we erected platforms about six feet off the ground and tethered the goats to them so the hyenas couldn't reach them there.

Sanjhalu and our team of crack Santali trackers brought from my hometown of Hazaribagh scoured the barren countryside searching out coverts where a leopard might hide. We thought we might be more successful by beating (driving) these animals than by hunting them from a blind. A man-eating leopard develops great caution, which makes setting up more difficult than beating. Two days later, news reached camp of a human kill 10 miles away. By the time we reached the site, often having to drive where there were not even trails, the remains of the victim had been cremated. Nearby, there was a dense, thorn-choked ravine that seemed to be an ideal place for any leopard to hide. Getting together 100-odd men, Sanjhalu laid out the cloth bunting used for stopping the flanks of the beat. The drive itself ran from east to west over a deeply scarred gravel hillslope. I took up my position on the ground behind a rocky outcrop. With drumming and clanging of tins, the beaters approached. Suddenly a cry went up, "The devil has turned back!" The leopard had broken back through the beaters.

The next day, in one of the newly prepared beats, another goat was killed by a leopard. Again the animal refused to be beaten out across the thinned shooting line. Five beats in succession drew a blank. All attempts at setting up proved fruitless.

During the following morning, we received news that a bullock had been killed about 20 miles away. I drove to the site. The heavy animal's neck had been cleanly broken, and it had been dragged straight up the steep side of a hill. At first glance, the kill seemed to be the work of a tiger. The ground was too gravelly to find pugmarks. The animal's neck was distended and the spacing of the killer's canines distorted. I had a machan erected hastily even as the red glow of sunset began to tint the sky and the twilight slowly settled about us. It was long past sunset before the shooters could take up their position. At 8:00 P.M., the leopard was on the kill and began to tug at the rope tether. Immediately the sharp beam of the flashlight flooded the spot. The leopard stood with its legs squarely placed on either side of the goat, tail high, defiantly staring with its shining green eyes at the machan. The shot was offered to my hunting companion, Dr. Harry Hech of Greenwood, Delaware. His 375 H&H Magnum was fitted with a high-powered scope, a thing I advise against in the dense Indian bush where fast and close shooting is involved, often at a charging beast. Worse still, the eye-relief on Doc's rifle wasn't working, and as a result all he saw in the viewfinder was a blank reticle. To add to all this, the only lit spot encompassed the leopard. Against these odds Doc was obviously rattled and missed the shot. In a flash the cat was gone. However, moments afterward it was back *under the machan*. Shooting down through the tangle of thorn wrapped around the base of the tree for protection was out of the question. The animal growled and rasped threateningly for the rest of the night, but nothing could be done since it refused to approach the kill again. In the morning I examined the spot where it had been shot and found a few cut hairs and some drops of blood. It had indeed been a close call for that leopard. Obviously, the cat had only been nicked; otherwise, it wouldn't have come back.

A few days after this disappointment, our luck changed. In a completely different region, a bait goat had been killed. This was important, since several human killings had occurred recently in that same area. The beat was a shallow basin encircled by a dense patch of babul thorn. Along the rim were loose heaps of rock boulders. One ravine ran in from the northeast and another from the southeast. Both met in the middle and proceeded downhill to the west. The goat bait had been killed and dragged off the platform and taken straight into the lantana thickets, which formed a tangle at the bottom of the ravine in the center of the beat. Once more, the tracks were of a male leopard of unusual size.

The beaters slipped silently into position and men climbed into trees along the flanks to act as "noisy stops." The shooters took position behind the rocky outcrop mentioned at the north end of the beat. A medley of Santal flutes rang through the glassy midday heat as the line of men advanced. All of a sudden we heard a few coughs right in front of us. Then we saw a blur of spots as the growling leopard swung back from the shooting line into cover. Moments later it was out, streaking along in a mettled saffron flash through the bushes. Even as the animal bunched up and stretched out impressively in flight, its tail straight out, ears flat, each sinew taut, muscles swollen with strain, the crash of a 375 smashed the stillness. The cat crumpled in midair like a felled woodcock. One of our guests, Jerry Hoch, had made an excellent shot. We taped the beast at 7 feet 6 inches.

♦ ♦ ♦

Later that summer, we had to hunt another man-eater. Namgaon village is a small group of huts situated on the edge of the network of ravines and dried-up watercourses that skirt the natural rock formation of Kalapatthar. On the top of a rocky hill stands a small temple, where a priest can be heard ringing a bell and chanting in the morning and evening each day of the year. Ram Dee, a local merchant, was returning to his home in Namgaon from Bhagalpur by bicycle late one night. In fact, during his trip Ram Dee had passed through our camp and spoken with the cook, Yakub. He did not know then that it was the last time that he would speak to anyone. From the scant evidence found next morning (a strip of his loincloth and his slippers) and the footprints and pugmarks available, we learned what had happened. As Dee had been pushing his cycle across a streambed, a leopard stalked and killed him. In the dark, the man could not have seen the animal until its fangs were closing on his throat. There were no remains to sit over, since the area abounded in hyenas. There wasn't any cover nearby that I felt would hold a leopard, so doing a beat was ruled out. The killer's track identified it as a big male, so at last I had some identification of it.

A few days later, this leopard killed one of my goats near Kalapatthar. When I visited the kill around 7:30 A.M., the flies that are usually present were conspicuous by their absence. I immediately concluded the leopard had been disturbed by me while it had been feeding. Bending back some branches to form a camouflage, I climbed into a makeshift blind and told the two trackers accompanying me to go away talking and imitating the bark of a dog. This is a great trick to use on a leopard that is hanging around its kill. Minutes after my men had left me the leopard could be heard coming out of the bushes in the ravine below the kill. I expected to get a shot at any moment. I held my breath and waited. For a full minute there wasn't another sound, and then, a slight rustle behind me caused me to swing around. Within arm's reach, in the foliage behind me, I caught a glimpse of yellow. The cat vanished.

Some weeks later, another goat was killed about a mile south of Kalapatthar temple by this same leopard, judging by its tracks. The goat, however, had not been dragged off the platform into cover. There was a lot of lantana scrub in the nearby beat area that we had prepared, but since the kill hadn't been dragged I decided not to beat. I had a machan constructed in the only big tree nearby, which happened to be a mango. The distance from the kill was about 40 yards. The platform where the kill lay was in ideal range from the machan, which I had built well above the ground. I've never relished the idea of sharing a tree with a man-eating leopard! I had thorn bushes wrapped around the base of the tree as an additional safeguard. By 5:00 P.M. we were in the machan. As the sun sank below the low line of Banka hills, a jackal howled and night fell. Hyenas could be heard chortling away in their awful laughter. Under the tree, on the dried leaves that I had spread earlier, the soft, padded footfall of the big cat brought us to attention. Moments later, there was a soft thud as the leopard landed on the platform where the goat lay. The light flashed on but in an instant the cat was gone, scrambling down on the other side. At around 8:00 P.M. there was a soft scraping sound on the bark of the tree. I was glad I had put the thorns around it. There wasn't any more excitement during the night.

I devised another plan to get this wary animal. Leaving the old machan up in the mango tree, I had a ground hide constructed to the north of the kill. Again, I had plenty of thorn put around it, with shooting loopholes in front. As the velvety darkness closed about me, my attention was caught by a low, rasping sound coming from the direction of the kill. After a while it stopped, and a long silence ensued. A smooth, scraping sound behind my left ear jerked me to earth: The breathing of the great cat was deep, throaty, rhythmic, unreal—like the sound of tides rolling in a shell. The mosquitoes were terrible, but I dared not move, hardly breathing. Being hunted by a man-eating leopard on the ground in the dark is a hell of a thing. Sweat gathered along my forehead and dripped down onto my spectacles. There wasn't a thing I could do. Somewhere in the dark, only inches away on the other side of the thorn, the leopard, too, was listening intently. That enclosure was only four feet high in order to blend in with the other bushes. I understood again the perfect uselessness of sophisticated modern firearms when hunting really dangerous game in this way. As the seconds ticked away, there was another sound—on the platform. I put on my torch, and as the light fell on the kill, I could make out the top of the leopard's back as it crouched, feeding. Before a shot could be taken again it was gone down the other side of the platform. The rest of the night was quiet.

I put into action another plan the next evening, since half the kill remained uneaten, and I expected the leopard to return. I had a white goat tethered behind the hide. After I got into the blind, the animal was brought and tethered to the peg by my trackers. Immediately after they walked away, it started bleating. The time was 5:00 P.M. At exactly 7:00 the animal stopped bleating abruptly. Around 9:00 P.M. I decided that the leopard must have arrived, since the goat had begun a low, moaning bleat. I strained my eyes through the loopholes in the back of the hide, and after a while I could make out the goat's form doubled up on its knees only 15 feet away, as it faced away from me. I concluded that it was looking at the leopard before the leopard attacked it. What a surprise lay in store for me; suddenly, as if unreal, a blackness closed up the opening of the loophole and I could feel the stale smell of the man-eater's breath. In another instant it was gone. My breathing had stopped. For another half-hour I sat completely still. (From tracks found the next morning, the leopard had gone on to inspect the old machan on the mango tree.) At 9:45 P.M. it came back to the hide. Back and forth, round and round it padded softly, trying to determine if there was anyone inside it. Luckily there wasn't a breath of wind.

At 10:00 P.M., at last satisfied there wasn't anything to fear, it finally jumped onto the platform and started feeding on its kill from the previous night. As I switched on the flashlight, the animal could be seen standing with the kill in its mouth. Dropping the meat, it lifted its head up and looked straight at the old machan in the mango tree. I offered Doc the shot, and his 375 Silvertip took that man-eater squarely in its left shoulder. Backing off the platform with a vicious snarl in a flurry of fur and fury, the leopard turned backward in an arc, falling into the bushes. Moments later it was right out in the open and coming for us at remarkable speed for such a heavily wounded beast. I slipped the safety forward on my 470 double. Doc got a grandstand view, as he had the action magnified six times in his scope! Just before the cat was on top of us, my 500-grain bullet smashed into its chest. Veering to one side, the animal crashed into the enclosure, dead.

This leopard measured seven feet long. Upon its death, there were no more killings near Kalapatthar. Both leopards were officially declared man-eaters.

••• *The boating editor of* SPORTS AFIELD *for two decades, and a New York editor before that, Zack Taylor resides in Easton, Maryland, gateway to some of the finest waterfowl hunting in North America. What better way to convey the joys of duck hunting than through the eyes of a well-used decoy?*—OCTOBER 1987 •••

LIFE OF A DECOY

by Zack Taylor

My first experience of life was smell. With quick movements of his hands, a man I came to know as Harry Shourds of Tuckerton, New Jersey, gouged out the nostrils on my bill and joined me to the world by scent.

What scents there were! The smoky smell of burning wood. Pine and cedar shavings as fragrant as flowers. The pungent odors of turpentine and linseed oil.

Then, suddenly, I could see . . . first from one eye, then the next. There was a man on his decoy bench. Knives and chisels were all over the place. A potbellied stove, black as ink, was located in the center of the room. Cans of paint and brushes beyond counting were evident. The floor was awash in wood shavings. And there, stacked on shelves, were other decoys . . . some like me. A man was talking.

"Ducks don't have ears, Harry," he said, laughing.

"Know it, John. But I like my decoys right." Defiantly, he fashioned a nail on the end of my bill.

"Take them glass eyes. Others make 'em outta tacks. By the time any black duck gets close enough to see my decoy's eye, glass or tacks, he's in my boat.

"I just like 'em right. Like 'em to have a pretty shape. Like to have 'em ride just right." His hands turned me over, and molten lead poured into a cavity cut in my belly. That'll keep him upright in a blow, eh, John?"

Then there was paint: black-brown for my body, yellow-green for my bill. My feathers were painted on by a feather used as a brush. Finally, a leather thong tied to a long lead was tacked to my breast. Then I was stacked on a shelf in the barn, and the long wait I came to know and hate began.

One day Harry's coarse hands grabbed me. Onto the wagon I went, in the company of a round, brown, curious-looking boat—a sneakboat, Harry called it. I was nestled breast down, tail up with a dozen brothers on the sneakboat's afterdeck. Harry whistled to his horse, and down the sand road through the pines we went.

It was dark the next morning when I felt the boat bob, then saw Harry's dark shape begin weaving the boat through small channels in the marsh.

What a day that first one was! No sooner was I in the water with my brothers and sisters than I heard wings whistling in the dawn glow. Harry's gun barked, and two ducks fell into the water. His retriever plunged after them. The sounds of other guns echoed over the marsh. Harry lay in the sneakboat, hidden in the grass; as ducks flashed by, his call would reach out to them and I would use the wind to bob and weave as realistically as swamp cedar and pine and paint could. It was thrilling.

The scene was re-created many times over the years. So were the long waits in the barn. Then the days in the marsh became fewer.

"Slowing down, are ye, Harry?" I noticed the other man was also creased and bent with age.

"Reckon. It's a lot warmer and drier just to carve 'em; and 75 cents apiece ain't bad." His eyes lit up. He nodded at a small boy at his side. "But I'm breaking in young Harry here. He's already a pretty fair shot."

Young Harry was a decoy's dream. H wouldn't quit. We hunted day after day. In the storms he hunted the high marsh. On the low tides we staked out on the open points. We often slept with snow blankets.

There were stormy days when the ducks went wild and we all dragged our anchors. And there were "bluebird" days, as Harry called them. With no birds flying, we'd snooze in the sun, with hardly a trace of a breeze to allow us to "work" on our leads. But they were all days of ducking. They were what my life was all about.

But the years began to take their toll on my master. Trips to the marsh became fewer. Then we didn't go at all. Year after year we gathered dust in the barn.

One day a violent thumping and banging startled us from our dormancy. A stranger entered the yard in a contraption that ran without a horse. Harry came out of the carving shed to greet him.

"We're opening a new duck club on Currituck Sound," the stranger said. "Currituck is easy to get to now that the railroad is in. Bought 10 miles of barrier beach with the prettiest broken marsh you ever saw. Need decoys, though. I was told you could fix me up."

"Sure, I'll carve you up any kind you want; $2 apiece," said young Harry, only he was young no more.

"Fine for next season, but we've got to get some for this season. I'll give you $1.50 apiece for any you've got in the barn." We were thrown into the back of the noisy contraption and rattled off.

Currituck was different. Bigger water. Ducks by the thousands. We were stored in special buildings, branded on our bellies with our owner's initials. The sportsmen came across the sound in their stovepipe hats. Servants awaited them. Local watermen set us out and gathered us up. The sportsmen never wet their hands. Still, we were out in the elements, where we belonged. And I'll say this for them: Bad weather never deterred them. Many were crack shots. They'd come and go. We'd work dawn to dusk every day for a week straight, then take a rest. They brought guests. (One got excited and put three No. 4 shot in my side.) Yet, along with my brothers and sisters, I was doing what I was created to do. Ducks by the score, even the hundreds, spotted us and came pitching in to join us until the guns spoke.

Then things went wrong. There didn't seem to be any young men. We heard talk of war, heard explosions at sea off the barrier beach. The club was boarded up. My owner died. A local man offered $4 apiece for us. We went off to another barn. Instead of storms and blizzards and ice, dust and cobwebs shrouded our bodies. The seasons slipped past. We stayed in our stacks.

One day that all changed. A stranger had me in his hands. "Even though it's branded, this isn't a Currituck decoy," he said to his companion. "Look, it's hollow with the inlaid keel. Been used hard. See the shot holes?" Now the other man was examining me with a magnifying glass. "Original paint. Old as hell. Pine head. Glass eyes. Leather thong. Inlaid ballast. By golly, a nailed beak! This is a Harry Shourds block!"

"Junior or senior?"

"From its age, I'd have to guess old Harry. I'm going to offer $10 apiece."

So I came to live not on a shelf in a barn, but on a shelf in a den. It wasn't a bad life. Many admired me. Complimented my graceful shape, the skill of my maker. "An artist, a natural folk artist." I smiled inside. Old Harry Shourds an artist! He probably wouldn't know what the word meant. Might take it as an insult. Sure, he was proud of his blocks and, like the other decoy makers, carved in a distinctive way. Folk artists? The waterman's way of life was too hard. It left no time for art.

One night in the den, a place of cigars and brandy instead of winds and waters, I was on display. "This Shourds with the shot holes and the brand fascinates me. I've got to have it. Name your price."

"Well, I do have a dozen like it. I won't be too tough on you. How's $500?"

There were more years on display, days in a sneakboat's decoy rack long ago in the past. Would I ever hear wingbeats and guns again? Would the retrievers ever churn past? I was afraid I knew the answer. I did not approve.

I learned a lot at my first auction. Hollow "Barnegat-style" decoys were collectors' dreams. Harry Shourds's name was magic. (If the excited novice could only know how his shot holes made me stand apart!) Men could hold me in their hands, and the marsh years of old sprang to life. I thought of Shourds's life lived on the edge of poverty. At $1500 the hammer fell. It would have been a fortune for him.

My last sale was different. I was X-rayed, examined under fluorescent light. The paint that Harry made with lamp black and linseed oil and a spoonful of red lead (a secret he shared only with his son) was chemically analyzed. The exchange was brisk.

"This is an authentic Harry Shourds original, circa 1890, certainly carved before the turn of the century. It is in fine condition considering years of abuse. [Abuse! What was I created for?] The museum simply must add it to its collection. I'm prepared to make you an offer you can't refuse—$7500." (I thought of Harry Jr. whacking me with an oar to rid me of ice, how he carelessly threw me onto the stacks. He could have gone through college on $7500. Not that he'd have traded a life on the water for a college degree.)

So now I sit in a glass display case. Hundreds who have never held a shotgun or even seen a duck fall from the sky march past me daily. Freezing winters on the marsh, blistering summers in the barn, tempered me. Now the moisture in the air around me is kept at a constant level; the temperature never varies. Every year my insurance value increases.

Never again will a sneakboat rock beneath me. No more will I nestle against my fellow blocks. The glowing dawn sun can no longer brighten my life. The wind in the marsh grass is but a memory. The slap of the waves against by breast is gone forever.

I've even heard that the breed I was created to entice is vanishing from the skies.

••• *An editor with* SPORTS AFIELD *since 1979, Jay Cassell has written about topics as diverse as caribou hunting in Alaska and mayfly identification on Eastern trout streams. In this story, he writes about his 6-year-old son's initiation to hunting.*—DECEMBER 1992 •••

THE RACK *by Jay Cassell*

"I found his antler, Dad," the throaty voice of my 6-year-old son, James, crackled over the telephone. "I saw it in the woods when Mom was driving me home from school, right near where we went hunting! Are you coming home tonight?"

When I told him that my flight wouldn't get in until 11:00, and that I wouldn't be home until midnight, there was a disappointed silence over the phone. Then, "Well, okay, but don't look at it until morning, so I can show you. Promise?"

I promised. We had a deal. I told him I'd see him soon, then asked to talk with his mother.

"Love you, Dad."

"Love you too, James."

Unbelievable. My son had found the shed antler of the buck I had hunted, unsuccessfully, all season. The big 10-pointer I had seen the day before deer season, the one with the wide spread and thick beams. He had seen me that day, having winded me as I pussyfooted through some thickets for a closer look. I think he somehow knew that he was safe, that he was far enough away from me.

I had scouted the 140-acre farm and adjoining woods near my home in suburban New York, the farm that I had gotten permission to hunt after five years of asking. "You can hunt this year," Dan the caretaker had said to me during the summer, when I asked my annual question. "I kicked those other guys off the property. They were in here with ATVs and Jeeps, bringing two and three friends every day they hunted, without even asking. Lot of nerve, I thought. Got sick of 'em, so I kicked 'em off. Now I'll let you hunt, and your buddy John, three other guys, and that's all. I want some local people on here that I know and trust."

When Dan had told me that, I couldn't believe it. But there it was, so I took advantage of it. Starting in September, I began to scout the farm. I had seen bucks on the property in previous years while driving by, but now I got a firsthand look. There was sign virtually everywhere: rubs, scrapes, droppings in the hillside hay-fields, in the mixed hardwoods, in the thick hemlock stands towering over the rest of the woods. I found what were obviously rubs left by a big deer. In a copse of hem-locks near the edge of the property, bordering an Audubon nature preserve, were scrapes and, nearby, about five or six beech saplings absolutely ripped apart by antlers.

With James's help, I set up my tree stand overlooking a heavily used trail that seemed to be a perfect escape route out of the hemlocks. James and I also found an old permanent tree stand, which he and I repaired with a few 2x4s and nails. This would officially be "his" tree stand—or tree house, as he called it.

Opening day couldn't come fast enough. James and I talked about it constantly. Even though he's only 6, and can't really hunt yet, he couldn't wait for deer season. He knows what deer tracks and droppings look like; can tell how scrapes and rubs are made; can even identify where deer have passed in the leaf-covered forest floor. My plan was to hunt the first few days of the season by myself while James was in school, and then take him on a weekend. If luck was with me, maybe I'd take the big buck and could then concentrate on filing my doe tag with my son's help.

Opening day came and went, with no trophy 10-pointer in sight, or any other bucks, for that matter. A lot of other days came and went too, most of them cold, windy and rainy. Three weeks into the two-month-long season, on a balmy Sunday in the 50s, James and I packed our camo backpacks with candy bars and juice boxes, binoculars and grunt calls, and at 2:00 P.M. off we went, on our first day of hunting together. When we reached the spot where I always park my car, on a hillside field, I dabbed some camo paint onto James's face, which he thought was cool. Then we started hiking up the field and into the woods, toward the hemlocks.

We saw one white tail disappear over a knob as we hiked into James's stand. I didn't really care, though. This was the first time I was taking my son hunting! It would be the first of many, I hoped. I wouldn't force it on him, just introduce him to the sport, and keep my fingers crossed.

At James's stand, we sat down and had a couple of candy bars. "Can I blow on the deer call now, Dad?" I said yes, and he proceeded to honk away on the thing like a trumpet player.

"Do it quietly," I advised. "And remember, always whisper, don't talk loudly. And don't move around so much!"

What with James honking on the call and fidgeting—checking out my bow, looking around, pointing to the hawk soaring overhead, crumpling up his candy bar wrapper and stuffing it into his pocket—I was sure no self-respecting deer would come within a mile of us. None did, not to my son's stand, or to mine, or to the rocks where we later sat, overlooking a trail and those ripped-up beech saplings, until darkness finally settled over the woods. But that was okay.

Hiking out of the woods, we met my friend John coming from his tree stand.

"I saw that 10-pointer today," he began, giving James a poke in the ribs with his finger.

"Where?"

"Up near those hemlocks, the same area you and I have been hunting. We were probably 100 yards away from each other."

"Well, what happened?" Part of me was saying, *Great, he got the buck!* The other part of me was saying, *Pleeeease tell me you didn't shoot him.* John looked at me sheepishly.

"I was watching that trail, and I saw a doe headed my way, right where I always put my climbing tree stand. Then, right behind her, I saw a buck—you know that 6-pointer we've seen over by the lake? Well, I started to draw back on him—he was only 30 yards away—but then I saw some movement to my left. It was HIM! Cutting through the hemlocks. That 6-pointer and doe got out of there fast, and the 10-pointer got to within 10 yards of my stand, stopped broadside to me, and then looked up straight at me!"

"Did you shoot? Did you shoot?"

"I couldn't. I was shaking too much. I mean, I could even hear the arrow rattling against the rest. Eventually, he just took off down the trial. Man, he was something. Must weigh 200 pounds!"

Later, driving the short ride home, James said, "Hey, Dad, how come John didn't shoot that deer?"

"Shooting a deer is a lot harder than many people think. Even if everything else is right, sometimes you can get so nervous that you just can't shoot, no matter how much you want to. John's time will come, though. He works at it."

• • •

I didn't see the buck until two days after Christmas. Hunting by myself, I left my normal tree stand and circled around to the backside of the hemlocks. At 4:00 P.M., I was wedged between some boulders that overlook a well-used trail. It was 20°F, getting dark, and I was cold and shivering uncontrollably. But I kept hearing a rustling behind me. *Another squirrel.* But it wasn't. Suddenly, 60 yards through the trees, I could see a big deer headed my way. It was moving with a purpose. It stopped at what appeared to be a scrape, and I could see a huge symmetrical rack dip down as the buck stuck his nose to the ground. Then he stood up, urinated into the scrape, turned, and headed back into the hemlocks. If he had kept coming down the trail, I would have had a clean 15-yard shot. It wasn't meant to be.

That was my season. I didn't see that 10-pointer again, and I missed my only shot of the year, a 35-yarder at a forkhorn that sailed high. Such is deer hunting.

• • •

So now I was returning home from my trip. I walked in the door at midnight, quickly read through some mail on the counter, soon slipped into bed. My wife rolled over and whispered, "Don't forget to wake up James before you go to work. He really wants to show you that rack."

The alarm went off at 6:30, and I got up to take a shower.

"Psst, Dad, is that you?" came a sleepy voice from my son's room.

"Yes, buddy, how are you?"

"Wait here, Dad!"

Before I could say another word, he jumped out of bed, put on his oversized bear-paw slippers, and went padding down the stairs to the basement. When he returned, he had the biggest grin on his face that I've ever seen.

"Look, Dad!"

And there it was, half of the 10-pointer's rack. A long, thick main beam, four long, heavy points, the back one eight inches. Amazing. And that buck will be there next year.

"Dad, can I put it on my wall?"

"Of course."

"And can we go look for the other half of his antlers tomorrow, because tomorrow's Saturday, and I don't have school, and you once told me that their antlers usually fall off pretty close together. Please?"

"Sure, James. If you're good in school today."

The deal was made. We never found the other half of the shed, though. It snowed, and we couldn't really look. Mice probably ate the other half.

But you know what? I think maybe my future hunting companion was born this past season.

••• *A hunter and gourmet who has traveled the globe on expeditions with world-class sportsmen, Guy de la Valdéne has been a contributing editor of* SPORTS AFIELD *since 1994. The following is from his 1995 book,* FOR A HANDFUL OF FEATHERS.—NOVEMBER 1994 •••

FOR A HANDFUL OF FEATHERS
by Guy de la Valdéne

> "The more I see of the people's
> representatives, the more I
> like my dogs."
> —COMTE ALFRED D'ORSAY, 1850.

No one can have the part of me I give to my dogs, a gift as safe as loving a child; a part of me I guard carefully because it bears on my sanity. My dogs forgive the anger in me, the arrogance in me, the brute in me. They forgive everything I do before I forgive myself. For me, the life and death of a dog is a calendar of time passing. I dream about my dogs, but recently the dreams have been turning into nightmares. One recurring scenario finds me hunting with Robin, the spaniel, on the ridge of a steep talus slope overlooking the Snake River in Idaho. The bitch runs after a cripple and follows the bird over the edge of the cliff. In my dream I watch Robin fall away, seemingly forever, a small, tumbling figure against a mosaic of sage brush, wheat, alfalfa fields and water thousands of feet below. More recently I dreamed that, without warning, the same dog began shrinking, shrinking and barking and running in tiny circles around my feet, her eyes huge and brown and imploring. I threw my hat over her mouse-sized body but missed, and when she was the size of a fly she flew away.

I don't know what these dreams mean, but if they are meant to prepare me for my dog's eventual death I would like to remind my psyche that the bitch is only five years old. On the other hand, perhaps these dreams are preparing me for my own death, or are fed by the guilt I feel when I kill something as beautiful and enviable as a bird. In any case, I'm sure that the communion I have with dogs should be channeled to my peers. However, since I think of man as the creator of desolation and not the center of reality, I don't; and as a by-product of that choice I accept the longing of loneliness, and the dark dreams that follow.

•   •   •

December 1, 1989: I wait in the front seat of my car, next to a 4-month-old puppy, for ducks to fly out of a flooded hardwood marsh on the edge of Lake Jackson. A cold fall morning without a gun. This time I hunt with a different perspective on life after spending time in southern Florida. I do this by sitting and watching wild things pass by. The sun, which broke quickly into the pale, gray sky, now hangs a few inches above the lake, shedding clouds until the water turns red. When the clouds burn off, the white sun resumes its ascent. The desperation I feel every time I venture into cities passes, even though not a duck creases the sky. The young dog, Robin, sits next to me with her head out the window, her ears opened to the fecund sounds of the marsh.

Back at the lake by 5:00 P.M. The puppy sits on my lap and stares out the front window, trembling. When the darkness gains weight the wood ducks fly back from the open water of the lake to roost, and Robin follows their outline until the upholstery blocks her view. The ducks become long-winged shadows falling from the sky. In the backwater under the hardwoods, the ducks squeal and stir the mud, exciting the puppy. Wood ducks are my favorite table duck, and my least favorite to shoot because they are beautiful and dumb: male-model ducks.

Lake Jackson has turned purple, purple water supporting a red horizon. Robin stares through the windshield at mosquitoes as big as birds. I am at my best when the sounds of civilization are at their lowest decibel, and I envy the fellow who, along with his Nagra tape recorder, hunted for and found all the places in the world where the sounds were purely natural and nonhuman. He found only a handful, but there he made beautiful music.

A cold wind pushes night into the car. Robin shivers and curls up on my lap. On the way home the headlights play under the pine trees. Rock and roll fills the cab. I feel young again for having been alone with the dog, the birds and now the music. At home, just before I fall asleep, the puppy lays her head on my chest to let me know our day together is over, and then she moves as far from my restless turning as she can and still share the bed.

My second dog, Mable, is a 7-year-old lemon-and-white English pointer I bought four years ago as a broke bird dog. Mable lived in a kennel before I bought her and now sleeps in a chair in my bedroom. I have spent four years hunting for Mable instead of hunting for birds; four years of howling at her to come and watching her run 180 degrees away from me into the quagmires of neighboring counties. The dog doesn't mean to run away, but the moment the terrain is at odds with her ability to see me, she becomes confused and then lost, incapable of figuring out from which direction I am calling. This happens because Mable is dumb, dumb as a knot, dumber than the dumbest human being I have ever known, and a graduate of Spark College, the modern, electrically oriented school of dog training.

I should have sent her back to her previous owner, or at least given her to a retired social worker. The dog loves children and women; they, in turn, enjoy dressing her up in their clothes. I persevered in thinking that because she loved me she would one day recognize the sound of my voice as a rallying point and not the echo of dementia. She never has, and now that she is middle-aged she has taken to peeing in the puddle of water she drinks from, licking the fertilizer in the flower beds, and eating toads. I, of course, have taken to feeling sorry for her.

It has been said that a pointer that comes when called is rarer than an honest judge, to which one should add that compliance is not the compelling reason for owning a bird dog in the first place. Bred and trained to hunt with their senses screwed to the bone, they are designed to raise the level of quail hunting to an art form, and when things are right, they do. A breeze ruffling a handful of feathers carries enough weight to enslave a dog to a bird in a covenant of uneasy immobility. Setters, Brittanys and German shorthairs face quail as if their lives depended on it, but when a good English pointer faces a bird, he does so with all but one foot on the coals of hell.

To counteract two demanding and jealous bitches, I have recently brought into the house an 8-week-old equalizer—a roan-colored male with white whiskers, a black nose and black eyes. His name is Carnac, the first male dog I have owned since I was 16 years old. Carnac is a French Brittany that looks like a suckling pig, a roan-colored suckling pig that keeps its eyes on mine or on my hands, the hands that feed him and smack his butt. The little man-dog already likes to bite the females' behinds and then run like hell, barking with joy. Once in a while the bitches catch him, pin him down, and make him pay, but because he is a male they mostly put up with his puppyhood. Carnac is a happy dog, willing and able to pee on any carpet, and hump a woman's leg, displaying via the abandon of his grasp the keenness of his will. Now, if he will only hunt . . .

Great Dogs

I remember when southern quail were abundant and time was cheap and hunting was an honorable diversion; when bird dogs spent most of the year as glorious bags of teats and bones, raising their pups under slat-board porches until the sounds of acorns crackling under the tractor tires snapped them to their feet, fired up their genes, and drove them to the woods. Dogs were bird dogs, English pointers whose real reason for being was to stop the instant the scent of a quail crossed their olfactory paths. What actually happened in terms of training between the time the bitch rose from her eight-month slumber to the time she addressed covey after covey of bobwhite quail, forgetting everything except the birds and the men she was hunting for, was not specified, leaving me with a picture of synergetic aplomb and grace.

Once in a great while, albeit not for very long, I have a desire to own an all-age, field-trial dog, a crackerjack flamenco dancer with quick feet, a flaring nose and a whalebone rib cage; a dog that owns the ground on which it runs and the wind on which birds fly. I want a dog whose cast gives reason to the landscape, a dog that shakes at the delirium of discovery and imposes on birds the fortitude of its resolve. I covet the bag of bones that each fall metamorphoses into a greyhound. I covet the magician, the trickster, but I also want it to come when I call, and that is asking too much. All-age dogs are the savants of the field-trial world, and asking them to do something as mundane as coming on command is like asking Van Gogh to add a cow to the landscape.

Twenty years ago, I hunted bobwhite quail from horseback behind those kinds of dogs. Memories return in the shape of thin, black men riding fast southern horses, men who worked the flanks and signaled points by raising their caps above their heads, and uncanny dog handlers who smelled birds before the dogs did. I remember galloping to points with my heart in my throat for fear of not getting to the covey before it blew up. I hunted behind all-age dogs that had competed in, and in some cases won, National Championships; dogs that trembled at the mere mention of birds; dogs that presented to the guns a quarry whose head they were given to eat. Memories of those days also include races between horsemen and deer across broom sedge fields; old dogs found pointing swamp-birds under the radiance of a cold winter moon; and gentlemen who killed only male quail.

A quote from the guest book at Sehoy Plantation, Alabama, December 13, 1967:

◆　◆　◆

Flushed 27 coveys of quail, shot over 23. Filled two limits. My companion missed all but one bird. Pointers, stretched to a beautiful attitude. Kennel mates backing in perfect unanimity of opinion. Tipped a bobwhite or two out of each covey rise. Moses (name of black dog-handler) exclaimed, "Gents, that covey's powerful close." Ate fried quail, collard greens with pepper vine-

gar, lima beans, hot rolls and French wine. Port with dessert, cognac later. Bid six hearts, finessed the jack, and made the slam. A day to remember.

◆ ◆ ◆

Dogs, like men, lose their range and enthusiasm for life from having the wildness in them questioned. In the case of dogs, trainers these days ask the questions with single-digit probes of electric trauma, trauma that reaches its destination faster than the trainer's thought. When sustained, and with the range to reach across field and dale, this bolt of bionic inhumanity will scramble a dog's brains and walk him to hell and back. In the hands of most men the electronic collar serves a number of purposes ranging from suppressed hate to a genuine training tool. The obvious shortcut electricity provides is not unlike sound bites and fast foods, and allows questionable trainers to postpone working a client's dog almost indefinitely. In the hands of a good man the collar removes the boot and the leather strap from the routine of training, and when it's applied just right the dog can be made to believe that God is watching and its salvation rests with its trainer. A thin line. One application too many, and the client owns a round-eyed dog that pees in the water it drinks.

I am a terrible dog trainer because the traits I like in a dog are the same as those I like in men: namely, civil disobedience. Training is repetition, hell is toeing the line. I have witnessed extreme punishment applied to dogs with instruments ranging from a 30-second hold on a number five button, to a two-by-four. When I was much younger and fresh out of Europe, where field trials were, and still are, thought of as civilized sporting contests between reasonable men and women and their dogs, I sucker-punched a dog trainer at a field trial in Pennsylvania for jerking a full-grown Labrador off its feet by its ears. The dog had swum the wrong course at a dead duck. I drilled the trainer in the ear, and he pitched face-first into the mud. My British host, without so much as raising an eyebrow, patted the dog on the head, looked down at the man, and said, "Well, as he's in no position to answer you, we might as well be moving along. Cruel bugger, what?"

Young Dogs

The best dog is the one that adapts to its master's temperament and style of hunting, and while I marvel at the English pointers and setters, such dogs have always tip-toed beyond the reaches of my hearing

Within hours of my owning them, and from that moment on I have had to blow my face up to get their attention. Now that I have retired my sneakers, this type of dog is no longer right for me. I want a dog that comes about 100 yards or so on either side of me and passes within gun range each time it checks in. I usually have an idea where the birds are and would just as soon have Biff go where I tell it to. Not a workable agenda when dealing with the tightly strung violins of dogdom.

Now, when I hunt, I like to think about things, like how the trees have grown, the last time I slept with a woman, the direction of the wind, what wine I'm going to drink with dinner. Killing is a formality. When I hunt with another person, I want to listen to and talk with that person—otherwise I wouldn't be hunting with him.

I want to stop if I choose to without losing the dog or having to hack at it to keep it on a level course. I have done all these things, and after a decade of getting just as frustrated as I did when I played golf, I bought the Brittany with the hope that I won't feel the fingers of retribution crawl up my backside each time the dog is out of sight. It all comes down to the man and what he wants from his dog. In my case, I plan to hunt behind pointers and setters until the day I retire my guns, but they will belong to someone else.

• • •

One can argue that, performed with a measure of dignity and restraint, hunting is just as important an issue now as it was 300 years ago, but for opposite reasons. Hunting is no longer a survival issue for man, but it has become a survival issue for the game; while we have multiplied like rabbits, the game has dwindled tenfold. Our importance as hunters lies in the fact that we as individuals, having no affiliations with anything or anyone other than the sport, witness and assess the condition of the game and habitat in this country. Our credentials are that we are out there, in nature, when others are not, and that we are out there because we want to be, not because we have to or are paid to be. Our eyes solicit the traceries of spoors on the earth and of birds in the sky. Our spirits are conscious of ravens and long for the restitution of wolves and bears to the land. We are the wildlife thermometers, poking about in rivers and swamps, in the shadows of forest canopies, under the flashes of desert suns, and the force that drives us is our soul.

We hunters, more than any other group on earth, should understand the symbiotic relationship between species and how it has come to pass that, thanks to our destructive meddling, the reflection of a teal on a pond is no longer free of charge. Those of us who understand the complex nature of a teal's life—and what it takes, in terms of protection and food, to grow the feathers that send that image darting over the water—also understand what the chase and the kill do to the spirit of man, its rewards and its shames. Because we understand and feel these things more acutely than our peers, it is sacrilegious of us not to protect with all our might what resources remain to be saved. If we neglect our obligations, we stand to incur the contempt of generations to come.

• • •

I have done some shameful things in the name of sport in the past 40 years, and recognize in my not-so-distant past the genetic chimpanzee in me. When Robin wasn't quite a year old I picked her up by the scruff of the neck and, with just enough anger in me to make the act sickening, threw her to the ground. The dog had been running around in a dove field enjoying her youth, the sounds of gunfire and the sight of falling birds while I, infuriated at her disobedience, wanted her to sit by my side. When I threw her, Robin fell wrong and screamed like a baby. She wasn't so much hurt as she was terrified that the one being in the world she loved unconditionally had suddenly and for no apparent reason turned on her. It scared me for all the appropriate reasons, not the least of which was that I recognized in me the dog trainer I had knocked to the ground years before, and nowadays when the little bitch lays her head on my shoulder in the dark of the night it is because I have called her to me, waking from the nightmare of that act; waking from the dream in which I had broken her neck.

The same crass and impulsive behavior incited me to shoot sparrows and swallows as a child, crows and hawks when I should have known better, and, more recently, a bobcat in the back and a raccoon in the face. My unbecoming and violent nature as a child doesn't concern me anymore. I have forgiven myself for being a young man with a young man's rules. But now that I am, for better and for worse, tired—no, exhausted—from witnessing the insipid violence in men, these questions of ethics so easily dismissed a few years ago weigh me down for reasons of principle, age and change. I fully understand the nature of hunting and being hunted, eating, sleeping and procreating. In fact, my inclination toward reclusiveness nudges me closer and closer into the world of animals, and I have to be constantly on guard not to let myself regress into a state that functions with even less thought than the one I see in the streets and watch on television. On the other hand, I know deep in my heart that there is something basically wrong about killing for pleasure.

The day I shot a bobcat instead of a turkey I altered the natural progression of life by killing for no reason. The cat walked out of the woods, I raised the gun and pulled the trigger. The act was simple. A response to the knowledge of the cat's predilection for turkey, but one I deeply regretted when I ran my hand over the tawny-colored coat of the adult female, tough and sinewy from making a living and dropping litters, but now lifeless and flat on a bed of dirt in the shade of a sweet-gum tree with a .22-caliber Hornet hole in her heart. There was a time when killing the bobcat would have pleased me. I would have felt like the protector, the benevolent despot of the forest. Now I question what it means to meddle in things that are so much more natural than what I see on the news. I feel like a half-wit to possess the same senseless traits I reproach in others, particularly as I am no longer convinced that I am better than the cat. Killing for no reason is killing with malice.

A month later, driving down a dirt road overlooking a pasture, I stopped and, from inside the car, shot a raccoon in the face while it watched me from inside the fork of a dogwood tree. The raccoon fell slowly, raking the bark with its claws, holding on until gravity took hold and pulled it to the ground where it would eventually rot. I had just finished reading an article about how raccoons rob quail nests.

The seduction of the scope made for simple killing and emotional ambiguity. Physical magnification had stolen the life from the image and left me with a sharp target. The precision of glass is finite but the consequence of a senseless death is not, except in how it takes its toll on the psyche of man. Could it be that those unnatural killings—I didn't eat or use either animal—were attempts at killing the wildness in myself?

. . .

My Dog

By winter, Carnac, the roan-colored Brittany, didn't look like a suckling pig anymore. He was thin and fit, the bones in his face had sharpened, his nose had swayed and lengthened, and his hindquarters had filled out. Carnac had graduated from looking like a pig to looking like a jackal, a 24-pound jackal with a long nose, and at 24 pounds the perfect poacher's dog, built to jump into a game vest at the first sign of trouble. At a year old he enjoyed life to its fullest, at the expense of everyone else, particularly the bitches. Not knowing anything about kennels, shock collars or leather whips, Carnac has had no contact with the darker side of a hunting dog's life, so when I say "birds," stretching the b's and the r's, he looks at me, sits up straight as an arrow, and tests the air. His cheeks puff and unpuff, his nose checking the azimuth, and his eyes follow his nose. He is stationary hunting.

Carnac was a natural from the first day in the field. He loved the grass, the briers, the smells, and the sound of a gun—a sound he was taught to relish early on, beginning with the feral pigs that I sometimes shot in the rear with a .410 to move them out of the yard. Carnac has hated pigs ever since the morning he and Robin ran out of the lake house into the legs of a sow and her four piglets rooting up the grass for worms. The sow cornered Carnac against the side of the house and tried to eat him, scaring the stink out of both dogs, and me. I hit the pig over the head with a shovel, hard, until she finally turned on me, allowing the dogs to get away before rending any meat, but it was close. Carnac does not have a problem with guns.

He pointed a quail wing within a minute of watching it fly at the end of a fishing pole, but that doesn't mean too much. I bought some pen-raised quail, built a call-back pen, and began training the puppy. The only thing that didn't work was that the quail that were supposed to return to their plywood home before dark never did, choosing instead to join the wild ones. Can't say I blame them.

Carnac learned to run through a field chasing birds that smelled good, and one day, just like my trainer friend told me he would, the puppy realized he couldn't catch them and pointed. Pointed, solid as Excalibur.

A week after that the dog pulled a checkcord through the woods and learned to whoa, which he did only to please me. By late summer he began finding a few wild coveys and learned about the sound of a dozen wings. Carnac began to follow his long shovel nose, which rarely deceived him. If he smelled birds, he trailed them until he found them. The dog is stubborn.

Meanwhile, my doltish pointer, Mable, managed to fall asleep under a truck and, oblivious to the engine noise, allowed herself to be run over, dislocating her hip. Once it was mended she did what she had always hoped for: She never left her chair. So much for her vacuous career. Mable has since moved in with a lady who doesn't hunt but enjoys dressing her in Victorian clothes. The age of the big-going dogs is over for me.

Now I sneak around with a tiny dog that walks on his hind legs to see over cover and looks goofy when the smell of feathers passes his way.

I introduced a blank pistol into the picture a few weeks into fall, and Carnac is now convinced that life is one big bowl of food, field and birds. When the sounds of wings and gunfire became inseparable entities in Carnac's mind, and I was able to hold him on point through the flush without raising my voice, I started calling friends up, praising the poacher dog's abilities. I lied a little, too, just to make sure they knew what a fine animal had graced my jubilee year, the dog that will hunt me to my 60s.

At home, Carnac missed few opportunities to display the flip side of his character. He kept right on eating rugs, shoes, the springer's tail and whoever else was handy. Carnac is not popular with those who don't know or care about his split personality. He is with me.

Graduation day came on an overcast winter morning, full of fog and pale shadows. I released him into a section of the farm I had seen, and watched proudly as the little dog cast back and forth, looking at me for direction, moving with a special eagerness, as if his instincts were telling him that this was what all those weeks of training had been about. The terrain sloped down through a mixed cover of grass, year-old oak saplings and myrtle bushes, leading to a small cornfield cut into an open bench in the middle of the woods. Half the corn was standing. The rest had been mowed down. There was grain on the ground. The deer had taken to the field, as had the turkeys and at least two coveys of bobwhite quail. The wind was right, it was early in the day, and wild smells sprang out of the dew.

Carnac worked on, 50 yards ahead of me, looking pretty sure of himself. Quail had always been easy for him to find before, and he saw no reason why they wouldn't be on this day.

When he stopped, he had a face full of bird scent and, except for a speeding tail and his cheeks that puffed, he stared ahead and didn't move. The scene warmed the cockles of my heart. This was the first of our salad days together. I walked up behind the dog, quietly reminding him to stay, walked to a piece of low cover, and watched a good covey of bobwhite quail hurl itself off the ground and fan over the cornfield. No doubles today, I thought and, assuring the shot, dropped a bird 25 yards away.

"All right, little man," I said. "Fetch it up." I was feeling pretty good about the developments.

The Brittany broke for the bird while I reloaded and thought about having a glass of wine for lunch, a big one, to mark the occasion and adjust my personality. Carnac ran behind a stand of tall dog fennel. I must have crippled that bird, I thought to myself, heading his way. What a good dog I have. I encouraged him from the far side of the fennel stand, and when I got around to where I could see, there he was, facing away from me, muzzle in a bush, tail wagging. It looked to me that he had the bird, so I told him to fetch it back. He didn't, so I told him to sit, which he did in his ramrod fashion. No problem, I thought; he pointed, held, and then found the bird. I didn't expect as much on his first day out; after all, perfection is elusive. I broke the gun, walked up behind the puppy, and reached around his head for the quail in his mouth. The only thing my fingers encountered were two scaly feet that, when pulled on, surrendered, and came free.

The rest of the bird shot straight down Carnac's throat.

Fishing

SPORTS AFIELD *has covered all the major happenings*

in the fishing world—the taking of the world-record

*largemouth bass (*THE WORLD RECORD BASS, *Vic Dunaway,*

*1969), the opening of Russia to fishing (*FISHING ON TOP OF

THE WORLD, *Thomas McGuane, 1995). But we've also found*

*that there is adventure (*NORTH UMPQUA STEELHEADS, *Zane*

*Grey, 1935) and mystery (*GHOST TROUT, *Nash Buckingham,*

*1945) to fishing—plus a lot of fun (*BREAMERS STOP AT

NOTHING, *Havilah Babcock, 1950).*

••• Adventurer, writer, outdoorsman—Zane Grey was known the world over for his books about the Old West (such as RIDERS OF THE PURPLE SAGE), as well as for his articles. Fishing was his passion: He held records at one time or another for tuna, marlin, sailfish and dolphin. He fished for tarpon and bonefish in the Florida Keys, bass in the Delaware River, pelagic species across the globe; but he always came back to his beloved North Umpqua, for steelhead.—SEPTEMBER 1935 •••

NORTH UMPQUA STEELHEADS by Zane Grey

Fifty miles or so above its junction with Steamboat Creek the Umpqua has its source in the high ranges and probably receives most of its ice-cold water from an underground outlet in Diamond Lake. For many miles down this rushing river seldom feels the sun. Great fir trees and canyon walls shade it halfway down. Numerous small brooks and creeks augment its flow. There are two big waterfalls and innumerable rapids. Ten miles above Steamboat cutthroat rainbow trout up to five pounds are abundant. We know that steelhead run up at least that far. There is a good trail up the river, and two homesteaders. Not until you reach Steamboat on the way down does the Umpqua know anything about fishermen, or automobiles. It is virgin. It has unsurpassed beauty. Deer and bear and cougar, wolves and coyotes are abundant.

From Steamboat an auto road makes the Umpqua accessible to anglers. That is to say it is easy to *see* the river from the road. But there are only a few places where you can get down to the river without great exertion and a risking of your neck, and a very decided chance of your being hit by a rattler. There is a succession of long channels, cut in solid granite, and white rapids. We call many places pools. But they certainly are not eddies.

The Umpqua is the most dangerous river to wade, and therefore to fish, that I know this side of Canada. In June it is high, swift, heavy, and cold. It would be bad for any fisherman to slip in. And the rocks are slipperier than slippery-elm. July it begins to drop, half an inch a day and by August you can reach most of the water. This summer was hot and dry, making the Umpqua lower than ever known before, so it was possible for some young and vigorous fishermen, like my boys, to wade it without waders. At that I have seen them come back to camp, blue in the face, shivering as if with the ague, and yelping for the fire. I would not advise wading the Umpqua very much without waders.

It is not a good river for spoon and bait fishermen. I watched upwards of several dozen hardware fishermen this summer and very few of them caught steelhead. Some of them got good bags of small trout. I am not one of the many who advocate closing the Umpqua to spoon-fishermen. That is arbitrary, and would be inclined to affront many Oregonians who live near the river. My idea has been to educate spoon-fishermen, and I have succeeded with several. There are two reasons why this should be easy; first, a spoon-fisherman, by a few casts in any stretch of water, spoils the fishing in that particular place for fly-fishermen all the rest of that day. A good angler with the fly, especially the dry fly, can spend all day in a 100-yard stretch of water. It is obvious that only a fish-hog, or an unthinking fisherman, will go on down the river, spoiling all the water for others who start in behind him. The second reason has no ethical or sporting side. It is merely that even a novice can, as soon as he learns a little about casting, get more rises, hook more steelhead and have infinitely more sport than the spooner. Only the expert spoon-fisherman can contend with an expert fly fisherman, and even the very best ones would get nowhere in a contest with Burnham or my son Romer. The question of tackle is negligible. You can buy usable fly tackle almost as cheap as spoon tackle.

But if the spooner waives this and tells me where to get off I come back at him thusly. If you must fish with a spoon, O.K. But don't flog all the river, and be a sport enough to give the fly fisherman a wide berth.

I have had many requests by letter and otherwise to tell what kind of tackle we use and how we fish. Romer, like Burnham, is partial to light tackle. This summer, as usual, he started with 5 1/2-ounce Leonards and Grangers, Ashaway lines, and 357 Hardy leaders. These English leaders are tapered, nine foot in length, and they cost plenty. In spite of his skill, and delicate handling of big fish, and his wonderful daring in wading, and in a pinch swimming the Umpqua, Romer began right at the outset to lose many steelhead. He broke two tips, and many leaders. He graduated down to six-ounce rods and 345 leaders. And when he quit on September 21, his last fish an 11 3/4-pound steelhead, about which I will tell later, he was using my favorite leader, 341.

Romer fishes fine and far away. He is a disciple of Burnham. He can cast 100 feet with ease. But he begins on a pool by keeping out of sight and fishing close. He is like an Indian in his wary approach. He never scares any trout. He preferred always, until this summer, small flies No. 6 and 8, and he used a good many English flies.

As is well known, the Parmachene Belle and Hair Coachman are the best flies on the Umpqua, during June and July. But toward the middle of this month they let up a good deal rising to these patterns. The old Turkey and Red failed to raise fish, and the Turkey and Gold, that Joe Wharton had made for me, soon lost its effectiveness. I had Wharton make a pattern after the New Zealand Gold Demon, adding hair and jungle cock. It was good for a while. Then that too slowed up, and we were hard put to it to find flies that would raise fish.

I had always been partial to larger flies, No. 4 and No. 3. And I had Loren and Joe Debernardi get busy with the fly-tying kits. It was my idea, but Loren hit upon a fly that beat any I ever used, and it was quite different in pattern and color from all the others. With that fly, and others almost similar, we had the most magnificent sport that I ever heard of on a steelhead river. We really made the Umpqua steelhead fishing no less than salmon fishing. And I mean Atlantic salmon fishing.

My bag of steelhead was impressive. Sixty-four in all, including three over 11, five of nine, a dozen around eight, and so on down to five pounds. Of course, I let a good many fish go. We never kept any we could not use, except a big one that we wanted to photograph. And these we smoked. Steelhead properly smoked, and salted correctly, are most delectable.

But that number 64 does not say anything. It was the steelhead I raised and could not hook, and those that I hooked and could not land, which counted. My favorite rod was a Hardy, seven ounces, with an extension butt I used after I hooked a fish. It was a wonderful rod. I do not see how it stood all the fights I had. Some of the steelhead I caught took over an hour to subdue. One that I did not catch and never even saw in all the 2 1/2-hour battle took me half a mile down the river where I would certainly have drowned but for Joe.

Curious to relate this fish and the two largest I got fast to were all hooked in the same place—a pool we called Island Pool. It was a channel in a bend with rocky islands here and there. The water was swift. Below was a rapid, then a long succession of small islands, and then a series of white rapids. The one I caught out of this hole weighed 11 1/4. I was one hour and five minutes on this bird. At that I never got him fairly, for he ran down the river so fast I could not follow. He took 160 yards of the 192 yards I had on my reel—this was the Crandall new camouflage salmon line, G.B.H. with 150 yards of the strongest and finest silk backing—the most wonderful line I have ever used.

Joe ran down river and wading out to the islets below he succeeded in catching hold of my line. He held the steelhead for a while in the swift current, then carefully handlined him up river, until the fish took a notion to run again. This happened three times, and the last time he got the steelhead close up to him or even with him, then he had to let go.

"Big pink buck!" yelled Joe. "He's tired. Put the wood on him!"

I was over 100 yards above Joe. How I ever pumped that steelhead up to me, inch by inch, I cannot tell. But eventually I did, and led him ashore and beached him on a flat rock. Then breathless and wet and exhausted by excitement and exertion I sat down to gaze spellbound at this magnificent steelhead. He was over 30 inches long, deep and thick, with a tail spread of eight inches, and a blending of silver and rose exquisitely beautiful.

Joe and I, naturally, overestimated his weight. We said surely 13 pounds. But I was happy, no matter what his weight.

The second whale I hooked in that hole I did not see rise. I felt a heavy drag and thought my fly had caught. It had, as a galvanizing vibrant pull proved. I saw a long white fish wriggle and jerk in the shadow of the green water. Then he came up stream slowly. He swam all the way up the Island Pool to where it was shallow. And there in scarcely three feet of water he fooled around in plain sight. Joe nearly fell off the rocks in his frenzy to get that fish. I nearly collapsed. For we could see him, and he was 40 inches long, 10 deep, a pink fresh-run steelhead that must have been lifted over the salmon racks by the netters at the hatchery. Sometimes they dip out a few steelhead and release them up river. Gus, my driver, saw them lift out six, all over 20 pounds, and one they said would go 28. No other way could those giant steelhead get above the racks. Well, this one was so big that I could not do anything but keep the rod up and let him bend it. To make a long and agonizing story short this monster swam there in plain sight for over a half hour, until the hook pulled out. I have lost 1000-pound swordfish with less misery! Joe swore he would get drunk.

The third one I hooked there, of these huge steelhead, must have been even larger. We never saw him once. The first one, I forgot to tell, had leaped prodigiously and often. This third one made my reel shriek and smoke as no Newfoundland salmon had done. He ran 100 yards, then stopped in the current. We ran, fell, waded, climbed, all but swam. At times Joe had to hold me up. I got half or more of that line back, then the son-of-a-gun ran again. This happened five times during that half mile. At last down at the head of a fall above what we call the Divide Pool he hung for half an hour more, then took his hardest run. I was glad he got off, but Joe was sick. I shall never forget what thrills and pangs that steelhead packed into the 2 1/2-hour battle.

Loren put up a remarkable and enviable record of 100 steelhead for the three months of our stay. A third of these, at least all the small ones, he carefully unhooked and let go.

During July I used to sit in camp with my glass and watch him fish the Z. G. Pool. Out of this water he caught 43 steelhead, and here he learned the fine points of the game. He developed. His luck was nil at first. For weeks it was all he could do to raise a fish a day. But he stuck, and that's the answer. After that he would get up at daylight and try to beat everybody to the Ranger Station Pool at Steamboat. Half the time he beat the fishermen who were camped right on the bank. And did he snake steelhead out of that strange and wonderful hole? I'm telling you. Twenty-seven he caught there, and lost twice as many. When they start down it's time to weep.

But Loren's best work came in August in the pools down the river. He would leave early in the afternoon and come back at dark, wet, tired, but with shining eyes. And once only do I recall that he came without fish. For that single exception he had a story that even I dare not tell. Allowing for the exaggeration and inaccuracy of a youngster it still is the most remarkable fish yarn I ever heard. Some days he would climb down the almost unscalable mountain, kick rattlers off the rocks, raise from 10 to 20 steelhead, hook some, fight them, and catch one or two, or more.

One night—the night—he came back with Gus packing a huge red steelhead that weighed in camp, hours after it had dried out, a little over 12 pounds.

"Here he is, fellows," he flashed with vibrant voice. "Look him over. Thirty-two and one-half inches! Look at that spread of tail. . . Look at me. Soakin' wet. An' look at this skinned place on my shin! An' look at Gus!—He swam out above that bad rapid—you know the hole, *my* hole, where I have hooked an' lost so many— Gus swam out to save the line. I thought he would go over the falls. But he didn't. An' this darn fish then swam up stream again. He'd done that a dozen times. Jump? Oh, it was terrible. Right in our faces! He splashed water right on me. He shook himself—tussled, like a dog. All silver an' red—jaws like a wolf! . . . Oh boy, I'm tellin' you, it was great!"

I didn't need to be told that. It was. And not all the greatness was in the sport, the luck, the fish itself. It is the spirit that counts. The boy or man who can be true to an ideal, stick to a hard task, carry on in the face of failure, exhaustion, seeming hopelessness—he is the one who earns the great reward.

As for Romer, dynamic drama always attended his fishing activities. He could not keep out of trouble with fish. One day he spent the whole long day trying to raise a big steelhead that lay dark against a green rock in the Z. G. Pool. This fish was so big he could be seen from the automobiles on the road, high above the river. Romer must have tried 100 flies over that fish. He must have rested him almost as many times. He did not come in for supper. We yelled and waved. No use! Finally I sent Joe out to drag him in. But Joe forgot that—forgot all in the passion to raise this steelhead. I interpreted Joe's wild wave to us to mean that Romer had, some-time or other that day, raised this fish.

I sat in my camp chair with my glass trained on Romer. And I was watching when he at last persuaded or drove this steelhead to rise. I saw the great boil on the water, then the angry upcurl of white. Romer's piercing yell of triumph and Joe's hoarse yell of exultation came to our ears above the roar of the falls.

I yelled like a maniac, and then all of us lined up on the cliff to watch in intense excitement. That steelhead ran up the river. The channel was tortuous and impossible to wade in a straight line. But Romer and Joe followed as best they could. Once a great splash far up stream warned me that this steelhead was going places. He did not show again. He ploughed through two rapids before he broke off. Romer stood as one dazed, looking up the river. Then he turned and waded back toward camp.

We were all sympathy. Romer was pale and grim. His big dark eyes burned. "Eighteen pounds!" he said. "I raised him at noon on a New Zealand fly. And tonight he took a Turkey and Gold—after all that time. I think he got sore, like an Eastern salmon does when you cast a lot over him."

Another evening I was just getting back to camp when I heard yelling. I ran. When I got out where I could see, the crowd was lined up on the cliff, greatly excited. They yelled and pointed. Then I saw Romer pile into the deep swift channel above the big falls. Long ago I had ceased to be scared when he pulled some stunt like this. He is a champion swimmer. He waded out on the other side, his bent rod held high. He could not stop the fish. It went over the falls. Romer plunged in to swim back to the point he had started from. And then straight down the middle of this wide reach in the Umpqua he ran with great strides. We knew, of course, he had hooked another of the bad fighters. There was a ledge of rock extending across the river, with the heavy fall at the far side, and a lesser one on our side. Romer piled right off this ledge to swim the few yards to the head of an island. There he ran again, winding his reel like a madman. Evidently the demon of a fish kept on. At the foot of this island Romer waded a bad rapid that he had never attempted before. He reached another island, where we thought he would be marooned. We hurried along the cliff, kept even with him, climbed down to the bank, yelling encouragement. There was a white mill race between Romer and the shore on our side. He leaped in with bent rod, and swam. We saw the rod wag with his powerful strokes. He came out safely, crossed the shallow rocky place, ran to the gravel bar below, and at length clear round the bend he stopped that fish in a deep eddy.

And there, for 20 minutes longer, by my watch, Romer pumped and worked on that steelhead before he could lift him. We were all dumbfounded to see the fish which had put up that fight. It was one of the smallest size. In fact it weighed 4 1/2 pounds. But what a rare, colorful, quivering, magnificently built steelhead!

"What do you—know about that!" ejaculated Romer, when he could talk. "Froze stiff—for this little fish!"

I happened to be with Romer when he got fast to a big steelhead that like this little one was almost unbeatable.

It happened at the Takahashi Pool, near sunset, on our last day of fishing. We had been far down the river. No luck! I had not even had a rise. Romer whipped the lower reaches in Takahashi while I watched. The sun set. The river sped by, shimmering in amber-green light. The mountain slope was bathed in gold. Insects had begun to chirp. The air had grown cold.

As last Romer climbed a high rock at the head of this Takahashi Pool and cast from there. This is at the foot of a heavy rapid. The waves were white-crested and big, the current fast. Few trout fishermen would ever try such a place. But we raised steelhead out of such water. When your fly dances over these waves steelhead will rise straight from the bottom in a rush, and come clear out. Sometimes they miss the fly; seldom do they hook themselves; but when they get fast—what a wonderful experience!

I was watching the fly when a vicious splash flew up and Romer's yell pealed out. I ran to a more advantageous point. This steelhead ran up stream against that current so that the line seethed cuttingly, audible to the ears. Romer stood high with a long line out. He reeled fast, but there was no need, for the bag in the line was as tight as a wire. I ran on up beside him, and got there in time to see this steelhead leap fully six feet out of that white water. He looked enormous and he caught all the gold of the setting sun.

Turning he made down river with extraordinary speed. I could not keep pace with Romer. At the foot of that long stretch there is a ledge where all hooked steelhead foul the line. This one did. We had a moment of despair. Then the reel sang again. The line was around the ledge but it fouled. Romer got out on the platform of poles Joe had built there for the purpose of releasing our lines when caught. Romer worked there carefully to get free. He reached out so far with his rod that I feared he would fall in. With sunset the canyon had begun to fill with shadow and soon the line was hard to see. But we could hear the reel clear enough. Jerk by jerk it warned us that the line was nearing the spool. Presently it ceased.

"There!—All—out," cried Romer, tragically.

"What? Not all your line!"

"Yes. What'll I do now?"

The old poignant query in moments of baffled effort!

"My heavens. All that 190 yards!" Then I bethought myself of the long forked pole Joe and I had used before we built the platform. Finding that, I waded as far as I dared and reached out. The pole was heavy. When I got it extended it sank of its own weight. Another desperate try while Romer called huskily: "Hurry, Dad!"

I released the line. It sang like a telephone wire. Romer plunged off the platform and made the water fly. I followed. We came out upon the flat ledge round the corner to a long deep stretch of river. Here had always been the ideal place to have it out with a big steelhead. Dusk had mantled the gap between the wooded slopes.

"He's stopped. But I can't get—any line," panted Romer.

"You've got to. It's now or never. What kind of leader and hook have you on?"

"That short salmon leader you gave me—and a big hook. I put them on—to try in that rough water."

"What a break! Lam it into him before he takes a notion to run again."

"Hook'll tear out. . . . Oh, he's heavy."

"No it won't. Not this time. Put the wood on him, Romer."

The moment was one of severe strain for more than the tackle and steelhead. But nothing broke. Romer got him headed upstream. Little by little he recovered line. What an endless task it seemed! I believe he was half an hour on that fish before he got to the enameled end. Forty-two yards from the steelhead! I begged Romer not to be afraid to pull him. In a long fight the hook wears out of the jaw!

The moon came up over the mountain—a full moon, bright as silver, and it made a vast difference. We could see. But another quarter of an hour passed before we saw the first white flash of the big trout. He was far from whipped, at least as badly whipped as Romer wanted.

We were standing in a foot of water with the fish close, weaving and turning right in front of us. Every time he moved his tail he took line.

"Don't let him have an inch! Hold him!" I remonstrated. "Romer, that steelhead is as tired as he will ever get."

"Oh—Lord!" was all my son replied.

Moments dragged by. And we saw the steelhead on each turn. In that black water, when he flashed in the moonlight, he looked monstrous. Everything was magnified. I never saw such delicate handling of a big fish. Afterward I acknowledged incredible patience and judgment. But I could not have done it. And I began to sag under the strain. Fifty-five minutes on that ledge! I had not noted the hour when the fish was hooked. However it was at sunset. Finally I could not endure any longer.

"My God—son! Pull him in."

"Not ready—yet," panted Romer, hoarsely.

"Romer, you *know* some of these steelhead *never* get dead tired. Take that 4 1/2-pounder of yours the other afternoon. Take the story Burnham tells. He saw an angler, a novice, to be sure, hook a fish. Burnham went on down stream. An hour later he came back. The fellow was fighting a fish—another one, Burnham thought. Burnham went on up the river. Came back in three hours. 'Say,' he yelled to the fellow who was on another fish. 'You're having sport. What fly are you using? How many fish have you been into?'

"'Only—one,' was the reply. 'Same—fish—I had on—this morning!'

"'Whoopee!—Turn your back, put your rod over your shoulder, and walk up the bank. That steelhead won't ever be any more licked than he is now.'"

"All right, Dad. I'll horse him," replied Romer, and tightened up a little. "Never—did this—before. . . . God help you—if I lose him!"

Romer worked the steelhead up on the ledge and approached the shore. I could see the fish and I would have yelled to Romer if I had not been panic-stricken. Why is it a big fish always has this effect upon a fisherman? I believe it is a regurgitation back to boyhood.

I kept wading in behind the steelhead, determined to fall on him if he got his head turned out again. Presently he lodged on a hollow place to turn on his side. Gaping with wide jaws, his broad side shining like silver, he galvanized me into action. With a plunge I scooped him out on the bank, where he flopped once, then lay still, a grand specimen if I ever saw one.

"How—much?" whispered Romer relaxing limp as a rag.

"Fourteen—thirteen pounds!" I pealed out. "Oh, what a fish! Am I glad you got him?"

"Whew!—Is he that big? . . . Gosh, what'll Loren say?"

"It'll be tough on the kid. He's so proud of his record. And that 12-pounder! But Loren can take it."

"Dad, don't weigh this one. We'll say 11 3/4!"

••• *Nash Buckingham was the most famous outdoor writer of his day. From Tennessee, he wrote for many magazines, and came out with such books as* THE SHOOTIN'EST GENT'MAN *and* GAME BAG. *His works appeared in* SPORTS AFIELD *in the 30s and 40s; in this piece, he got a bit more than he bargained for.*—APRIL 1945 •••

GHOST TROUT

by Nash Buckingham

Names of persons and places in this yarn may be coincidental, but its facts are not fiction. If clues crop out in this episode or escapade (or whatever you choose to call it, including a damned lie) have it your way. You may be right, but it happened just like Billy Mex and I saw it. We left the Springs before daylight to ride across Colorado's White River Plateau and down to our ranch on Beaver C'rick; a long day's cow-ponying in those days before automobiles stenched our Valley. Ours had been a week's holiday three months shy of haircuts. Swims in the hot sulphur pool untied a lot of kinks from range riding, too, to say nothing of cooling libations and waltzes (yep, I said waltzes) with lovelier partners than many of today's "Pin-Ups!"

That afternoon on the Flat Tops was unpleasantly warm. We ambled along half asleep on the bronchos, Prince and Cub. Behind us thunder muttered at intervals, but that wasn't unusual. In those altitudes you could get snowed or hailed or rained on at the drop of a five-gallon Stetson. Northward, a magnificent panorama of peaks and lesser humps piled mountain ramparts across the horizon. Great flashes and patches of sunshine and shadow chased themselves across seemingly half a world beneath us. Midway toward the Bear's Ears across the Wyoming line, Sleepy Cat's overlording heights towered like a blue-black gun sight. Billy Mex nodded awake, yawned a look-around, and birthed an idea.

"Tell you what I'll do with you—just once—Cowboy."

"Speak up, Little One, you are among friends."

"We'll turn off here, drop into yonder gulch toward Lost Solar, and ride a bee-line across country toward Sleepy Cat. Just to see where we strike the Valley. Are you on?" He checked Cub and squinted the proposed cutoff's angle as against the road's 30-mile loop. "Jes' up-an'-down an' up-an'-down—like that," he added.

"You're on compadre, let's ride to High Adventure." The sun was suddenly doused and on three sides we found ourselves being walled in by increasingly dense, black clouds. A hot, sulphurous breath stole across the Flat Tops. Crossing the open, we stiff-legged the ponies off a steep hogback and hopped them on down through thick buckbrush and a smattering of blue spruce into some elk-weed parks. Smack dab into a bunch of elk, too. Billy waved to the heavily-beamed herd bull and promised to look him up, come open season.

Lower, we came onto a great spring, gushing from beneath a precipitous cliff, with quite a bunch of cattle hanging around its apron. Follow water downhill long enough and you're bound to come out—somewhere. Lightning began jabbing at us, and thunder, jarring shale-slides, stampeded the critters. Billy and I tightened our saddle bags, which were full of candy and magazines, and donned fishskin slickers.

"It's fixin' t' rain wuss'n' th' town pump on wash day," opined Billy. "Let's us git under sumpn' thick—quick."

Ten minutes down hill, we struck a small corral, remnants of drift fence and dim cart tracks. The big spring above had by now become a gorgeous trout stream. Along the trail well above it, along the side hill, we raced pell-mell. But a trout fisherman's eye somehow takes stock of willowed reaches and meadowed cut banks where he just knows swirling waters break into glassy pools. We dove into a canyon and beneath its walls visibility dwindled to practically nil. Our mounts, warned by animal instinct of impending trouble, whinnied with increasing nervousness. Ranch outposts appeared and the canyon dwindled. It took all we could do to restrain Prince and Cub from bolting in wild-eyed terror. We emerged into a meadowed valley, rock-rimmed on both sides and all but blotted out from wall to wall.

"Look," shouted Billy, pointing across the c'rick. Looming through the gloom, a pretentious ranch lodge was visible against a conifered cove let into the valley's rim. Just then two jagged clouds met head-on above us and a tremendous reverberation all but jarred us from our saddles. A storm of hailstones the size of walnuts slugged us half groggy in an instant. With singing heads we spurred under a shed providentially hard by. We risked lightning, but anything was better than getting one's brains beaten out.

The meadow, heaped with hail, whitened. Leaden light struggled through a rising ceiling and the stones ceased in favor of a cloudburst. Two hundred yards from our shelter, we saw the trout stream leave its banks and spread toward us. Uprooted snags dotted the swirling flood. Half an hour of that and the overhead became a sodden drizzle. I favored hitting for home, but Billy decided to see who lived in the big lodge. After a while he caught up with me.

"I had to swim that c'rick—damn if I know whether anybody lives in that joint or not—it's all boarded up—I don't like the dump. Looks to me like there's something spooky about it."

There was a lot of lightning damage to haystacks in our valley; we saw the fires, because it took us till long after night getting home.

Next morning, while repairing fences down the meadow, Billy blurted: "Buck, when I rode up to that lodge yesterday afternoon, there were lights in it, I could see 'em behind the boards across the windows—sort of blue lights. When I got closer they dimmed out. Who th' heck you suppose lives there, anyway?"

I said I didn't know or care, but I knew that c'rick sure looked like virgin big-trout water to me, and that for two cents or less I'd ride all the way back up there just to ask permission to fish in it. All they could do, I argued, would be to turn us down. In such case, we could go on down the main White and try to snake a record rainbow out of heavier water. Billy said that would suit him to a Tee-Y-Dee-summa cum if Hughie could spare him off a few days. Hughie said that would register in the affirmative with him, provided we cut across under Burro Mountain and scouted some deer country against open season. With a pack horse along, we dropped into the strange valley from behind and, judging from the number of big bucks we jumped in the high down timber country Hughie wanted inspected, the territory looked prime.

We hit the c'rick about two miles below the strange lodge. There were still traces of the cloudburst, but the water was crystal again and tumbled along as though nothing ever had happened to roil its beautiful bends, shelving riffles, open-meadow spirals, cut banks and willow chasms. Some of the log jams were helter-skeltered and piled higher onto others. At one particular inviting stretch of water we succumbed. Billy kept remarking the absence of horse and used wagon tracks. "Whoever these dudes are," he muttered, "they sure keep pretty much to themselves—funny we've never even heard of this layout."

With the nags on picket in a grassy gulch, we set coffee water to boil and spuds to freshen. Then we jointed up our rods for an all out assault on fresh meat. When we'd creeled four "keepers," we'd quit and start munching. It didn't take long. Billy put his Royal Coachman into the throat of a log jam's inlet and an instant later I heard him bawling. Just above him, I walked out onto a tiny sandbar and shot across at a beautifully solemn slash of cut-bank water. Three floats and I wristed as gallant a two-pounder as ever tackled a Heather Moth. We just barely made away with those two fish. A post luncheon snooze and we packed up and climbed the wagon road until the ranch lodge valley came in sight. In brilliant sunlight, we paused for a comprehensive survey of the premises. Lodge, stables, barn, carriage shed—all deserted. But they were packed with farming equipment and rigs.

Billy whistled softly to himself. "There ain't a human bein' much less any critters, on the whole place. It's a ghost ranch. But I'll swear I saw lights, blue lights, in that house the other night."

"That was lightning you saw reflecting through the windows."

We rode along a spell, and Billy kept muttering to himself.

I'll always recall that stretch of trout water at the foot of which we finally camped as about the most beautiful tumble-jumble of exciting fishing mileage I've ever seen; a pretty broad statement, considering. We left the cart tracks where they began to climb steeply and wound around under increasingly brooding cliffs into a point of shelving meadow with aspens and a few spruce in its lap. It was a high, wildly lonesome spot, with the true canyon pinching in sharply up above and a view down-valley off to the north that was entrancing.

We hobbled old Blue, the pack horse, just in case, but turned Cub and Prince loose to ride herd on him. Billy spaded out the fire pit and laid the wire grill over a touch-off of pine knots. Then he laid by wood enough and to spare for a three-meal stay. I waded into a fern bed and accumulated a mattress of them for our bags, with a foot push-log for good measure. The tarpaulin was laid handy and our chuck box put at kitchen-alert. Chores finished, we reassembled our rods, slipped into creel harness and set off upstream to explore.

The canyon's jaws pinched in abruptly half a mile above camp, and we heard heavy water slamming through what turned out to be long, sinuous, glassy pulls broken by shark-tooth granite dams. Through and over these, muslin cascades bounced and spread into paradise pools where quiet caught its breath again. We tramped as pygmies beneath towering cliffs and along pint-sized sandbars hashed with deer and elk tracks.

You, too, doubtless have walked the banks of virgin trout water unable to select a beginning stretch. Nowadays we wisely fish by well devised solunar tables which foretell with amazing competence the annual day by day mess call for minnow and leviathan. Not all do, however, because the "early" and "late" schools of thought along such lines will remain forever and aye unreconstructed. But in those early days all we had to go by was the "feel" of the barometer, and lore passed on to us by old colored folks back home who had taught us when the "sign" and the "moon" were right. Billy and I had an agreement to keep only extremely worthwhile fish. The "sign" must have been right, for soon we were throwing back trout that would have popeyed the average tourist.

In those primal trouting years I packed the biggest creel made. It was braced with belts of green rawhide that shrunk it into a powerfully gripped basket. On its top was sewn a leather-and-felt fly and leader carrier. I never used a landing net but wore, instead, a thin cotton pallbearer's glove on my left hand. Wet, this would clamp and hold the slippery big 'uns like a vise. And with the fly-book handy, I could stand in heaviest wading water and change, if need be, without having to do several other things at once. The capture of Billy's five-pounder that afternoon was an epic. It was coming half-dusk and, by pressing them down somewhat, I had kept four trout that more than filled my basket end-to-end. Just then I ran onto Billy, fixing to negotiate his fly into a magnificent pool. I can shut my eyes and live it all over again, like yesterday. And when the spell has lifted, I'll be as limp and tingly as I was then, too.

Emerging through one alder around a rocky pool-head, I spotted Billy clambering over a huge boulder at its foot and dropping onto a sandy spit. From the way he let his creel down, I knew it was fish-heavy. On either side of the stream 50 yards of alders, young conifers and willow-tangles matted back to cliffs sheer 300 feet above us. Billy hadn't seen me and I could tell from the way he carefully stripped off line and measured the breaking-belt twixt drop-water from the dam and its out-running, greenish spirals that he was licking his chops and figuring heavy on making his first presentation in this stretch count.

His fly landed precisely where I wished it to, and was whisked off down along the off-ledge suction. Billy's rod tip whipped upward and bent almost before a flash of sullen cream and crimson went off like dynamite where I'd last seen that Royal Coachman. I suppressed a longing to yell my head off, but Billy had all he could attend to right now—and then some. Veteran and cool head that he was, I saw Bill's mouth form a big "O" the first time that rainbow saluted. Then his lips set and he leaned back on the Leonard. His left hand fingered slack like a harpist and he settled down to the struggle he realized lay ahead. He had aboard the kind of trout he liked to skin and mount against lacquered alder bark, and then bake and work on with some spuds and cornbread. He had beach room, but if that fish ever beat him over the dam—his horse would change colors. I yelled too late and Billy never saw the stick of driftwood he tripped over.

Hitting a belly-whopper in the wet sand, he lost slack and came up cussing a blue streak and grabbing for it. But by then the big rainbow was over the falls, with Billy stripping line frantically and dashing for the roaring water gap through which the fish had disappeared. I was within 10 feet of Billy by then and realized instinctively what he intended doing. The quarry was still aboard, I could tell by the tight line. Deliberately seating himself on a roller of that glassy chute-the-chutes, Billy held his rod high above his head and disappeared in the thunderous smother below.

Rushing to a brink-way boulder, I held on against the current's draw and watched the grand finale; fully prepared to have to go in after Billy in case, as was more than probable, he had hit a sunken rock and been knocked cuckoo. But to my relief, he shot out of five-foot water down the pool, got good footing, shook himself and waded shoreward, snatching in slack. That fish must have been deeply snagged for it was in the shallows on the far side and still trying. Gradually Billy worried it into a beachy cove, slid it onto the hard-packed sand, laid down his rod and let go an Indian war whoop. I joined up about then and we sat down for Billy to blow and admire that pretty fish. There was no creeling that fellow, so Billy cut a forked willow.

Walking home wet was nothing in our young lives. While Bill's duds dried around an extra bonfire, we dished up a highly satisfactory bait of vitttles. Dishes done, Billy stuck two candles in a hip pocket and said, "Let's ride down and give that lodge an inspection. I believe the dump is sort of loco."

A nigh full moon climbing over the valley's east wall lit up the stone stairway to the lodge's main terrace. The place was deserted and boarded tight. In the rear an extension "I" obviously housed the service end. We pried open a window with Billy's belt axe and stepped into what proved a butler's pantry. Our candles led us into a dining room. His flare aloft, Billy stopped and whistled softly. A mahogany sideboard flashed with tarnished silver and heavy cut glass. Places for eight were laid at a table loaded with rare old china, costly napery and massive flat silver. Drawers were loaded with damask and exquisite linens. But over everything lay a deep dust film and rat droppings.

Much subdued, we eased into an enormous, round living room, coupled in dull glass. Passages to bedroom suites opened north and south. Magnificent Navajo rugs, powdery and rat-chewed, and streaming cobwebs set off the weird interior, like something from Edgar Allan Poe. Sporting prints adorned the log walls and great elk and deer heads grinned down at us. Billy stumbled upon an enormous music box.

"Maybe the damned thing will play—it'll be more cheerful if it does."

A few turns of the crank and "The Blue Danube" set the rafters waltzing. Half-filled decanters of Scotch and bourbon, poker chips and recklessly flung cards littered a table. Fine hats for men and women hung upon antlered racks. A gun cabinet held fine, rusted rifles, and in a drawer were many handsome revolvers. The four bedrooms revealed closets hung with men's and women's clothing. The bathrooms were exquisitely finished. On one dresser lay a gold and silver-mounted Colt six-gun with solid ivory Bisley grips.

"Brother Buckingham," whispered the awed Billy Mex, "I've a notion to urge that gun to let me and you see it safely home." The music box had played itself out during our brief cruise of the remaining rooms. Having refastened the burglarized window, we walked to the steps leading from lawn to valley floor.

"Jeeps, Buck," gulped Billy, squeezing my arm. "Look back—do you believe me—now?"

A dull, bluish glare was sifting through the boarded lodge window chinks. Billy's fingers crushed my biceps. The next thing I knew we were scrambling to our feet at the bottom of that stone stairway and racing streamward. Neither of us spoke until well past the bridge and at the horses.

"It's gone," gasped Billy, "but we seen it didn't we?" I said we sure seen sumpn'. But the lodge was now just a black blob against the cliffs. I puzzled over the business a long time before dropping off to sleep in my bag. Whatever *thing* that lodge held, I hoped it wouldn't get sore and follow up to pounce on us in our sleep. Just before he dropped off, Billy muttered, "Buck, I didn' know you could sprint that fast, you almos' kep' up with me."

There is something ineffably nostalgic in remembering one's awakenings in fishing camps amid the high Rockies. The last thing one has in mind, lying warm and comfortable in a sleeping bag, is the silvered serenity of moon and stars probing a deep well of black fastnesses, replete with the sounds of nature and wildlife. There is realization that within one's neighborhood some silvertip lumbers or beds, elk and deer feed, and the tinier populations scurry and battle. You hear the sound of strong horse teeth chomping meadow grass, the light thud of shifting hoofs, soft nickers of companionship. You see the dying pin-point of camp fire, as you pull the heavy tarp closer in case a storm blows up.

A pine squirrel's chirruping gradually alarm-clocks one from the void of deepest rest. You lie in utter peace while rearranging a sense of earthiness. Stars are fading into false dawn, nature's night shift is going off watch. The tarpaulin is frost covered, and so is your bag. A gradually graying meadow lies beneath a pall of dull mist. Comes the soft whirr of a daring camp bird's wings. One resolves to be afoot, just as the stream's musical score steals through a still sleep-ridden tolerance. Its tinkle becomes a fortissimo summons, so one sits up, reaches for one's boots, towel and toothbrush. The water will be icy but comforting and, as one passes, a foot prod to the other sleeping bag fetches a grunt of agreement to rise and shine as to breakfast fire. Smoking coffee, bacon grease, rainbow steaks and flapjacks. Take back your king's ransom; we are free men.

Matutinal dishes sanded and soaped, there was a period of silence while tackle was adjusted and hobnailed wading boots laced.

"How many flies you takin', Bill?"

"I never pack but six. When I played baseball all they ever gimme was three strikes. So I'm over liberal with trout when they come up to the home plate. If they don't, or won't hit them six varieties, they're out with me. But I jes' keep fishin' an' hopin' t' outwit their mess call. Fish have their feedin' periods, jes' like us—if we can ever out-figure 'em." I watched him pin Heather Moth, Black Gnat, Royal Coachman, Queen-o-the-Waters, Gray Hackle and California Coachman into his own creel-top fly book.

"Fishin' upstream or down, Billy?"

"Makes no never-mind t' me, Buck. This valley runs north and south, so th' mawnin' sun bein' over your shoulder is jes' a matter of the' c'rick bends anyway. Besides, each pool's an individual nut to crack. Les' meet back here by 11, eat a snack an' hit f' home. An'—le's jes' keep th' real big 'uns."

Writing this, I wonder what the stretch of water I fished that glorious forenoon nearly 40 years ago looks like today. Pretty much the same, perhaps, and I hope to the Red Gods there are fish in it today as heavy and as game and as worthy of their honorable ancestor which rose and gulped my Heather Moth. For I lost one of the three priceless such lures I had along.

Chances are that Valley is full of tourists nowadays, with the c'rick well gamewardened and restocked regularly—which is as it should be. There'll be flamboyantly arrayed dudes riding and packtraining all over the hills and peaks and, God of our Fathers, sheep all over the once restful horizon where our critters roamed untainted. But the sun and moon and stars will be the same, the heights still as overlording, some game left and the air as clear and clean and sweet off the spruce and chockcherries as I ever knew it.

I'll bet the coyotes still sit on their measly thigh sprockets and rifle titled nose anthems against a blue moon, and I'll wager that big spring still gushes from beneath those awe-inspiring cliffs. And what's more, I hope that all the dudes who ride that range and those who come after them have as much fun thereabouts as Billy and I had.

I lost my Heather Moss less than half an hour after I waded a broad, pelting riffle half a mile below camp and cast mouse hackles with silver body trim into a deep, green pool cupped in behind an almost clean-across log jam. I watched the current's swing race the sinking pin point toward me, and held slack at hair-trigger. Half instinct, half surface boil made me strike heavily. And only those who know the sensation of hanging one's fly into a submarine know the "no-give" that challenges wrist and biceps and warns of trouble ahead.

Something whispered I was on the trail of a big trout, but if this fellow got below me into heavy twisters and rapids I was a blowed-up sucker. Once he was almost under the log jam, but I put the pressure on and turned him up the still water. At its end was a pebble beach that I welcomed with open arms. I slid the fish into its shallows and he was a sight for sore eyes. But just as his nose struck some protruding stones and I tightened the leader gently, I saw the fly leave the cat-gut snell. All I held was the leader. Apparently sensing reprieve, the great trout flipped his tail and half-rolled. I lost my head and tried to kick him ashore. But I kicked myself off balance, fell flat, and the last glimpse I caught of Mr. Rainbow was a fleeting flash of white and red disappearing into rapid green depths. And my Heather Moth went with him as the drag pumped dominant life through his gills.

The shame and frustration of that moment still lingers dull red, facially. But from some source I gathered strength to continue, with a brand new Heather Moth and leader to bolster a cheap alibi and a prayer to high heaven to sustain a sense of humor. I must have hooked and released 40 worthwhile fish that morning. But when I sopped into camp there were only six end-to-enders in my rawhided basket, and Billy, vociferous of his luck, had kept eight. Meanwhile, we had accumulated some company.

I recognized Sheriff Sam Himes' red, four-seated buckboard, with its span of rangy roans feeding nearby. Mort Davis, one of Sam's ranch foremen, was along and they were exclaiming over Billy's big trout.

"I stayed at you fellows' ranch last night," said Sam. "Hughie told us where you'd be, so as we were comin' here anyhow, it fitted in."

"Whut you doin' up here, Sam?"

"Well, I'm gonna have t' sell this outfit nex' month, an' as I ain't been here but once in five years, thought I'd better drive up an' check inventory; th' last watchman I had up here run off four years ago. Said th' place is haunted." Billy Mex, cutting up some rainbow chunks, rolled a wise eye at me and winked. The sheriff and Mort were busy helping with Dutch-oven biscuits and hashed spuds with onion, for dinner.

"Haunted?" chuckled Billy. "Whut giv'm that idea Sheriff?"

"Well, 'bout eight years ago I fixed up a deer and bear hunt through here for a wealthy dude and his new young wife, from th' East. Met 'em over at the Springs. They hunted again next year and the boy bought three sections in here, filed on some more land, and put in a big outfit. That lodge cost him a slug of dough. Brought out a lot of expensive and wild city folks every summer; they were really high rollers. Reports of wild parties drifted down to town. Then came some kind of accidental, but fatal, shootin'. The young wife was th' victim. They pulled out the minute the coroner's verdict came in; and no one ever came back. My dude closed the ranch, sold his cattle, put the property in my charge with instructions to just leave it lay. All taxes and upkeep charges have been coming through regularly from some trust company. The dude died recently, and I got orders to sell at auction. The old fellow I had living in the bunkhouse run off."

"Whut did he claim ghosted 'im?" asked Billy. The sheriff stepped over and peered into Billy's deep skillet of sizzling fish cuts. Said he liked his rare. Then he added: "Aw, old Gilley imagined he saw blue lights come and go in th' lodge at night, and heard women folks screamin'." Billy's mouth sort of flew open.

"You boys want t' buy th' layout an' open a tourist joint?"

"Might be an idea, at that," said Billy. "An' that ghost dope would make grand publicity but I'd hate to turn a lot o' dudes loose onto such fishin' water as this." The chuck was all dished so we set-up.

"How about you and Billy helping me and Mort take stock? We can finish by tomorrow noon and I'll give you both time off to fish late and early; in fact, me and Mort will join you."

"We'd have to charge you a pretty stiff fee, Sheriff."

"How much?"

"Oh! We'll take all the firearms, fishing tackle and leather goods—if any—that ain't rusted and ruined."

"Gosh! You're easy pleased, you're on." Billy sighed.

Sitting around that evening munching crispy sow-belly and more rainbow cutlets, the sheriff said:

"Boys, that was an adventure, wasn't it, but I still don't believe what I saw." Billy said, "I still don't believe this fishin'." He grinned and went on cleaning that gold-mounted Colt with the ivory Bisley grips.

"Sheriff," he said, very seriously, "we forgot t' tell you, but me an' Buck seen them blue lights in th' lodge, night befo' las'. But we didn' hear no wimmen folks screamin'. We was jes' fixin' t' look th' place over when she lit up." The sheriff's mouth, full of grub, sort of spilled, but he chewed on through.

"What did you-all do when you saw them blue lights?"

"We run."

••• The father of the Solunar Tables wrote many articles, mostly on eastern trout fishing, for SPORTS AFIELD in the 1930s and 40s. He resisted the normal "rules" about flyfishing, including the one about always fishing above your position in a stream.—MARCH 1949 •••

UPSTREAM OR DOWN?

by John Alden Knight

When, I wonder, are folks going to learn that it is a dangerous thing to attempt to lay down hard and fast rules about fishing? It's been tried many times, always with embarrassing repercussions. No sooner does a fellow arrive at a nice, neat set of common-sense rules of fishing and, still worse, make these rules a matter of public record, than the fish hold a meeting, conspire, and proceed to upset the applecart. Let's take a quick look at a couple of these dicta. Some of them have been found, rather quickly, to be unsound. Others have persisted down through all too many years. It is contrary to human nature to doubt the veracity of the printed word, especially when it's reprinted over and over, time without end.

In his day and age, Dr. J. A. Henshall was No. 1 man on black bass. His book, *Book of the Black Bass*, published first in 1881, was for many, many years—and still is, for that matter—generally accepted as the standard work on the subject. His famous line, "I consider him, *inch for inch*, and *pound for pound*, the gamest fish that swims," no doubt will live forever. Yet in that very book the good doctor makes this astonishing statement.

"It is folly for the angler to cast his flies upon a smooth surface, if the water is clear enough for fishing."

No hedging there, no side-stepping; there it is, an outright, flat-footed pronouncement. In view of what we know of bass fishing today, it is needless to comment on that rule of fishing, save to remind you of the power of the printed word. To show you its lasting effect, this same sentence was used as the keynote of the instructions on fly-fishing for bass in the *Forest and Stream Sportsmen's Encyclopedia*, published in 1923, 42 years later.

Or consider the admonitions we used to receive on the futility of fishing anything other than fast water in a trout stream, especially if we happened to be using dry flies. Fish the fast water if you really want trout. Leave the pools alone. In fast water a trout must decide quickly to take or reject a fly; in a pool he can look it over and take his own sweet time about making up his mind. Don't waste your time in the pools.

Fortunately for some of us, it took the general run of trout fishermen about 25 years to find the holes in that one. Meanwhile we unbelievers had the pools to ourselves. Today it is apt to be the fast water, not the pools, that is fished by the minority.

There are many other instances of exploded theories, but there is neither space nor need here to explore them. Let's take a look—a good, close look—at one of the *un*-explored ones.

Ever since the introduction of the dry fly, we have been coached in the ritual of its use. Fish always above your position, so that your fly will drift like a natural insect. Let the current carry it without motion imparted to it by the leader. Avoid drag at all costs. Always that bugbear DRAG is held up before us as the constant danger signal. Drag, they tell you, is a sure-fire way to put down your rising trout. Shun it as you would the plague. What they don't tell you is why it is common practice to drag a wet fly—and, incidentally, catch plenty of fish by so doing—and not to drag a dry fly. Both wet flies and dry flies simulate, theoretically, natural insects. Why differentiate?

When you come right down to cases, I don't know a better way to put down a big trout than to cast a leader and, still worse, a line over him. Even in a small stream, where the trees and bushes on the bank make it impossible to cast any other way than directly upstream or directly downstream, it is better to approach a large trout from the upstream side. You can say all you wish about curve casts, but the light disturbance that is caused by the fall of a leader and line often will ruin your chances and put down a big fish.

Even though a large fish decides to ignore the leader, an upstream cast often is hazardous. Leaders are hard, resilient things, entirely foreign in "feel" to the sensibilities of a trout. Thus, when a big fellow rises, if his nose happens to touch the leader as he takes your fly the resultant frightened splash will put down every feeding fish in the area.

One June day I was fishing one of the smaller streams in central Pennsylvania. The weather was fine, a solunar period was in progress, and a liberal hatch of big

May-fly drakes was coming down from the riffle above the pool. As I rounded the bend at the tail of the pool, moving upstream, I saw that several large trout were feeding actively to the hatch. Wishing to plan my approach before casting to them, I watched them feed for a while, making careful note of their locations as they rose. There were seven of them, all big fish, and I was pleased to note that the one nearest me was the best of the lot.

This pool is a long, narrow affair, quite deep, and flanked by overhanging trees. It can be fished only from directly below or directly above. I knew that in any event it would be a long cast, as the water was low and gin-clear. The probabilities were that it would be a one-cast job. By detouring through the woods, I could have approached the pool from the upstream side, but I knew that my fly would then be taken by one of the lesser fish upstream, and I wanted to hook the big fellow. After thinking it over, I decided to risk a wide, right-hand negative curve cast, and see if luck would favor me.

Slowly I made my way as close to the feeding fish as I dared. When I was still 50 feet or so from them I began to work out line by false casting. When I had the range, I let go the final cast. It was a good cast and I could see that it was going where I wanted it to go. Unfortunately, at that moment a puff of wind came up the valley, caught my big fly, and straightened the right curve so that my leader flanked the feeding lane, perhaps two feet to the left of the big fish's location. However, the fly looked edible, so he drifted over to take it. Up came his big nose and the leader lay right across it as he opened his mouth. The frenzied splash he made as he discovered the deception sounded like that of a beaver slapping the water with his tail. And that was that.

I reeled in my line and waded over to the bank. There I sat for more than an hour while the May-fly hatch drifted down past me unmolested. During that full hour's time not another fish fed in the pool. Then the hatch was over and all was quiet. Had I approached the pool from above, I am quite sure that, barring unforeseen misfortune, I would have had at least one large trout to show for my pains, and would have saved a full hour of good fishing time.

In the big rivers it is not always possible to take your position directly above a feeding fish. These streams are too sizable for indiscriminate wading. Thus, the downstream technique often must be elaborated with the use of curve casts. Only occasionally, however, do we find an instance where the fly cannot be brought down to the fish with the leader point extending upstream. In these rare instances we cast to the side of the trout's location and, if we do this often enough, usually we can persuade him to leave his feeding station and move toward us. This, of course, places the leader point in line with his direction of motion, still unobtrusive and out of the way so that he can take the fly without touching the hard gut.

Taking big brown trout on light tackle with what have come to be called "orthodox" methods often is somewhat of a paradox. If your tackle is large enough to hold the fish, he refuses to take; if your tackle is fine enough to interest him, more often than not he will smash your terminal gear as though it were gossamer. By using the downstream technique, you can eliminate at least part of this hazard. With your fly coming to him first and the leader and line out of sight upstream, it is not necessary to use extra-fine leader points. Thus, I never fish anything finer than 3-x points, and in the early season I use 2-x points quite successfully.

Here and there in our big Pennsylvania streams there are long, reasonably shallow "flats." These places almost always hold their full share of big brown trout. During broad daylight, it is impossible to come within casting range of a big fish in such water. No matter how much care is used, he will stop feeding while you are still 70 to 80 feet away, and you can cast your arm off for all the good it will do you. Reasoning that there must be some way to take these fish, we evolved the method of drift-wading.

The procedure is to wade out into the feeding lane at the head of the flat. The location of this feeding lane is usually well marked by the line of riffle foam extending right down through the entire pool. Once in position, we cast downstream as much line as we can. Then we strip off line and perhaps 20 to 30 feet of backing. This done, we wade right down through the flat, our fly, leader, line and backing drifting ahead. If the fly is well oiled and the line and all but two feet of the leader well treated with line dressing, we can fish for 200 or 300 feet before reeling in and recasting. The current in these places always is slow, and it is possible to wade along at the same speed so that the tackle won't be pulled under by current action. When we first tried this method, we were surprised at the number of good fish we were able to take—fish that otherwise would have remained untouched from one season to the next.

Even in the fast water, we no longer fish above our positions. Instead, we use curve casts and fish directly across or slightly below. It is not as easy or pleasant fishing as it is to fish upstream, but we do take more trout that way with a dry fly.

Last spring I had the dubious assignment of doing the fishing scenes for a motion picture that was being made for one of the film rental services. Knowing the approximate date of the annual caddis hatch on our streams, I arranged to have the cameraman here at that time. As we had hoped, the caddis hatch showed up on the appointed day and the weather was sunny—sunny but very windy. The trout fed freely to the drifting insects, but the strong wind was blowing upstream. The water had been chosen for its photographical excellence, and was too deep to permit unhampered wading. We had to fish where we could, not where we wished.

With the upstream wind, it was virtually impossible to throw a downstream curve. Never have I seen so many leadershy trout. Just let one of them catch a glimpse of a leader and he would stop feeding for 15 to 20 minutes.

Though the wind was strong, it was slightly puffy and irregular. We adopted the expedient of waiting for a lull, and then getting a curve cast on the water as quickly as possible. After that it was merely a case of selecting the trout you wanted, waiting for a lull, and then drifting the fly to him with a downstream curve. Not once did one of them refuse a fly that was presented to him in that manner. So long as the trout could not see the leader, he took without hesitation.

Inevitably, in downstream fishing there comes a point where drag sets in. What then? If drag does all the horrible things that they tell us about, each trout would resolve itself into a one-cast proposition. After some experimentation I have learned that it is quite practical to utilize drag and convert it from a liability into an asset. I found this out more or less accidentally many years ago. When fishing big water, I would cast across and up (in the correct "orthodox" fashion), and allow my fly to drift down opposite me before picking up to recast. Now and then, in the hope of picking up a fish which had refused my offerings, I would allow the fly to drift down past me. Then when drag set in, I would skip the fly in short jumps across the current in a semicircle until my line was directly downstream. To my surprise, I found that I caught fish that way, but I had heard too many expert instructions to believe that drag could be utilized as an effective method for taking extra-selective trout. Utilize drag! Take fish on a dragging fly! Why, that was nothing short of pure heresy.

One day I was fishing the Brodhead with a friend of mine. We had come to a pool that is a right-angled affair. You know the kind. The current comes in from the side, sweeps across the top of the pool up against the far bank and then down along that bank to the next riffle, leaving a deep backwater eddy to form the center of the pool proper. My friend remarked that he had never caught a trout from that pool.

"Why?" I inquired.

"My fly drifts only about two feet. Then it starts to drag. One cast, and I've put every trout down."

"There are all sorts of drags," I told him. "Why don't you utilize your drag? There must be fish in that pool."

He looked at me as though I were a little mad, and told me to see what I could do. Fortunately, I had on a palmered fly at the time, so I cast it to the edge of the fast water. The line rested on the still water, not moving, so of course the fly began to drag before it had drifted more than a few feet. When drag set in, I raised my rod tip and brought the fly skipping toward me in erratic jumps about eight inches or a foot long. The fly made about three jumps and socko!—up from the bottom of the deep eddy came a nice brownie and took it into camp. A glance at my friend's face showed that a great light had dawned.

◆ ◆ ◆

For a while, when we were investigating the possibilities of a dragging dry fly, we contented ourselves with fussing around with "skater" or "Skitter" flies—big spiders with stiff hackles, sometimes reinforced about the hook shank with an application of clear lacquer. We used these only when we were "bump casting." This highly unorthodox procedure consists of casting in rough water with a fairly short line. The forward cast is aimed so that it terminates at least two or three feet above the water. Then, as the fly drops, the rod tip is raised rather sharply, causing the fly to strike the water at an angle and to bounce once or twice toward the caster before coming to rest.

Bump casting, however, is effective only in rough, broken water. Smooth water requires a longer line, as you can't crowd your trout without scaring them. Thus, the next logical step in this unethical series was the use of a well-greased line and leader, and skittering the big skater flies across perfectly flat water. Strangely enough, this method seems to have unusual appeal to large trout.

Exactly 18 minutes by car from the desk where this is being written is a stretch of trout water that is nearly always surprisingly productive. Year after year it holds its full quota of trout. The area is hard-fished but it is discouraging to the rank and file of the trout fishermen because the trout therein quickly develop a degree of super-selectivity that often is difficult, if not impossible, to combat. A great deal of the time these fish feed on midges, of which there seems to be an inexhaustible supply. When they're doing that, you may just as well fold up your tent.

It so happened that I had located an unusually large trout in this water. Not one of the two- or three-pound ones, but a real old buster of a fish. Naturally, I spent much more time in that pool than was compatible with finished manuscripts and publisher's deadlines. One fine June morning I suffered at my desk until I could stand the pressure no longer. A glance at the solunar tables showed me that I could just about make it, so I climbed into my car and set sail.

♦   ♦   ♦

Sure enough, the solunar period had brought a scattered hatch of flies down from the riffle, and I saw my big fish rise and take one of them. So that I wouldn't disturb the water, I made my way up the bank before wading in quietly to my casting position. There I waited until the big trout fed again.

The hatch was mixed, and I had not been able to see which fly the trout had taken, so I showed him a selection of five imitations of the drifting naturals. Nothing doing. The flies were well tied and they were presented properly, still he wasn't interested. At last, despairing of raising him, I made my way upstream in the hope of picking up a mess of lesser fry. My best effort failed to raise so much as one single trout.

When I reached the top of the riffle, still fishless, I sat down on the bank to think things over. Then I happened to recall that skittering spiders sometimes took big fish, so I tied on a big brown bivisible spider. At that location, using a long, well-greased line, I heaved this cart wheel diagonally across-current and brought it back again below me in a series of short, well-spaced jerks. On the second cast a two-pound rainbow engulfed it with high gusto.

Having dealt successfully with the rainbow, I tied on a fresh spider, oiled it thoroughly, and went down to the home of my big trout. Fearing to crowd him, I cast as long a line as I could, and then started the spider on its erratic journey across the pool. The spider passed over his feeding station without incident and was well out toward the center of the pool when the big boy decided that he wanted it. Over he came, top speed, his dorsal fin cutting the water, and he fell on that spider like a wolf on a rabbit. That he came unhooked after a 10-minute tussle is of little consequence here; what is important is the fact that in water where "orthodox" methods had produced nothing, a skittering fly had hooked two large trout.

Since then, things have been going from bad to worse. We have elaborated the skittering method, combining it quite successfully with the downstream technique. Believe it or not, it really works wonders. This is the system as we now use it.

Suppose, for instance, there is a hatch of insects that look like Gray Quills drifting. Naturally we tie on Gray Quills. These we fish across and down so that the leader stays away from the fish. When the end of the natural drift is reached, we make the fly skitter its way to a point directly below us before picking it up. Should a fish refuse a quietly drifting fly, as a last resort we skitter the fly as it approaches the trout's feeding station. Believe it or not, we have taken more trout on dragging flies than we have on orthodox drifts.

When there is no hatch on the water, we don't resort to the big skaters any more. Instead, we use a palmered version of the hatch which is currently due, and employ the downstream-skittering technique. You'd be surprised how much action we can kick up among a group of nonfeeding trout.

This season it was our pleasure to have as a guest an editor of one of the outdoor magazines. I told him that we had been flying in the face of tradition by taking plenty of trout on dragging flies. He regarded me as though I had lost my mind. Despite his obvious reaction, I showed him the method and then stood back to watch him raise 24 trout to dragging dry flies in about an hour's fishing.

In case you do decide to turn pagan and try out this highly irregular procedure, let me give you a word of warning. *Don't* strike a downstream trout. Light gut simply will not stand the strain. When you raise a fish that is below you, merely lift the rod tip and tighten. That way, your days astream will be long and happy ones and your terminal tackle bills reduced by one half.

••• *A contributor to* SPORTS AFIELD *from 1935 to 1960, Havilah Babcock was the Chairman of the English Department of the University of South Carolina for many years. He wrote mostly of hunting and fishing in the South, in a homey, easy-to-read style.*—JUNE 1950 •••

BREAMERS STOP AT NOTHING by *Havilah Babcock*

When I came to South Carolina 24 years ago, there were three things I swore never to do: eat grits, drink okra soup, and turn catalpa worms inside out. As regards the first two, I have remained stanch and uncompromised. I am still a virgin Virginian. But as regards the third . . .

Well, here I squat above a spillway, with my legs dangling over a tiny maelstrom 10 feet below. And I am straining my bifocals and trying to persuade a three-inch caterpillar that he looks handsomer with his pajamas on the outside of his pants. Which shows how the strongest characters will degenerate in time.

Regardless of how adroitly it is done, catalpa-turning is not recommended for aristocrats, or for prudish souls with overnice stomachs. The catalpa caterpillar is a juicy and overco-operative critter. When turned or squashed in the fingers, it exudes a greenish and bilious-looking substance that leaves an ineradicable black stain on hands and fingernails. A glance at a man's hands will tell you instantly whether he is an addict. It is the badge of the brotherhood of turners.

But there are times, especially in June and July, when the saucy redbreast sun-

fish, which we call the redbreasted bream down here, will disdain all other entice-
ments. During March, April and May, he is not so fastidious. A big green catalpa,
whether turned or unturned, is an irresistible hors d'oeuvre. Inside-out business is
gilding the lily then. But in late season the prized redbreast can be consistently
seduced only by a freshly turned catalpa.

Squatting beside me are two other bream fishermen engaged in a similar
enterprise, and apparently meeting with undistinguished success. They are both
doctors, and their fumbling endeavors in this new field of surgery tickle me no end.

"How are you doing it, Henry?" one asks the other.

"With a matchstick," the other replies. "A fellow told me to push the stick
through the worm lengthwise, then slide 'im off onto the hook."

"How does it work?"

"Nothing to write home about. They turn all right, but won't slip off onto the
hook. I've been arguing with one customer here for five minutes. How are you doing it?"

"With a nail. A fellow gave me the same directions, with a nail. Sounded plau-
sible, but ain't worth a tinker's. Besides, a damned caterpillar just squirted in my
eye and it stings. Wish I had brought my surgical instruments along."

"What we really need is a first-class chiropractor," clucked the other doctor.
"Wouldn't a job like this be duck soup for a chiropractor!"

"What method are you using, Professor?" They both turned to me.

"Gentlemen, your operative technique is wrong," I gravely counseled. "You are
endeavoring to turn them inside out. That is a mistake. Turn them outside in. It is
somewhat disillusioning to hear two more or less reputable physicians confess their
ineptitude at such a simple procedure. When I think of the confidence your patients
repose in you, and your intimate knowledge of anatomy—"

"We don't turn our patients inside out, thank you. Now quit stalling, Prof, and
show us how to do it."

"How much is it worth to you?" I bargained. "When I consult a doctor, I get a
bill for professional services. If each of you will knock off a five-spot from what I owe
you—"

"Go ahead, Shylock. No chance of collecting your bill anyway. I've already told
my secretary to deduct it from my income tax as a bad debt."

"Then if you sons of Hippocrates will come closer, we'll conduct a clinic in
worm-turning. First, remove the head. If you are a stanch States'-Rightist, bite it
off. If you are a sissified Junior Leaguer, pinch it off like this. Then take a small,
long-shanked hook—say a Carlisle No. 8—and place the rounded bottom of the
hook—not the point—into the tail of the patient and press gently, slipping his pet-
ticoat up the shank with thumb and forefinger. Like this.

"Now your caterpillar is upside down, inside out, and outside in, and he
doesn't know his what from a hole in the ground. In other words, he's in a hell of
a shape. Now jab the point of your hook against your thumb to clear it. Like this,"
and I displayed a black-dotted and well-punctuated thumb as evidence of my skill.
"Then you flip this anatomical anomaly into the current 30 feet away and—"

My rigmarole ended abruptly as the line cut a fast monogram across the frothing pool into a foam-capped eddy, and back through the swirling current again. Quite a dancing master he is. Cocky as a bantam rooster. But a moment later a 16-ounce gamester flashes in the sun beside me.

Tricked out in the scarlet finery of spring, the redbreast sunfish is perhaps the most gorgeously hued of the fresh-water game fishes. Its brilliance is always startling, like a resplendent jewel instantly drawn from its case.

And there are two other distinctions I ungrudgingly accord the red-breasted bream: the pluckiest and the most flavorsome of all the pan fishes.

Whenever I am fishing for bream in still water, I use a three-ounce glass fly rod, a leader almost invisibly small, and neither float nor sinker. I want the lure to waft downward with disarming gentleness, precisely as if it had fallen from an overhanging tree. In fast water I make two adjustments: sufficient sinker to carry the hook down under the cypress knees and swirling hammocks, and a leader *stronger than my hook*, so the hook will straighten out to disengage itself when hung.

Otherwise I would be continually replacing tackle, for the handsome reds and the big copper-headed bream (bluegill) hang out in the identical places a hook is most likely to get snagged. A slender hook thus straightened may be readily pressed back into shape between thumb and forefinger. When a body is lost in the mazes of a cypress swamp, a tiny hook can be a precious possession.

The catalpa caterpillar has certain unique advantages as pan fish bait. First, it is not commonly molested by hook-robbers and undersized feeders, as are crickets, earthworms, May flies, wax worms, honeybee and wasp pupae, and other small insects. When you get a strike, the probabilities favor a nice fish. Secondly, the catalpa is so tough-skinned that it will cast almost as well as an artificial fly.

And thirdly, it is so durable and water-resistant that several fish may be successively taken on the same bait. I have taken as many as four without rebaiting.

The necessity of identifying the red-breasted bream, and distinguishing it from the copper-headed or bald bream, would hardly occur to even a tyro in the Deep South. So traditional are these rival species, and so immemorial the arguments as to their relative merits, that any 12-year-old boy from the Carolina low country can write you an "A" theme on either—and probably take you where you can catch a mess.

But for the benefit of those who have never angled in the unreconstructed kingdom, it might not be amiss to say that although the red-breasted bream

(*Lepomis auritis* Linnaeus) and the copper-headed bream (*Lepomis macrochirus* Rafinesque) are both sunfishes, they differ in color, body conformation, habits and habitat.

The redbreast is instantly recognized by its flaming breast and sides, and by its extremely long ears, contrasting sharply with the somber hues and the short ears of the copperhead, which may flaunt a bar of burnished copper across its forehead. The redbreast is also the larger-mouthed and gamier of the two. It shows a marked predilection for rivers and creeks, while the copperhead bream attains its maximum size in ponds and lakes. And the redbreast is regarded as the more palatable, although it is hard to distinguish between two such incomparable table delicacies.

In size, they are similar. The largest redbreast I took this spring ran 21 ounces, the largest copperhead 24. It is always a mistake to weigh a fish, particularly a bluegill, which is undoubtedly the most eye-deceiving and overestimated fish in the world.

When you take a 10-ounce bluegill, you swear that it weighs 14. When you take a 12-ounce specimen, you swear that it weighs a pound.

Our low-country creeks and spillways are famed for their fishing. A serpentine black-water creek that steals its way through a brooding cypress swamp is to me a thing of dark enchantment, a mystic and primeval region where the strangest things happen naturally. And nowhere else on the habitable globe, I think, will one find such an amazing variety of game fish in comparable water.

Although I have fished these swamp creeks for years, I am perennially surprised by the size of the fish that sometimes thread their way up the log-jammed and tortuous channels. In a creek that a boy could jump without splitting his britches, an astute angler might hook a ponderous bowfin, a lithe chain pickerel, or a tackle-wrecking bass.

I have yet to return from an extended swamp foray without fish, and a tale or two to tell. But creek fishing is not without danger and discomfort, especially in late summer. For then the swamp is so infested with mosquitoes, horse flies, deer flies, chigoes and snakes that only a hardy or misguided wayfarer will venture far into its singing recesses.

I am not particularly snake-conscious, proceeding on the theory that a snake is as uncomfortable in my presence as I am in his. But only a witless wight will go blundering through a semitropical swamp in late summer with his eyes shut. There are rattlers and big cottonmouths aplenty, and in July and August the cottonmouths hang head-high from bushes and drop ponderously into the water as you pass.

I have had few upsetting encounters with snakes myself, but last summer I did get into one rather ticklish situation. A rusty cottonmouth blocked the narrow path ahead of me and refused to budge. There he lay hissing his displeasure and insisting on his privacy. Not a blessed stick or rock presented itself. That's one thing I dislike about this Carolina low country: no rocks. You can't for the life of you find one to flatten a chunk of lead, turn a tack-point in your shoe, or throw at a snake.

Well, the big cottonmouth was still coiled and insisting on his rights under the constitution. I was confronted with what a diplomat would call an impasse and a taxpayer would call a hell of a fix. My little glass fly rod had a big catalpa dangling from the tip. Maybe I could tickle this peevish gent into vacating my parlor.

A moment later I rued my impulsiveness, for I had a heaving cottonmouth on a $60 fly rod. It was a brand-new situation for me, and probably for him. I didn't know what to do, but he did. With one massive lunge, the gut leader snapped and Mr. Cottonmouth suddenly remembered a business appointment and highballed it through the swamp, with a hook in his mouth and a green catalpa worm for a chin whisker.

There are people who can detect the presence of snakes by the sense of smell. I have no such gift. There are others who have a strange immunity to marauding insects. I have one swamping acquaintance who swears he has never been bitten by a mosquito, another who is blithely impervious to chigoes. The Lord failed to endow me with such talents.

Whenever I get chigoe-infested, I hit a beeline for 803 Sumter Street and diligently anoint myself with each of the seven brands of guaranteed insect lotion on my shelf. Alice regards such wholesale therapeutics with disfavor.

"That's the trouble with you," she lectures. "When you get sick, you use so many remedies you never know which cures you. When you get chigoes, you use so much different junk you never know which one does the work. Anybody with an ounce of gumption would use one at a time in the interest of science. A good education was sure wasted on you."

Our precious catalpa worms are sometimes hard to get. Incredibly plentiful at times, they are incredibly scarce at others. As a matter of fact, they seem to be scarcest when fish bite best, and most plentiful when fish bite least, but I reckon that's the way the world is run. The trees in my section normally produce four crops of caterpillars a year, with a three-week interval between egg-laying cycles.

During the dearth period between cycles, an ardent breamer will canvass a whole countryside for 100 worms. One friend of mine drove 170 miles on a caterpillar quest. Another had a supply shipped by air from Alabama.

Caterpillar dealers can supply only a fraction of the demand, although many fishermen raise their own worms, or have sources of supply about which they are highly secretive. A man might tell you his wife's age, how he is going to vote, or how much money he owes the bank, but he will lie ingloriously to protect the source of his bait supply.

Catalpa worms, which are universally called "catawbas" down here, retail for three cents apiece in the spring, but during scarce periods a good bargainer can get almost any price he asks, especially around full moon in May, June and July. A full moon seems to affect breamers as well as bream. During May I saw a levelheaded banker pay $5 for 100 caterpillars. During full moon in July, I heard a party of distraught breamers on the Santee-Cooper offer $1 a dozen for the horrendous critters that many benighted folks spray to get rid of.

The worms can be successfully refrigerated for two weeks and thousands of breamers keep emergency supplies in their iceboxes, in spite of indignant squawks from their long-suffering wives. After considerable experimenting, I have discovered a method of preserving the caterpillars almost indefinitely. But try to get me to tell you about it! My most coveted possession right now is the 15 cartons of caterpillars snugly reposing in my deep-freeze, each carton conspicuously labeled for Alice's benefit: "Worms: do not cook."

This spring an 80-year-old South Carolinian fell from a tree and broke his leg—while picking catalpa worms to go fishing. Catalpa trees are notoriously brittle-limbed. Worms were pretty scarce at the time, and after I had related the story to a group of bream fishermen on the Cumbahee, the comment of one clownish fellow broke up the party:

"Wonder if he got 'em all?"

"Every loyal South Carolinian has three ambitions," opines a waggish friend of mine. "He wants to re-fight the Battle of Gettysburg, run for governor on a States'-Rights platform, and inherit a grove of catalpa trees. And he thinks maybe that Gettysburg affair might turn out different, now that we've got the atom bomb factory in Confederate territory!"

••• *Ted Janes wrote for all of the major outdoor magazines in a career that spanned the 1950s, 60s and 70s. And while he covered such varied topics as pickerel, trout, grouse and woodcock, he seemed to reserve his best writing for creatures of the salt.*—JULY 1958 •••

THE SAGA OF VEENIE HOLBROOK by Ted Janes

I stood on the desolate, surf-swept beach watching the helicopter dwindle away like a fat beetle into the September skies. I felt like some latter-day Robinson Crusoe marooned on a desert island. I even had my man Friday in the person of Charlie Drake, who had come over on the first trip and now stood on the shore surrounded by our camping equipment and tackle. Very soon, though, I realized that I had my metaphors mixed. I was Friday, with Charlie doubling in brass of Crusoe.

"Now then," he said briskly, picking up his surf rod, "let's get the duffel up under that dune. That's a good place to pitch the tent."

It all started a few weeks before, when Charlie unfolded a worn newspaper as carefully as if it had been an old treasure map—which in a sense is what it turned out to be.

"I found this in the library while I was looking through some newspaper files for this year's historical pageant. I'm on the committee, you know."

I glanced at the yellowed pages curiously, noting the date, August 10, 1907 . . . "President Theodore Roosevelt To Visit Provincetown . . . Fire Razes Dyer Homestead . . ."

"There," Charlie said impatiently, stabbing a forefinger at the middle of the page. "That's the one."

"CHAMP DOES IT AGAIN," it was headed. *Our champion fisherman, Veenie Holbrook, has broken his own record. The 70-pound striped bass which he brought into Lombard's Market Wednesday morning is the largest bass ever handlined on Cape Cod and outweighs by almost five pounds the 65 1/2-pound "whale" caught by Holbrook two weeks earlier. Congratulations, Veenie.*

I felt my eyeballs twitch as I read it. "Gosh!" I breathed enviously. "Seventy pounds! That's almost the world record. I wonder where he caught it."

I'd have left it there, but not Charlie. "So do I," he declared earnestly. "And I'm going to find out."

It was a project which took some doing, as it turned out. Veenie Holbrook was no longer around to be interviewed and only a few of the older townspeople remembered him and his monster bass. A lot of water had gone over the dam since men had stood on lonely beaches flinging handlines into the surf—summer folks, automobiles, movies, radios and other diversions had come along to change old ways.

But Charlie is persistent. Once he gets an idea he follows it relentlessly, like a slow-but-certain hound on the trail of a running fox. Besides, this sort of research fascinates his legal mind. And one day he came to me in triumph.

"Well, I've found out," he said.

"Found out what?" I asked. I'd forgotten the paper.

"Where Veenie Holbrook caught his bass. It was quite a job. I'll bet I've talked to every old settler in town and I've read the newspaper files for 50 years, but it finally paid off."

"And where was it?" I asked him, a little embarrassed at having the hard-won information dumped in my lap so easily.

"Gull Island," Charlie said, enjoying my surprise. It was his reward for his hours of work. "Right under everyone's nose, including ours."

"Well, not exactly," I objected. "Gull Island isn't exactly accessible."

Gull Island is located off the New England coast, but it might as well be in the South Seas; which would be better because then it might have shady palms instead of being just a treeless sweep of sand dunes and beach grass shimmering under the noonday sun. Once, it was a fairly respectable island, represented on older maps by a good-sized dot which, today, like the island, has shrunken to a pin point.

Once, it boasted a population of 20 families, a church and a school, but men and buildings both had been forced to retreat before the inexorable advance of the sea. At one time a halfhearted attempt had been made to save what was left of the eroding island by constructing a breakwater at one end, but the sea would not be denied and quietly began eating in from the other side.

Several dwellings, along with the church, had been rafted across to the mainland, and the rest had long since been abandoned to the seabirds, which were now its only inhabitants.

"How in the world did Veenie get there?" I asked curiously. "Boats can't land there because of the shoals."

"Apparently they still could in 1907," Charlie said, "because Veenie went in a dory. He used to go at night and for a long time nobody knew where he was fishing."

"And now that you've found out," I said, "it doesn't do us much good, does it? Except for your satisfaction."

"Doesn't do much good!" he echoed indignantly. "Are you crazy? It just means that you and I will inherit his mantle and will probably catch a world-record bass."

"And just how are we going to get there?" I inquired sarcastically. "Fly?"

"Exactly. There's a guy in Chatham that sprays gypsy moths and mosquitoes from a helicopter. For 10 bucks apiece he'll set us down on Gull and pick us up the next day."

My backbone quivered a bit but the moment demanded caution. "That was a long time ago, Charlie, when Veenie caught the big bass."

"Sure it was," he agreed, nodding, "and no one remembers anything about it. Even if they did they can't get there now except by helicopter. It's a natural. We can't go wrong."

I wasn't so sure and I looked for the flaw in Charlie's scheme, for experience has taught me that a flaw there must be. Charlie takes the large view and frequently overlooks a few important details, like Napoleon forgetting about the hidden road at Waterloo. But he seemed to have the angles pretty well figured in this deal—even to the transportation.

"But Charlie . . ." I objected weakly.

"But me no buts," he said firmly. "Bring along some good stout tackle and prepare to have your name in the paper."

And, as it turned out, I nearly did.

But when we were finally all alone on a half-mile strip of sand which was slowly disappearing beneath the sea, I was glad we'd come. I thought of Nauset Beach, Newcomb's Hollow and the other hotspots, jammed with beach buggies and fishermen shoulder-to-shoulder. Here there was plenty of room to swing a surf rod and no sound except the surge and resurge of the surf and the mournful cries of sea birds overhead. This was pioneering, practically virgin fishing on a beach all our own.

"Where do we fish?" I asked, picking up my rod.

"We'll handle this the way Veenie Holbrook did," Charlie said. "It is surmised that the veteran angler reached his chosen spot shortly before high tide."

"Do you have to sound like the *East Chop Bugle* to answer my question?"

"Sorry," Charlie said, "I was just explaining that Veenie fished near high tide. It's low now. Let's explore and see what we can find."

"Okay," I agreed, and shouldering our light spinning rods we headed down the beach.

What we found was a school of bluefish slashing into a shoal of bait just beyond the breakers. A flock of terns wheeling and screaming beyond a sandy point revealed the presence of the fish and sent us scrambling through the soft sand. I got there first and sent a long cast to the edge of the flurrying ruckus. The sand-eel jig hadn't moved two feet before—wham!—a solid strike bent the rod into a dancing bow. At the same time I heard Charlie's panting shout.

"Fish on!"

Pumping and reeling, I brought the battling blue in and slatted him off on the beach, out of reach of the breakers. The next cast brought a jolting strike that missed, and a second later another smashing hit that didn't. Casting, reeling, stumbling up the beach and casting again, we worked the school for the next 30 minutes under a canopy of wheeling birds. The sun felt warm on my back and shoulders, the surf creamed cold around my legs, and when the school went down at last we had nine blues flopping on the sand, blues weighing from four to six pounds apiece.

"This alone has been worth the trip," I exulted as we picked up our fish.

"All this," Charlie said expansively, "and stripers, too."

As we wandered back to camp we found something else. Charlie saw them first. He looked a bit puzzled and I saw him bend over in a couple of feet of water and come up with something in his hand.

"Oysters!" he shouted. "Dozens of 'em!"

And there were. We estimated there must have been 100 barrels of shellfish in the backwater, just waiting to be picked up. We filled our tackle boxes and pockets with them and wished we'd had a bucket.

The sea birds were coming in as we slogged back through the soft sand—gulls and terns along with flocks of sandpipers and yellowlegs that whirred up from the beach at our approach to wheel and settle again behind us.

The last lavender banners of sunset were aswirl in the western sky and a chill had crept into the air when we got back to the tent. Sweaters, trousers and boots felt good. We pumped up the gasoline stove and lantern, and while Charlie opened oysters I dressed a couple of fish. Oysters on the half-shell, bluefish, spuds, corn on the cob and some brownies Charlie's wife had sent along.

"I wonder if Veenie Holbrook ever hit the blues like we did," I mused dreamily, forking up another plateful. "And if he knew about the oysters."

"It is so surmised," Charlie said with his mouth full.

It was dark by the time we'd washed the dishes. Winking stars overhead merged with pin points of light on the mainland, and off to the north at five-second intervals the flash of Highland Light's four-million-candlepower beam stabbed the night sky. In the sputtering glare of the gasoline lantern we rigged our tackle and I felt a sort of tension in the air, a sense of mighty events close at hand. So must Veenie Holbrook have girded himself for the battle half a century before. Charlie glanced at his watch.

"Time to get going," he declared. "We'll have to cut this fine. Tide's high at 11:20. It's now 7:45. We can't stay over high water . . ."

"Can't stay where?" I demanded in surprise.

"On the breakwater," Charlie explained. "That's the secret of Gull Island. That's were Veenie caught his fish!"

"Gosh!" I said doubtfully. I didn't like the glimpse I'd had of the surfswept breakwater that afternoon. "Is that definitely surmised?"

"And alleged and stated," Charlie asserted. "It's perfectly safe if we time it right. We'll have to get out of there about an hour before high tide. That will give us a couple of hours to fish."

The 70-pound striped bass he brought into Lombard's Market . . .

"All right," I said. "But let's get going."

It was dark as a pocket as we began threading our way by flashlight over the slimy, weed-grown, barnacle-encrusted rocks of the breakwater. We had to leave our tackle boxes on the beach and we carried a couple of spare plugs, snap swivels, knives and gaffs hitched to our belts. Even then it was rough going and as we neared the half-way mark, flung spray from pounding breakers made the slippery footing even more hazardous.

We had to wade gingerly up to our knees across a low spot, and half the time we had to crawl on our hands and knees pushing our surf rods ahead of us. Only the thought of those huge stripers kept me pushing forward, that and the thought of Veenie Holbrook making his lonely way along this slippery breakwater by lantern light. It took longer than we'd planned, but at last we stood on the breakwater's end and we could hear the sucking undertow of the rip punctuated by the hissing surge of breakers exploding against the rocks.

I snapped on a big popping plug and flung it into the black witch's cauldron of the rip. Out of the darkness came a muted plop . . . plop as I jerked the rod tip. Behind me I could hear Charlie cursing softly over a backlash. The plug came back and I cast it out again. Once, I heard a heavy splash out in the black water and my heart bounced into my mouth but nothing happened. After a while I changed to an amber plug. I was just snapping it on when Charlie yelled.

"Fish on!"

I could see him silhouetted against the night, bent backwards against the arc of his rod while line streamed from the reel. Then he began pumping and cranking while I watched with fast-beating heart.

"How does it feel, Charlie?"

"He feels all right, but he's acting funny. He's in the rip and . . . here he comes!"

Pumping and reeling frantically, Charlie worked the bass into a rolling breaker which swept it right up onto the breakwater and left it flopping among the rocks. It might have weighed 10 pounds.

"Damn!" Charlie muttered, holding the fish in the beam of his flashlight. "I didn't come out here to catch minnows."

"How big was that fish Veenie caught?" I asked gently. "Was it seven pounds?"

"Seventy," Charlie snapped. "Seventy pounds and . . ."

And then it happened. I'd laid the amber plug far out on the rip and given it a couple of twitches while I kidded Charlie. All at once it stopped moving. If it hadn't been a surface plug I'd have thought it had caught on a boulder. I yanked back instinctively and as I did so my line started rolling out.

You couldn't call it a strike, not the hard, jolting smash you expect from a striper. Instead, this was a ponderous, deliberate engulfment of the plug by an over-whelming force which now surged irresistibly seaward. It didn't even go very fast—it just kept on going.

"Charlie," I said shakily, "I've got on the biggest bass in the ocean."

"You've . . . no kidding?" he gasped, climbing over the rock. "Hang onto him."

That was easier said than done. The fish was still moving out obliquely to the current with no sight of stopping, and I had to lighten the drag against the weight of 150 yards of line. Only 50 yards remained on the spool and that was going fast. It was time for a showdown.

I laid back hard on the rod and the tremendous flurry out in the darkness throbbed up my arms right into my backbone. But the fish turned. Even now he had me at a terrible disadvantage. I couldn't move with him as you would along the beach. All I could do was jam my boots among the slippery rocks and hang on, reel-ing and giving line to the great fish's ponderous surges. With a stout tarred codline I might have been able to hold fast and haul, but not with the tackle I was using.

And shortly I noticed something else. The water which earlier had been around my ankles was now over my knees and some of the breakers were bursting right in my face. Charlie noticed it, too.

"Hurry it up, can't you?" he said anxiously. "It's after 10. We'll have to get out of here before long."

"You can't hurry this baby," I said through clenched teeth. "We've still got half an hour."

I knew I was going to need it, too. I'd had the fish on for half an hour already and he showed not the least sign of tiring. My wrists, arms and shoulders ached and I was drenched from head to foot. But I had got some line back, and given any breaks, I thought now, I might somehow land the fish. And I knew it was a record bass. I've had big fish on before, fish in the 50-pound bracket, and I knew this one was bigger.

I got the breaks but they were bad ones. The water crept higher and a rolling breaker knocked me backward among the rocks. I realized then I'd never make it. Chariles was in high G by now, jittering on the jetty.

"We've got to get out of here," he declared in real concern. "It's after 10:30. Come on."

It was the biggest bass I've ever hooked, probably the biggest bass I'll ever hook. And the cards were stacked against me. I knew now that I was licked. I pulled my knife from my belt and held it in my teeth as a breaker burst over me. For a wild second I decided desperately to stay there and fight it out whatever happened, and in the same instant I knew it couldn't be. The bass saved me the final ignominy. As I hauled back hard against a floundering surge, the taut line sawed across a barnacle-encrusted rock and parted with an audible twang. Reeling in, I clambered after Charlie over the rocks.

It wasn't until then that we realized what we were in for. Coming out had been tough enough, but going back was a triple-plated nightmare, crawling over the greasy rocks with the surf boiling around us, trying to snatch us off into the sucking undertow. I turned to look back once, and the end of the breakwater where we had stood was entirely covered now with bursting surf.

I didn't think we'd make it. When we came to the low place, we had to flounder, half-swimming, half-wading across it, scratched by barnacle and bruised by sharp rock. That was the worst moment, but there was still some rugged going before we finally stumbled half-drowned onto the beach.

Back at the tent we took off our sodden clothes, dried ourselves as best we could and rolled up in our sleeping bags. I was still shaking, not entirely from the cold. My mind kept going over and over the battle with the monster bass but I didn't care about losing him anymore. I was glad to be alive.

"All I can say," I declared slowly at last, "is that Veenie Holbrook certainly earned his record fish and his reputation. It's a wonder he wasn't drowned."

Charlie sat up in his sleeping bag. "Oh, he was," he said brightly. "The next summer. Apparently he pushed his luck and stayed too long. They found his body washed ashore below the breakwater. That's how I found out where he fished."

••• *Vic Dunaway wrote for this magazine in the 1960s and early 70s before giving up his freelance career to become the editor of* FLORIDA SPORTSMAN *magazine. In this story he writes of a record that stands to this day . . . and maybe forever!—*MAY 1969 •••

THE WORLD RECORD BASS
by Vic Dunaway

Thirty-seven years ago, on June 2, 1932, an avid but meagerly equipped young bass fisherman named George W. Perry flipped a plug into the dark waters of Montgomery Lake, Georgia. His topwater lure bobbed on a lake surface rippled by a stiff wind and pelted by intermittent driving rain. Perry thought then (and he hasn't changed his mind over the years) that the weather conditions were the worst imaginable for fishing. But he and companion Jack Page had gotten up before daylight and labored mightily to reach the fishing hole; so in a halfhearted effort to convince themselves it was all worthwhile, Perry gave the big plug a couple of light twitches.

"I don't remember many details," Perry says today, "but all at once the water splashed everywhere. I do remember striking, then raring back and trying to reel. But nothing budged. I thought sure I'd lost the fish—that he'd dived and hung me up. I had no idea how big the fish was, but that didn't matter. What had me worried was losing the lure. It was the only one we had between us."

To Perry's great relief, the "snag" soon began to move. The rest of the tussle, he recalls, was suspenseful enough, though certainly not spectacular. Using all muscle and no finesse, the fish bulled around until exhausted. Perry had known since shortly after the strike that he was tangled up with a bass of extraordinary size, but he was not prepared for the monstrosity he hoisted into the boat.

Later that day, in the town of Helena, the bass was weighed in at 22 pounds 4 ounces. It has stood ever since as the accepted world record for largemouth black bass.

Today, the catch ranks, by all odds, as the most impressive angling record ever set, and the toughest to overcome. Older records and larger ones are in the books but no record has stood so long against such massive assault. America is a nation of bass fishermen. Largemouths swim in every state except Alaska, and it would take a battery of computers to calculate the number of bass taken in the country during the past 37 years, let alone the number of man-hours expended in pursuit of everybody's favorite game fish.

Records are made to be broken, it's said, but this one seems made to frustrate.

What are the chances that heavier largemouth bass will ever be caught? Many anglers and authorities say the odds are surprisingly good, despite nearly four decades of fruitless flailing. They can point out any number of *reported* catches of 25- and even 30-pound bass made over the years but, for one alibi or another, not authenticated. Almost every area of the South has a legendary big bass that would be the world record, if only . . .

Also, several stateside anglers stoutly maintain that a bearded spectre named Fidel Castro—not Lady Luck—has barred the path to a certain new bass record. These folks were privileged to sample the fabulous bass fishing in Cuba's Treasure Lake before Castro shut the door. For a short while, Treasure Lake turned out 15-pound bass by the gross, and it was a rare visitor who did not claim to have hooked and lost a 25-pounder.

Right now certain bass fishermen in the land check their newspapers hopefully each day for some sign that Castro is on the skids. I'll wager that the very first tourist flight to post-Communist Cuba will be at least half booked with panting bass fishermen, each expecting to hook the new record on his first cast.

Unfortunately, the scientist qualified to give the most expert opinion of all sticks pins into the ballooning daydreams of the Treasure Lake fans, for reasons which we will take up a little later. This same authority, Icthyologist Luis Rivas of the University of Miami, believes the record will someday be broken in the southern United States—probably Florida.

With Rivas' prediction to bolster his enthusiasm, how does the bass fisherman begin his calculated assault? Logically, he should explore all details of George Perry's catch for any little item that might be profitably emulated. The location of the famous catch is an obvious starting point.

Several Montgomery Lakes are in the state of Georgia and, in the neighborhoods of each, residents lay stout claim to the record—not in a deliberate attempt to fraudulently advertise their home water, but because they simply assume that *their* Montgomery Lake is *the* Montgomery Lake.

Let George Perry clear this important point.

"Montgomery Lake where I caught that fish," he says, "is sort of a big horseshoe bend in the Ocmulgee River, in Telfair County between Jacksonville [Georgia] and Lumber City."

But Perry discounts the possibility that Montgomery Lake may harbor another record. "It's been filling in ever since. Now it's pretty shallow and weedy."

No encouragement here. Perhaps if we listen to Perry reminisce, we can uncover some subtle clue.

"I was 19 years old that year, and I'd just become my own man. My father died the year before. I had my mother, two sisters and two brothers. We lived three creeks farther back in the woods than anybody else, and in those depression days it was pretty difficult making a living

"As I said, that was the first year I had things under my own control. I took money we should have eaten with and bought myself a rod and reel and one plug. I've never regretted it either.

"I'd fish every chance I'd get, usually with my brother Jim or with Jack Page. We never had more than one lure at a time, because money for a bait was a long time coming.

"One day Jim and I were taking turns rowing the boat and casting with the only bait. One of us—don't remember which one—got a strike, and the lure broke off. Well, we just sort of sat there looking at each other and wondering what to do. We'd come a good way and had hardly started fishing.

"Must have been a t least 15 or 20 minutes later when a big jack [chain pickerel] came up, thrashed his head, and left our plug floating right alongside the boat. We just tied it back on and started fishing again.

"I fished for fun all right, but I always like to bring fish home, too. When I caught that 22-pounder, the first thing I thought of was how nice, a chunk of meat to take home. It was almost an accident that I had it weighed and recorded. It created a lot of attention that day in Helena. The old fellow who ran the general store weighed it. He was also a notary public and made the whole thing official.

"I never even thought about mounting it, or even taking a picture. I just took the fish home and we ate it."

Perry never received much in the way of tangible dividends for posting the top angling record of all time, but recognition has built slowly over the years. A common question he hears nowadays is: "Say . . . you aren't the George Perry who caught that record bass, are you?"

"I suppose if I caught the same fish today," he muses, "I could realize all sorts of gain from it. But that doesn't really bother me."

A pilot, Perry now leases and operates the Municipal Airport in Brunswick, Georgia, and is owner of Perry Aircraft Service.

"No," he says, "I'm afraid there's not much in my story that could help anyone catch a new record. I wish luck to anyone who wants to try, but I won't make any prediction. It seems to me there just aren't as many big fish as there used to be. Over the years I've only caught two other really big ones—both around 15 pounds."

The most serious assault on Perry's record was waged in an all-too-short period of time late in Batista's regime in Cuba, and in the days when Castro was still being hailed as the great liberator.

Appreciable numbers of American sportsmen made the trip and proved beyond doubt that Treasure Lake bass fishing was out of this world. One wide-eyed visitor was Charlie Ebbets, a well-known Miami outdoors photographer who made the trip with writers George Laycock and Buck Rogers.

"Frankly," Ebbets says, "we went down there with the idea of breaking the record, but the fish made monkeys out of us. All of us had fish on that might have topped 25 pounds, but we lost them. In my case, at least, it was a simple matter of getting excited and going to pieces. We must have caught about three dozen fish that weighed over 10 pounds."

A similar tale is told by Lefty Kreh, manager of the metropolitan Miami Fishing Tournament and free-lance outdoor writer, who made a jaunt to Treasure Lake in 1960.

"I've never seen anything like it," he says. "Every few casts you'd have a bass, and the majority of them weighed between four and 10 pounds. On each of two days, the party must have caught a dozen bigmouths from 10 to 15 pounds. And both days I saw much bigger fish than I caught.

"The guide showed me a picture of a 33-pound bass that had been speared by a native fisherman."

With authentic tales like that floating about—and there are many others— how can anyone doubt that Cuba will produce the new record once sportsmen return there?

Ichthyologist Rivas, the most qualified authority to comment on Cuban bass, stocked largemouths into Treasure Lake. He explains his doubts this way:

"The largemouth bass is not native to Cuba," he points out. "It was introduced there. And in every instance where bass were introduced to new waters, the fish have shown a fantastic growth in both size and numbers. All the stories you hear about monstrous bass in Cuba are true—anyway, they *were* true. But histories of other introductions show that this growth explosion reaches a peak eventually, and then the population begins to level out.

"I'm afraid that when fishermen get back to Cuba they'll find the bass fishing, at best, pretty ordinary. In some cases where bass were introduced to waters in Latin America, they boomed and then later died out."

The scientist's remarks concerning great bass fishing in newly stocked waters—followed by an eventual settling down—are supported by experiences in almost every new impoundment in the States. Whether natural or introduced, bass populations in newly impounded lakes invariably flourish—producing many fish of an average size much greater than is the case several seasons later. Lake Mead is perhaps the best-known example of this phenomenon.

So bass fishing in Treasure Lake, today, might range from very good to poor. But Rivas sees little likelihood that it will even approach the bonanza proportions it enjoyed in its pre-Castro heyday.

Inasmuch as Rivas tabs Florida as the most likely area to produce a new record, let's hear his advice on how to fish for it.

"Any bass that reaches 20 pounds," he says, "is a real patriarch. Only a very rare one grows to that size, although I'm sure an occasional specimen might go as high as 30 pounds or so. They're capable of reaching such weight only in warmer regions, and Florida is the best state of all for raising bass.

"Naturally, the record fish would be a very old fellow. He'd be likely to pick out a comfortable spot, and stick pretty close to it. His food would mostly have to swim within snapping range of him.

"This record fish might possibly be caught on a surface plug thrown above his head. But much more likely he'll be taken on a lure or natural bait fished right on bottom and pretty slowly retrieved."

Florida fishermen have always been pretty much rankled that Georgia claims the world record, even though Florida is widely acknowledged as the best bass-fishing state. Should Rivas' prediction come true, we will hear rejoicing south of the Georgia line.

George W. Perry, the current record holder, is no doubt correct in his casual observation that there just "aren't as many big fish as there used to be."

Many waters in Florida are now turning out more big bass—10-pounders and up—than they ever did. But the record threateners are undoubtedly in shorter supply than they were in the good old days.

Dr. James Henschall, America's first great authority on black-bass fishing, in 1904 in the revised edition of his famous *Book of the Black Bass* wrote, "I have taken the largemouth bass in Florida up to 14 pounds on the artificial fly, and as heavy as 20 pounds with bait. It is obvious that where the largemouth black bass does not hibernate, as in Florida, and is active all the year and constantly feeding, its size and weight will be much greater than in northern waters."

Henschall also reported catching "in a clear, deep, lily-bound lake near Altoona, Florida," a bass weighing 23 pounds 2 ounces. How this one escaped the record books is not clear.

Maybe in some other deep, lily-bound lake in Florida or perhaps again in Georgia or another southern state—a bass will one day be taken that tops George Perry's catch.

If it is, don't bet against another 40 years passing before angling's toughest record is broken once again.

••• A native of New York City, Nick Lyons is the founder of Lyons & Burford, a publishing house that specializes in sporting literature. A former professor of English at Hunter College, Lyons has written and edited more than a dozen books, many on fishing, and has written hundreds of magazine articles. In this tale, he writes of a man's life, and what he left behind.—MARCH 1971 •••

THE LEGACY *by Nick Lyons*

I had never known Ed Halliday, of course—neither personally nor by reputation. For a while afterward I tried to find someone who had: someone who had fished with him, someone who could tell me how he approached a pool, what rivers he loved, how softly he could lay down a dry fly, what size stripers he took from which lonely beaches, whether he preferred flat water or the riffles, whether he fished often, in the early mornings, weekdays, autumns, or when and where and how.

But I was not very successful and to tell the truth I didn't try very hard. After that evening I had may own image of the man and whatever he actually was has by now been transformed in my imagination. That's how it will have to remain. I have never even seen a photograph of him. I was once tempted to ask Tom for one, but never did, not even after he finally saw his father. After all, his legacy was not mine.

My former student Tom Halliday had called late one night to ask my advice. His father had died a few months earlier and there was, he said, a certain amount of fishing equipment in the estate. Would I come over and give him an educated opinion?

"Doesn't anyone in the family fish?" I asked. I was rather too busy that wet December to go tramping around the bleak cold city looking at some poor dead bloke's cod rods. I knew Tom had never cast a line, for I now and then make allusions to trouting in my classes: There are metaphors in it for most of what goes on in the world. He had never risen, except once, to ask a sharp and probing question about the "morality" of trout fishing. He had never mentioned his father to me, though the number of times he came to me for certain advice might have suggested he had no father to ask. I knew he was searching for values, for a guide; he was not by nature a rebel and his solitary nature kept him from joining the fashionable student mobs. We shared certain solitary habits of mind.

No. None of the family fished: neither of his two sisters, certainly not his mother, none of his uncles. And they didn't want to bring in a dealer until they had some idea how much the lot was worth. The man had fished a great deal, Tom told me, and his sisters thought his equipment might have some value.

"Are any of the rods in metal cases?" I asked. "Tubes?"

Tom did not remember. He only knew there was now a mass of it in several closets where his sisters lived, and that he had been given a quick look a few weeks after the funeral.

"Didn't you see it in the house?" I asked. "When your father was alive?"

"I didn't live with my father. My parents were divorced. I was only allowed to see him three, maybe four, times."

I agreed to take a quick look and, to the best of my limited ability with such matters, let him know if it had much value. The next evening I met him in the lobby of a dowdy apartment building on the Upper West Side.

The apartment itself was a shambles. Beer cans were littered everywhere; clothes and newspapers were carelessly heaped in the corners; I thought I detected the odor of marijuana. The television was blasting from the other end of the living room and lights were dimmed. A seductive but sleazy girl in her mid-20s was scrunched down into the shoulder of the couch and, as we came in, a bearded young man moved over to the opposite arm rapidly, frowned, and then stared back at the set.

Tom said that the girl was Clarise, his older sister; he'd never seen this particular friend. He brought me directly into a large cluttered room and told me to wait a moment while he fetched his younger sister, Julie. I pivoted slowly in the dim room, trying to find some logic to this bewildering mess. I could not.

A few moments later a whole spate of fishing rods, clustered and extended like lances, came thrusting into the room. There were eight or nine of them together, with one long stick projecting ahead of the others. Even before I saw who was carrying them, I saw the long rod catch against a cardboard crate and bend suddenly in a sharp arc. I leaped for it, shouted wildly, and managed to shove the crate back. I was too late.

"Damn," I muttered. "Clean split."

The girl—quite short, scraggly, and obviously very hip—was unruffled. "Did something drop?" she asked.

"No," I said after a short pause.

"What was that sound. Like didn't you hear something, Tommy?"

"You broke one of the rods," I said. I still couldn't see, among the mess of sticks, which one had snapped. Most of them were thick salt-water affairs.

"I couldn't have!" she announced.

I turned the light on, went over to the pile of rods she'd dropped on a daybed, and showed her the split tip section. I shut my eyes. It was a fine light-ocher bamboo.

The girl looked at it closely, running her fingers across the severed strands. Then she proclaimed, in the miraculous tone of admitting something she rarely admitted: "Like you're right!"

Tom had come over, and he, too, wanted to see the rod.

I disengaged it carefully from the others and held it out, the splintered tip hanging limply where it had broken. It was fly rod—about eight feet, I judged—and a fine one. I grasped the cork handle instinctively, thumb ahead, and moved it gently back and forth. Fine fly rods come alive in your hand. This one leaped, then died. I could feel it in my stomach.

Then my eyes darted to the butt. The signature read:

Dickerson   7604
Ed Halliday

"No. No. No."

"Is it a good one?" asked Tom.

"One of the best," I muttered. "Custom made, too. Is there another tip for this?"

The girl said she'd look and skipped out of the room.

Tom could see that I was upset and asked if the rod could be fixed. I told him it couldn't, not anymore, but that a company on the coast could probably match the broken section from their stock, or build another. It would be expensive, and the rod would probably never be quite the same

"I don't like to see fine things destroyed," Tom said soberly. "I don't know a Dickerson from a Morgan, but if you say it's one of the best . . ."

"It should have been in a metal case. I can't imagine why it was set up like that," I said, bending the splintered tip gently so that the pieces came together—*imperfectly*.

"Julie!" called Tom. "Have you found a case for this rod? Or another . . . another . . ."

"Tip," I said quietly. "Tip section."

"Another tip?"

She came into the room with a heaping armful of tackle, cases and boxes, dumped them onto the daybed, and went back for more. "No cases yet. But I think I saw some near the radiator."

I shuddered visibly and Tom asked me if I wanted a drink.

"Two."

"Let's go into the kitchen."

Several quick shots of Jack Daniels didn't help. And I was anxious and troubled about returning to the room. When we got back the pile had grown substantially. Julie was bringing in, she said, the last of it. She did. She dropped a couple fly boxes, a handful of empty reel cases and a net upon the rest, sighed, and said: "I never realized Ed had so much junk. Clarise brought over some the day we closed up his place, and I took some over in a duffel bag on Harvey's bike, and the uncles carried some. I never saw it all together like this before. There's a regular mountain of it, isn't there, Tommy?"

Though the equipment was in wild disarray, and most of it buried, it was simple enough to see that it had substantial value. There were seven or eight Wheatley fly boxes, six or seven aluminum-rod tubes in canvas or leather carrying cases, a fisherman's carryall, a fine pair of Hodgman waders, a lovely English wicker creel, seven or eight expensive salt-water reels to go with the heavy rods I'd seen. And more. Much more.

It was also simple enough to see that though the equipment was heaped now, the man himself had been meticulous. One quick look into the opened top of a Wheatley box disclosed that. Here and there were corners of his fishing life untouched by his pelican daughters.

I held out my arms, smiled, and said, with as little irony as possible: "How can I help?"

Tom explained that the provisions of their father's will had simply said that all his worldly possessions were to become, jointly, the property of his two sisters and himself. His mother, Rena, had gotten some cash and, when it was secured, had gone off on one of her frequent trips—this time, one of the girls thought, to South America. But they weren't sure. They had decided to sell all this "fishing junk" and divide the proceeds equally—if indeed it had any value; but Tom could have his choice of several items if he had any use for them; the girls certainly didn't. They had heard hostile talk about fishing from their mother for as long as they could remember. "I suppose what we'd like is some evaluation of it all," said Tom, "and perhaps some help for me in choosing one outfit. I didn't want any of it at first, but there's something fascinating about it, isn't there? I doubt that I'll ever use any of it, but I guess that since these things obviously meant something to him, I should keep something."

"All right," I said, "let's unravel some of it."

I began by extracting the salt-water equipment. The big rods were good fiberglass; I suggested their commonness and minimal resale value. Some of the big-game reels looked expensive and I mentioned several places that dealt in such used equipment; I told the confused legatees to try them all and to take the best offer. In a half hour we had gone through all of the heavy gear—surf-casting rods and spinning reels, boat rods and reels, carryalls full of hooks and lures and wire leaders. It all probably had cost in excess of a thousand dollars, but I told them to be satisfied with several hundred. Through private sales they might get more; but they would have to advertise, and without someone knowledgeable on hand, it would be a cumbersome business.

The fresh-water tackle was another matter. Nothing here was cheap, nothing was less than choice. The gear was all for trout, and it was the best. I could not quite reconcile it with the heavy salt-water tackle, but realized my problem: The world of trout has seemed mysterious enough to me for my short lifetime.

I said nothing for a long time while I carefully laid out the fly rods, cases, boxes and miscellaneous gear, each separately and in a safe section of the room. Several times I thought I detected Tom's eyes searching mine while I fingered a particularly fine item.

None of the rods were in their cases. One other besides the Dickerson was fully joined, and I began with these first, trying to match up odd tips with mid and butt sections, some of them warped from heat, nicked badly and otherwise damaged.

"Why weren't they in their cases?" I asked without looking up, as I laid out the three sections of a handsome 8 1/2-foot Orvis.

"We——ll," said Julie. "Like my friend Harvey was over and he wanted to see it all . . ."

"Does Harvey fish?"

"Only from the piers at Sheepshead Bay now and then. He drives this motorcycle, see, and he likes to go down there and sit on the piers and drink a few beers on a hot summer evening."

"Why didn't he put them back?"

"Well, a couple of weeks ago we had it all out, every stitch of it, and well, we were having a little fun with the rods and then it seemed like one helluva lot of trouble to . . ."

"Fun?"

"Some of us were . . . a little high, and were like fencing with the really thin jobs."

"Like this one?" I asked her, holding up the extra tip to the Dickerson. It had several bad nicks in its finish and one guide had been ripped off, but it looked straight and solid still.

"Guess that's one of them."

"And what was this piece of heavy wool doing on the end of this one?" My God, the fully joined rod was a Payne, 7 1/2 feet.

"The cat."

Tom had grown strawberry red. "What about the cat?"

"We were fishing for it."

I closed my eyes and rubbed my forehead. Then I disjointed the rod, running my fingers along its smooth red-brown surface. With old Jim Payne gone, his fine rods had recently tripled in value; in 10 years they would be priceless.

There were no reels to be found for any of the fly rods: No one knew what had happened to them. And there was one case for which we could find no rod. It had been an Orvis midge. Julie finally admitted she had given it to Harvey.

"The motorcyclist? The guy who fishes off piers?" My voice was high and shrill.

"Look mister. Don't talk that way about him. I can do what I want with Ed's possessions. What did he ever do for me? Clarise knows and she couldn't care less. Who are you to come in here making snide remarks? This is my apartment and my junk and I can do exactly what I want with it."

"Shut up, will you!" said Tom abruptly. "I invited him here to help us. The rod you gave away may have been worth a few hundreds dollars. And it was Dad's."

"Well, it's not Ed's any more. I don't care if it was worth 10 thousand bucks. Like it was Harvey's birthday and I told him to pick out a couple of things. He liked that skinny little stick."

"Look, Tom. Maybe I'd better go. This is family business. This equipment was obviously the man's life. It's the very best, and since I take it he wasn't very rich he probably bought it with every spare nickel he had, out of the deepest kind of passion and love. It has financial value. A lot. The demand for a number of these rods will continue to increase, like blue chips. Make the lot of it neat, get a dealer in, or a couple of them, and get bona fide appraisals. Maybe it will end up in someone's hand who will appreciate what's here." I straightened my jacket and asked where my coat was.

"Stay a little longer," said Tom. "Julie, shut your mouth for ten minutes, will you?"

The girl balled up her fist and stamped out of the room.

When she was gone I breathed deeply in and out.

"It's a disaster, isn't it."

"It's criminal," I said quietly. "Look at these fly boxes: They've been left on a radiator, or under a radiator—they're all rusted and most of the flies are ruined. See this fly-tying equipment? The man probably tied each one of those several thousand flies himself. It's meticulous work. Look closely at this Hendrickson and see how carefully it's made. See how straight the tail comes off the shank of the hook? The neat uprightness of the mandarin wings? The delicate pink in the body? The neatly tapered head knot? And look at all these feathers scattered around. Ripped out of the necks. Look. Blue dun hackle—excellent grade; you can't buy blue dun necks like this today. Mashed. Ruined. The net's broken but you could bind up the wood carefully with bait-casting line; you can't buy another old miniature net like this anymore: It's a beautiful little thing and probably helped the man with hundreds of memorable trout. Broken rods, missing reels, fishing for cats with a Payne! My God, Tom, whether you fish or not, this is absolutely criminal to treat fine equipment like this; it's like trampling on someone's white linen with muddy feet."

Clarise came in then, let her shoulders slump a full five inches, put a strand of hair in her mouth, and mumbled, "Oh goddam: this will take months to clean." Then she said: "Look, Tommy, there are a couple of dozen legal matters I gotta talk over with you and Julie since Rena's skipped, and she wants to get out and meet Harvey. So if you can spare 10 minutes maybe we can get them done. Already it's time to be finished with this lousy cheap junk—or are you falling in love with it, like Ed did?"

Tom agreed to go and asked if I'd mind staying alone for 15 minutes.

"Not at all. I'd like to look it all over closely."

"Be back soon," he said and walked out the doorway. Clarise went after him, took his arm, and whispered loudly: "Can we trust him?"

"No," said Tom loudly.

I picked up a couple of the rods and waved them slowly back and forth, perpendicular to my waist. I popped open a few more fly boxes. Perhaps I should make a low offer for it all and try to steal the whole lot, I thought. In a week they'll mash it all anyway.

I picked up the vest, carried it over to an armchair, sat down wearily, and began going though the pockets.

Leader material. Spare leader, dyed. Penknife, small and sharp. Fly dope.

Leader sink. Rubber pad. I put my hand into an inside pocket. What's this? I fished out a little black notebook.

I thumbed through it slowly and saw in a neat fine hand, that it was a record of trips. There was a date, the abbreviation of a stream, a few scattered comments about the condition of the water, an emergence record, and finally, for each day, a list of trout caught and the fly that had taken them. He had done well.

It was a pleasant, valuable little book—with a wealth of stream information it. I would have liked to study it carefully and half thought of taking it. Who would miss it? Who would understand it? Toward the end of the book he had written something else; it took the last six or seven pages. I cannot remember it all, but some words riveted themselves to my brain.

◆   ◆   ◆

"Raining. Sheets and sweeps of it. River growing browner by the minute. River pocked with the bubbles and the lines slanting in. So I sit under this ledge, with pipe and pen, with my good Dickerson taken down and lying across my knees. Gulleys of brown water washing down around me. But it's dry here and there are two nice trout in my basket and I released four more this morning, which started so quietly before sunup, alone, with the mists hovering over the river. Rena would never understand. Never did. Not Clarise. Not Julie. Not ever. Not even the shrill crisp of the morning or the quick disappearance of a dry fly. Not the swallows sweeping down the stream's alley, the stream birds beginning to work while a good hatch gets under way. Not the deep satisfaction of laying down a good cast, a per- fect hook cast, several in a row, 60 or 70 feet of line poised in the air and then reach- ing toward the eddy behind the midstream rock. Not the squirrel who shared my snack a half hour ago. Not the colors of the water or the sharp tug of a fat native trout. They never did. They never will. I was never able to tell them the slightest small bit of it, not any of them. And Tom I do not know.

"One calls it butchery while she butchers everything private and holy in her and everyone near her; another finds it merely boring. Rena tells me I am fleeing my responsibilities. And Tom, they have never let me know.

"Good ladies, I find myself here. The confusions disappear. The sweet mystery of it envelops me. It is full of sweet noises, the air. Perhaps I have failed with you all. You certainly have failed me—and perhaps yourselves. And no doubt Tom. No doubt. I wish to God he could have been here this morning with me, whispering while we suited up in the dark before dawn, talking about flies and stream conditions, and a certain partic- ular trout one or the other of us raised six weeks earlier. He is the one person I would truly have loved to fish with, to communicate the loveliness of being alone with the trees and the streams and the mysteries under the surface. He is the one person I should have liked to tell this morning to. He is my only son, and I can give him nothing. He will not call now that he is a man; he cannot call, he cannot speak to me. I cannot even hope that some day, some how, he will find me, or this piece of bamboo, or this corner of the world where a man can still husband that sure and gentle legacy that is every man's . . ."

◆   ◆   ◆

I closed the little book and waved it back and forth vigorously. Then I rose, still holding it, and began to walk swiftly to the door.

I heard voices coming toward me. I picked up the vest, slipped the little black book into its hiding place, and dropped it casually on the heap.

"Well, I've seen it all, Tom, and there's nothing more I can say. This trout equipment is valuable. The Payne, even thought it's been used for cat fishing, is probably worth $400 or more; the Dickerson somewhat less; the flies can't be sold; the net and boots, this and that, have no resale value."

"What would you suggest?"

I hesitated. "I know you don't fish . . ."

"I think I'd like to try, perhaps this spring."

"It could be arranged."

"I might have to reimburse my sisters if I took it all. Should I?"

"That's your affair, Tom. But there's something of a man you never knew, who you've wanted to know, I think, in all this."

"Perhaps."

"Well, take the Dickerson," I said, "and, if you can get it, the Payne. But if you fish, don't use them for a full five years. Learn on a good glass rod and use it until . . . well, until it seems to be part of your arm. I can show you a little about it this spring if you're really interested. Buy an inexpensive reel for the glass rod, and then, when you're ready, the best reel you can afford—a Hardy or Orvis. The flies might still be good. Some of them. Go through them carefully some night when you have a few hours. But put away one of each pattern, in cork, for a reminder. The waders are ruined. Keep the net."

"Anything else?"

"Yes. Take the vest," I said quietly, picking it up and handing it to him. "It has no value. No value whatsoever. But there are a few items in it that will show you what a proper vest should contain. Your father wore it often, I think, and perhaps you'll find something in it that will help you understand who he was. Otherwise, it has no value."

••• *A Pulitzer-winning syndicated sports columnist for the* HERALD TRIBUNE *until its demise in 1967, and then for the* NEW YORK TIMES *from 1970 until his death in 1982, Red Smith was the most widely read sportswriter in the world. He wrote a number of books, including* RED SMITH ON FISHING *and the critically acclaimed* STRAWBERRIES IN THE WINTERTIME *and* TO ABSENT FRIENDS. *His only story for* SPORTS AFIELD *was written in the third person, as was his style when he was involved in the story.*—SEPTEMBER 1972 •••

A FLING ON THE FLATS
by Red Smith

Posted on the restaurant door is an admonition that the management of New York's Cote Basque has not yet deemed necessary: "Shirts, please," but in spite of that formality the interior decor is casual—plastic walls of a slightly seasick green, formica-covered tables with paper napkins. Ushered to a seat, the guest has a minute to admire a hand-painted picture of roseate spoonbills before Ziggy Stocki, his host, arrives. Ziggy wears a short-sleeve white sports shirt and an air of quiet weariness. He stands leaning against the wall, eyes fixed on a point two feet above the horizon.

"We have some items not on the menu," he says. "We have grouper Senegalese, that's grouper in a brown sauce with almonds, shallots, apples, raisins and curry served with chutney and rice on the side . . ."

This is not a commercial, but the place is The Conch (pronounced Konk) and anybody bent on piscicide in the Florida Keys is advised to fortify himself first with dinner there. It stirs the juices, refreshes the spirit, lifts up the heart and braces a man for whatever indignities the bonefish and permit have in store for him.

Having prepared himself thus in the evening, an incompleat angler presented himself the following morning to Jack Brothers at the Islamorada Yacht Basin. Jack Brothers began life in Sheepshead Bay, Long Island, wandered south shortly after World War II and eventually set up as a fishing guide, thus saving himself from a career as an architectural draughtsman. His invulnerable amiability is proof even against the sports who employ him, and his ability to see fish is admired by Ted Williams, whose own eye could count the stitches on Bob Feller's fast ball.

Loading a skiff with Brothers was Arnold Sobel of Chicago, still walking several inches off the ground after setting a world record for light tackle by taking a bonefish of 12 pounds 2 ounces, on 6-pound-test line. These two have fished together every year since Brothers started guiding, and they have shared some big days.

"In the Miami Metro tournament four or five years ago," Sobel said as Jack steered away from the dock, "I took a big bone on a fly. We headed for home right away so the fish wouldn't dry out and lose weight. The first weighmaster checked it out at 12 pounds 12 ounces, an all-time record for the tournament.

"That tall man on the dock when we left just now, that's Bart Foth, easily the best man with a fly rod around here. He was leading the tournament with a bone of 12-6 taken on a fly. From his boat he could see us come in and he saw a crowd gathering so he came in to find out what was going on. 'Hey, Bart,' they were calling, 'come take a look at a real fish.'

"We had to wait an hour for the second weighmaster, and the photographers wanted pictures so we let that fish lie in the sun on the concrete. When it was weighed again it had shrunk to 12 pounds 10 ounces. We won the tournament but lost the record."

It was an almost windless day, and the sea was a medley of colors Winslow Homer never dreamed of—turquoise and chartreuse, royal blue, lime green, beige and mauve. Brothers steered through a crooked cut to the Atlantic side.

"This is Tavernier Creek," Arnold Sobel said, "where pirates hid out in the old days."

"And rumrunners later," Jack said.

He shut off the motor in an area called Rodriguez Flats, baited two spinning rods with shrimp and began to pole through the shallows. This is what sets bone fishing apart from most other kinds of angling. Sneaking up on the spooky critter is like stalking game in the woods. There is the same sense of stealth, suspense building like steam in a pressure cooker until the dark underside of every wavelet looks like a fish to the unpracticed eye. It takes a fish hawk like Jack Brothers to spot the pale puffs of mud stirred up by feeding bones, the tail of a bottom feeder breaking water or the shadowy torpedoes cruising over coral.

"Fish ahead," Jack said quietly. "No, see that motion? It's a shark. Swishes the tail like a blonde on Fifth Avenue. There's something at 11 o'clock, Arnold. Try it."

Sobel cast a little white jig, his line tightened for an instant, then came in slack. A barracuda had hit the lure, his wicked teeth severing the leader. Twice more Jack saw fish, twice more Arnold cast and two more barracuda had lures for souvenirs.

The other passenger let fly two or three times with one of the rods Brothers had baited. The guide watched with interest as a shrimp shot straight up or splattered into the water a dozen feet away. Quietly he reached for the other rod and set it at his feet.

They moved on to an area called Newport, off Key Largo, and the hunt began again. Jack stiffened. He stopped poling and pointed. Sobel cast straight ahead, dropping his jig with a tiny *plip* in front of a shadow moving from left to right. Then there were two shadows, three, half a dozen . . .

A shrimp splotched into the water close to the boat. At that moment, Arnold struck. He had a fish on, but still the shadows kept coming—a dozen of them, two dozen. Bones came thronging, trooping, traipsing by. Even to the unschooled eye, it was like Times Square at lunch hour.

"Take this," Jack said. He had cast the other shrimp and now he handed the rod over. In a moment a fish was on. "Don't horse him," Arnold said, still playing his cautiously on the 6-pound-test line. The bone that had grabbed the shrimp took off like a blonde in a logging camp. At length he eased to a halt, and with the first turn of the reel the rod straightened. Sharp coral had cut the line.

"Is there any way to prevent that?" Brothers was asked.

"Just hold the rod tip higher," Jack said, "and try to keep pressure on."

With exquisite care, Sobel brought his fish in. "Ten pounds?" Jack guessed. "Where's that Mickey Mouse scale of yours?" The fish went nine pounds. Holding it just above the tail, Jack lowered it into the water and applied artificial respiration, moving it gently back and forth. Each time he drew the fish backwards its gill covers spread. When he let it go, the fish moved tentatively at first, then swam strongly away.

"It's years since I've seen a school like that," Arnold said. "Must've been a hundred of 'em."

Hour after hour the search-and-destroy mission proceeded—all search and no destruction. Once the sport sitting amidships managed to get a cast out in front of cruising bones. He could see nothing, but Jack said a fish paused over bait and went on.

"That tackle you're using belongs to Ted Williams," Jack said. "He checks it out for the manufacturer all winter and when his ball club goes to training camp he leaves it with me. 'See if you can bust it up,' he tells me, 'and let me know how it works.' "

As the afternoon wore on, visibility diminished. A freshening breeze rumpled the surface and the reflection of clouds—"them big white snow sails," Jack said—made it difficult even for him to see fish before they saw the boat.

"We'll still-fish 25 minutes," Jack said. Thrusting his pole into the mud he snubbed the boat against it and flung handfuls of shrimp downwind. Arnold Sobel, a purist, shipped his tackle without impatience. After half an hour he said, "Five o'clock, Jack."

"Five minutes more," Jack said.

Sobel grinned. "Yesterday," he said, "the wind was blowing like hell and we decided to quit. I said, 'One more cast' and took a 10-pound redfish."

"So," it was suggested, "the moral is clear: Always take one more cast and fish five more—ooops!"

The rod tip was a quivering bow. Monofilament peeled off the reel and disappeared as a bonefish raced to the Azores. For 38 minutes by Jack's watch, single combat raged hand to fin. Muscles barely fit to carry a portable typewriter were aching when the fish came in, worn-out but quivering with rage.

"Would you believe 13 pounds?" Jack said. Considering that the American record is 15—it was the world record until a 16-pounder was caught off Bimini last year—the answer has to be no. Still Jack and Arnold sang their hosannas of praise, never once hinting that in still-fishing it is not necessary to stalk fish, it is not necessary to present a lure and a retarded chimpanzee can hold a rod.

Back at Islamorada, Mary Frances Dressing weighed the fish officially—12 pounds 5 ounces.

"When you see Williams," Jack said, "tell him you caught it on that Mickey Mouse reel of his and then step back and hear him scream. You don't have to tell him how you caught it."

Two hours later Ziggy lounged over and leaned against the wall. "We have some items not on the menu," he said. "We have Oysters Bienville, that's oysters loosened in the shell, wrapped in crab with capers and baked under a blanket of Parmesan cheese with 12 or 14 seasonings, I'm not sure what-all. I've got three chefs, a Bavarian, a French-Canadian and a Dane, and they like to surprise me."

Next morning Jack, who had another commission, introduced his friend Eddie Wightman. By local terminology Eddie doesn't qualify as a conch because he foolishly got himself born in Miami up on the mainland. However, before he was a year old he mended his ways and moved down to the Keys. Those green gobbets of coral and mangrove have been home ever since, but Eddie keeps informed about the outside world and its burning issues, from Indo-China to the forced busing of schoolchildren.

"Would you like to try for permit first?" Eddie asked. In the estimation of Florida guides, the permit or great pompano is Stanley Ketchel with fins. He offers a challenge no man of spirit could resist.

"Let's go," said Eddie's new acquaintance.

In a shallow bay within earshot of trucks howling down U.S. Route 1, Eddie shut off the motor and began poling. He said, "A sport I had here asked how a spooky fish like permit could be so close to the highway. I told him the fish were coming through this passage long before there was a road, or men to travel on it."

He had baited a spinning rod with a crab the size of a silver dollar, thrusting the hook through the very edge of the shell so the crab would stay alive. "Want to be strictly on your own or should I back you up?" he asked.

"By all means back me up." He baited a second rod with a crab.

In a little while he saw permit —a school of four or five—or smelled them, for the breeze was fresh and it didn't seem humanly possible to see beneath the ruffled surface. He pointed. The sport took aim. Caught in a crosswind, the little crab sailed wildly. Eddie plucked up the other rod and fired in a low line drive. In a moment he spoke in a hoarse stage whisper.

"A big one's looking at it. No, he passed it up. Must've weighed 40 pounds." The great permit hunt was over.

Eddie started the motor and headed into Florida Bay, the shallow sea between the Florida peninsula proper and the scimitar curve of the Keys. From a cluster of pilings, resentful cormorants took flight.

"Look," Eddie said. "Beautiful!" Softly lustrous in pastel pink, three roseate spoonbills flew across the bow. "They seem to be growing more numerous here," Eddie said with satisfaction.

An osprey sailed by high against the blue. In a treetop silhouetted against the sky, Eddie pointed out the untidy clutter of sticks and seaweed that these fish hawks call home. "You wonder how it stays up there in a wind storm," he said. A merganser flew by, going hell for breakfast. "See if those are white pelicans," Eddie said, handing over binoculars.

Ankle deep on a submerged bar stood a dozen big white waders. The white pelican is a poor mixed-up kid, a saltwater fisherman that breeds in the northwest from Minnesota to the Rockies and vacations in Florida along with tourists from Council Bluffs and ball players in spring training. "They don't dive like our brown pelicans," Eddie said. "Just scoop up fish while swimming."

"There seem to be brown ones on each side," the other said, focusing the glasses. "What are they? Native guides or bodyguards?"

"The brown ones live over there on the mainland," Eddie said. "They were bused over here."

He had been cruising past tiny keys apparently traveling without a plan, but now he pulled up in shallows that looked no different from 10,000 other spots. Might get anything from redfish to snook here, he said. He rigged the rods with little white bucktail jigs.

It was weird. Even for the dude, every other cast produced a fish. Four snook came in cursing foully. Eddie watched one thrash the sea to froth. "He's fighting for something near and dear to him," he said, "his butt."

The same little lure deceived big redfish, alias channel bass, alias red drum. They were overpowered and released. The sport caught a shovelnose shark, a speckled trout and even a sheepshead wearing the prison stripes that used to be *de rigueur* on Florida's chain gangs.

Sea and sky were alive. There were great white heron, blue heron, one black-crowned heron and probably some kippered heron. Small flocks of snowy ibis cruised by, their hooked noses red as rum blossoms.

"Want to go sightseeing?" Eddie asked. He turned toward the mainland and pointed the skiff up a milky creek meandering through brush. "This is Taylor River. All this brush with the thick-root construction is the common red mangrove. That tree with the rumply bark is a buttonwood and over there is a very large black mangrove. See that big spiny air plant up there? I'm surprised some tourist hasn't cut it down. Those are orchids starting to grow on that limb. All along theses banks there used to be alligator lodges. That was one, that hollow there."

They went stalking redfish in the flats. Nature designed the redfish to shore up an angler's shrinking ego. You must hunt him as bones are hunted, but the redfish is patient. Botch up a cast, and instead of spooking off he'll wait around for a second cast, or a third. With such co-operation, failure isn't easy but it can be accomplished. At length Eddie allowed himself a small sigh. "I know a redfish hole that will restore your confidence," he said. He was right. Casting blindly into the area he indicated, his passenger became once more a mighty angler before the lord.

"Does this jig look like a live shrimp to the redfish?" he asked.

"Nine out of 10 of those interviewed," Eddie said, "reported that they didn't know what the hell it was but it was small and they thought they could whip it."

"You cast alright," he said generously, "especially when you can't see the fish you're going after."

"When I get home," his passenger promised, "I'm going to perfect my spin casting on the lawn."

"Won't do any good," Eddie said, "unless you go fishing some more." They were on the way home.

"How long have you been guiding?" Eddie was asked.

"Professionally, 12 years."

"That's a long time to keep your patience."

"It gets easier," Eddie said, "as you grow older."

That evening Ziggy leaned against the wall. "We have some items not on the menu," he said.

`••• Book and magazine author, conservationist, filmmaker, inventor
and founder of the Wulff flyfishing school in Lew Beach, New
York, Lee Wulff was one of the best-known sportsmen in the United
States. He passed away in 1991 at the age of 86. In the
following story, Wulff reminisces about his early days, fishing in
Alaska.—NOVEMBER 1977 •••

THIS WAS MY ALASKA by Lee Wulff

It was like a daydream. Waters were swirling around my waist, making that special sound they make when they slide right over my chest waders. I could feel the pressure of the water at my back, firm and solid, as I held my footing for the cast. The banks on both sides were overhanging with high grass and great pieces of turf hung down, dragging the grass into the flow. There were patches of willows and scattered birches and spruces along the banks, some still secure, others succumbing to the undermining process and hanging from the bank into the stream.

I could picture the insects, even the mice and moles, tragically caught in the shifting sod and sliding down into the steady undercutting sweep of the run, helpless before the trout that lay there. There were indentations in the bank, cutout places between the tangled logs that still clung to the soil.

In each of these cut-bank pockets, I knew a trout would lie. It would be a big trout and a hungry one. A trout that would not quibble as to whether the fly was a 6 or a 2 or a 4, or worry whether the hackle was a true Andalusian blue or a blue-dyed white hackle from Fresno. I knew that just a few yards farther downstream, in the next bank pocket or under the next leaning log, there'd be another, just as eager to take a fly. These dream fish would be primeval trout, untutored by many releases or escapes from an angler's fly. They would strike with the sure abandon of the king of a prime pocket of water. Then, being rainbows, they would shake their heads and leap in bewildered fury. They would run to the open water then dog their way back to the bank where the snags would worry me, where I'd have to slack off and hope their love of speed and the open reaches would call them back to the main flow where I could tire them out.

It would take a long cast but they would take the streamer I had just tied on, a beautiful big Kulik Killer on a No. 2 hook of flashing gold. And when they finally came in with appropriate reluctance, my fingers would take the hook and set them free.

I knew, before I cast, exactly what flow of power it would take to reach the first fish. It was like being in a dream...but it wasn't a dream. It was real. I was back in Alaska again.

I had just stepped into the American River. I could touch the flowing water and feel its coolness. I could see the eddying sand and silt that the current picked up every time I moved a foot. I could hear the birds and see the bear trails on the banks . . . feel the wild loneliness of the land around me. I was back in Alaska, and it was as I'd dreamed this homecoming would be.

Although, according to the Department of the Interior, I am not a "native Alaskan," I was born at Valdez at 2 P.M. on the tenth day of February 1905, just as the steamship *Excelsior* was steaming into the bay and sounding her whistle to alert the town's inhabitants. My earliest memories are of fishing. My mother used to tell me that I was fishing with a bent pin on a piece of string as soon as I could crawl to the "crick" behind the house.

Valdez was a great town for a fisherman's boyhood. The streams had huge runs of trout and salmon, and there was a good smelt run in the winter. From the bay we could catch not only salmon but cod, flounder and halibut. Each fall, when the salmon and trout runs were on, every family in town wanted to salt down at least a couple of barrels of those fish, and a kid who liked to catch fish could fish endlessly and never catch more than his family and his neighbors needed.

There were hundreds of sled dogs in town, and if you add the needs of the dogs to the human demands in that town of 1700 souls the total was staggering. There were no game laws. There was only a vital need and a seemingly endless supply of fish, runs of trout and salmon that streamed into the fresh waters over and beyond the take of the canneries that operated farther out in Prince William Sound.

Early fishing memories come back across the years when I let them. Memories of early summer days when the fields on the way to the two-mile creek were covered with a mottled red blanket of Johnny Jump-ups and shooting stars. But I took only fleeting notice of the flowers.

In spring there were only trout and salmon parr in the streams. This was the time when fish were few and hard to catch. We young fishermen carried some hooks and a length of line. I'd find a place where a log or tree leaned out over a pool and

I'd quietly let my line down to where the trout or parr were moving in the slow current. I'd twist the line to adjust the small single hook and wait till a fish swam over it. Then I'd yank. The yank would carry the small fish right out into the air and up on the bank.

From there on my fishing was more conventional. Now there were two eyes for bait and I'd add a sinker to the line and swinging it over my head, send it out to the deep eddies to rest on the bottom where the bigger trout were. Each fish caught had two more eyes to take out, so the supply of bait from that point on was never-ending.

Fishing with hook and line was fun but there were other methods of catching fish that were more certain and equally entertaining once the main runs came in. These called for different gear and much more stealth and skill. I could fasten a short length of soft copper wire to the end of an alder pole.

Forming the wire into a loop a little larger in diameter than that of the trout I was trying to catch, I would move it down cautiously over the fish's head and fling him out onto the bank. The trout were wild, and the problems of seeing them, then stalking carefully and finally getting the snare in place, were far more challenging and effective than throwing a sinker and bait into the pools.

We made gaffs with a 14/0 shark hook wired to the end of an alder or a bamboo pole. In gaffing the fish we liked to see them first and, as with a snare, drift the gaff gently into position and yank it into the fish. A gaff would bring ashore bigger fish than we could take with a snare, because the soft copper wire wouldn't take the heavy weight and hard twisting. The great value of the gaff lay in its effectiveness in cloudy or turbulent waters. Even though the fish couldn't be seen, if you could read the water and your stroke was good you could connect.

By the time I was 8, I was proficient with the handline, spear, snare and gaff. I was wet to the hips all summer long, either wading wet or soaked over the tops of any boots I wore. We'd wade down a stream, and when the trout that had congregated in the tail of the pool tried to race past us to get to safety we'd strike them with a spear or nail them with a gaff. It took a lot of judgment. We had to be able to see the fish in the twisting eddies (something most anglers never have to learn to do), then, as a trout became a fleeting shadow sweeping by at full speed, we'd strike him with a spear or gaff while allowing for the reflections and refractions and the speed of the water. As with the old market gunners, once you really became skillful you were so deadly that your catch was basically limited only by the number of fish in the waters you worked.

The commonest method of taking salmon during the run was by snagging with a 3/0 treble on a heavy line tied to the end of a 15-foot bamboo pole. Such an outfit gave one a 30-foot reach, and when the fish were thick, the catching was easy. Most of the citizens who were looking for their barrel or two of salmon caught them that way. I thought snagging was too haphazard, and liked it even less when, in my ninth summer, I hooked a big coho on the back fin, pulled back hard and then had the hook pull loose. The big tackle snapped back across my shoulder, looped around my neck and dragged a hook-point across my open lift eye, directly over the pupil. For the better of a year I had a white scar there.

The year I was 10, most of my fishing was done with a character called "Slop Jack." He was the town indigent and handyman. Small and cheerful, he hauled garbage and did odd jobs at the saloons. He boozed a bit, never seemed to have a dime, and lived alone in a small weatherbeaten shack. Slop Jack's main industry, and the one that tied us together, was feeding the sled dogs in the summer.

To most sled drivers, their dogs were just a nuisance in the summer. They required food but they couldn't be worked when there was no snow. So Jack boarded them and fed them. What better ally and companion could he have than a fishing-freak kid who'd go along for just a little gear, an occasional bag of fruit or candy and some wonderful free lunches that came from the saloons where Jack carried out slops.

Spearing, I think, was the prime sport of all. It was more exciting and more deadly than any other method. Anyone who has ever become good at it realizes that it became too deadly to be allowed as pressure on the fish increased. I'm glad I lived at a time when I could learn and enjoy it. Jack and I would work a stream together, sneaking upstream on the banks on each side and spearing the fish we could see from shore. Then we'd wade back down, side by side, taking as many of the fish we hadn't seen on the way up as possible.

Jack was not my only older fishing companion. A friend of my father's, a guard at the local jail named Rosy Roseen, also took me under his wing. Rosy was a displaced Englishman and devoted flyfisherman.

In my ninth and tenth summers I spent a good many hours with him, using first a bamboo pole with wire guides and waxed mason line attached to a six-foot, three-fly silkworm gut leader. In my tenth year I had a combination lancewood and greenheart rod and a fair assortment of flies, some of which I'd tied under Roseen's supervision. When the big runs weren't on, I divided my time between the superb sports of spearing and gaffing with Jack and casting flies for the smaller fish with Rosy.

Such were the days of my youth. Then calamity seemed to fall, and my father gave up the newspaper he ran in Valdez and moved the family down to the States, where my fishing in New York and Pennsylvania, and later California, was far, far different.

While I was reminiscing about my youth I was fishing today's Alaskan dream, a 30-rainbow day on the American River with a few arctic char thrown in for good measure. Our group met at 4:30 where the river flowed into a lake, and with my companions, Dean Hadcock, Jerry Jacob and young Bill Jacob, I climbed aboard the Cessna and flew back to Kulik.

.   I had made that trip to Alaska to be with Jerry Jacob and, in memory, with his father, Jake, a longtime friend with whom I'd often fished the wild trout and salmon waters of Labrador. Jake was a man who loved deeply, both his friends and his fishing places. His angling was worldwide but best of all he loved this Kulik area, the river valleys, the big brown bears that walked the banks and sometimes watched him fish, the bright flashing rainbows that struck his flies. Each year, with a group of friends, he came back to the Kulik area in September. Each year, too, he asked me to join him but that had been a bad time and I hadn't been able to make it . . . until this year. I'd worked out a way to be free and join him in September. When I called to tell Jake he could count on my joining him, Jerry had answered the phone. I said, "Jerry, tell your dad I'll fish with him in Alaska this year come hell or high water."

Jerry said quietly, "You can't fish with Dad, Lee. He passed away three weeks ago." He paused, then added quickly, "But you can come and fish with us. I'm taking Billie for the first time. He's 12 now and he'll be as pleased as I will if you'll join us."

So I joined Jerry and Billie and their friend, Dean Hadcock, another wide-roaming fisherman, to make the pilgrimage that Jake had loved so much.

On a quiet morning, soon after our arrival at Kulik, Jerry and Billie climbed to a long ridge that overlooked the river. There, as he'd wanted it, they put Jake's ashes in a cairn that watched over the valley where he'd found a high point of happiness. When they came back to camp Jerry said simply, "Let's go fishing," and we got into our waders and fished the Kulik.

One day the plane took us to the Battle River, beaching where the Battle flowed into the lake. We made our way over soggy sand to the inlet. The others took the tundra trail to meet the river a mile or so upstream. I inched my way across to an island with an occasional drip coming over into my waders. From here I worked up the main branch through some low and swampy ground.

Working upstream on a big river, where the banks overhang, is awkward. The steelhead weren't seriously interested in dry flies, and trying to work a wet fly or a streamer while backing upstream doesn't give the fly the same teasing approach to a fish he'll get if it gradually moves down from upstream. I leapfrogged upstream for a quarter mile and fished down to the spot where I'd started.

There was none of the rich deep soil we'd found on the American river along these banks. This was rock and gravel with only an occasional pocket of settled-in sand. There appeared to be far less food for fish, too. The major salmon runs were over, and only a few carcasses lay in the water or lined the banks. I didn't expect to find too many rainbows hanging on. An hour and a half gave me neither sight nor feel of a fish.

It's a long way to these wild, uninhabited streams of Alaska, and it's a little surprising to find, after you've dreamed or remembered so long, that it's usually feast or famine. Strike a river when the run is in, and the action is hot. Hit it after the run is over, and it can be dead. I hoped for a straggler and kept fishing, letting my mind drift back.

It was the summer of 1923. I was back in Alaska on my summer vacation as a sophomore at San Diego State . . . to drive a Model T Ford truck over the road from Valdez to Fairbanks, to work as a stevedore on the Valdez dock, and to have a hunting trip in the mountains back of Rapids on the Fairbanks road. Late in August we took the S.S. *Alaska* to Seward to meet the first train to come over the brand-new Alaska Railroad, with a fishing trip afterward. The track had finally been laid all the way to Seward but the grades south of Anchorage were so steep that the inaugural train had to be broken down to two cars, leaving the others in Anchorage and hooking on two engines for the two-car train. When the train pulled in we were part of the small crowd on hand to shake hands with President Harding and his secretary of commerce, Herbert Hoover.

While President Harding went on by ship to sickness and death in San Francisco, my father, his friend Judge Wickersham, a pair of guides and I boarded the train for its trip back to Anchorage. Our guides were Andy Simons, one of Alaska's most famous, and Henry Skilak. We left the train with our canoes and duffel for a trip down the Kenai and up Turnagin Arm to Anchorage.

Judge Wickersham made periodic trips to check the lesser settlements and the backcountry of his district. Dad, as an old friend from his newspaper days, had been invited to go along and he'd run me in to give me what Judge Wickersham had said would be the best rainbow fishing he could offer. The trip had been planned for a long time and I was prepared for it.

I'd been tying flies throughout the winter months and among them was a brand-new idea in flies. It was the *streamer.* I'd copied it from a photo in that year's Abercrombie & Fitch catalog. It was called the Rooster's Regret and was made with a few hackles wound around the shank behind the eye and four long hackle feathers streaming out behind the hook for a startling innovation. The catalog said it was designed for the fighting smallmouth of the Belgrade Lakes but that big trout, too, would take it.

Our first camp was at the mouth of the Russian River where its clear water poured into the cloudy Kenai. This was my father's promised Rainbow Heaven. Andy caught trout after trout on his salmon eggs for a total of 64 in our two-day stay. I caught three times as many, mostly on the newfangled streamers, and one of my fish was by far the biggest. Big enough, it turned out, to take a fishing magazine's contest prize that year.

Two days of pure delight on the Russian and then we took our outboard-powered canoes and went on down the Kenai and up the arm to Anchorage, where we found a few saloons, a church, a small scattering of houses, and, as an added attraction, a cow moose walking down the street.

My musings on the past were interrupted by a solid and unexpected strike . . . and the leap of a four-pound rainbow. In the Battle's fast flow he put on an exciting display before I brought him in and released him. I checked the bear trails and scanned the hillsides but I saw no bears. I listened to the gulls. I watched an eagle. A flock of ptarmigan landed at the stream edge but, for the rest of the morn-ting, I didn't draw another strike. It wasn't till noon, when I had the rest of the group in sight upstream, that the next fish struck.

T his one was a male, beautifully colored, weighing close to 10 pounds. When I brought him to the campfire where the others sat, I found that Dean had caught his twin, a silvery female. They were a beautiful pair. Dean was as elated as an angler can be. His was a bright new moment. Mine was an echo of an old memory.

For our last fishing day we flew back to the American River. Billie was working down ahead of me with a big orange Woolly Worm he had tied the evening before, under my tutelage. He was a quiet boy, old for his 12 years, and very keen about fishing. Jerry had given him a good outfit to use, one of his impregnated split-bamboo rods with a matched line and leader. He had picked up casting easily and was fishing his fly well.

Fishing parties had been flying in to the American almost daily and although the fish had been plentiful and eager on our first visit, they now seemed scarce and very reluctant to take a fly. A lot of the river's stock of rainbows had undoubtedly been caught and released, for, like ourselves, the other parties brought few fish back to camp. As a result we weren't going out in a blaze of glory. I was acutely aware that Billie hadn't caught a very big trout and I kept hoping he'd get one.

I was watching his fly when it bounced off the far bank and dropped to the water just ahead of a half-submerged log.

"Nice cast," I said to myself under my breath.

Then I saw the swirl and sensed rather than saw the lift of his arm and the tightening of the line. My eyes had stayed on the swirling water, for there was a long bright rainbow flash near the log.

For an instant the reel made no sound and all action was frozen. Then the reel sang and the fish raced downstream, leaping as he went. He was a good, big fish and I felt a warm ray of hope for Billie.

Just then I had a strike. A two-and-a-half pound rainbow, like the half dozen we'd caught already, hit the fly and zinged out across the pool. He completely absorbed my attention by ending in a submerged tangle.

Periodic glances told me that Billie was still fast to his big fish and was slowly wearing him down. While I waded out and gingerly pulled and twisted the snag enough to free my fish, Billie had worked down under the high overhanging bank as far as he could go. He was wedged in against the earth wall on a slim shelf under a tangle of willow.

My fish was played out and I reached down to free him, so that I could go and help Billie, when I heard his call.

Pulling the hook free quickly I rushed toward him. He was half-standing, half-falling back against the willows. He had the big rainbow in his arms and he was shouting, "The hook's come out. He's loose! He's loose!"

Handling a big, lively and slippery rainbow isn't easy even for a grown man and Billie was losing his grip. We carried no nets but I had my rod in my left hand and the fly I'd just removed from my fish in my right.

Reaching Billie, I hooked my fly into the rainbow's mouth with a quick motion milliseconds before he slid back into the stream. I handed the boy my rod and picked his up from the mud.

The rainbow rested upright in the shallow water, fanning his fins a little. "Billie," I said, "that's a beautiful fish. He's about as big as any we've taken on this trip. He'll look great on your wall at home."

The boy just stood there for a moment, watching the tired fish. He said, "Grandfather Jake always told me, 'It's the big ones we want most to catch that we should leave in the rivers to breed more big fish for us.' He said the smaller ones may never grow into a really big fish like this."

Now my mind went back to the pristine Labrador brook trout waters Jake and I had pioneered in my seaplane and how great that fishing had been. Together over the years, we'd watched the runs and the fish diminish in size to where two- and three-pound fish were "trophies." They'd cleaned out the big ones and left the runts to breed. I could picture Jake telling all this to the boy.

Billie spoke again, "You *helped* me, too. I know I'd have lost him alone."

He bent down over the fish and worked my fly out of his mouth. Then he gave him a little push and the big rainbow disappeared.

Jake, whose mortal remains were finally at rest on the ridge over the Kulik, had taught his grandson well. I wished with all my heart Jake could have been there at that moment. Come to think of it, he was.

••• *The editor in chief of* SPORTS AFIELD *from 1978 to 1994, and the saltwater fishing editor before that, Tom Paugh loved to write about the big three of the flats: bonefish, permit and tarpon. In this tale, he tells of a special fish that only a chosen few get to see.—*NOVEMBER 1978 •••

MYSTERY FISH AT TURNEFFE ISLANDS

by Tom Paugh

The first day it was E. L. "Wayne" Wheeler all the way. Was it 18 or 20 bonefish he caught? He told us he "lost count, exactly." I didn't lose count of mine. I caught one. But, I discovered, Wheeler, 73 years old and celebrating his 50th year of sportfishing, had a unique bonefishing secret.

Wheeler and I and our wives plus nine other venturesome souls were wetting lines in the Caribbean waters surrounding the Turneffe Islands 30 miles off the coast of Belize (formerly British Honduras) in Central America. With 126 islands in this group, all virtually uninhabited, the place is like the Florida Keys must have been 100 years ago. The Turneffe Island Lodge provides the only facility for visiting fishermen, and the only other humans I saw were a couple of natives keeping lonely watches over lobster pots and fish traps.

We were experiencing what an old friend of mine refers to facetiously as "bonefish weather"—which is to say it was blowing like hell. Because of the wind I had found the fish difficult to see, spookier than usual and generally off their feed. When I did see a fish within casting range and when I did make a cast worthy of a hookup, the bonefish would just pass over my bucktail jig even though it was tipped with a tempting piece of fresh soldier crab or conch.

The second day Wheeler was again camp champ—16 bonefish this time. The Wheeler numbers were actually the total catch between Wheeler and his charming, hard-fishing wife, Dorothy. Dorothy's exact share was not revealed, leading some in camp to speculate that it might have been high. Actually, the first day Dorothy confided in me she had caught only three of the 18 or 20. Wheeler admitted he was now keeping careful count. All eyes in camp were focused on these top rods.

The third day, Tuesday, the wind continued its unrelenting sweep across the mangroves and flats, and the surf pounded white and heavy on the protective barrier reef—second in size only to Australia's Great Barrier Reef. Wheeler and wife showed they were human by catching "only" nine bonefish. They could easily have become the object of jealous suspicion, misplaced despair, outright hate, if they had not been such pleasant, jovial, open folk. Also, as my guide, Burley Garbutt, kept pointing out, the Wheelers never talked about the *size* of their bonefish, only the *number*. We were after quality, not quantity, Burley assured me.

Wheeler proudly showed me his secret. He was using little ball-headed, barehooked jigs. He dressed each hook with a small Mister Twister or similar plastic tail, a favorite of freshwater bass and panfish. The *only* color he used was a translucent chartreuse. I don't know what the bonefish thought it was, but it was working. Tipping it with conch or crab wasn't hurting. But there was more. To the eye of each jig Wheeler attached a tiny Sampo-type ball-bearing swivel with split rings (or a snap) on either end. I, personally, still doubt this was necessary, but it was Wayne Wheeler who was catching the bonefish, not me. On the other hand, Anne and I were not getting skunked. And, Burley kept insisting, ours were bigger.

Wednesday was an important day for me too, not because of anything particular that happened, but because of something Burley said. We were wading a nice flat off the east side of Calabash and had come almost to the end of it when he told me in the lilting dialect of the country (the only English-speaking country in Central America) about the "yellow bonefish."

Actually, I was only half listening. I didn't need a yellow bonefish, I needed a 10-pound regular bonefish. Or, better still, a permit. We had already seen a few permit working the edges, and I had caught a couple of these outstanding gamefish in the past in other areas along this very same reef. But yellow bonefish? When you travel around a lot, fishing here and there, you hear tales. You take them with a grain of salt.

Burley said that there were only three areas he knew of where yellow bonefish had been seen and Calabash was one of them. There was never more than one yellow bonefish in a school, he said. They were very rare and some of the guides in camp had never seen one. Even Burley, guiding every day for so many years, said he had observed one on only six occasions. The other two places to look were Lighthouse Flat and the Mud Flats (located on the west side of the islands).

"'Dis lady come," said Burley, "and she didn't want to fish, jus' look for de yellow bonefish. So we look all week and finally I show her one and she tol' me, 'Now I believe.'"

I am glad Burley told me that story even though I didn't pay it much heed at the moment because Thursday, the very next day, I was to have an incredible rendezvous.

Thursday was memorable for other reasons. The first was that when Wayne Wheeler returned from his day of fishing he reported, "You are looking at a skunked skunk." They hadn't caught a single bonefish. Inwardly, quietly, there was great rejoicing throughout the camp.

Another nice thing happened Thursday. Dr. Russell C. Johnston of Santa Rosa, California, who had been arduously flailing his fly rod in the strong winds all week, caught his first bonefish ever on a fly. He smiled all evening, even while he was eating.

But, I wouldn't have traded places with the good Doctor or any other fisherman in camp that day because Anne and Burley and I had a very mystical experience out in our little boat. We were working the Mud Flats. The bonefish there run in singles, pairs or groups of four, seldom more. And, while you do not see as many fish, certainly fewer schools than in the other areas of Turneffe, the fish do run bigger.

On the Mud Flats you fish from the boat—no wading because you'd sink out of sight in the soft bottom. Wading for bonefish is fun, but, unless the fish are tailing, they are tough to see because you are too close to the water. Standing on the casting platform on the bow of our skiff as Burley poled us along the edge of the mangroves, I could see everything that was happening on the bottom through polarized glasses. We were seeing a lot of barracuda, but not many bones.

I had a rod prerigged for cuda. It was just a basic bonefish setup, actually, but with a little piece of wire to fend off the famous cuda teeth that sever six-pound monofilament as neatly as nail clippers. I use six or seven inches of No. 2 coffee-stained wire with the tiniest saltwater swivel I can buy on one end and a white or pink bucktail bonefish jig on the other, tipped with natural bait if I'm lucky enough to have some. The beauty of such a rig is that if you see a bonefish when you are about to cast to a cuda you can change your mind in midcast. With luck, the bone won't be spooked by the light wire.

I made a cast to an arm-long barracuda that shied away just long enough for a yellowtail snapper to sneak in and grab the hook. Only an instant later, a bigger cuda zapped in from nowhere and grabbed the snapper. I got one jump and a lot of reel screeching out of him before he let go and gave me back the head of the snapper.

As I reeled in, I saw a school of bonefish off to my left and was just about to point it out to Burley and Anne when I noticed the yellow fish in its midst. Because of my previous conversation I knew exactly what I was looking at. The rumor, the wild UFO-type tale, was being confirmed by my own eyes. Then Burley saw it too, and Anne.

The school was in about three feet of water, and all the fish were near the bottom except the yellow bonefish which swam just above. Burley told me later that it is usually that way. The yellow one seems to be the leader or lookout fish for the school. Subsequent interviews with others who have observed this phenomenon (all guides) resulted in the following information and speculation:

• • •

1) No one has ever seen a yellow bonefish dead. There was a rumor that one had been caught and the angler had sent it back home to Florida to be mounted by Pflueger's taxidermists. A call to Jesse Webb of that company squelched that one. Never heard tell of such an animal he told me. Also, Burley, who has seen thousands of dead bonefish netted for the Belize market, but never a yellow among them, speculates that perhaps the fish is only yellow temporarily and loses this color when killed. Perhaps, he theorizes, a bonefish that is yellow one day may be normal in color the next, especially if another takes over leadership of the school. (A new law now protects bonefish and snook from commercial exploitation in Belizian waters.)

• • •

2) A guide by the name of Kent Lesley was the first ever to report seeing the yellow bonefish. Other guides did not believe him at first until more reports came in. I was unable to substantiate the exact date of Lesley's first sighting but it was probably after 1970. I found no reports dating back before that time.

• • •

3) This same Kent Lesley reportedly had a yellow bonefish pick up a hermit crab bait he cast to it, but then drop it before he could set the hook. The former owner of the Turneffe Island Lodge offered a $25 reward to any guide bringing one in. None did. Present owners, André and Phillippe Job, wisely have withdrawn this offer but do want one photographed.

• • •

4) One guide for a fishing camp in Belize told me that he had seen as many as three yellow bonefish in a single school. All guides agreed that the yellow bonefish had been seen only in the Turneffe Islands even though a much greater area off the coast is regularly fished for bonefish. There have been no other sightings reported.

• • •

The school was moving away so I told Burley to try and pole up on the fish, and Anne kept her eye on it as I quickly snapped a 300mm lens on my camera, the most powerful telephoto I had with me. The school was easy to follow with that bright yellow fish to flag it, but they began swimming to deep water and I knew Burley would have no chance to keep up. Starting the motor, of course, would have sent them out of sight even faster. I clicked off three quick shots. I didn't have time to put on a polarizing filter which would have cut the surface glare. The wind was still brisk enough to rough up the surface. In other words, even though the sun was bright, visibility conditions were not that good and photographing conditions were impossible. Even so, when I got my shots back I could see that there was something yellow there—a mysterious, almost alien presence beneath the surface of the water. But a bonefish? You couldn't really tell.

I realized that I was not getting the shot I wanted at the time, yet I could not have been more elated as I watched the school vanish over the edge. For I had seen something rare and felt privileged.

"Now," I said, "I believe."

••• *A regular highlight of* SPORTS AFIELD *in the late 1970s and early 1980s, A. J. McClane's "notebook" series, featuring such gamefish as brown trout, northern pike, smallmouth bass and brook trout, was an especially popular series with the magazine's readers. Known as well for his 1158-page tome,* McCLANE'S STANDARD FISHING ENCYCLOPEDIA AND INTERNATIONAL ANGLING GUIDE, *"Al" McClane passed away in 1991.*—OCTOBER 1980 •••

McCLANE'S NOTEBOOK— BROOK TROUT
by A. J. McClane

In 1734, the Common Council of what was to be the City of New York passed a law that restricted trout fishing in then-popular Collect Pond to "Angling with Angle Rod, Hook and Line, Only." Although the island of Manhattan was laced with ponds and streams, the early settlers had already netted some of these waters to near depletion. Even back then, fishing regulations had to be imposed.

During the next century, the ponds were filled, the streams were funneled into conduits, and the whole island was gradually covered with asphalt. Seemingly, all the ghosts of the past were forever sealed from view. When a water main broke on 58th Street and Madison Avenue in 1956, however, plumbing expert Jack

Gasnick found a brook trout flopping in the gutter as water poured down the street. Like most of his compatriots who work the city's underground, Mr. Gasnick has taken a variety of fish over the years, including pickerel (which are especially prone to getting lodged in fire hydrants), carp, goldfish, smelt, catfish and eels. But this was his first trout—possibly a relic from the Turtle Bay Stream, which still meanders under the East 50s. According to Mr. Gasnick, who has since netted trout in the flooded basements of 301 and 325 East 52nd Street, the stream is audible as it whimpers behind walls and below cellars. Plumbing suppliers and troubleshooters Charles J. Hassel and J. Henry Kling have also collected numerous specimens, adding yellow perch and striped bass to the Big Apple's abyssal checklist.

In the eyes of its nomenclator, *Salvelinus fontinalis* is a "fish of the fountains" and, indeed, there is modern proof. One brook trout erupted from the outlet pipe of a lobby fountain in a newly built Greenwich Village apartment house, which straddles the site of what once was another productive stream—Minetta Brook. I won't speculate on the underground life of salmonids, as I can't even imagine what the pH of a Manhattan water main might be, and heaven knows how trout feed or reproduce in a no-photoperiod environment. Maybe they just wander down from the Catskills along some labyrinthian path and get mugged by a bib faucet. The point is that this beautiful native American char should have vanished from its range years ago—but its spirit is indomitable.

The brook trout was the first species to invade the streams being formed by melting ice in the last Pleistocene epoch of the Appalachians. In her master plan, Nature sent along a companion foodfish, the sculpin, which is also tolerant of extremely cold water. As the ice melted, lakes formed behind barriers on the slopes of the mountains. Then, when the water levels dropped and currents warmed, fishes such as the minnow and sucker began their upstream journeys. In many places, rock slides and impassable falls blocked their entering brook trout habitat in the headwaters. The trout remained in safe havens.

When man (the original Mixmaster) eventually introduced alien brown and rainbow trout to the native, however, a variety of problems began. And in the social fabric of our trout family, the brookie now hangs by a bare thread. Except for certain still-isolated strains, it generally has a shorter life span (five years) than the rainbow (seven years) or the brown trout (10 years). It is much more susceptible to angling and cannot withstand competition from the other species for resting and feeding sites. If you've ever seen a hatchet-faced rainbow nipping the belly of a brook trout in swift, corkscrew attacks, it becomes painfully evident who is boss. The rainbow gets the turbulent, food-rich oxygenated water, while our delicate native gets an inferiority complex.

Pioneer fish culturist Seth Green probably had the greatest impact on the streams of Appalachia through his experiments with an early-maturing domesticated strain that promised a quick solution to our already declining brook trout populations in the 19th century. The intangible, however, was that his stock had a genetic flaw: It had a short life span. These fish were widely introduced and soon dominated what was left of our "wild" trout fishing. Even Ray Bergman, the Dr. Spock of a whole generation of trout anglers, in writing of his experiences during "horse-and-buggy" days in New York waters, felt need of a footnote to the effect that "at this time restocking streams was very uncertain and legal-sized fish were not used for this purpose."

Today, brook trout in eastern upland streams seldom make it beyond three years of age, with a climax size of about 10 inches. The largest native I ever caught in the Catskills was exactly 14 inches long, and that was back in the 1930s. I have taken stocked fish of greater size, but their only bona fides were a club membership and access to a ton of Trout Chow. During the halcyon era of squaretail fishing in Maine, from the 1880s to the 1920s, five-to-seven-year-old brook trout (weighing three and one-half to five pounds) were not uncommon. Presumably, some of this genetic stock has survived as the state continues to produce an occasional trophy fish. In Canada, there are even longer-lived brook trout populations such as the Assinica strain, which attains an age of 10 years or more, and weights of nine to 11 pounds. However, our native trout lives in the delicate balance everywhere because of habitat destruction and overfishing. Foam-flecked rivers running through forests where the logger's ax has never echoed do hold trophy-sized fish, yet any of these could be wiped out tomorrow. Fortunately, enlightened resort operators such as Ray Cooper, who honchos the Minipi River camp in Labrador, offer their angling on a catch-and-release basis. This is the only hope for the last frontier.

Ted Williams and I have a long-standing donny-brook over which is the superior gamefish. Ted batted .400 in his salad days at Fenway Park, and as an angler he scores .500 in my book; when he narrows things down to Atlantic salmon, bonefish and tarpon, the argument is formidable. I can't tell him how to hit a knuckleball, or cast a fly, nor am I able to squeeze the steelhead into third place on his list. I'm tempted to put the South American dorado in first place, and the sea-run brown trout in second place. Tarpon, no. That's where the magic of a name, like the cut of the emperor's clothes, protects a reputation so well established as to seem inviolate. About the time I put my elbow in the spaghetti sauce, I resort to the old homily that there's more to fishing than the fish. To Ted, this is similar to sending in a Little League pitcher, right-handed at that. The truth is, I've never been able to make up my mind. If I named three today, they'd probably be different tomorrow. By his measure, I'd have trouble placing the brook trout in the first 10.

The squaretail may jump gracefully through the air on magazine covers, but in reality it usually flops, squirms and tail threshes at the surface, seldom becoming airborne. A big brook trout is much more likely to dive for the nearest obstruction in powerful surges; in the thunderous rapids of a river like the Gods, or the Broadback, you have your hands full. The squaretail learns his lessons badly, too. He is sometimes seen with a mouthful of rusting flies and broken leaders. I once caught a five-pounder in a small Quebec lake that had a half-dozen hooks in its jaws; if nothing else, the larger fish have needlesharp teeth. But this lack of guile may be a point in the brookie's favor. There is solace in finding at least one salmonid that occasionally lets me feel that I've learned something about fishing. It's not all *that* easy in civilized waters, though, as those natives that survive can be as spooky as any other trout.

For that matter, we had a near wipeout one snowy day in a remote Argentinian lake, where huge brookies swam about in plain sight and ignored every pattern that three anglers could muster. We managed to hook a few, but those were charitable fish. The following day, the weather turned bright and warm as we drove south to camp at Lago Generale Paz. There we caught brook trout in numbers and sizes that still boggle my mind. Fish of four pounds were par for the course, and several exceeded eight pounds. Johnny Dieckman, who was then International Casting Champion, took one that weighed nine and one-quarter pounds. I doubt if his casting impressed the trout so much as his unflagging devotion to hooking and releasing fish from dawn until dusk. He didn't even stop to eat. Originally from Maine, these trout were planted in a noncompetitive vacuum during the 1920s where an abundance of crayfish, freshwater crabs and galaxias minnows composed a rich food supply. I don't know what the present status of Lago Generale Paz might be; on my last visit we had an access problem with Chilean border guards at the productive outlet end of the lake. Our guide was a suspected gun runner (which he later bragged about) and the *soldados* were as friendly as snarling cougars. We decamped with self-congratulations. So whether a record trout is possible at Paz must for me at least wait in the hold file.

In 1916, Dr. William J. Cook caught a 14 1/2-pound brook trout on the Nipigon River in Ontario. This region was famous long before the skilled doctor began his piscatorial operations. His world record is well documented. The other celebrated brook trout, said to be equally as large, was captured by Senator Daniel Webster in 1823. Webster's fish, immortalized in a Currier & Ives lithograph, and with its dimensions traced and then carved into a weathervane for the Brookhaven Presbyterian church, makes a charming legend. Though the facts are confused, it is said that the Senator got up during a sermon and hastened to the stream, where he hooked the great trout while a gathering congregation cheered or chorused hallelujahs. Invocation from the Scriptures may have been part of Webster's technique, but where did he catch the fish? In one version, it was the Nissequogue River and by another, more logical account it was Carmans River—one on the north and the other on the south shore of Long Island, New York. The size of the weathervane was also deliberately exaggerated by its artisan for better visibility. And while both streams have access to salt water, an environment where brown and rainbow grow to record sizes, the anadromous brook trout seldom attains a weight of more than five pounds even after debauching in the bounty of the sea. Worse yet, the sea-run brook trout comes back looking like a used car salesman in a mail-order suit. Although Webster's fish was entered into our Congressional Record many years later, it appears to be an exorcised hobgoblin, lending verisimilitude to an amusing incident—exactly what, we'll never know.

In 1961, the church was moved to nearby Bellport, where both the original weathervane and Currier & Ives version of the faithful black slave Apaius Enos netting Webster's trout (as he captionally exclaims, "We hab you now, sar!") can be seen at the Bellport Historical Society Museum.

The indomitable spirit of a brook trout is challenged in a river such as the Gods. From its top at Kanuchuan Rapids down through Big Bear to Red Sucker, the deep pools and glides give way to bouldery, torrential chutes, which only the expert Cree canoemen can negotiate in their 20-foot canoes. The river narrows and virtually explodes in pebbles and foam at Farting Rapids (the Cree language is often pictographic) and it's a miracle that any fish survive. Below Red Sucker, the river becomes broader and shallower, and here "small" trout of two to three pounds are more numerous. From where the Gods joins the Hayes River, down to York Factory, the water is silted and the mosquito-drenched country dismally barren on the shores of Hudson Bay. Although the upper 50 miles of the Gods is larded with stoneflies, there are few places where one can successfully fish with floating patterns; in most trophy waters, you must send down a big streamer for consistent results. Whatever promise there is for a rise, it usually occurs in the evening, which in my experience is generally true in northern trout country. Morning fishing is best resolved by an extra hour in the sack and another bout with the flapjacks and bacon. At dusk, you might find surface-feeding squaretails in eddies and backwaters; then a bushy Brown Wulff works its magic.

In the northern refugium of *fontinalis*, it appears to me that the largest fish are still found in headwater populations. This is not only true in the Gods, but in other streams along the Hudson Bay shore as well. Many of the smaller rivermouths are badly shoaled or blocked by gravel accumulated over the centuries and only floods or extreme tides make the passage of fish possible. In this land, where all streams flow north, one might assume that the more "remote" pools downstream hold larger trout. The reverse is more likely. You can catch tremendous numbers of two-to three-pound sea-run brookies in some estuaries, but after awhile one is apt to feel like a racehorse delivering a milk route. For trophy fishing, you must still go inland to the "fountains." This brings to mind another kind of brook trout fishing, which in some respects is the best of all.

Ben Hecht once said that the finest country in the world is Youth, and I suppose if that's gone, its corollary is the Country of our youth. When my daughter was about 6 years old, we began visiting a certain brook, far away from the road, that flows down a mountain through dark hemlocks and windfall tangles before joining the river. A stranger wouldn't know the brook exists, because in the last 100 yards or so its voice is silenced where it flows under a vast pile of gravel deposited by countless floods. But up the mountain for about five miles, there is a series of fern-fringed pools connected by bubbly runs and even infant waterfalls. We would pack our sandwiches and spend the day probing greeny pockets with dry flies to find the colorful little jewels that sparkled and danced in the sunshine. I had made Susan a fly rod from a four-foot fiberglass tip section, and although her casts were limited, there were always a few innocents willing to splash at her Coachman. The fishing didn't matter, really. Often we'd just sit on a ledge and watch the trout, who in the pale amber of a pool looked like Chinese mandarins in their jade robes, speckled with blood-red gems, as they swayed in some stylized ritual.

Once, in a drought summer, we followed the brook with dip nets, rescuing those fingerlings that were left stranded in drying, shallow riffles and moving them into permanent pools. I can still see her blonde head bobbing under the rhododendron as Susan netted a fish and ran frantically for the nearest deep spot shouting "Daddy, I got one!" I realized, then, that our brook was literally what philosophers had in mind when they wrote of a stream of consciousness, where a moral obligation is recognized—no matter how abstract. Two decades have passed and nothing much has changed, except now, on the homeward trek, I don't have to carry Susan piggyback anymore, or empty her pockets of salamanders. Or dry her pants.

The lady sits patiently and waits for the old man to get his second wind.

••• *The editor in chief of* SPORTS AFIELD *from 1970 to 1977, Lamar Underwood established the Almanac section that runs in the magazine today. Underwood is still hunting and fishing, but with more wisdom with each passing year, as you'll see from this story.* —FEBRUARY 1983 •••

MIDSTREAM CRISIS
by Lamar Underwood

As the year began, I decided to embrace the advice of my friend Sparse Grey Hackle, who told me "Let the wolf out!" He was dead right. It was the only way to go. No more Mister Nice Guy! My New Year's resolution was a notice served on all creatures, great and small, that in the open seasons ahead I was going to fill my hand. I was fed up with two-trout days, three-bass weekends, and no-deer vacations. I'd had it with calling to bird dogs that wouldn't stand still and turkeys that would (two ridges away!). I didn't want to see another pheasant getting up 200 yards away down a corn row or another bay full of ducks and geese rafted up and preening their feathers under skies that had flown in from Palm Springs.

Government wags told me that in the previous season some 2.5 million hunters had shot 12 million ducks. The calculator that lives beside my checkbook told me that works out to five or six ducks per hunter. I didn't get any five ducks! Who the hell shot my ducks?

All-around, the previous year had not just been bad; it had been a disaster. I zigged when they zagged. The northeasters and I booked into the same places at the same times. I frightened the spots off brown trout while bass slept through my offerings. The deer left the mountain country I hunt; but those from the woods alongside my house found my tulips and peas in the spring, then shredded two young pines during rub-time in the fall. Plenty of geese crossed the pit blinds I hunkered in all season, but they were so high they were a menace to aviation—and they held express tickets.

My dismal performances afield forced me to face what the late John Foster Dulles called "an agonizing reappraisal." Clearly, my tactics were lousy; my timing stank; my equipment belonged in a museum.

I knew better than to seek some all-embracing formula as my game plan. Each subject would have to be tackled separately, tactics and gear made precise. The geese, I felt, would be the simplest problem to deal with. I began squirreling away the bucks to purchase a 10-gauge magnum automatic, with which I intended to wreak havoc on the Eastern Shore. My more-immediate problem—and infinitely more complex—was what to do about those trout.

Since the Romans knew nothing about split-cane rods and matching the hatch, they invented a calendar that starts the new year off from the pit of winter. For me and millions of other fishermen the real new year begins on the opening day of trout season. My usual opening-day scenario looked like this:

An already-pudgy figure, bulked further by enough clothes to outfit the Klondike gold rush, stands hip-deep in a flow of black water torn into sudsy rips by protruding rocks and bearing of the countryside what the winter snows have been holding in storage: sticks, leaves, tires, a bloated cat, the occasional beer can. Overhead the sky is a glowering mass of putty, against which the bare branches of the trees snap and creak with iron-hard stiffness as blasts of wind arrive from Siberia. For hours our man alternates making casts, peering intently at the jaunty little flies that ride the current like miniature galleons, and fumbling stiff fingers through his flybox in search of new offerings. To find a greater fool, you would have to look inside an icefishing shanty.

The bottom of a trout stream is its food factory, and on this day it will not be violated by anything except the soles of el piscator's waders. Although he will soon abandon his dry flies (how quickly the credo fades "I'd rather catch one on top than five down deep"), our man will make only tentative probes into the depths. His wet flies, streamers and nymphs will sweep harmlessly over the heads of the stone-hugging trout. Troutless by 3 o'clock, he will seek the solace of the lodge where fire, firewater and kindred snake-bit companions will be waiting with tales of woe and livers in various stages of distress.

Long before opening day dawned last season, I was determined to never again be a part of this demented tableau.

For weeks I hit the books with an intensity seldom mounted in my professional life. Schwiebert, Whitlock, Marinaro, Swisher-Richards, Caucci-Nastasi—the great masters of flyfishing for trout were devoured. Their instruction manifested itself in a barrage of catalogs and small packages of flies arriving daily from every corner of troutdom. My wading vest bulged with trinkets. Latin names of bugs came trippingly off the tongue.

Opening day. I stood thigh-deep at the head of a pool of black water, frigid and swollen with runoff. Coming to the stream, I had received the usual assortment of reports that the fish were in a coma. The voice on the car radio had said something about snow. None of these things intimidated me at all. This year I was ready.

To meet this early and elemental trouting condition, I pried open a box of nymphs. These were not ordinary nymphs, but masterpieces of illusion—caterpillar-like, hairy-leggy-juicy-looking. Each was weighted with enough piano wire to outfit a Steinway. Never mind that they would hit the water with the finesse of a slamdunk. They would go down, my friend, down, down to the very noses of those frozen wisenheimers. I would fish these creations with a leader hacked to three feet. (Long leaders, I had learned, rise in the pushing and swelling of the current.) The whole outfit would ride down with a high-density sinking line topped by a fluorescent strike indicator to tell me when I had a customer.

You don't cast such a rig. What you do is sort of heave the whole mess out and to one side, paying close attention that a hook in the ear is not the immediate result of the effort.

I watched the curls of line and leader straighten downstream toward a boulder that slashed the smooth flow. I tried to form a mental image of what the nymph was doing—sinking, tumbling, ticking over rocks. The line straightened past the boulder. I paid out three more long pulls from the reel, watching the strike indicator bob on downstream. Suddenly I thought I saw it dart forward. I came back with rod and line and felt the weight of a trout. As the brown—a lovely 15-incher—darted and splashed on the way to the net, my elation soared. My patience and virtue and hard study were to be rewarded. The masters of the game were indeed wise and learned men.

After that, you can imagine my hearthammering excitement when the next 30 minutes yielded two more fish, about the same size as the first.

Then the devil sent his disciples to descend upon me, like a plague of locusts. First one, then two, then three other anglers were crowding into my stretch of water. Not one asked what I was using. They simply assumed I had found "The Place."

Never mind, I told myself. You can afford to be generous. I waded from the stream and pointed up toward uninhabited water. In a few minutes I was sloshing, much too fast, through a bouldery run of pocket water when I felt my right foot sliding down an eel-slick ledge. I lurched hard to the left, but that leg would not bear the burden. I went down into the water on my back with a teeth-jarring crash. Totally submerged for a second, I stood up and cursed my luck and the worn felt soles of my waders. I was drenched, achingly cold, and clearly out of action for the rest of the day.

As I waded to the edge of the stream, I discovered another result of my accident with dramatic suddenness. As I made a little sideways move with my left leg to step around a rock, I felt a nauseating wave of pain. I did not want to feel such a shock again, ever, so now I picked my way gingerly along, trying to protect the knee.

Yuk! Yuk! See the man all soaking wet and limping toward his car. Fat-ass must've fallen in. Yuk! Yuk!

A prominent physician whom I trust sentenced the knee to six weeks of healing. Because I could not wade the stream, I could not fish for trout. The great fly hatches of early spring for which I had prepared myself so diligently came and went: the Blue Quills, the Hendricksons, the Grannon caddis, the March Browns.

My mood was foul and depressed. Without my jogging program, with which I had successfully been losing weight, I quickly regained 10 pounds. Going to work in New York on the train one day I was struck by a thought as morbid as any I've ever had. The obituary page of *The New York Times* named very few males in their 90s. No, the ages of the boys getting their names in the paper were in the 70s and 80s. At age 45 I had the startling realization that in all likelihood I was more than halfway to the barn. Life begins at 80? Give me a break!

Okay, my somber mood told me, so you've lost some of your good moves and speed. You can't hit a 60-yard mallard or sink a three-foot putt. On the tennis court children who can't get into an R-rated film have you gasping like a beached whale. The guide can show you a tarpon at 60 feet, and you may or may not be able to get the fly to it (probably not, given any kind of wind). But relax, buster. For the years have given you wisdom. Look at what you did with those opening-day trout!

I was still clinging to this slightly uplifting notion when I finally got back to the river in late May. One of the year's best hatches remained. According to the grapevine, the Sulphurs had arrived in tentative numbers two days earlier, and all signs pointed to their major emergence late that evening.

The hatch of *Ephemerella dorothea*, which goes on with diminishing consistency for about six weeks on good eastern streams, ranks as a favorite because it stirs smart, self-respecting trout into an unusual orgy of gluttony. Unlike some mayfly hatches, which deliver more sizzle than steak, the appearance of the No. 16 yellow-and-dun flies in the last hour before darkness produces fishing so fast and exciting that it is the stuff for cool hands and stout hearts.

My favorite slick-water was flat empty that evening. My recent misfortune was all forgotten as I waded into position and made a few desultory casts while waiting for the hatch to begin. The air was heavy with humidity, and low clouds on the ridges promised that darkness would come early and perhaps a thunderstorm with it.

The time that passed seemed interminable. Nothing came off the darkening water, not even caddis. A kingfisher flew upstream, scolding my presence. I heard a great horned owl up on the mountain and an answering cry from nearby. Then I saw the first delicate yellow mayfly climbing steeply toward the trees. In a few moments there was another, then another, and then I actually saw one in the instant it left the water—and beyond it the swirl of a trout.

My line arched through the growing dusk. I saw my artificial Sulphur begin its jaunty ride down the feeding lane where the trout had swirled. It floated on downstream unharmed. There were other rises all over the pool now—not splashy waterthrowing slaps, but subtle bulges and swirls.

I really started worrying when my bogus Sulphur made three more rides through the melee without interesting a trout. What was wrong? The fly? The leader? My thoughts screamed as I watched the hatch and rises go on. You've been out of action so long you don't know what you're doing!

In the middle of this burst of self condemnation I saw something—flashes of darting trout just beneath the surface. That was it! The trout were not taking the surface duns! They were nymphing, gulping the insects as they rose to the surface and in the film as they emerged into winged shape.

I was prepared for this, but my hands trembled as I opened the flybox and got out a floating nymph. The light was going fast, but I managed to tie on the fly without digging out my night light. In my excitement, however, I dropped my reading half-glasses into the stream. Klutz! Fool! I should have had them on a cord around my neck.

No matter. I had the right ammo now, and the fish were still going strong as I roll-cast the nymph to the top of the pool. Instantly a trout was on, and I felt a flush of ultimate satisfaction.

The fish was a strong pulsating weight as it struggled upstream for a few seconds. Then the line went slack as the trout bolted downstream almost past my legs, a momentary shadow that caused me to gasp: I was into my largest trout ever.

The reel screamed appropriately as the fish bolted downstream. He reached the lip of the falls that terminated the pool and turned to face the current. The steady pressure on the 5X felt unbelievable. I had the feeling of the fish backing up, backing to the edge of the tumbling water. He was going to be washed over the lip! I had to do something! I palmed the flange of the reel, increasing the drag, and thereby succeeded in instantly breaking off the trout as surely as though I'd been trying to.

I reeled in the sickeningly slack line and looked at the 5X tippet. So many trout were still taking the sulphur nymphs all over the pool that the excitement smothered the loss of the big fish. I quickly had another floating nymph out, ready to tie on. I felt my shirt pocket for my reading glasses and remembered where they had gone. I held the fly at arm's length against the gloom of the darkening sky. No way. I could not thread the eye of the hook in that dimness.

No problem. My night light had a magnifying glass that fit over the top of the light. No sweat, just stay cool.

I was deeply aware of the rises continuing all over the pool as I pulled the light out and draped its cord around my neck. I felt deeper into the pocket for the magnifying glass. It wasn't there! I flipped the switch on the light. Nothing! *Click, click. Click, click.* Still nothing! Okay, the batteries are dead. You're on your own. Now just hold the fly very still against what is left of the sky and tie it on.

My panic rose as I tried unsuccessfully to tie on the No. 16 Sulphur. I tried a No. 14. It would not go. In a final burst of madness and inspiration, I dug out a No. 10 Blonde Wulff, the biggest fly in my vest. Maybe it would work on these feeding fish.

Perhaps it would have. I don't know. I never got the Wulff tied on. My vision is 20/20, but at age 45 I could not see close up well enough to tie on a fly and resume fishing a hatch that I had waited for all winter.

I reeled in slowly, felt the end of the leader reach the reel, then broke down my rod. The splashes of feeding trout popped out from the darkness. I could not see the rises now, but they were distinctive above the murmur the current made as it tailed from the pool downstream.

Slowly the disappointment drained away. The easy moves, the good speed. Going, going with the years. Yet it was true you were wiser, vastly richer in the things you knew. Such as realizing right now that what made fishing so great was that on any given outing, things could happen that you would remember all of your days. Few other times in life could offer that.

That is the easy part of change—the knowing, the feeling. The other side is that you have left something precious behind—something you had used up and would have to go on without.

Flashes of lightning came across the ridgetop, then the roll of advancing thunder. The feeding grew quieter, then died out completely. The bursts of lightning helped me find my way up the hillside to the lane that led back to the car.

I did not know if I had reached the end of something or the beginning.

The wind blew on the high ridges, gusting along the slopes, coming down to the river.

••• *The fishing editor of* SPORTS AFIELD, *from Missoula, Montana, Anthony Acerrano has been writing for the magazine for almost 20 years. He professes a fondness for trout in streams near his home, but he has a special place in his heart for another fish.*—MAY 1987 •••

A GLIMMER IN THE WATER
by Anthony Acerrano

I n bed that night I lay awake and wondered if the silver fish had come in from the ocean. The picture was easy to form: a black night with surf lapping and tide rising, a mist down low on the water. And beneath, in the dark mouth of the river, the shad darting nervously in the swirl and tumble of current, packed tightly, waiting for the signal to plunge upstream.

The school would be large and, if caught by sudden light, would glimmer as one piece of silver, the main body wavering, a few stray individuals flicking here and there at the edges, adjusting position.

It was easy to imagine them this way and then to lift the camera eye up and out, back into the damp and foggy night. Then there was only black water and mist and the sounds of surf, with no hint of the nervous school below. Here the world split into distant, distinct halves. The fish could not see a man on the bank; he in turn would be ignorant of them. Though it was the thinnest of membranes—a mere skin of surface film—the barrier, perceptually speaking, was as thick as a rock wall.

As I lay in bed, in the middle of a dark and chilly night, listening to the rhythmic moaning of a foghorn, this seemed a shocking, even a profound revelation, as though I'd stumbled onto a fundamental truth of nature. If the profundity seemed to leak a little when the light of morning came, it leaked even more when we got to the damp banks of the Umpqua and learned that the shad had not come in. Or if they had, the itch was stronger than normal, sending them far upstream. But this seemed unlikely, or, at least, against the pattern. Terry, who knew the river better than most, cast intently for an hour before issuing the final degree: The fish were definitely not in.

"Nothing to do but wait," he said. "Just keep pitching. Sooner or later, they'll come."

Waiting is a singular fact of the shadding game, and it can be pleasant or exasperating, depending on your outlook and the mood of the weather. Spring on the Oregon coast runs from damp to sodden, sodden to miserable, and before long miserable becomes such a standard way of life that it's considered normal. A visitor to these parts must become adept at translation. When a local says the weather has been "pretty good," he means it's drizzled steadily for a week. "A little on the damp side" means the drizzle has turned to cold, beating rain, and "not too good" tells you the rain has been icy and ceaseless for a month. This underplaying of the weather is not so much an intentional deception as it is a practical adaptation. The locals don't sweat the rain for fear of going mad. Better, after all, to make oilskins, hip boots and rainsuits a part of daily life than to end up babbling in a rubber room.

Actually, once you've dressed against the cold and have a good shell of waterproofing between skin and rain, the continual gloom and leakage isn't all that bad. It can even be cozy if you adopt what is known as The Right Attitude. Then you can enjoy the sensation of standing calf-deep in the river, casting tiny jigs for shad while rain patters on your hood and little rags of cloud hang like smoke in the folds of the mountains. Naturally it helps if the shad are in and the action is steady. When you have three- to five-pound fish jumping and flashing all over the place, putting respectable bends into a light spinning or fly rod, rain is only the gentle mist of the gods.

Other days are not so lucky, and The Right Attitude dims quickly as a chill crawls beneath your clothing and too much rain leaks down your neck and up your sleeves, and the constant pattering on your hood is calculated torture. Sniffles and a distinct lumpiness in your brainpan forecast the arrival of a sinus cold. The river is empty of fish, and you wonder why you get involved in these kinds of things and make solemn oaths to go south rather then west next spring, down to where the sun shines hard and the days are lastingly warm.

Then—sometimes—the shad rip in, as if from nowhere, and for an hour or so your rod rarely stops dancing. Later you make plans to come back next year, to this precise spot, at precisely the same time. By now your sinus cold has arrived but is more or less ignored. A little sniffling, after all, means nothing whatsoever to a real fisherman.

◆ ◆ ◆

Now we move back several years and down a few hundred miles into California, where we see a beginner on shad, one who's heard about these fish for years and who now wishes to catch some. He reads the daily newspaper and finally finds a little squib announcing the arrival of the first runs. He cancels work for the day, perhaps the week, and drives off to discover the Sacramento River. Our boy is from Montana, and it's with some moodiness that he realizes the Sacramento, even in its best moments, is a far cry from the Big Hole. "Hey, you don't like it, go back where you came from," someone says, when he mutters aloud. Fair enough. But first there's the matter of these shad, the chunky silver fish with a reputation for being aquatic hand grenades on a fishhook, just the thing to cheer a homesick fisherman in desperate need of salvation on light tackle.

The first rule of shad fishing was not long in coming and was relayed by a baitshop owner who not only enjoyed the certainty of his convictions but also displayed an enviable talent for rolling a cigar around in his mouth, from one corner to the other, without using his hands. He dipped dead minnows from his bait tank with a tiny net and lectured as if to a gathering of the hearing-impaired.

"You gotta be there when the *shad* are there, or it don't mean squat!" he yelled. "Best fisherman in the *world* can't catch them if they ain't there. I know. Been fishing here for 50 years, and believe me, I know." I believed him. But I was curious: How *does* one know when the shad will be in?

He rolled the cigar in a quick circle and glared at me. "When you lived here 57 years like me, you know. Don't ask how, you just know."

Now, I was willing to pay my just dues, but 57 years seemed a little excessive. Originally I'd been thinking in terms of three days to a week.

My next informant looked even older but was in fact younger, a victim of a hard lifestyle that included vast quantities of cheap wine and damp nightly lodgings in a local culvert. He wore a floppy, trail-beaten felt hat and a grayish scraggle of beard. His face was long and pale, and his eyes had the sheen of liquid chocolate. He was said to be the best shad fisherman in town.

"You want to catch shad," he said, "you want to hit the really heavy runs, there's only one way to do it. *Live* on the river. Every morning I get up, I make a few casts into the pool. I do the same after my nap in the afternoon. And again just before dark. You do that every day for a month, you'll hit it right, sooner or later. That's the trick."

Since spending a month on the river, much less in a culvert, was not entirely practical, or even desirable, I had to forgo his advice and continue floundering about in my own way, trying the best pools, casting proven lures into the current, over and over. Still, try as I might, I did not catch, or even see, a shad.

Two days later my luck improved, when I learned about a multilinked phenomenon known as the Shad Grapevine. It extends throughout the northern West Coast and explains how thousands of fishermen manage to show up suddenly at the first sighting of a silver scale in the water. The arrival of shad coincides with a thunderous ringing of phones.

In my own dim and outsider's way, I plugged into one of the minor currents of the grapevine, and soon I was knee-deep in the American River, near its confluence with the Sacramento, standing alongside a few dozen other hopefuls. It wasn't long before I felt my first West Coast shad perform gymnastics against the ultralight rod. Unfortunately my hand was too heavy, or the fish's mouth too light, or both, and the little shad dart came back empty, save for a spongy white particle of oral tissue skewered near the barb.

"Don't horse 'em!" the guy next to me screamed. Apparently my lost fish was a direct affront to his integrity. Blushing I pretended not to hear. I cast four or five times before hooking my next fish, which I coaxed in softly despite its leaps and splashes. The guy who had screamed was catching nothing, and maybe I took a little longer than necessary to remove the hook and release the fish, turning it broadside toward him for excessive lengths of time.

This petty display at least served to shut his mouth, though it failed to stop him from inching closer and closer with each cast, until it seemed we were both fishing from the same pair of waders. I endured this coziness because by some unknown quirk of fortune I continued catching shad, one after another, while he took none. Finally, when his breath grew too warm on my neck, I splashed out of the water to find a less-peopled run.

The last time I heard from the grapevine it was a voice from Oregon saying, "Yeah, get on down here. The run is on." So I packed the truck and headed for the Umpqua. It was a day-and-a-half drive, and by the time I got there conditions had changed. Heavy rains filled the river, and the shad, by all appearances, had fled back to sea.

It was still raining hard the next morning when Terry and I hit the water, a dismal fact I compounded by having forgotten to pack my rainsuit, which is about as sapient as forgetting your boots on an elk hunt. It didn't take long for the chill rain to soak into the depths of my underwear. From here it was only a matter of hours before the first sniffling and sneezing forced a Kleenex break. I shrugged and kept casting. I had not been a steelheader all these years for nothing; a cold in the Oregon rain was like coming home.

That night I lay awake and sniffled and listened to the foghorn and pictured the silver fish moving up into the dark mouth of the river, but the fish had moved only in my imagination. In the morning the river itself seemed empty. I cast until the process became mechanical. I watched the low clouds hang in the green, sodden hills and heard the staccato drill of a woodpecker. The Ump ran full and cold, yet lovely in its dips and washes and boulder runs. Scotch broom—the shadbush of the West Coast—bloomed in bright yellow clusters up and down the banks. I sneezed and blew my nose. I listened to the rain fall on my parka and huffed warm breath on my hands and struggled to maintain The Right Attitude. At least, I told myself, I'm *fishing*. The word itself was somehow restorative, if I didn't think about it too closely.

Terry disclaimed responsibility for the state of inaction. "They were biting like crazy two days ago . . . ," he began, but I waved him quiet. Out of tissues, I mentioned a pilgrimage back to the truck, which soon became an excuse to quit for the day. A half hour later we were back at Terry's log home, nibbling smoked shad on crackers and chugging beer from the can.

Dawn found us once again on the river, but the shad weren't in, or weren't biting. The early clouds soon parted and drifted east, and the rare spectacle of a blue sky made the Umpqua glow in a kind of jeweled green. By late morning shad began appearing in a narrow current lane between two rock ledges. A jig drifted just right, free-spooled at the last moment, then snubbed up and swung around in the current, brought strikes on every second or third cast. I whooped and hollered. Terry, a taciturn man, wore a permanent grin and even allowed himself a modest "hey-hey!" now and then, when a large fish made a particularly high spinning leap over the surface. Shad were thick in the narrow free-water lane, and they hit the darts hard; beefy silver fish, fresh from the sea, full of muscle and spirit and flash.

Then they were gone, a bright shimmer lost from the water, and the jigs drifted unharmed and unseen, time after time, until we reeled up and quit, shaking our heads. The shad had moved on, upriver or back down, a few miles or a few yards, unpredictable as a swirling wind. We rested for a while on the streamside rocks, chatting and watching the dark clouds blow in from the sea. Then we went back to it, casting patiently into the flow, waiting for the rain to begin. Waiting, and wondering what would happen next.

••• A contributing editor to SPORTS AFIELD since 1994, Robert F. Jones is the author of eight books, including the classic BLOOD SPORT. His often-hilarious articles on the outdoors have appeared in a number of major publications, including SPORTS ILLUSTRATED. He has also refined the art of catching weird and ugly fish!—MAY 1994 •••

WAMPUS CATS & OYSTER TOADS
by Robert F. Jones

If you've spent a lot of time fishing, as I have, sooner or later you're going to catch the big one—marlin or muskellunge, tarpon or brown trout, bonefish or striped bass or bluegill . . . maybe even the Wampus Cat of a lifetime, so big that it's probably the world record.

If you're a politically correct, ecosensitive kind of guy, you'll unhook your Wampus Cat as gently as possible, make sure its gills are pumping, and release it to swim off, stunned and sullen but with little harm done.

If you're a true gentleman, you'll never utter a boastful word about this encounter, nor of the fearsome battle the great fish gave you on the lightest possible line.

And if in the future you should happen to see another angler subdue a particularly large specimen of the same kind, and hear him exult in his triumph that it must surely be the largest ever taken—anywhere—on rod and reel, you will bite your tongue and nod in smiling agreement.

Sure you will.

Men compete—it comes with the testosterone. Maybe even before that, as in "Mine's bigger than yours."

That's what records are for.

David Goodman, a flyfisherman, was brooding over a solitary supper one foggy March evening at his home on Nantucket. A ceramic tile setter—a craft he pursues to keep body and soul together between fishing excursions—Goodman had just broken up with a longtime girlfriend, and he still ached at the broken places. He was dining that night on a mess of white perch he'd caught earlier in the evening on nearby Sesachacha Pond, where he'd gone, as was his wont, to knit up with flyrod and feathers the raveled sleeve of his care. Now, as he picked at the platter of bones before him, it occurred to him that these perch were among the largest he'd ever caught on the island. Someone at his fishing club, The Nantucket Anglers, had recently posted a list of gamefish available on the island, along with the current world-record weights for them. Goodman checked the list.

He'd just eaten a couple of world records—white perch that no doubt exceeded the existing marks in at least two flyrod categories. He felt pretty good about it. But why hadn't he weighed them—and submitted them for recognition—before scoffing them down?

Well, there'd be bigger perch available tomorrow—they were thick on their spawning beds right now. But did he really want a world record? At the age of 43 David Goodman was old enough to remember the 60s, when the ego trip ranked right up there with short hair and male chauvinism as a bête noir of the Boo Decade. This was 1991, though, and his ego needed a little inflation. A modest ego trip was clearly in order. After all, it wouldn't be so gross a sin. Even if he broke a world record, David Goodman would hardly be breaking Lefty Kreh's rice bowl, much less that of the world's most obsessive billfish and tarpon angler, the redoubtable Billy Pate.

I mean, a white perch, *Morone americana* . . . No big deal.

Goodman sorted through his collection of tapered fly leaders, found a fresh one that maxed out at 10 pounds, and decided to go for it—in the 12-pound tippet class, which at that time stood at a measly 1 pound 1 ounce. By sundown the next day, March 26, without even breaking a sweat, he owned the new world angling record for white perch taken on a flyrod: 1 pound 12 ounces.

But of Course That Wasn't Enough.

"I'd always kind of wanted to hold a world record," he says now, looking back on it all, "but it's like one of those deals where you can't eat just one. Suddenly I wanted all of them, all six of the tippet records in the white perch category. When it comes to compulsion, Ahab had nothing on me."

Over the next five months—sometimes rising at an ungodly 4:30 or 5:00 A.M. to be on the water when the fish started feeding—Goodman flailed Sesachacha Pond to froth, caught white perch hand over fist, muttering to himself whenever he fell just a silly milligram short of the mark, exulting whenever one of his catches broke the record, and virtually rewrote that chunk of the book, filling the 2-, 4-, 8-, 12-, 16- and 20-pound tippet classes. His biggest white perch, caught on July 20 on 4-pound tippet, was a whopping 2 pounds.

Was it worth it after all?

Well, during the course of his marathon assault on the record book, David Goodman found himself a new lady (this time one who shared his love of flyfishing), moved to a new address, and landed a satisfying new job as fishing columnist for Nantucket's 170-year-old *Inquirer & Mirror*. Go figger.

The International Game Fish Association, founded in 1939 and headquartered in Pompano Beach, Florida, currently maintains all-tackle catch records on 498 species. They range from the subtropical agujon (8 pounds 3 ounces) to the subarctic zander (25 pounds 2 ounces), with stops at such aquatic marvels as the Chinese seerfish, South African geelbeek, Austrian tolstolob and Swedish vimba. They include the largest fish of any species caught so far on rod and reel—Alfred Dean's 2664-pound great white shark, taken while surfcasting near Ceduna, Australia, 35 years ago—and the smallest, a 1-pound grass pickerel landed at Dewart Lake in Indiana by Mike Berg in 1990. (Yes, smaller fish have been caught—I've caught plenty myself—but the IGFA requires that any fish submitted for a record weigh at least a pound.) Some of the better-known and more glamorous marks, like oilman Alfred C. Glassell Jr.'s 1560-pound black marlin, caught back in 1953, and Dr. W. J. Cook's brook trout of 14 pounds 8 ounces, taken in 1916 on the Nipigon River in Ontario, seem unassailable, if only for their longevity.

The fiercest competition occurs in the IGFA's line-class slots, covering 328 "game" species, fresh water and salt, caught by means of conventional tackle (trolling, baitfishing, plugcasting or spinning) or by flyrod. In the conventional categories, separate records are maintained for men and women. Flyfishing, however, is democratically unisex (like those baggy chest waders de rigueur among trout anglers regardless of gender). Every year nearly 700 anglers apply for new records, and about half of those usually pass the IGFA's scrutiny. (Record applications must be accompanied by photographs of the fish, measurements of its length and girth, readings by an impartial weigh master from approved and accurate scales, corroborating reports by two eyewitnesses unrelated to the angler and an intact sample of the line-class leader or fly tippet used in landing the fish.) Of the 3588 IGFA record slots available, hundreds are still vacant, mainly in the flyfishing category.

Until recently, the most prestigious records were those set for billfish—black, blue, striped and white marlin, broadbill swordfish, and Atlantic or Pacific sailfish—usually taken on heavy line up to 130-pound test. Big tuna, especially "granders" (bluefins of 1000 pounds or more), used to make headlines in the sporting press. But tuna of all colors and dimensions are getting scarce in the waters of the world, thanks to the appetites of sushi-snarfing Japanese. Tokyo fishmongers pay hefty fortunes for fresh-caught horse mackerel, and their agents wait on our docks, cash in hand, for sportboats to come in, ready to buy any tuna for the equivalent of a year's wages.

Diehards and Maniacs

In the early years of this century, big tuna outranked even marlin or broadbills for bragging rights among gentlemen sportsmen. When Zane Grey, that indefatigable angler, joined the Catalina Tuna Club in 1914 and began catching broadbill swordfish in the waters off Avalon, old-boy members merely sniffed. Time enough for handshakes when this brash "young writer of Westerns" (he was 39 at the time) should manage to boat his first Blue Button tuna (100 pounds or better)—a feat Grey couldn't accomplish until 1919.

In 1917 a fellow club member, William C. Boschen, added injury to insult by catching a bigger broadbill than "Pearl" Grey had ever hung: a 463-pounder the Tuna Club promptly proclaimed a world record. Stung to the quick, Grey retaliated by spreading word that Boschen's hook had penetrated the big fish's heart, thus rendering the fight "unfortunately" one-sided. Boschen did not deign to reply.

Then in 1920, Grey caught the biggest broadbill of the season—418 pounds—and went around the club boasting that his fish, though 45 pounds lighter than Boschen's, had been hooked in the lip, not the heart. He buttonholed anyone who would listen, boring them stiff with blow-by-blow details of his fight, explaining ad infinitum how he worked out on rowing machines all winter to get into shape for the big fish, even soaking his hands daily in salt water to harden them for the arduous piscatorial battles ahead. But the following summer a female Tuna Club member landed a broadbill that outweighed Grey's by eight pounds. Gleeful members took turns phoning Grey every few minutes that night to suggest that perhaps he should give up salt water and try soaking his hands in Jergen's lotion.

Grey resigned his membership and fished only with sycophants from then on—though in the 1930s he tried to line up Ernest Hemingway for a *mano a mano* fishing trip around the world on Grey's 52-foot cruiser, *The Gladiator*.

Hemingway—just reaching the apogee of his career, while Grey's was already in decline—wisely said no. If Grey, who was 24 years older than Hemingway, had outfished him, Hemingway knew he would never have lived it down. You can't help but wish that the trip had come off, though, both for the fish and the potential fireworks.

During the filming of *The Old Man and the Sea* in 1956, Hemingway talked Producer Leland Hayward into a month's fishing on the famous marlin grounds at Cabo Blanco in Peru, hoping to come up with appropriate footage of a big blue marlin jumping for background shots of Santiago's battle. But Papa's luck ran as poorly as the Old Man's. The seas were as steep as the Andes. For 10 days, while the wind off the Desierto de Sechura blew sand into everything, Papa's crew saw not a single fin. Then it calmed and they got a few hookups. Hemingway whipped a 680-pound marlin in eight minutes flat (no mean feat for a man in his late 50s—or any man, for that matter), then let it run again to get jumping shots for the camera. But it was too small. Later he boated another of 915 pounds, but the bigger fish refused to jump. Hayward was finally forced to pay $250,000 for film of Alfred Glassell's fight with the record 1560-pound black marlin, caught three years earlier in the same waters.

But to film the marlin alongside Santiago's skiff, Warner Brothers concocted a mechanical fish 20 feet long with a motor inside to make the tail and fins wiggle. Hemingway, who had been paid $150,000 for the rights to the book along with his services as technical adviser, dubbed the rubber marlin "The Condomatic" and swore he would never work for Hollywood again.

"No picture with a rubber fish ever made a dime," he said.

The Cabo Blanco marlin fishery collapsed in the late 50s, done in by a combination of overfishing for marlin and overnetting of the *sardinas*—baitfish—they fed on, plus (some said) a shift in the Humboldt Current that took the big fish elsewhere. The focus of billfish record action shifted to Cairns, Australia. For 30 years now, wealthy big-game and tournament anglers have been seeking The Double Grander, aka The Big Mamu or The Wampus Cat—the legendary 2000-pound black marlin—somewhere off northeast Australia. A friend of mine, Joe Judge of Centreville, Maryland, spent three months a year (September through November) during 1973 and '74 bouncing around off Lizard Island, in the company of such fishing nuts as Australia's Peter Goadby and actor Lee Marvin (who owned the ultimate fishing platform, a converted U.S. Navy minesweeper) in pursuit of The Double Grander. The biggest black marlin he could come up with was 1143 pounds.

"You know he's out there," Judge says, "and he could hit you at any moment. So you have to keep alert all the time, day in, day out. One lapse, one momentary foul-up, and you might have blown the only shot you'll ever get in your lifetime." The hopes of these diehards were—and still are—fueled by reports of huge marlin well over the one-ton mark, blue as well as black, caught and processed in both the Atlantic and the Pacific by long-liners. Yet with each year the commercial fishing pressure increases, and the supply of big fish—marlin or tuna or you name it—continues to shrink. Glassell's record may well stand forever.

In recent years the focus in angling has switched to light tackle and less spectacular fish—ones that don't carry swords on their snouts. But while it lasted, there was nothing to match the quest for big tuna or billfish, either in grandeur or expense. Not to mention sheer arm-deadening, back-breaking hard work. An old-time 14/0 Vom Hofe reel, finished in German silver, weighs 13 pounds. The short, stiff greenheart or bamboo big-game rods of the 1920s and 30s, before fiberglass or graphite came along, were as thick as broomsticks and about as limber. Just by itself, the 700 yards of Ashaway 54-thread (162-pound test) linen line that a big broadbill or marlin was likely to peel off in a single scorching run weighed more than all the trout a latter-day trout fisherman will catch in a whole season.

The pursuit of today's glamour fish—tarpon, permit and striped bass in salt water, Atlantic salmon, brown, rainbow and brook trout, as well as largemouth bass in fresh—isn't nearly as expensive as tuna and billfishing were in the Golden Age. For one thing, you don't need a big seagoing boat. Back in Depression-strapped 1934, Hemingway paid $7500 for the *Pilar,* his black-hulled 38-foot Wheeler. Now you'd pay $10,000 to $20,000 a linear foot. An equivalent boat today—Hatteras, Rybovich, Luhrs or Bertram—could cost up to half a million or more.

By contrast, an Avon raft or Mackenzie boat for floatfishing a Western trout river like the Big Horn or the Madison might cost you $1500 tops. Even a Hughes skiff replete with 150-horse Johnson for fishing permit or tarpon or bonefish on the Florida flats, or a Ranger bassboat "loaded" (i.e., with GPS navigation system, side-scanning fishfinder sonar, pump-fed livewell, Astroturf no-skid carpeting, single-sideband radio and a plug-in fridge to keep your brewskis chilled) would cost no more than $20,000.

Yes, small-game fishing is the poor man's sport—that's why so many writers take up the flyrod. I've been fishing for more than 50 years now, with a canepole when I was a kid growing up in Wisconsin, then graduating to a baitcasting rod for muskies and a flyrod for bass, trout, salmon and the saltwater species. Along the way I've managed to catch five world-record fish—or at least they would have been if I'd chosen to submit them.

Two of the fish were respectable—a 125-pound sail taken off the Bat Islands in northwest Costa Rica on 20-pound flyrod tippet in 1991, the first year that the IGFA slot was open, and this year a decent pink salmon on the same outfit while I was fishing for 30- to 40-pound chinooks in British Columbia.

But if the IGFA had a category for ugly, three more of my record-size fish would have made the book in that slot as well. I'm proudest of them. I was throwing deerhair poppers for largemouths into Lake Champlain not long ago when the world's biggest rock bass smacked the bug. The rock bass, for those unfamiliar with it, has a mouth like the late Totie Fields's and the colors of a recovering burn victim, with maybe a little psoriasis thrown in for texture. Its dorsal fin is a fright wig with spikes. This guy—or probably gal, since the biggest fish of most species are female—weighed well over a pound, closer to two. I shook her off when I had her at my waders and cursed her back to her lair. Rock bass will drive you crazy by slamming your fly before the fish you really want has a chance to make up its mind.

Later that night, though, I was leafing through the IGFA's annual *World Record Game Fishes* and noticed that all the tippet slots for rock bass were vacant. I thought of going back to that spot the next day, à la David Goodman for his white perch. The notion had its appeal. Holding the world record for a really goofy-looking fish, one of angling's undesirables, would be more fun than holding a trout, say, or even a tarpon record. Then I remembered my friend George Reiger, author of such books as *Wanderer on My Native Shore* and *Profiles in Saltwater Angling,* who while trolling the Virginia coast for sharks had suddenly snagged what he took for the bottom. But no, it moved. When he finally cranked it in, it proved to be a "monstrous oyster toadfish."

As a joke, Reiger submitted the fish to the late Elwood K. Harry, longtime president of the IGFA, for a new all-tackle record. "Elwood, the sweetie, wrote back very apologetically to say there was no category for *Opsanus tau* just then," Reiger recalls, "but he hoped I wasn't too upset by this news. I wrote back and told him I was. It's shameful, I said. The oyster toad is as noble and valiant a battler as any fish in the sea. Beauty should have nothing to do with it. Now I notice that the IGFA has indeed added the oyster toad to its all-tackle list. But the spot is held by a lowly 3-pound 10-ounce specimen caught off Okracoke. Why, my toad could have et that one for breakfast—and begged for more."

Of course, ugly as she was, my rock bass could never have contended with an oyster toad for ugly. I promptly forgot about the record.

Another time, fishing from the rocks around the power station at Port Washington, Wisconsin, I landed a huge brown trout on a 4-pound flyrod tippet. This was during the fall, when the browns spawn, and it was a hen fish. She leaked roe as I unhooked her and weighed her. Never has there been an uglier brown trout, nor a more sluggish one. She was little more than 24 inches long but with the girth of a medicine ball—like a lady dwarf two months overdue with sextuplets. She weighed 18 pounds 10 ounces. Since the brown trout fly record for that tippet class was only 10 pounds 13 ounces back then, she would have been a cinch for a legitimate glamour-species mark—one that would have held to this day, when the record stands at only 12 pounds 3 ounces. But I have sympathy for the ugly, a kind of grudging respect tinged with awe—a feeling of kinship renewed each morning when I shave—so I slogged out into the surf (the water temperature was about 52°F that late September day, and I wore no waders) beyond the breakers and held her head-on into the waves until her strength came back. Then I shooed her back out to the sand flats where she'd been digging a redd. Perhaps one of her daughters is out there in Lake Michigan right now, growing to record size. I only hope she doesn't favor her mommy for looks.

The Best I've Ever Done

But my personal best for ugly, as well as big, weird and hazardous, came nearly 30 years ago in East Africa. I was writing the post-Uhuru stuff for *Time* magazine back then, and I'd been taking a look around Kenya, Uganda and Tanzania to see how independence was faring. It wasn't faring well. Sick of cooling my heels in Nairobi, waiting for an interview with Jomo Kenyatta that never came off, drinking too many chota pegs at the Long Bar in the New Stanley, I chartered a bush plane and flew up to a lake on the Northern Frontier, where I'd heard the fishing was good.

Some lake.

Some fish.

Imagine a six-foot turbojet engine painted in camo colors—olive drab on the top, silver on the belly—that's fallen from a fighter bomber at full blast into a 150-mile-long trough full of bitter green water. There's a sandstorm blowing over the trough, the temperature is 120 in the shade, 15-foot crocodiles bask on the banks, and wildmen called *shifta* are waiting out in the desert for night to fall so they can shoot you full of holes with Russky bullets.

That was Lake Rudolph in 1964. It's called Lake Turkana now, but it's not that much better, despite the politically correct name change. The shifta are Somalis, poachers of elephant and rhino armed with Kalashnikovs, and they feel—perhaps rightly—that the whole northern end of Kenya belongs to them. (The colonial powers were arbitrary when they sliced up the African pie.) The turbojets are Nile perch (*Lates niloticus*), close relatives of the hard-hitting Australian barramundi. They range from Egypt to Nigeria and Benin, and clear on down into Lake Tanganyika. Recently they were introduced into Lake Victoria, where they're said to be thriving on an abundance of tilapia. They grow to more than 200 pounds, and larger fish, up to 500 pounds, have reportedly been netted but have never been officially recorded.

There was a fishing camp on Rudolph at that time—perhaps half a dozen thatch-roofed, open-sided bandas and a kitchen with makeshift bar—run by a most happy fellow named Guy Poole, his Kenyan wife, his children and an Italian named Tony, an ex-POW from World War II who served as the camp mechanic. We fished from an ancient, round-bottomed, single-screwed African Queen of a vessel with split-cane boat rods that were even more venerable, and rust-pitted Penn 12/0 reels spooling what looked like miles of 130-pound DuPont monofilament line.

The wind died toward sunset, and we started hooking turbojets. The Nile perch came up from the greasy green depths, smashed the foot-long wooden plugs we were trolling, and took off on long screaming runs reminiscent of marlin or wahoo—300 or 400 yards at a whack. Our gaffer was a tall young El Molo tribesman, imaginatively named "Molo," who harpooned the big fish when we finally got them alongside. He was deadly. No catch and release in East Africa. The largest Nile perch I caught that bloodred evening—and I pulled them until my arms went dead—weighed 187 pounds 8 ounces on Guy Poole's scale when we brought them ashore. My record would have held for 27 years.

But I didn't bother to submit it. Instead we ate it for supper that evening—Guy Poole, his wife and kids, Tony, my pilot, Dick Prewitt, and a talented *Time-Life* photographer named Priya Ramrakha, who was killed by a sniper in Biafra a few years later. The whole bowlegged El Molo tribe, root and branch, joined us at the table. Only the bones remained when we'd finished.

That night, which happened to be my 30th birthday, I lay full bellied under the mosquito netting in my banda while hyenas whooped me to sleep. Eighteen months later shifta fell upon the camp, tortured and killed Guy Poole and a Catholic priest who was there to fish (Poole's wife and children had gone to Nairobi for supplies), shot up the radio, generator and three of the trucks, and burned the camp. They disappeared into the desert in the fourth camp truck, the El Molo said later. Tony was driving with an AK pointed at his neck—once again a POW. But not for long.

They were bound for a well called Gus, the El Molo said. When they got there, they filled their water bottles, burned the truck, banged Tony on the head, and skinned him out like a catfish. They took the hide for a trophy.

That's a real fishing story. Forget the records.

••• *The author of eight books, including the recent* AGE AND GUILE BEAT YOUTH, INNOCENCE, AND A BAD HAIRCUT, *P. J. O'Rourke is a reactionary and humorist, the past editor of* NATIONAL LAMPOON, *the current foreign affairs desk chief of* ROLLING STONE, *and still a budding flyfisherman.*—JULY 1994 •••

MY FIRST-TIME
FLYFISHING
DISASTER *by P. J. O'Rourke*

I'd never flyfished. I'd done other kinds of fishing. I'd fished for bass. That's where I'd get far enough away from the dock so that people couldn't see there wasn't any line on my pole, then drink myself blind in the rowboat. And I'd deep-sea fished. That's where the captain would get me blind before we'd left the dock, and I'd be the one who couldn't see the line. But I'd never flyfished.

I'd always been of two minds about the sport. On the one hand, here's a guy standing in cold water up to his liver, throwing the world's most expensive string at trees. A full two-thirds of his time is spent untangling stuff, which he could be doing in the comfort of his own home with old shoelaces. The whole business costs like sin and requires heavier clothing. Furthermore, it's conducted in the middle of blackfly season. Cast and swat. Cast and swat. Flyfishing may be a sport invented by insects with flyfishermen as bait. And what does the truly sophisticated dry-fly artist do when he finally bags a fish? He lets it go and eats baloney sandwiches instead.

On the other hand, flyfishing did have its attractions. I love to waste time and money. I had ways to do this most of the year—hunting, skiing, renting summer houses in To-Hell-and-Gone Harbor for a Lebanon hostage's ransom. But, come spring, I was limited to cleaning up the yard. Even with a new Toro every two years and a lot of naps by the compost heap, it's hard to waste much time and money doing this. And then there's the gear needed for flyfishing. I'm a sucker for any-thing that requires more equipment than I have sense. My workshop is furnished with the full panoply of power tools, all bought for the building of one closet shelf in 1979.

When I began to think about flyfishing, I realized I'd never be content again until my den was cluttered with computerized robot flytying vises, space-age Teflon and ceramic knotless tapered leaders, sterling-silver English fish scissors and 35 volumes on the home life of the midge. And there was one other thing. I'm a normal male who takes an occasional nip; therefore, I love to put funny things on my head. Sometimes it's the nut dish, sometimes the spaghetti colander, but the hats I'd seen flyfishermen wear were funnier than either, and I had to have one.

I went to Hackles & Tackle, an upscale dry-fly specialty shop that also sells fish-print wallpaper and cashmere V-necked sweaters with little trout on them. I got a graphite rod for about the price of a used car and a reel made out of the kind of exotic alloys that you can go to jail for selling to the wrong people. I also got one of those fishing vests that come down only to the top of your beer gut and look like you dressed in the dark and tried to put on your 10-year-old son's three-piece suit. And I purchased lots of monofilament and teensy hooks covered in auk down and moose lint, and an entire L. L. Bean boat bag full of flyfishing do-whats. I also brought home a set of flyfishing how-to videotapes. What better way to take up a sport than from a comfortable armchair? That's where I'm at my best with most sports anyway.

There were three tapes. The first one claimed it would teach me to cast. The second would teach me to "advanced-cast." And the third would tell me where trout live, how they spend their weekends and what they'd order for lunch if there were underwater delicatessens for fish. I started the VCR, and a squeaky little guy with an earnest manner and a double-funny hat came on, heaving flyline around, telling me the secret to making beautiful casting loops is . . .

Whoever made these tapes apparently assumed I knew how to tie backing to reel and line to backing and leader to line and so on, all the way out to the little feather and fuzz that fish sometimes eat at the end. I didn't even know how to put my rod together. I had to go to the children's section at the public library and check out *My Big Book of Fishing* and begin with how to open the package it all came in.

A triple granny got things started on the spool. After 12 hours and help from pop rivets and a tube of Krazy Glue, I managed an Albright knot between backing and line. But my version of a nail knot in the leader put Mr. Gordian, of ancient-

Greek-knot-legend fame, strictly on the shelf. It was the size of a hamster and resembled one of the Woolly Bugger flies I'd bought, except it was in the size you use for killer whales. I don't want to talk about blood knots and tippets. There I was with two pieces of invisible plastic, trying to use fingers the size of jumbo hot dogs while holding a magnifying glass and a Tensor lamp between my teeth and gripping nasty tangles of monofilament with each big toe. My girlfriend had to come over and cut me out with pinking shears. I've decided I'm going to get one of those nine-year-old Persian kids they use to make incredibly tiny knots in fine Bokhara rugs and just take her with me on all my fishing trips.

I rewound Mr. Squeaky and started over. I was supposed to keep my rod tip level and keep my rod swinging in a 90-degree arc. When I snapped my wrist forward, I was giving a quick flick of a blackjack to the skull of a mugging victim. When I snapped my wrist back, I was sticking my thumb over my shoulder and telling my brother-in-law to get the hell out of here, and I mean right now, buster. Though it wasn't explained with so much poetry.

Then I was told to try a "yarn rod." This was something else I'd bought at the tackleshop. It looked like a regular rod tip from a two-piece rod but had a cork handle. You run a bunch of bright orange yarn through the guides and flip it around. It's supposed to imitate a flyrod in slow motion. I don't know about that, but I do know you can catch and play a nine-pound house cat on a yarn rod, and it's great sport. They're hard to land, however. And I understand cat fishing is strictly catch and release if they're under 20 inches.

After 60 minutes of videotape, seven minutes of yarn-rod practice, 25 minutes of cat fishing and several beers, I felt I was ready. I picked up the fin tickler and laid out a couple of loops that weren't half bad, if I do say so myself. I'll bet I cast almost three times before making macramé out of my weight-forward Cortland 444. This wasn't so hard.

I also watched the advanced tape. But Squeaky had gone grad school on me. He's throwing reach casts, curve casts, roll casts, steeple casts and casts he calls "squiggles" and "stutters." He's writing his name with the line in the air. He's pitching things forehand, backhand and between his wader legs. And, through the magic of video editing, every time his hook-tipped dust kitty hits the water, he lands a trout the size of a canoe.

The videotape about trout themselves wasn't much use either. It's hard to get excited about where trout feed when you know the only way you're going to be able to get a fly to that place is by throwing your flybox at it.

I must say, however, all the tapes were informative. "Nymphs and streamers" are not, as it turns out, naked mythological girls decorating the high-school gym with crepe paper. And I learned that the part of flyfishing I'm going to be best at is naming the flies: Blue Wing Earsnag; Overhanging Brush Muddler; Royal Toyota Hatchback; O'Rourke's Ouchtail; and PJ's Live Worm-'n'-Bobber.

By now I'd reached what they call a "learning plateau." If I was going to catch a fish, I had to either go get in the water or open the fridge and toss hooks at Mrs.

Paul's frozen haddock fillets. I made reservations at a famous fishing lodge on the Au Sable River in Michigan. When I got there and found a place to park among the Saabs and Volvos, the proprietor said I was just a few days early for the Hendrickson hatch. There is, I've learned, one constant in all fishing, which is: The time the fish are biting is almost—but not quite—now.

I looked pretty good making false casts in the lodge parking lot. I mean, no one laughed out loud. But most of the other 2000 young professionals fishing this no-kill stretch of the Au Sable were pretty busy checking to make sure that their trout shirts were color-coordinated with their Reebok wading sneakers.

When I stepped into the river, however, my act came to pieces. My line hit the water like an Olympic belly-flop medalist. I hooked four "tree trout" in three minutes. My backcasts had people ducking for cover in Traverse City. The only thing I could manage to get a drag-free float on was me after I stepped into a hole. And the trout? The trout laughed.

The next day I could throw tight loops, sort of aim, even make a gentle presentation and get the line to lie right every so often. But when I tried to do all of these things at once, I looked like I was conducting "Flight of the Bumblebee" in fast-forward. I was driving tent pegs with my rod tip. My slack casts wrapped around my thighs. My straight-line casts went straight into the back of my neck. My improved surgeon's loops looked like full Windsors. I had wind knots in everything, including my Red Ball suspenders. And $200 worth of fly floatant, split-shot, Royal Coachmen and polarized sunglasses fell off my body and were swept downstream.

Then, *mirabile dictu*, I hooked a fish. I was casting some I-forget-the-name nymph and clumsily yanking it in when my rod tip bent and my pulse shot into trade-deficit numbers. I lifted the rod—the first thing I'd done right in two days—and the trout actually leaped out of the water as if it were trying for a *Fly Fisherman* playmate centerfold. I sounded like my little sister in the middle of a puppy litter: "Ooooo, that's a baby, yessssssss, come to Daddy, wooogie-woogie-woo." It was a rainbow, and I'll bet it was seven inches long. All right, five. Anyway, when I grabbed the thing, some of it stuck out of both sides of my hand. I hadn't been so happy since I passed my driver's-license exam.

So I'm a flyfisherman now. Of course, I'm not an expert yet. But I'm working on the most important part of flyfishing technique—boring the hell out of anybody who'll listen.

••• *Barry Hannah, the author of 10 books, including* AIRSHIPS, *teaches writing at the University of Mississippi. The following piece of fiction, the only story he's written for* SPORTS AFIELD *(to date), has solid roots in his childhood.*—SEPTEMBER 1994 •••

A CREATURE IN THE BAY OF ST. LOUIS

by Barry Hannah

We were out early in the brown water, the light still gray and wet. My cousin Woody and I were out wading on an oyster shell reef in the Bay. We had cheap baitcasting rods and reels with black cotton line, at the end of which were a small bell weight and croaker hook. We used peeled shrimp for bait. Sometimes you might get a speckled trout or flounder, but more likely you would catch the croaker. A large one weighed half a pound. When caught and pulled in, the fish made a metallic croaking sound. It is one of the rare fish who talk to you about their plight when they are landed. My aunt fried them crispy, covered in cornmeal, and they were delicious, especially with lemon juice and ketchup.

A good place to fish was near the pilings of the St. Stanislaus school pier. The pier gate was locked, but you could wade to the pilings and the oyster shell reef. Up the bluff above us on the town road was a fish market and the Star Theater, where we saw movies.

Many cats, soft and friendly and plump, would gather around the edges of the fish market, and when you went to the movies, you would walk past three or four of them who would ease against your leg as if asking to go to the movies with you. The cats were very social. In their prosperity they seemed to have organized into a watching society of leisure and culture. Nobody yelled at them because this was a small coastal town where everybody knew each other. Italians, Slavs, French, Methodists, Baptists and Catholics. You did not want to insult the cat's owner by being rude. Some of the cats would tire of the market offerings and come down the bluff to watch you fish, patiently waiting for their share of your take or hunting the edges of the weak surf for dead crabs and fish. You would be pulling in your fish, and when you looked ashore, the cats were suddenly alert. They were wise. It took a hard case not to leave them one good fish for supper.

That night, as you went into an Abbott and Costello movie which cost a dime, that same cat you had fed might rub against your leg, and you felt sorry it couldn't go into the movie house with you. You might be feeling comical when you come out and see the same cat waiting with conviction as if there were something in there it wanted very much, and you threw a jujube down to it on the sidewalk. Jujubes were pellets of chewing candy the quality of vulcanized rubber. You chewed several during the movie, and you had a wonderful syrup of licorice, strawberry and lime in your mouth. But the cat would look down at the jujube, then up at you as if you were insane, and you felt bad for betraying this serious creature and hated that you were mean and thoughtless. That is the kind of conscience you had in Bay St. Louis, Mississippi.

This morning we had already had a good trip as the sun began coming out. The croakers swam in a burlap sack tied to a piling and under water. The sacks were free at the grocery, and people called them croaker sacks. When you lifted the sack to put another croaker in, you heard that froggy metal noise in a chorus, quite loud, and you saw the cats on shore hearken to it, too. We would have them with french fries, fat tomato slices from my uncle's garden and a large piece of sweet watermelon for supper.

It made a young boy feel good having the weight of all these fish in the dripping sack when you lifted it, knowing you had provided for a large family and maybe even neighbors at supper. You felt to be a small hero of some distinction, and ahead of you was that mile walk through the neighborhood lanes where adults would pay attention to your catch and salute you. The fishing rod on your shoulder, you had done some solid bartering with the sea; you were not to be trifled with.

The only dangerous thing in the Bay was a stingaree, with its poisonous barbed hook of a tail. This ray would lie flat, covered over by sand like a flounder. We waded barefoot in swimming trunks, and almost always in a morning's fishing you stepped on something that moved under your foot and you felt the squirm in every inch of your body before it got off you. These could be stingarees. There were terrible legends about them, always a story from summers ago when a stingaree had whipped its tail into the calf of some unfortunate girl or boy and buried the vile hook deep in the flesh. The child came dragging out of the water with this 20-pound brownish black monster the size of a garbage can lid attached to his leg, thrashing and sucking with its awful mouth. Then the child's leg grew black and swelled horribly, and they had to amputate his leg, and that child was in the attic of some dark house on the edge of town, never the same again and pale like a thing that never saw light; then eventually the child became half-stingaree and they took it away to an institution for special cases. So you believed all this most positively, and when a being squirmed under your foot, you were likely to walk on water out of there. We should never forget that when frightened, a child can fly short distances, too.

The high tide was receding with the sun clear up and smoking in the east over Biloxi, the sky reddening, and the croakers were not biting so well anymore. But each new fish would give more pride to the sack, and I was greedy for a few more since I didn't get to fish in the salt water much. I lived four hours north in a big house with a clean lawn, a maid and yard men, but it was landlocked and grim when you compared it to this place of my cousin's. Much later I learned his family was nearly poor, but this was laughable even when I heard it, because it was heaven; the movie house right where you fished and the society of cats, and my uncle's house with the huge watermelons lying on the linoleum under the television with startling shows like *Lights Out!* from the New Orleans station. We didn't even have a television station yet where I lived.

I kept casting and wading out deeper, toward an old creosoted pole in the water, where I thought a much bigger croaker or flounder might be waiting. My cousin was tired and red-burnt from the day before in the sun, so he went to swim under the diving board of the Catholic high school 100 yards away. They had dredged a pool. Otherwise the sea was very shallow a long ways out. But now I was almost up to my chest, near the barnacled pole where a big boat could tie up. I kept casting, almost praying toward the deep water around the pole. The lead and shrimp would plunk and tumble into a dark hole, I thought, where a special giant fish was lurking, something too big for the croaker shallows.

My grandmother had caught a seven-pound flounder from the sea wall years before and she was still honored for it, my uncle retelling the tale of her whooping out, afraid but happy, the pole bent double. I wanted to have a story like that about myself. The fish made Mama Hannah so happy, my older cousin said, that he saw her dancing to a band on television by herself when everybody else was asleep. Soon—I couldn't bear to think about it—in a couple of days they would drive me over to Gulfport and put me on a bus for home, and in my sorrow there waited a dry red brick school within bitter tasting distance. But even that would be sweetened by a great fish and its story.

It took place in no more than half a minute, I'd guess, but it had the lengthy rapture and terror of a whole tale. Something bit and then was jerking, small but solid, then it was too big, and I began moving in the water and grabbing the butt of the rod again because what was on had taken it out of my hands. When I caught the rod up, I was moving toward the barnacled pole with the tide slopping on it, and that was the only noise around. I went in to my neck in a muddier scoop in the bottom, and then under my feet something moved. I instantly knew it was a giant stingaree. Hard skin on a squirming plate of flesh. I was sorely terrified but was pulled past even this and could do nothing, now up to my chin and the stiff little pole bent violently double. I was dragged through the mud, and I knew that the being when it surfaced would be bigger than I was.

Then, like something underwater since Europe, seven or eight huge porpoises surfaced, blowing water in a loud group explosion out of their enormous heads, and I was just shot all over with light and nerves because they were only 20 feet from me and I connected them, the ray and what was on my hook into a horrible combination beast that would drag out children who waded too far, then crush and drown them.

The thing pulled with heavier tugs, like a truck going up its gears. The water suddenly rushed into my face and nose. I could see only brown, with the bottom of the sun shining through it.

I was gone, gone, and I thought of the cats watching on a shore and said good-bye, cat friends, good-bye, cousin Woody, good-bye, young life. I am only a little boy and I'm not letting go of this pole—it is not even mine; it's my uncle's. Good-bye, school, good-bye, Mother and Daddy. Don't weep for me; it is a thing in the water cave of my destiny. Yes, I thought all these things in detail while drowning and being pulled rushing through the water, but the sand came up under my feet and the line went slack; the end of the rod was broken off and hanging on the line. When I cranked in the line, I saw that the hook, a thick silver one, was straightened. The vacancy in the air where there was no fish was an awful thing, like surgery in the pit of my stomach. I convinced myself I had almost had him.

When I stood in the water on solid sand, I began crying. I tried to stop, but when I got close to Woody, I burst out again. He wanted to know what had happened, but I did not tell him the truth. Instead I told him I had stepped on an enormous ray and its hook had sliced me.

When we checked my legs, there was a slice from an oyster shell, a fairly deep one I'd gotten while being pulled by the creature. I refused treatment and was respected for my close call the rest of the day. I even worked in the lie more and said furthermore that it didn't matter much to me if I was taken off to the asylum for stingaree children; those were just the breaks.

It wasn't until I was back in the dreaded schoolroom that I could even talk about the fish. My teacher doubted it, and she in goodwill told my father, congratulating me on my imagination. My father thought that was rich, but then I told him the same story, the creature as heavy as a truck, the school of porpoises, and he said that's enough. You didn't mention this when you came back.

No, and neither did I mention the two cats when I walked back to shore with Woody and the broken rod. They had watched all the time, and I knew it, because both of them stared at me with big, solemn eyes, a lot of light in them, and it was with the beings of fur that I entrusted my confidences then, and they knew I would be back to catch the big one, the singular monster, on that line going tight into the cave in water, something thrashing on the end, celebrated above by porpoises.

I never knew what kind of fish it was, but I would return and return to it the rest of my life, and the cats would be waiting to witness me and share my honor.

••• *Known as Uncle Homer to many readers, as Mr. Bass to others, Homer Circle has been writing about fishing, mostly bass fishing, since he started with the magazine in 1955. Here, our bass editor looks at his old tacklebox, thinks about days gone by, and comments on what's truly important in life.*—JANUARY 1995 •••

THIS OLD BOX
by Homer Circle

For years, my very first tacklebox has sat in a corner of my workshop, neglected. Made of Canadian cedar, the box has 80 aluminum, cork-lined compartments that hold over 200 lures. How proud I used to be to open it, savor that rich aroma, and have anyone and everyone view my vast lure selection.

Now, some 60 years later, I haul it into my office, spread-eagle the cantilevered trays, and gaze at the contents. As I lift various lures from their sanctuaries, and whiff that cedar again, a montage of memories floods my mind.

The bronze tag on the lid bears my name and reminds me the box was made by the Dickson-Clawson Company (now long out of business) in Kansas City, Kansas. At $45 it was the Cadillac of tackleboxes back then—when I was making $14 a week managing the fishing-tackle department in a Springfield, Ohio, sporting goods store.

Those were deep Depression years and such a luxury was unthinkable. But I got the salesman to trade one for a spare fishing rod I had hand made. He was a kindly old gent who sensed my yearning. How I wish he were here now, so I could thank him for the companionship and the memories this tacklebox has given me.

In one corner of the bottom is an odd item, a duck call. My boyhood fishing buddy, Homer Darbyshire, loved duck hunting, rating it just one notch below fishing. We took our tackle along on opening days of duck season, just in case the birds weren't flying. We made the best of those duckless days by fishing for bass.

Darbyshire taught me much of my fishing lore in southern Ohio's smallmouth streams. Our pet lures were crayfish imitations that I had turned out on my grandfather-in-law's wood lathe, using 100-year-old walnut he had salvaged from aged church pews. The wood was so hard I had to drill, rather than punch, screw holes for the two treble hooks. For every 10 I would painstakingly turn out, maybe two would have that mysterious, magical beat that smallmouths go for.

But the lure caught more than bass. It opened the door to my career in the fishing-tackle industry. As I gazed at it I remembered the first fishing trip my wife Gayle and I took after the war.

We were ensconced at Pleasant Lake in southern Michigan and the wind blew at 40 knots for three days straight. On the morning of the third day I said to Gayle, "You know, the Heddon company is less than an hour away and I just might sell them that crab bait. Let's try, and meantime that wind might settle down."

I chatted with the two vice presidents and told them I had made a bass lure so good I would challenge their best fisherman to a contest. If I couldn't catch more bass on my crab than he could on Heddon's best plugs, I would hush and hurry back to Ohio. To make a long story short, the company bought me instead of the crab, and I worked hard for a dozen years to attain the vice president's chair.

In the top shelf of my old cedar box is a vintage Lucky 13, one with glass eyes in a white cedar body. It was given to me by then plant manager Jack Welch, who shared with me the story of how this venerated surface lure came by its name.

Charles Heddon had challenged him to make a lure with the same action as South Bend Bait Company's hot-selling Bass Oreno, but not a look-alike. Welch simply cut the face slot in the opposite plane to avoid the design patent while preserving the odd, wavering action.

One Friday, Welch took Heddon bass fishing on Pipestone Lake to show him how the new lure worked. At day's end they had two limits of bass laid out on the dock for pictures. Welch said, "Not a bad catch, Mr. Heddon, when you remember today is Friday the thirteenth."

Heddon replied: "Hey, that's a good name for the bait, 'Lucky 13.'" Thus, history was made.

Another glance into those trays reveals a rather homely metallic lure with most of the paint worn off, a Sonar. It has three holes in the head for action control in varying river currents, and is a veritable all-species lure.

Gayle and I were fishing for salmon in the Tatshenshini River in the Yukon Territory and for some unknown reason, Gayle just couldn't latch onto a good fish. She kept at it, though, with her characteristic tenacity.

At the last minute of the final morning she was standing on a rocky point and made one long cast with a Sonar. As she coaxed it back, her rod tip suddenly whipped downward and she yelled, "Got one—and it feels big!"

The fish leaped skyward and the guide whispered, "At least 50 pounds!" Three more frantic jumps in the fast-flowing river, and it hit the heaviest white water below. Gayle jammed her thumb onto the disappearing line, pulled it away quickly and licked its burned surface. "I can't stop it," she grunted.

Suddenly we heard a loud pop and she held up a naked reel spool. "Well," she said, grinning, "what a wonderful keeper-memory to take home with us!" That's my fishing buddy—and latching onto her has to be the greatest, quality catch of my lifetime.

Another glance into that portable cedar attic and I see a tray of tiny white jigs, which brings back some tender moments from when I was teaching a group of orphans how to catch panfish off an old dock. One winsome lad, about 8, kept his blue eyes locked on mine as I described how to impale a cricket on a hook.

As I talked, from the corner of my eye I saw a small hand ease into the tray of jigs and withdraw a couple. His eyes never faltered. I said nothing, but later observed him drop the jigs into his shirt pocket.

When we finished the session and the kids were heading for the bus to return to the Rhodehaver Youth Ranch, the same youngster sidled close, wrapped his arms around my thigh, smiled up at me and asked, "Uncle Homer, can you take me home with you?" Both moments still tug at my heartstrings.

As I gaze down at the old cedar tacklebox crowded with lures for most species of fish, I'm reminded that today's high-tech boxes are a lot more practical. They're more durable, waterproof and leakproof, and the compartments can be arranged to fit any fisherman's peculiar choices of lures. Tackleboxes have come a long way since the simplistic design of my old container.

But come to think of it, this box has come a long way, too. And it has brought with it something modern tackleboxes will never have in my lifetime . . . the woodsy scent of cedar . . . and the afterglow of memories made in the camaraderie of some of the world's finer folks . . . fishin' buddies!

••• *Coming aboard the magazine as contributing editor in 1995 was Thomas McGuane, whom many know from his novels, including* NINETY-TWO IN THE SHADE, *which was nominated for a National Book Award, and his film work about the West. Here he fishes another frontier, perhaps the wildest one left.*—MARCH 1995 •••

FISHING ON TOP OF THE WORLD

by Thomas McGuane

The tarmac at Murmansk was under repair and so we were diverted into a military airport. We were a small group of American and English travelers. We stood near a plywood shanty, awaiting transport to the Soviet helicopter, red star painted out, that would carry us to 67 degrees north latitude, above the Arctic Circle, to our camp on the Ponoi River, 350 miles of Atlantic salmon water springing from a tundra swamp and flowing to the Barents Sea.

We took the time to inspect the very advanced looking pale blue fighter planes parked in front of bulldozed gravel ledges. They looked like state-of-the-art military equipment; but canvas had been thrown over the canopies and there was at least one flat tire. They now belonged to a discarded chapter of world politics and other cerebral fevers. The hearty, cheerful Russian woman who was our translator, for the moment, gestured to the airplanes and asked, "You like some military secrets?"

We boarded the enormous helicopter and put in our earplugs. We sat on benches amid duffel bags and rod cases. The Russian crew nodded in that enthusiastic, mute way that says, *We don't know your language.* The helicopter lifted off to an altitude of about two feet. I looked out the window at the hurricanes of dust stirred by the rotors. Then the helicopter roared down the runway like a fixed-wing aircraft and we were on our way.

In very short order, the view from the window was of natural desolation, rolling tundra wisps of fog and alarming low-level whiteouts. Even through my earplugs came a vast drumming of power from the helicopter's engine. As I often do when confronted with a barrage of new impressions, I fell asleep, chin on chest, arms dangling between my knees. I looked like a chimp defeated by shoelaces.

After an hour and a half's flight, we stopped at a rural airfield and got out to stretch while the chopper refueled. Parked on this airfield were the enormous Antonov biplanes, built in the 1940s. A Russian mechanic told us that some of them had American-made engines. These were great cargo hauling workhorses in Siberia and from time to time we would see them flying over the tundra at a snail's pace.

◆ ◆ ◆

We reboarded. A very pretty Russian girl boarded with us, carrying an armload of flowers. She smiled at everyone with the by now familiar mute enthusiasm while the helicopter roared into flight once again. We all mused on this radiant flower of the Russian north, working up theories about her life and dreams. Everything was so wonderfully foreign, we were later slow to acknowledge that she and her husband were our talented cooks from Minnesota.

We landed on a bluff above the Ponoi River. From here we could see both the camp and the river. The camp was a perfectly organized congeries of white tents of varying sizes and, when I was installed in mine, I briefly stretched out on my bunk to take in that bright sense of nomadic domesticity that a well-appointed tent produces. At this far-north latitude, I knew the sun would be beaming through my tent day and night. In one corner was the small Finnish woodstove which, in the sustained spell of warmth, we would never use.

We were briefed about the angling at our first dinner. An amusing and slightly imperious Englishman named Nicholas Hood picked the first pause between syllables during the official briefing to forego dessert and descend to the river with his 16-foot Spey rod. I was impressed by his deftness in effecting a warp-speed fisherman's exit without getting caught at it. I had just given an old household toast of ours, "over the lips, over the gums, look out stomach, here it comes," when Hood said, "Cerebral lot, your family," and was out of there. One of my companions, Doug Larsen, a superb outdoorsman, remarked that Hood slept with one leg in his waders. I do like to hit the ground running in these situations, but by the time I could disentangle myself, Hood was stationed midway down the home pool cracking out long casts and covering water like one who'd bent to this work before. "Any sense of the protocol on fishing through here?" I asked.

"Go anywhere you like," said Hood, far too busy to get into this with me. So I went, I thought, a polite distance below him and began measuring several long casts onto the tea-colored water. English salmon anglers think that our single-handed rods are either ridiculous, inadequate or simply bespeak—especially when combined with baseball hats—the hyperkinetic, sawed-off spiritual nature of the people who use them. One Englishman, fishing here earlier in the season, stated plainly that he didn't think Americans should be allowed to fish for salmon at all.

At end of one quiet drift, a salmon took, ran off with my flyline and, well into the backing, cartwheeled into the air. He put up a strong, fast flight. I had to follow him down the beach to a small cove, where I tailed him. I looked down at the fish, not a big salmon, but a wonderful, speckled creature of eight pounds, a pure and ancient product of the Russian Arctic. I slipped the barbless hook from the corner of his mouth and this brilliantly precise creature, briefly in my hand, faded like an image on film, into the traveling depths of the Ponoi.

When I returned to my spot on the pool, there was Hood, beaming and fishing at once. "Well done!" he said with surprising pleasure at my catch. As we would see, Hood was much too able a fisherman to be insecure about someone else's success.

• • •

In addition, there was the talented Doug Larsen, who fascinated me with his expansion of the carp family: The specklebelly geese so popular among Texas gunners were "sky carp"; the grayling with their tall dorsal fins that darted out after our flies were "sail carp." I know he wanted to place that enormous salmonid of the Danube and other waters, the taimen, into some remote branch of the carp family. But it wouldn't go. The Russians who fished for them, he explained with ill-concealed disgust, waited until the taimen made his first jump then let him have it with a 12-gauge. It was the only way to land them. It made aesthetic or even polite tackle out of the question. You would be at one with the shark assassins of Montauk and other brutes.

Larsen had brought with him a third companion, a Mr. Duff who listed among his shadowy achievements giving investment tips to Mookie Blaylock. During the course of our week's angling it became clear to me that the suave, well-dressed, neatly coiffed Mr. Duff—introduced to me as one who had warmed up for Atlantic salmon by float-tubing for bluegills on their spawning beds—was a werewolf. His attempts at angling innocence, like asking whether a Near Nuff Frog would be a good fly to tie on, didn't fool me even in the beginning. There was something about the space between his eyes that put me on the *qui vive*. He was into fish all week and stood on the banks of the tundra river at evening and howled like a Russian wolf to commemorate each fish. Not quite physically powerful enough to pinch down the barb on his hook, he had other strengths. It wasn't long before I began to make my middle-of-the-night excursions that I realized that when I reached the river, the wolf would be there.

In the end, we accepted "Mr. Duff" as he was: a wild dog, saliva glistening in the corners of his mouth, chastely marcelled locks of blond over his forehead and an almost gymnastic ability to fish up to you, around you, past you, nibbling continuously at your water, with an unswerving, otherworldly need to catch the most fish. In other words, a werewolf.

Larsen and I were no longer comfortable with our considerable experience in angling for sea-run fish. We were being hunted down by this bluegill jock and had to exhaust our reserves of strength and knowledge to stay ahead of him. And the Ponoi frequently rewarded him as he gazed reflectively through his cigarette smoke. Incidentally, while he always had a smoldering cigarette between his lips, I never saw him light one. This primeval or eternal cigarette ought to be a final clue for any reader who needs one.

After a few days, I imagined I would be on the river forever. This is one of the few places I have ever fished where salmon seemed truly eminent. I fished with ongoing concentration, trying to throw strikes with every cast, mending as exactly as possible, and looking into my fly book like a fortune teller. The world of the river became more enclosing, the hurtling power of the fish ever more emblematic of the force of wild things and the plenitude of Nature undisturbed.

One afternoon, I fished in the trance state of repeated casting. The river was so comfortable that I fished without my waders. The clouds were long, thin streamers in a sky of northern summer. On the cliff face above me was a nest of Arctic gyrfalcons; the parents wheeled around the nest bringing food while the screams from the pale, fierce youngsters echoed across the canyon.

Our group stopped at a place where villagers had come out and built a fire. There were empty vodka bottles and pieces of roasted reindeer tongue. The ground was trampled around the fire. The people of that village had been there for thousands of years and had some old habits, not readily discernible to our eyes.

The fish came with a slow rolling motion and started back to his lie with my Green Highlander in the corner of his mouth. I let him tighten against the reel and raised my rod. Now, we were off to the races, running over the round river rocks in wading shoes, while the fish cart-wheeled in mid-river, the thread of Dacron backing streaming after it and the reel making its sublime music.

We had earlier noted Nick Hood bounding like Nijinski behind a fish, springing from stone to stone, and I felt more than the usual pressure to stay on my feet. But my fish was landed in a slick behind boulders. I released him without ever taking him out of the water. He flickered away into the depths of his ancestral river. Larsen continued to catch fish steadily while Mr. Duff showed some of the deficits of his otherworldly auspices. He would catch fish at a good clip, then become possessed by a "hoodoo." By this time we had become well enough acquainted that he could share some of the special problems he experienced. A hoodoo evidently is some sort of bird—possibly a bat. When it settles, imperceptibly, between the shoulderblades of the unsuspecting angler, it becomes impossible to catch a fish. It is possible to hook a fish, but it always gets off. So, for a while, the wolf's echoing howls were less frequent. Sport that he was, though, he finally shook it off. From time to time, the hoodoo settled on Larsen and me. In attempting to provide companionship and sympathy, we began to acquire some of Mr. Duff's quirks. By mid-week, Larsen himself had begun taking great pains to make the part in his hair precise.

That night, when I left the dining tent with its many pleasures of good food, pleasant companionship, and a fly tying table where the silliest notions may be brought to life, I knew I had to keep fishing. It had been a long day and so a small nap was in order. Mr. Duff, now transmuted into a bon vivant, refilling the drinks of the guests, telling golfing stories and smoking the very cigarette I had watched glow all week, was occupied in the dining tent for the foreseeable future. He and Larsen were being corrupted by an English farmer, James Keith, who promoted late card games and a general shore-leave atmosphere. I could see that Hood was all in: There was every chance I would have the magnificent Home Pool—one of the greatest salmon pools in the world—to myself!

♦ ♦ ♦

I awakened at three and gulped the cup of cold coffee I'd left beside my bunk. I was soon walking through the sleeping camp with my rod over my shoulder. Snores were coming from several tents and the sun was shining merrily. Wagtails had seized this time to hop among the tents looking for food. I noted Hood's 16-foot Spey rod leaned up in front of his tent. I climbed down the path along a small stream, waving away the mosquitoes, and was soon casting out onto the great river, discovering how tired my muscles were.

♦ ♦ ♦

I caught a small grilse right away, a silver-bright fish only a day or so from the ocean. Then it got still. There were no fish rolling. Sleep kept rising through my mind but I was in the river and the casts were still rolling out. About half way down the pool, I had a jolting strike. After ripping 40 yards into my backing, a terrific salmon made one crashing jump after another well out in mid-river. Then it started back toward the ocean. I put as deep a bow in the rod as I dared and began following the fish downstream. I beached it on a small point, beyond which I may not have been able to follow. It was a big male with a lower jaw so hooked it had worn a groove in the upper. I was delighted to make certain this individual made it back to the gene pool.

♦ ♦ ♦

I've always thought that it would be nice after landing an exceptional fish to go straight to bed. This time, I did, drifting off in my glowing tent in a dream of sea-run fish.

We stopped in Murmansk for a couple of hours on the way out. I went to a small museum and looked at some wonderful paintings of submarines, some in the open sea, some in remote ocean coves with snow on their decks, portraits of their captains. This glimpse of military glory was at sharp odds with the beleaguered municipality all around us. As I looked at the cheerlessly monolithic public housing towering over raw, bulldozed ground, I remembered that the leading cause of domestic fires in Russia is exploding television sets. But no one in the world has wild, open country like the Russians, a possible ace-in-the-hole on a strangling planet. Poets and naturalists could have seen this so much more comprehensively than I did, dragging my flyrod (without which I would probably never have gotten there, or stood for a week in a tundra river bound for the Barents Sea).

Mr. Duff gazed at me with the faintest of smiles as I dragged my duffel to the boarding area. A thin plume of motionless smoke extended vertically from his cigarette. He looked away from me and resumed his scrutiny of a back issue of *Golf Digest*.

I was conscious of the weight of my duffel, which had come to seem tremendous. I dragged it from boarding area to boarding area that day and night, in Murmansk, in Helsinki, in New York, in Salt Lake City, in Bozeman. I had apparently become so weak, I could barely carry it. Finally home, I dragged it out of my car like a corpse. I hated it so much that I slept a full day before unpacking it. When I did I found, beneath the soggy wading shoes and dirty laundry, the most beautiful round river rocks. And I remembered a distant howl from the shadows along the far shore of the Ponoi.

••• *Ian Frazier has written for the* NEW YORKER *for 20 years, starting with a piece about selling fishing gear in Manhattan. He authored the national best-seller* GREAT PLAINS, *and most recently,* FAMILY. *In 1995 he moved from Brooklyn, New York, where he fished for large stripers in local waters, to Missoula, Montana, where he fishes for big and little trout.*—FEBRUARY 1996 •••

BIG FISH/LITTLE FISH
by Ian Frazier

Most angling stories involve big fish. For a fish to be literary, it must be immense, moss-backed, storied; for it to attain the level of the classics, it had better be a whale. But in fact, mostly that's not what we catch. Especially when first learning the sport, we catch little ones, and we continue to catch them even when we gain more skill and know how to find and fish for big ones. In the retelling, the little ones are enlarged, or passed over as if mildly shameful. There's just something not flattering about the contrast between over-equipped us and a trophy that would fit with five others in a King Oscar of Norway Sardines can. You rarely read a story in which the author catches a fish of five inches—it's as if a fisherman's numbers don't go much below 12. A recent euphemism is "fish of about a pound." When I hear of a slow day on the river where the angler is catching fish of about a pound, my mind corrects that estimate to "nine inches, tops."

I've told my personal big-fish stories so often to myself and others that now I may remember the stories better than the events they describe. The little fish I've caught remain unglazed by myth, and if I do happen to remember them they are perhaps in some ways more real than the big ones in my mind. Once on the Yellowstone River a pocket-sized rainbow trout startled me by coming clear out of a patch of riffle water to take a dry fly before it landed, when it was still about a foot in the air. Little rainbows are more vivid in color; this had a line like a streak of lipstick on its side. In a rivulet next to a campsite in northern Michigan, a friend and I heard small splashes one night as we sat around the fire. When we investigated with a flashlight, we saw a spring peeper frog swimming on the surface with one leg gone, and fingerling brown trout slashing at him from below. Near the campsite ran the Pigeon River, a brushy stream full of browns. During a Hendrickson hatch, I waded with great care toward a little sipping rise in a place almost impossible to cast to under tag-alder branches—just the sort of place you'd find an 18-inch fish. I hung up a fly or two, and broke them off rather than disturb the water. Finally, miraculously, I laid the fly in the exact spot; a four-inch brown hit so hard that his impetus carried him well up into the alder branches, where he remained, flipping and flapping and complicatedly entangling the line. Once in a river in Siberia reputed to hold *farel*, a trout-like gamefish, I found instead millions of no-name silvery fish about the size of laundry marking pens. They were too small to net, but would take a fly; I caught 15 or more, and a Russian friend wrapped each one whole in wet pages from her sketchbook and baked them, paper and all, in the campfire coals. We took them out and unwrapped them and ate them steaming hot, with river-temperature Chinese beer.

Little fish make my mouth water, like the mouths of the hungry cave-guys in the movie *Quest for Fire* when they see a herd of antelope across the plain. A seine net full of smelt looks delicious, almost as good as a dozen golden deep-fried smelt with lemon wedges on a plate. In Ohio we used to eat little fish by the mess—as in, a mess of bluegills or a mess of perch. My cousin and I used to catch white bass by the dozens in Lake Erie in the Painesville harbor, right by the docks of the Diamond Shamrock Chemical Company, and then take them back to his house for fish fries, which no doubt left certain trace elements which we carry with us to this day. Once I was fishing for shad in the Delaware River with a friend and somehow snagged a minnow only slightly bigger than the fly itself. I showed it to my friend, examined it, and popped it in my mouth. His face did that special deep wince people do when they watch you eat something gross. But the taste wasn't bad—sushi, basically, only grittier.

When I went to Florida on a family vacation as a boy, I was disappointed to find that no tackleshop carried hooks small enough for the quarry I had in mind. Like everyone else I went out on the bottom-fishing boats in the deep water over the wrecks and the reefs. I cranked up a cobia longer than my leg, and a man from Cleveland in a scissor-bill cap caught a shark which the captain finally had to shoot with a handgun. On later trips I remembered to bring small hooks, and a spinning rod light enough to cast morsels of shrimp with no sinkers. In the quiet shade beneath the new overpass at the Key West charterboat basin I fished for triggerfish, Frisbee-shaped fish with sharp dorsal spines and pursed, tiny mouths. They fought hard, turning sideways to the line and soaring among the riprap and the mossy bases of the pilings. From the boardwalks of docks and next to highway bridges I fished for mangrove snappers, grunts, porgies, and unidentified fish with colors luminous as an expansion team's. At a boat canal near our motel I spent hours casting to needlefish, little bolts of quicksilver on the surface that struck the bait viciously again and again without ever getting themselves hooked. If I happened to be near deeper water, sometimes the dark shape of a barracuda would materialize, approaching a little fish I'd hooked and then palming it like a giant hand. The moment the rod folded with his weight, the ease with which the line parted, the speed with which the rod snapped back, were as much of the monster as I wanted to know.

At times, catching even a single little fish has been far preferable to catching no fish at all. Often I have landed my first with relief, knowing that at least now I can say I caught something. One afternoon four friends and I rented boats to fish a Michigan pond supposedly full of bluegills and largemouth bass. In 20 man-hours of determined fishing, between us we did not catch or see a fish. One of us, however, drifting bait on the bottom, did catch a clam. About the size of a 50-cent piece, the bivalve had closed over the hook so tightly that it required needle-nosed pliers to dislodge. Of course it was of no use to us other than as a curiosity, and did not dispel the gloom with which we rowed back to the jeering locals at the boat-rental dock. But it did reveal its usefulness later when we reported to friends and family about the day. They asked how we did, and we said, "Well, we caught a clam." Such a statement will always set non-fishermen back on their heels (*You caught a clam? Is that good?*) and defangs the scorn that awaits the fishless angler's return.

I look for fish in any likely water I see—harbors, rivers, irrigation ditches, hotel-lobby fountains. Every decade, maybe, I spot a long snook lurking in the shadow of a docked sailboat somebody's trying to sell, or a tail among the reeds at the edge of a pond that connects itself to a body that connects itself to a head improbably far away, or a leviathan back and dorsal fin breaching just once in the Mississippi that even today I can't believe I saw. More often, I see nothing, or little fish. The two are not so different; if a big fish is like the heart of a watershed, little fish are like the water itself. I've taken just-caught little fish and put them in the hands of children watching me from the bank, and the fish gyrate and writhe and flop their way instantly from the hands back to the water, not so much a living thing as the force that makes things live. I've spotted little fish in trickles I could step across, in basin-sized pools beneath culverts in dusty Wyoming pastures, in puddles in the woods connected to no inlet or outlet I could see—fish originally planted, I'm told, in the form of fish eggs on the feet of visiting ducks. One of the commonplaces of modern life is the body of water by the gravel pit or warehouse district where you know for a fact not even a minnow lives. The sight of just one healthy little brook trout, say, testifies for the character of the water all around, redeems it, raises it far up in our estimation.

Near where I used to live in Montana was a brush-filled creek that ran brown with snowmelt every spring, then dwindled in the summer until it resembled a bucket of water poured on a woodpile. I never thought to look in it, or even could, until one winter when I noticed a wide part, not quite a pool, by a culvert under an old logging road. Thick ice as clear and flawed as frontier window glass covered the pool, and through the ice I saw movement. I got down on my knees in the snow and looked more closely; above the dregs of dark leaves and bark fragments on the creek bottom, two small brook trout were holding in the current. Perhaps because of the ice between us, they did not flinch when I came so near I could see the black-and-olive vermiculate markings on their backs, the pink of their gills when they breathed, the tiny red spots with blue halos on their sides. They were doing nothing but holding there; once in a while they would minutely adjust their position with a movement like a gentle furling down their lengths. Self-possessed as any storied lunker, they waited out the winter in their shallow lie, ennobling this humble flow to a trout stream.

Adventure

Beginning in 1926, with a Jimmy Robinson profile of Annie Oakley, and moving through such thrilling tales as Russell Annabel's $7,000,000 ADVENTURE WITH BEARS (1969), Peter Beard's crocodile hunting expeditions in EYELIDS OF MORNING (1974) and Jack Kulpa's THE MIST PEOPLE (1985), adventure has always been an integral part of SPORTS AFIELD. We've also included a few other pieces—an article on elephant guns by Ted Kerasote from 1982 and a sermon of sorts by Jim Harrison from 1995—just to make things interesting.

••• *The trap and skeet editor of* SPORTS AFIELD *for 60 years, Jimmy Robinson hunted with kings and queens, movie stars and celebrities. In this story, one of his first for the magazine, he covered one of the greatest women trapshooters of all time.*—DECEMBER 1926 •••

ANNIE OAKLEY RULED THE TRAPS

by Jimmy Robinson

Of the thousands of sport followers who roam the hills and streams, and visit the traps, there is none who have not read about the famous Annie Oakley.

Annie was known by the shooters all over the country. Although the present generation has but a rather vague recollection of Annie Oakley and her skill with the gun, those whose memory take them back a quarter of a century know what a wonder she really was.

She was born in Woodland, Ohio, and was never really famous until she defeated the famous Frank Butler in a shooting match in this little town years ago. Mr. Butler was at the time one of the country's leading all around shots, and he was touring the country, shooting exhibition matches against all comers. Annie was then a charming little Quaker Miss of only 15 summers, and she proved his downfall. She defeated him in a 50-bird exhibition match. Shortly after these two were married and traveled the country, shooting. They joined the famous Buffalo Bill show and traveled with this troupe for 17 years. Of the great collection of crack shots that Buffalo Bill had under his command, "Little Sure Shot," the nickname given Annie, was the greatest.

She traveled in 14 countries, gave exhibition matches, hunted and shot game in every one of them. She has been entertained by kings, queens and emperors. During her long regime with Buffalo Bill she missed but two performances. She shot two matches in 1888 on successive days at Gloucester and Trenton, N.J., and several sportsmen wagered $5000 that she could not kill 40 birds out of 50 at 80 yards. Annie killed 49. At Trenton, she shot with the famous Miles Johnson in a 50-bird race and defeated him before a crowd of 30,000 people.

Some of Annie's best shooting was done abroad, where she won over $9000 in several matches in England. She gave five special exhibitions in England at the request of the Prince of Wales, who afterward was King Edward. At one of these matches the ruling monarchs of five European countries and queens of four others attended.

At this particular match the Prince of Wales presented Annie with a gold medal inscribed, "You are the greatest shooter I ever saw, and America should be proud of you," to which Miss Oakley replied, "I am proud of America."

Some time later Queen Victoria sent Miss Oakley an autographed photograph of herself and Alexandria, who later became Queen of England. Miss Oakley has a book of autographs that is most interesting. Presidents of the United States, rulers of European nations, everyone of world fame in the last 30 years has written a line or two in this book. Mark Twain wrote in it, "You can do everything that can be done in the shooting line and then some."

The book of autographs is only a small part of her valued collection, for while abroad nobility showered gifts upon her. The Prince Regent of Bavaria gave her a bracelet containing 11 diamonds; the Baroness Rothschild, a diamond brooch; the Baroness De Molesticks of Vienna, a necklace of pearls. But the most treasured of all her collection is the head and dress uniform worn by Sitting Bull, the great Indian Warrior, in his fight against Custer. She taught Sitting Bull how to write and later on she was made his heir.

In her long and glorious career she has never used the word "champion" and always insisted that her friends not address her as such. She always did much charity work. She has taken care of and schooled 20 orphans, helped the Red Cross during the war and gave exhibition matches to the "Dough Boys" before they went to France. Miss Oakley met with a severe accident in Florida a few years ago, breaking her hip. Doctors said that she would never be well again. Annie thought differently, and the grit and courage she has always displayed is pulling her through, and we all hoped that in a short time we will see her as active as ever. This glorious Diana of the shooting world will always live in the thoughts of nimrods and trapshooters.

Editor's Note: A long-time reader of Sports Afield, *Annie Oakley passed away as the December 1926 issue was going to press.*

••• *As a field editor of* SPORTS AFIELD, *Jimmy Robinson covered all the shooting sports, plus wrote the waterfowl report for 50 years. He shared his duck blind on the Delta Marsh in Manitoba with a long line of guests, including the Hemingways, Hiltons, Olins and, here, his friend Clark Gable.*—JANUARY 1939 •••

A DUCK HUNT WITH CLARK GABLE
by Jimmy Robinson

The *boom, boom* of a shotgun shattered the stillness of the vast delta marsh on Lake Manitoba. Two canvasbacks halted in midflight, hurtled to the rushes and mud below.

A double!

The hunter was Clark Gable of Hollywood. He stood in a battered duck boat, grinning and happier, perhaps, than he had ever been before on a duck hunt.

"I've fulfilled my life's ambition, Jimmy!" Clark shouted. "I've always wanted to shoot the limit of canvasbacks in a single day—and boy, oh, boy, I've done it at last!" Clark almost tipped over the flimsy boat in his enthusiasm.

Gathering in the ducks and pulling in our decoys, we paddled through the tall rushes and wild rice to the channel which would lead us back to our little duck camp on the shore of Lake Manitoba, 60 miles west of Winnipeg. Hundreds of mallards, canvasbacks and widgeons whizzed over our heads to settle in the potholes and bayous of the great marsh.

Clark Gable insisted upon doing the paddling. All I had to do was sit on my seat and give steering directions!

It is a far cry from the glare of lights in Hollywood's studios to the solitude of the Manitoba marshes. The only artificial lights within miles of the boat in which Clark and I sat were the gasoline lamps in our hunting shack and those of our neighbors.

Gable liked our Manitoba marsh country. He stayed with us a week. Each day we visited a different section of the marsh. In spite of the warm September days, the birds were flying early in the morning and in the evening—the cream of the waterfowl population of the entire continent.

"I didn't know there were so many ducks in the world!" said Gable.

Clay targets brought Clark Gable to Manitoba. He loves duck hunting—it's one of the things he lives for. He's an upland bird shooter and big game hunter, too. Clay targets, however, are responsible for Gable's presence on the Canadian prairies. Clark does a lot of skeet shooting at the Santa Monica Gun Club in California.

Between rounds of skeet at Santa Monica, one winter day in 1935, I told Clark and Jack Conway, motion picture director and Gable's hunting companion, about our duck hunting on the Manitoba marshes. My tales attracted Clark's attention to such an extent that when I suggested that he should join me at Portage la Prairie, Manitoba some time, he accepted my invitation with alacrity.

Almost three years elapsed. Clark was busy in pictures. His shooting was confined to skeet, to ducks and doves in California, to doves in Mexico, to cougars in Arizona.

Grant Ilseng, top ranking skeet shot of 1938, and Ed Williams started Clark on the Manitoba duck trail. Having listened to my duck stories at the National Skeet Tournament at Tulsa, Oklahoma, where they were my roommates, Grant and Ed deluged Clark with yarns about canvasbacks and mallards when they met him at the Santa Monica Gun Club a few days after the Tulsa tourney.

On September 10, 1938, I received a wire from Clark in Los Angeles, addressed to the *Sports Afield* office in Minneapolis. It read something like this: "Met Grant Ilseng at gun club today. He informs me that you are going duck hunting at Lake Manitoba again this year. Have a week to spare so will take up invitation you gave me few years ago if convenient. Wire."—Clark Gable.

My reply urged Clark to wait until October, because we were experiencing an unusually warm September in Manitoba. His second wire advised me that he had to go to work on a new picture in October. I said: "Come anytime!"

Clark came by train from Hollywood directly to Portage la Prairie, Manitoba.

"I wish you had come a little later," I greeted him. "It's warm and the ducks are not flying so good."

"Shucks," Clark replied, "I just came up for a little holiday. If we don't get any ducks, that's O.K. with me."

Winnipeg newspaper men, who had been tipped off by Hollywood correspondents that Gable was coming to Manitoba, shot pictures of the movie actor even before the Canadian Pacific transcontinental pulled out. I had made an effort to keep secret Clark's coming, but to no avail.

"If we can get a few ducks for a feed or two, that'll satisfy me," Gable continued. "We can sit around the stove at night and talk about how many we should have gotten. That's what we do in California."

Clark insisted upon seeing Portage la Prairie before we headed for the camp. He bought his shells and hunting license at Cadham's hardware store, then visited the 5 and 10 cent store where he shook hands with all the girls. Our next stop was at the Leland hotel, operated by my old friend, Telf Miller. By this time a big crowd had gathered. Clark ordered Telf to "set them up" for all the boys.

We arrived at the camp—our hunting shack, we call it—at 3 P.M. Clark met the boys. Included in our party were Ernie Maetzold, Minneapolis, vice president of the Amateur Trapshooting Association; Walt Taylor, Minneapolis, of *Sports Afield*; Chuck Murphy, Joe Brush, George Hart, Ted Culbertson, Nick Kahler and Phil Fjellman of Minneapolis, and Phil and Rod Ducharme, local French-Canadian guides. Walter Peacock, Chicago, veteran trapshooter and member of the Illinois Racing Commission, was scheduled to be a member of the party but he did not arrive until after Gable had gone.

"This is swell," Clark declared, as he unpacked his grips, slipped on a pair of slippers and made himself comfortable.

"Take it easy," I said. "We won't do any hunting until tomorrow morning."

Clark rested only a few minutes. The marshes were close. His body demanded exercise after the long train ride.

"Let's go hunting now, Jimmy!" he exclaimed. "I want to take a look at those ducks I've been hearing so much about. Tomorrow's too long to wait."

So we set out to the marsh with Rod Ducharme, our French-Canadian guide. Clark paddled the boat.

Mallards, canvasbacks and widgeons winged their ways over our heads. The air was full of ducks. The huge marsh was alive with waterfowl. A golden September sun, reflected on rushes and wild rice, lent color to the scene.

"Boy, this is swell!" exulted Clark.

Fortune smiled at us. We set up our decoys in a little pothole, pushed our boat into the rushes, which are our blinds out here. Sleek barley and wheat-fed ducks, fattened by crops in nearby fields, decoyed obligingly. We garnered our limits within an hour.

Gable brought two shotguns with him to Manitoba. One was a double barrel Parker, the other a Winchester pump. The rest of his outfit was the kind you or I might wear: a battered Berlin leather hat, six years old, leather trousers and jacket which had seen plenty of service in the out-of-doors, light-weight boots, etc.

Gable was among the first up each morning. Usually it was the sound of his axe biting into the chunks on the woodpile that awakened me. Our typical schedule was breakfast at six, then out to the marsh, ready to shoot, by sun-up. At noon we returned to camp to rest, to talk about hunting and fishing trips, to play diamond-ball.

This man Gable is quite a ball player. He can handle himself well in the field and when his turn at the bat comes around he connects often enough to be classed as a fair hitter.

Gable is strong as a bull. He's six feet, one inch tall, weighs 200 pounds. He's fast as a cat—and in tiptop condition. Not only did he out-shoot me on the marsh but also he out-walked me in hiking to the marsh. In fact, he out-did me in almost everything except eating.

"Got to watch my diet," said Clark. His appetite ran away with him, however, when Mrs. Robinson served a canvasback hot from the oven, at the supper table each night. He insisted that the Lake Manitoba wall-eyed pike our guides caught were the best-eating fish he ever ate.

Clark's first canvasbacks in years of shooting were the ones he dropped that first afternoon, a few hours after he got off the train. Gable insisted that he was just a fair duck shot. He had no excuses to make about his shooting after he killed that first double that came in. Although he hasn't shot many ducks, he's an exceptionally fine duck shot. The speedy way he handled his gun surprised me.

Among the visitors who attracted Gable's attention was Jack Handily, Manitoba game warden. The pair did a lot of talking about hunting in the North Country. Several "mounties" stopped in to say hello to Clark.

The camp, a private one leased by the group of Minneapolis hunters, is located on the Delta Marsh on the south shore of Lake Manitoba, 14 miles north of Portage la Prairie and 60 miles west of Winnipeg. We can drive to the camp when it doesn't rain. It's two miles from the camp to the marsh and we drive it with lights when we go out for the morning shooting. It's a job, pushing our boats through the runways in the rushes and rice, but we get through. When we come to a pothole or to the big bay, we push our boat into the rushes, set out the decoys which the guides have whittled, and we're ready for the flight.

The camp—"shack," we call it—is an old farm house. We have a big kitchen, a dining room, and two bedrooms rigged up with triple bunks. A huge stove supplies the heat and another big woodstove takes care of the cooking.

Clark Gable is so long that his feet stuck out of the end of the bunk. Clark proved to be helpful around camp in other ways than chopping wood. He also helped Mrs. Robinson with the dishes.

The whole gang went to bed at 10 each night, except one night when we played poker for a 25-cent limit. That's Gable's top limit out in California.

Each afternoon when we'd finished playing dia-mondball we talked about hunting and fishing in other parts of the country. Gable revealed that he enjoyed hunting mountain lions. He makes frequent trips to the Kaibab Forest area in Arizona to shoot the big cats. He always has felt that this type of hunting is a genuine contribution to big game hunting. He claims lions such as he has killed take a terrific toll among deer. It is estimated that a big cat will kill 25 deer in a year.

In his Hollywood home Gable has three dogs, two cats, four canaries, seven turkeys and a cook. When he hunts doves he goes in his trailer, takes the cook and her husband with him. He does a lot of hunting in company with Jack Conway, the director, and Jim Smith, California trapshooter.

Nick Kahler, who puts on the Sportsman's and Outdoor Shows in Minneapolis and whose Chicago Sportsman's Show comes up in January, staged a party for Gable, attended by sportsmen and newspaper men, at the Nicollet Hotel in Minneapolis at the conclusion of the trip. Following an afternoon at Lake Minnetonka, near Minneapolis, Gable returned to Hollywood.

Clark Gable is an A-1 companion on a hunting trip—a first-grade sportsman. We would enjoy hunting with him again.

• • • Born in Wisconsin in 1900, Gordon MacQuarrie was the out-door editor of the MILWAUKEE JOURNAL from 1936 to 1956. During that time, he wrote innumerable stories for SPORTS AFIELD, most of them about the Old Duck Hunter's Association, a fictitious organization he invented for literary purposes.—OCTOBER 1956 • • •

THE OLD BROWN MACKINAW
by Gordon MacQuarrie

When the president of the Old Duck Hunter's Association, Inc., died, the hearts of many men fell to the ground.

There was no one like Mister President. When the old-timers go there is no bringing them back, nor is there any hope of replacing them. They are gone, and there is a void and for many, many years I knew the void would never be filled, for this paragon of the duck blinds and the trout streams had been the companion of my heart's desire for almost 20 years.

I made the common mistake. I looked for another, exactly like hizzoner. How foolish that is, as foolish as it is for a man to try to find another beloved hunting dog, exactly like the one that's gone.

In the years after Mister President's death I fished and hunted more than before, and often alone. There was a great deal of fishing and hunting, from Florida to Alaska, before a man came along who fit the role once occupied by Mister President. This is how it was:

I was sitting in the ballroom of the Lorraine Hotel in Madison, Wisconsin, covering the proceedings of the unique Wisconsin conservation congress. I became aware that a man carrying one of the 71 labels for the 71 counties of the state was eyeing me.

He held aloft the cardboard label "Iowa" signifying that he was a Big Wheel in conservation from that western Wisconsin county. He looked like Huckleberry Finn and he grinned eternally. One of the first thoughts I had about him was that he probably could not turn down the corners of his lips if he wanted to.

Each time I glanced at him his eye was upon me. This sort of thing is unnerving. Once he caught my eye and held it and grinned harder. I grinned back, foolishly. The beggar burst out laughing. I felt like a fool. He knew it and laughed at me.

Let me give you the picture more completely. In that room sat more than 300 dedicated, articulate conservationists. They were framing, no less, the fish and game code of this sovereign state for an entire year. Not in silence, you may be sure.

Up at the front table on the platform, as chairman of the congress, sat Dr. Hugo Schneider of Wausau, with a gavel in one hand and—so help me!—a muzzle-loading squirrel rifle in the other. Each time *Roberts Rules of Order* seemed about to go out the window, Doc would abandon the gavel and reach for the rifle.

In this delightful pandemonium, in this convention of impassioned hunters and fishers and amidst the shrieks from the wounded and dying delegates, Wisconsin evolves its game and fish laws. And if you can think of a more democratic way, suggest it. We may try it.

At one point in the milling commotion and confusion, I saw my grinning friend slip to the floor and on his hands and knees start crawling toward me. By this manner of locomotion he managed to evade the baleful eye and subsequent vengeance of Dr. Schneider, and he crawled up to my chair and handed me a scribbled note. Then still on his hands and knees, he crawled away. The note read:

"I've been reading your drivel for years. See me after school if you want to get some good partridge hunting."

Harry

Since then I suppose I've "seen him" 1000 times—on trout streams, on lakes, in partridge cover, in the deer woods, in the quail thicket, and yes, in the August cow pastures where the blackberries grow as long as your thumb, and in the good September days when you can fill a bushel basket with hickory nuts beneath one tree.

No outdoor event of its season escapes Harry. He is lean and 50ish. He is a superb shot. He ties his own flies, one a black killer with a tiny spinner at the eye made from special light material he begs, or steals from dentist friends. On a dare, once he shinnied up a 12-foot pole and came back down head first. Once he made me a pair of buckskin pants. All in all, an unbelievable person.

How natural then, just this last October, that we should rendezvous, not in Iowa County—we save those partridge until December—but at the ancient headquarters of the Old Duck Hunter's Association, two whoops and a holler north of Hayward, Wisconsin.

I got there first. This is not hard for me to do when going to this place. Some things do not change and this is one of those things. It's exactly like it was before the atomic age. On that particular day, late October's yellow shafts were slanting through the Norways on the old cedar logs of the place. A chipmunk which had learned to beg in summer came tentatively close, then scurried away, uncertain now.

All was in order, down to the new windowpane I had to put in where a partridge in the crazy time had flown through. The label was still pasted to the tiny square of glass. I must scratch it off some day but there is always so much to do at places like this.

I went to the shed at the rear to check decoy cords and anchors. When you open this shed door one of the first things to catch your eye is a brown, checked-pattern Mackinaw, about 50 years old, I guess. It belonged to the President of the Old Duck Hunters. I like to keep it there. It belongs there.

Flying squirrels had filled one pocket of the Mackinaw with acorns. They always do that, but these avian rodents, so quick to unravel soft, new wool for nests, have never chewed at the threadbare carcass of Mister President's heroic jacket. Perhaps this is because the wool, felted and tough, has lost its softness and flavor.

I launched a boat, readied a smaller skiff and screwed the motor on the big boat. I fetched three bags of decoys down the hill and placed them handy. I put an ax—for blind building—in the boat with other gear, and when I got back up the hill to the cabin Harry was there.

On the way —a 300-mile drive—he had hesitated, he said, long enough to slay two pheasant roosters.

"I see," he said, "that you have been here an hour and have killed 'ary a duck or partridge." He explained that he had felt my auto radiator—"She's cooled only about an hour." This man operates like a house detective. I explained that in the remaining hour and a half of daylight I would prepare him a kingly supper.

"An hour and a half of daylight!" He flung two skinned pheasants at me, dashed to his car and returned, running, bearing fishing tackle.

"D'ja soak the boat?" he cried as he passed me. I doubt if he heard my answer for he was soon down the hill and nearing the beach when I replied. Within two minutes he was trolling.

The man never lived who could fill up each moment of a day like this one. Nor was there ever a one who could, once the day was done, fall asleep so fast. He goes, I am sure, into a world of dreams, there to continue the pursuits of fish and game, man's life's blood—well, his, anyway.

I lit the fireplace. No need for the big steel stove, or was there? Late October weather in the north can be treacherous. I laid the big stove fire, to play safe. The provident Harry had made getting supper easy. You take two pheasants and cut them up. You save the giblets. You steam some wild rice for an hour . . .

It was long after dark when Harry returned. He had a seven- or eight-pound northern and a walleye half as big—"If we're gonna be here for four days, somebody around here has got to bring home the grub."

I set the table fast for fear he would fall asleep. He stuffed himself with pheasant and wild rice and mentioned that he must not forget to tell his wife how badly I treated him. Then he collapsed on the davenport before the fire, and in one yawn and a short whistle he was gone. I washed the dishes.

No, he is not a shirker. Before sleep afflicts him he will kill himself at any job which needs doing, especially if it pertains to hunting and fishing. To prove his willingness for the menial tasks, I recall a deer camp one night when one of the boys bought in a 300-pound bear—dragged him right through the door and dropped him at Harry's feet.

Harry was wiping the dishes, clad only in a suit of new, red underwear. He had sworn to be the first man in that camp to bring in important game, and because now he obviously had not, he turned, dishcloth in hand, eyed the bear casually and remarked:

"Johnny, that's a mighty nice little woodchuck you got there."

Even when I turned on the radio for a weather report he did not awaken. His snores, wondrously inventive, competed with the welcome report of changing and colder weather. Outside the wind was coming along a bit and it was in the northwest. But mostly it was the warm wind hurrying back south ahead of something colder at its back.

Iowa County's nonpareil was bedded down in the far room where his snores joined the issue with the rising wind which keened over the roof. A good fair contest, that.

When I arose I had to light the big heater for the weather had made up its mind. No snow, but a thermometer at 26 degrees and a buster of a wind. I hurried with breakfast because I thought we might have to build a blind on Posey's point. That point, the right one on this day, had not been hunted in the season. When I mentioned the reason for haste he explained:

"Man, I built that blind yesterday. You think I fooled away three hours just catching a couple fish?"

It is not possible to dislike a man like that. Furthermore, I knew this blind would be no wild dove's nest, but a thing of perfection, perfectly blended with the shore line.

A lot of people in this country think the Old Duck Hunters are crazy when they hunt this lake. We carry so many decoys that we have to tow them behind in a skiff. Fifty is our minimum, half of them over-sized balsas, and a scattering of some beat-up antiques more than 120 years old, just for luck.

Settling himself for some duck blind gossip, Harry began, "I was down on the Mississippi at Ferryville last week. Mallards all over the—"

"Mark!"

A hundred bluebills, maybe twice that, who knows, came straight in without once swinging, and sat. We never touched a feather as they rose. I have done it before and I'll do it again and may God have mercy on my soul.

"This," said Harry, "will become one of the greatest lies in history when I tell my grandchildren about it. I am reminded of Mark Twain. When Albert Bigelow Paine was writing his biography and taking copious notes he once remarked to Twain that his experiences and adventures were wonderful copy.

"'Yes, yes,' replied Mr. Clemens. 'And the most remarkable thing about it is that half of them are true.'"

He then set his jaw and announced he would kill the next three straight with as many shots. This he did, for I did not fire. While I was retrieving them in the decoy skiff, another bundle of bluebills tried to join those giant decoys and were frightened off by me. Walking to the blind from the boat, I saw Harry kill a canvasback.

He was through for the day and not a half hour had passed. Many Badgers will remember that late October day of 1955. Ducks flew like crazy from the Kakagon sloughs of Lake Superior to sprawling Horicon marsh, 300 miles away. Only one other day of that season beat it—Wednesday, November 2.

Harry cased his gun and watched. I cannot shoot like Harry, but getting four ducks on such a day was child's play. Many times we had more divers over our decoys than we had decoys. It was pick-and-choose duck hunting. I settled for four bull-neck canvasbacks.

Back at the cabin we nailed their bills to the shed wall, and over a cup of coffee Harry said the divers we'd seen reminded him of the "kin to can't day." Then he explained, the law let a man shoot the whole day through from as soon "as he kin see until the time that he can't see." I knew a place, Oscar Ruprecht's sugar bush, and we drove the eight miles to it.

This chunk of maple is on an island of heavier soil in an ocean of glacial sand, grown to pines. If its owner had the equipment he could tap 5,000 trees. Many know it and hunt it. We separated, for we are both snap shooters, or think we are.

The plan was to meet on a high, rocky bluff where the river Ounce passes by below, on its way to the Totagatic. Here was no dish like that easy duck blind venture. These were mature, hunted ruffed grouse, all the more nervous because the wind was high. On one of the tote trails where Oscar's tractor hauls the sap tank I missed my first bird, then missed two more.

A half mile to my right two calculated shots sounded, well spaced. Perhaps a double. Ah, well. . . . My fourth bird was as good as dead when it got out of the red clover in mid-trail and flew straight down the road. I missed him, too.

Three times more, and later a couple more times Harry's gun sounded. Then two birds flung themselves out of the yellow bracken beside the two-rut road and I got one. When I was walking over to pick it up, a third pumped up and I got it.

It was noon when I got to the high bluff. Deer hunters with scopes on their rifles love this place. From it they overlook almost a half mile of good deer country in three directions. My sandwich tasted good. I lit a little friendship fire and thought about other days on the river below me. It's a pretty good trout stream for anyone who will walk in two miles before starting to fish.

Harry came along. He'd been far up the valley of the Ounce, bucking fierce cover—no sugar bush tote trails in there, only deer trails. But he had five grouse. We hunted back to the car, and in his presence I was lucky enough to kill my third bird.

It was around 2:00 P.M. when we pulled into the cabin. My Huckleberry Finn who I have seen, on occasion, whittle away at a pine stick for 20 minutes without doing anything but meditate, was a ball of fire this day. He tied into the ducks and partridge. When he had finished cleaning them his insatiable eye fell upon the woodpile.

You can spot those real country-raised boys every time when they grab an ax. They know what to do with it. No false moves. No glancing blows. In no time he had half a cord of fine stuff split and piled for the kitchen range and he went on from that to the sheer labor of splitting big maple logs with a wedge for the fireplace.

He spotted my canoe and considered painting it, but decided it was too cold, and anyway, it had begun to snow a little. Then he speculated about the weather, and when I said I wish I had a weather vane on the ridgepole, he went into action.

He whittled out an arrow from an old shingle, loosely nailed it to a stick, climbed to the roof and nailed it there firmly. I suppose that if I had mentioned building an addition to the back porch he'd have started right in. He came down from the roof covered with snow and said he wished he hadn't killed those four ducks in the morning, so he could go again.

"But let's go anyway," he suggested. "No guns. Put out the decoys and just watch 'em."

Out there on the point the divers were riding that wind out of Canada. Scores of them rode into and above the decoys. Posey, the owner of the point, came along for a visit and decided we were both crazy when he saw what we were doing. Nevertheless, we had him ducking down as excited as we were when a new band of bluebills burst out of the snow. Only in the big duck years can a hunter enjoy such madness.

Our shore duty at dark that night involved careful preparations against the storm. We pulled up the boat and skiff higher than usual and covered everything with a weighted tarp.

Walking up the hill, I considered how nice it was to have one of the faithful, like Harry, on the premises. He should have been bone tired. Certainly I was. But before I relit the big heater he took down its 15 feet of stovepipe, shook out the soot and wired it back to the ceiling. He carried in enough wood for the remaining three days, stamping off snow and whistling and remembering such tales as one hears in all properly managed hunting camps.

He spied a seam rip in my buckskin pants and ordered me to take them off. While he mended them he complained bitterly about such neglect on my part— "There's nothing wrong with the workmanship on these pants."

He had made them himself, two months before, from two big chrome tanned doeskins. He just walked into my house one night with a gunny sack containing the skins, a piece of chalk and some old shears his wife used for trimming plants. He cut the pants out, fitted them to me and took them to the shoemaker's shop where he sewed them up and affixed buttons. I never in my life wore pants that fit so well.

This man should have been born in the same time as a Kit Carson or a Jim Bridger. Turn him loose anywhere in his native heath, which is Wisconsin, and, given matches, an ax, a fishhook and some string, he'll never go hungry or cold.

He is a true countryman, a species almost extinct. Each day of the year finds him outdoors for at least a little while. In trout season he hits the nearby streams for an hour or two around sunup. His garden is huge and productive. In the raspberry season you may not go near his home without being forced, at gun point if need be, to eat a quart of raspberries with cream.

He represents something almost gone from our midst. He knows the value of working with his own hands, of being eternally busy, except when sleeping. His last act that snowy evening was to go to his car and return with a bushel of hickory nuts. He set up a nut-cracking factory on a table, using a little round steel anvil he had brought for busting 'em. He had over a quart of hickory nut meats in jars when I put the grub on the table.

He almost fell asleep at the table. Then he yawned and whistled and looked out the door and said he was glad it was snowing hard—"Don't shoot at anything but cans in the morning." He flopped on the davenport and was gone to that far-off land where no trout of less than five pounds comes to a surface fly and the duck season runs all year.

I tidied up and washed the dishes. I smelled the weather and smoked a pipe. The fireplace light danced on the big yellow cedar beams. The snow hissed against the window. The President of the Old Duck Hunter's Association should have been there.

Maybe he was. At any rate, I went out to the shed and took the old brown Mackinaw off its nail and brought it in and laid it over Harry's shoulders. It looked just fine there.

••• *From Yonkers, New York, Gil Paust was a commercial pilot who wrote adventure stories for this magazine from the late 1950s through the 1970s. This particular piece, written five years after the incident occurred, illustrated how survival skills were critical even to old Alaskan sourdoughs.*—JANUARY 1960 •••

THE YEAR THE BROWN BEAR WENT MAD
by Gil Paust

The premature autumn blizzard of 1955 had blitzed the Alaska Peninsula with a four-foot fall, and in the light of the clearing dawn the tundra, topped with lightly drifted crests and troughs, was a bleached sea frozen in a gentle swell. Bill Hammersley's snowshoes trailed a thin, wavering wake across its waste.

Against a spit of snow dust raised by the storm's ebbing wind the rail-thin figure of the old sourdough plodded toward a curved finger of tangled spruces that beckoned from the bordering forest. His face, masked by a full graying beard, was Messiah-like, but his sunken, troubled eyes revealed a strange inner intentness. And in one scraggy hand he carried a short-barrel Winchester rifle.

Hammersley was 100 paces from the trees when he stopped in midstride. He heard a sudden unseen crashing—a harsh discord in the soft sigh of the air through the branches. He thumbed off the safety of the rifle, muting its click with his glove. A moose? Or one of the man-killers? His eyes hardened to blue ice, their corners cracked by deep lines. Kicking off his snowshoes, he dropped onto his stomach and wriggled his fur-clad body into the powder snow until only his head, arms and rifle remained clear. The animal, whatever it was, couldn't scent him. He was downwind from it. And the wolverine fur of his exposed parka hood was white enough to blend with the snow. Even his beard had been frosted to near-white by his steaming breath. He pulled off his dark snowglasses and slipped them inside his parka, then squinted across the sudden glare.

Hammersley wanted it to be a moose. He'd had little to eat in five days. If he hadn't needed food so desperately, he wouldn't have dared to leave his cabin to face an even greater hunger in the woods—that of the brown bears. That year starvation had driven the big bears mad. These giant carnivores had become the greatest menace to settlers on the Alaska Peninsula. And Hammersley had been marooned among them. He'd been ready to "come out" to escape them when he'd discovered after the first snow that they were too hungry to hibernate. But then the long blizzard had come unexpectedly, and escape had been impossible.

As the sound continued, grew louder, the old man dug himself deeper into the snow. He was no coward. The rigors of the frontier had strengthened his courage as well as his endurance, and at 63 these qualities had been preserved in him by some mysterious elixir from the same environment that nurtures the mightiest moose and bears in the world. But for the first time in his 30 years in Alaska's backcountry, he was afraid. While he'd prospected the remote river and lake benches for gold, he'd killed animals only when he'd needed them for food or fur. The wilderness and its wildlife hadn't been his enemies. They'd been simply the setting for his own life of solitude. He'd survived because he'd respected their hazards and prepared for them. The complaisant brown bears had been the least of them. The greatest was the arctic winter that could crush a man beneath its juggernaut of snow and cold. Then the bears had gone mad. And this time Hammersley had been prepared for neither.

The sound in the spruces ceased abruptly when a large dark form moved from the point of trees and floundered into the open snow, halting when it became mired to its brisket. The fresh breeze off the tundra became tainted with the noxious stench of a rutting bull moose. The animal was a giant. It arched its curved muzzle high, nostrils filtering the air for scent of danger, then the glossed palms of its ponderous antlers flashed in the early sunlight as it swung its head to look back.

Hammersley's taut figure lost some of its tenseness. He grunted with satisfaction. The bull's liver would be foul from the rut, but there would be all the steaks and chops he could carry. The predators could have what he left. Propping his elbows on one of the snowshoes, he lifted his rifle and sighted it on the lowest visible part of the bull's chest. Then he hesitated as his eyes studied the animal through the sights. The chest was whooshing like a great bellows, pumping out its breath in steaming billows. The hair on the animal's flanks was matted with melted snow, but the ruff bristled on its shoulders. The bull hadn't willingly left its sheltered runways beneath the trees and attempted to cross the tundra. Something had driven it. But an Alaska bull moose in rut has too much justified ego to know fear.

And it is too formidable to have any natural enemy. Its front hoofs are sharp sledge-hammers swung by 1500 pounds of brawn with the perseverance of a killer whale. Too lethal even for a wolf pack. It seldom fears even man.

Hammersley thoughtfully lowered his weapon. When the bull continued to stare toward the trees, ears cocked, the old sourdough cautiously spread the sides of the parka hood that muffled his own hearing. There was a new and different sound in the forest, a crackle of branches that was subdued and measured, not loud and continuous like that of the moose when it had crashed through them. An animal was stalking stealthily on padded feet. As the crackling came nearer, the bull panicked. It pranced farther into the open until it was only 50 paces from Hammersley and stood trembling, eyes red and wild and head stretched flat until the tines of its antlers brushed its ruff. A second dark form grew at the edge of the spruces. A moment later, with a grumbling roar, it charged the trapped bull.

The bull turned when it heard the roar, and tried to meet the charge of the huge bear, but was snowbound. Its stiltlike legs were so deeply spiked in the snow that they couldn't counter the bear's jaws and flailing paws, and the bear's broad furred feet gave it better footing, and the bull's antlers were too cumbersome for any combat other than a formal joust with another bull. The old sourdough blanched as he watched the duel between the giant animals, and he cringed against the snow. The stark violence of the scene, the snorts of the doomed bull and the savage mouthings of the bear overwhelmed him with their nearness.

But they ended quickly. Rearing upright on its hind legs, the brown bear towered over its kill, forelegs hanging stiff. The paws, with unsheathed claws as thick and long as a man's fingers, brushed across its stomach. It was a 10-foot-tall sow that would have weighed nearly as much as the moose if it weren't emaciated. The hide was drawn drum-tight over its bulging rib cage and was scraped hairless, as was its rump. Its belly, which should have been bulging with fat, was shriveled, and its flanks were blotched with bald spots, some marked by scars while from others the hair had simply "slipped" because of malnutrition. Lips curling over its fangs, it scanned the tundra suspiciously, a monstrous and vicious counterpart of a child's torn, mangy teddy bear.

All at once it looked directly toward Hammersley with a hiss, chomping its jaws angrily. Although it couldn't see or scent him, a subtle intuition peculiar to all wildlife, to the female especially, enabled it to sixth-sense his presence. Hammersley held his breath to smother its sound, and his hand crept toward his rifle. The little 270 bullet could drop a standing moose or discourage a surly brown bear, but it wouldn't be able to stop a bear in a charge, certainly not this hunger-crazed sow. And it would be fatal to run.

The sow stretched its neck, craning to see over the low drift separating it from Hammersley. But it was reluctant to leave its kill. It dropped to its forepaws as if intending to investigate him, but immediately reared up to stare once more. Then unexpectedly a shrill whimper came from the spruces and a stronger instinct over-came the sow's suspicion. Swinging toward the sound, she yapped once. Immediately two yearling cubs (they were so scrawny and stunted Hammersley could have carried one under each arm although they should have weighed at least 100 pounds apiece) bounced out across the snow and tore into the dead moose rabidly. In spite of their hunger, with the obedience characteristic of well-disciplined bear youngsters, they had been waiting under cover for their mother's all-clear.

Without visible movement the old sourdough kept flexing the muscles of his stiffening arms and legs, more often those of his right arm and fingers, which would have to work the rifle. He had no doubt he would have to try to kill the sow eventually when the cold became unbearable. The Winchester lay before him on the snowshoe, its muzzle tilted clear of the snow that could clog its bore. Several fast shots catching the sow unawares might drop it, ending the siege, because when physically unaroused the animal would be more vulnerable to the shock of a bullet. But with the sow's help, the cubs might survive the winter. They surely wouldn't without it. Hammersley's eyes became soft as they contemplated the starving bear feeding ravenously on the moose carcass. They were pitiful animals, and misfits, originally victims of one strange unbalance of nature and now fighting against another.

Although the brown bears were created vicious carnivores with capable jaws and teeth, any large animals they could prey upon either have become too scarce or are too fleet-footed for them to catch. In their evolution they learned to compromise for more abundant and less elusive foods, such as insects, ground rodents, green spring grass—and principally the millions of fat red-and-pink salmon that pack the rivers from June through September on their spawning runs.

But in 1955 the salmon runs on the Peninsula had been meager. Fewer spawning fish had returned from the Pacific to their home rivers, and only a small percentage of these had dodged the canners' nets. Hunger had gradually made the bears frantic. They had reverted to their forgotten predatory instinct, even attacking moose. One prey they found they could overcome most easily because it was puny with inadequate protective senses of sight, smell and hearing and was incapable of outrunning them—was man! The homesteaders, trappers, prospectors and Eskimos who lived in the outlands and had seldom carried firearms when traveling among their unaggressive bear neighbors were taken by surprise. Many fled with their families to more inland settlements. By autumn it was considered suicidal to walk the forests or tundra without a rifle of large caliber. The bears became increasingly menacing as their hibernating period approached. They began to stalk the settlers in their cabins, then raid the cabins.

To Hammersley the extermination of the bears, even in self-defense, was too drastic a solution to the problem. He had no doubt that the balance of nature would be restored the following year, and that the salmon would return in their customary numbers. But during the approaching winter the danger from the unhibernating bears would be too great. Hammersley had decided to come out—for the first time in 30 years.

The old sourdough had arranged to fly out with the bush pilot who brought him supplies and mail each month during the summer. The weather had been seasonal, with warmer days thawing the night freezes, but on the morning of the day the little floatplane had been scheduled to touch down on Nonvianuk Lake near his small sod-roofed cabin, the temperature had begun to skid. Snow flurries sifted from a ceiling of scattered cumulus and powdered the white veneer already covering the tundra. Then at noon an early blizzard had whipped down from the Arctic. It stormed for four days, isolating the Peninsula. When it had lifted on noon of the fourth day, Hammersley had shoveled out of his cabin and gone to the lake. He'd taken with him a bucket of ashes from his chunk stove. Although the water would no longer be open to permit a seaplane landing, the pilot would have gotten weather news of the storm and would have equipped his plane with skis, and if Hammersely found the ice solid enough to hold a plane, he would spell OK in ashes on its surface.

That afternoon the bush plane had flown high over Nonvianuk Valley between its flanking mountain ranges, but the pilot had seen only the snowcrested peaks studding the top of a solid overcast that hid the lake below. When he'd dipped dangerously into the cloud layer for several hundred feet and couldn't find its bottom, he'd climbed out of it and headed back to Anchorage. If he'd broken through it, he'd have seen the tiny figure standing near the lake to wave him off. The ice on the water was too thin, and the cover of snow shielding it from the cold air would prevent its freezing solid for many weeks. Even the snow on the shore and tundra was too treacherously soft for a landing. He would also have seen a different message Hammersley had written with the ashes—FOOD.

Since Hammersley was coming out, he hadn't stored extra winter rations as he had in previous years. Canned food left behind in his cold cabin would freeze and burst. Meat would be an invitation to a raiding bear. If not to a bear, to some marauding wolverine that would break in through an unboarded window it could see through, or would climb down a chimney small enough to admit its slinking body, or chew off the lock and tear down the door. On the plane's previous visit Hammersley had received just enough supplies for a month. On the day he was planning to leave, he'd put the leftovers on the shore several hundred yards from the cabin where the animals could get them. By the time he'd realized the storm was a blizzard, it had been too late for him to recover the discarded food.

Hammersley had done too good a job of ridding his cabin of everything edible. He'd searched everywhere for something he'd overlooked. In an old siwash prospecting outfit in his woodshed he'd found a small tin of flour, useless without the sourdough ingredient necessary for making biscuits, but with it had been a jar of instant coffee and a few sticks of "squaw candy," a neglected gift from some Eskimo. For each meal he'd drunk a cup of coffee made with melted snow and had eaten a stick of the rock-hard smoked salmon. The meager fare had lasted three days. When on the third day the blizzard had begun to lull and he'd tried again to recover the food he'd thrown away, he'd found only a pit pawed in the snow. Even the few cans had been ripped open by sharp teeth and emptied.

Whenever Hammersely had run out of food while prospecting, he'd always been able to obtain more. The lakes and rivers had been full of fish, and a moose would provide enough meat to feed an army. After the snow had stopped on the fourth day and he'd listened to the buzz of the unseen bushplane fading in the distance, he'd fished the fast and still-open water of a small river nearby that drained the lake. But the scattering of salmon it had contained had long since run the spawning cycle and died, and the rainbow, Mackinaw and Dolly Varden trout had disappeared. He'd had only one recourse—and had been trapped by the sow and its cubs.

The bear family had been feasting on the kill for over an hour while Hammersley huddled shivering beneath the snow. The morning sun had swung low over the horizon into a pale blue sky, and as its light had grown stronger, so had the wind. Hammersley studied it anxiously. If it shifted 180 degrees, as wind usually does following a storm, the bear would be able to scent him and the sow would charge him to protect not only its young but also its food. But it held steady.

The shrunken stomachs of the cubs were filled quickly, and the little animals became playful. They chased each other and tumbled in the snow.

Such scenes of domesticity, unknown to men who had never lived among the brown bears, weren't new to Hammersley, but they had never ceased to touch him. They were reasons he had always been content to allow these animals to live in peace. But when the cubs started to play, they became a real threat. Their romps widened. Some came dangerously close to where he was hiding. Finally one cub, pursued by the other, made a long dash that took it downwind from Hammersley. It caught his scent and stopped, staring inquisitively, then it walked toward him cautiously, its innocent eyes wide with wonder. Hammersley tensed. If he frightened the cub to drive it off, the sow would come running. The sow would already be coming if it had been watching, but its face was buried in the moose. The cub halted a yard from where Hammersley was hidden under the snow, its neck stretched forward to sniff. Then it woofed.

The sharp ears of the sow caught the sound even against the strong wind. The big bear's head snapped up. It looked at the other cub rolling happily in the snow near the trees, then at the one standing stiffly near Hammersley. It rose and lumbered toward him. Hammersley's best chance of dropping it would be a shot at point-blank range where he wouldn't be able to miss and the 270's muzzle velocity and shocking power would be greatest. He'd wait until the bear had almost reached him, then he'd snatch up the rifle and shoot before the animal could recover from its surprise. Perhaps he'd be able to fire twice before it lunged. Slowly the sow approached. At 25 yards it stood on its hind legs and looked down at him, trying to identify him. Hammersley pondered whether he should wait for it to come still closer. At that instant the cub playing near the forest gave a howl.

The sow wheeled, dropping on all fours, and charged off across the tundra, kicking up high geysers of snow. Another bear, an adult male as emaciated as the sow, had galloped from the trees, and ahead of it the cub was fleeing for its life. But the cub kept a safe lead because it didn't sink as deeply into the snow. The boar didn't know it was also being pursued until the sow, following in its tracks, caught up with it and hit it like a thunderbolt.

For a moment the two growling giants were smothered in an explosion of white powder. The boar emerged first and ploughed away over the snow. The sow was about to follow, but then thought better of it, called its cubs, and inspected them thoroughly to reassure itself they were uninjured.

The boar didn't go far. Several hundred yards out on the tundra it turned and stood looking back at the sow while the latter returned the look hostilely. Several times the sow dropped on its forepaws and with a bellow feinted a charge at the distant intruder, but the boar refused to be bluffed. At last the sow headed for the trees. It seemed Hammersley would escape the first danger only to be confronted by a second long wait on the tundra.

But the sow had no intention of letting the boar go unpunished. When it reached the nearest tall spruce, it nosed the cubs toward it. They would be safe in it out of reach of the boar, which was too heavy to climb. One cub went up quickly. The other hesitated, resenting the maze of stabbing branches. A clout on its backside sent it scrambling after the first. This accomplished, the sow started again for the boar. This time it wasn't a feint. Hammersley watched the two animals dwindle into distant specks and eventually veer into the forest.

As soon as they had disappeared, Hammersley drew himself stiffly from the snow, his body aching from the cold, and got into his snowshoes. He knelt on one snowshoe while he inserted his other foot in the second shoe, then, using his rifle as a staff, he jacked himself upright and slipped his first foot into the first shoe. It was a process that would have stumped an amateur, but he had done it often. He didn't head back to his cabin immediately. It would be some time before the sow gave up the chase and returned to its cubs. And it was doubtful there'd be still another bear close by. The bawling of the cub, not the smell of the dead moose, had attracted the boar because the wind was still from the wrong direction to have spread the scent of blood through the woods. He hurried to the carcass and carved off several steaks with his knife. Fortunately the bear hadn't appreciated the soul-satisfying virtue of moose tenderloin.

That evening Hammersley filled his stomach for the first time in five days. The meat was too fresh and strong to have drawn compliments from a stateside cheechako, but broiled over his wood fire it was manna to the old sourdough. He carefully cached what was left, even saving scraps for stew. But he would need more because he might be weathered-in for weeks. During the night he listened to the wind. It hadn't died with sundown and was still northerly. If it continued to blow from the same point, the predators from the forest wouldn't be able to scent the dead moose, although one might discover it accidentally. The sow and its cubs probably would have left after their scare by the boar. Come morning he'd try to salvage what remained.

The wind hadn't altered by dawn, so Hammersley retraced his steps toward the spruces, dragging a small sled. On it were his rifle and a woodsman's double-edge ax. Periodically he stopped to inspect the scene through his binocular. There were no bears in sight, only one dark spot on the white tundra, the carcass of the moose. When he reached it, he saw it had been pulled closer to the trees. The sow must have tried to pull it through the deep snow into the forest, then abandoned it when the task proved too difficult. Not much more of it had been eaten. There were many pounds of good meat left on it. Hammersley took a cautious look about him, then picked up the ax, the standard tool for cutting an Alaska moose into carrying-size portions.

He worked steadily, loading the sled with all it could hold and still be light enough for him to pull. Occasionally he glanced toward the spruces 30 yards away. The sled was almost filled when he noticed two eyes glowing redly at him from the undergrowth. He stiffened, but turned and kept moving as deliberately as before. The animal had been stalking him and wasn't ready yet to come for him, but if it realized it had been discovered, it would charge without delay. With no quick movements he propped the ax in the snow and picked up the rifle, and walking to the opposite side of the sled, he crouched behind its pile of moose meat, resting the weapon's barrel across its top. As soon as he was settled, the bear charged.

Although prepared for the attack, Hammersley gasped when he saw the monstrosity that lurched from the trees. It was a full-grown bear even more emaciated than the others had been, a caricature of the magnificent powerful boars he'd seen in previous years, no more than a hide covering a living skeleton. But it struggled fiercely through the snow to reach him. He sighted between its eyes. With the report of the shot, the animal dropped. But Hammersley was confused. It seemed the bear had fallen before he fired. After a moment he left the sled and walked warily to the animal, his rifle ready to shoot again. But he didn't fire it, even when the bear lifted its head with a vicious snarl. As he circled it slowly, the bear followed him with its eyes, tried to rise, and fell back. There was no blood on the snow near it, no sign of a fresh wound on its body.

It was an old boar. The fangs bared at Hammersley were worn nubs, and its hide was tattered. For several minutes the old sourdough stood looking down at the animal. His face was inscrutable beneath the beard, but his eyes were restless with indecision. His straight figure seemed suddenly to wilt under an unseen burden. He lifted the rifle to his shoulder and pointed it at the snarling death's-head. But his eye wasn't in the sight. Lowering the weapon, he returned to the sled for his ax. He hacked again at the moose until he'd cut off several large chunks. He dropped them several yards from the bear's jaws. One he tossed within its immediate reach. The animal pawed it to its mouth and devoured it eagerly. Hammersley was forgotten.

That afternoon the Arctic blew down a gale over the Alaska Peninsula, and when it died by nightfall, it left a -30° F cold. Two days later the chief pilot of a Northern Consolidated Airliner on its scheduled run from Dillingham to Anchorage glanced down on one of his checkpoints, Nonvianuk Lake. The gale had carried away the crust that had covered the lake, and the ensuing cold wave had sealed its waters under a layer of rock-hard ice. He noticed the OK on the shore of the tiny cover that marked Hammersley's cabin, and he saw the small silver-winged bush plane that was climbing out of the valley. He nudged his copilot, gesturing with a nod: "Bill Hammersley is coming out. The old sourdough must be getting soft!"

••• *Russell Annabel was a mainstay among* SPORTS AFIELD *contributors from the late 1930s into the 1980s. Adventure was his business, as most of his stories were about wild days spent on the Alaskan frontier. Here he relates how one man lucked out and struck it rich while getting slammed around by bears.*—FEBRUARY 1969 •••

$7,000,000 ADVENTURE WITH BEARS

by Russell Annabel

"They got me. I'm a dead Injun," hollered my youthful Denna assistant, Johnny Tyonek, otherwise known as the Millionaire Kid, when he saw the two giant Alaska brown bears swooping down at him."The s.o.b.s win at last."

Bill Weston, the current pilgrim, whipped up his .30-06. He was in my line of fire, which reduced me to spectator status.

Everything had gone screwball. It was a bizarre accident outrageously timed. The two brown bears, sportive brutes, were belly coasting down the middle of a steep mountainside snow stringer directly at the kid. Forty yards distant. Coming like breakneck bobsledders. They were also, no matter what Johnny thought at the moment, victims of circumstance. They had been coasting for the fun of it, a springtime custom of brown bears, and then they had busted around an alder bend and there was our Johnny.

The kid didn't have a prayer of getting clear of them. He had, while ranging ahead of Bill and me, broken through sun-softened snow crust and was bogged to his brisket. Moreover, he didn't dare shoot. When he fell he had speared his rifle into the snow. With its barrel plugged, the weapon would have exploded and probably blown his head off. Bill let go a shot at the bear and missed.

This drastic drama was taking place part way up the alder-jungled north wall of Chinitna Bay, under Iliamna Volcano, bright and early on a crystal morning in June. The bears, when we first sighted them from our beach camp, had been lying asleep 1000 yards above us at the base of a rimrock cliff. One of them, I estimated, was in the hallelujah 10-foot class. The other looked pretty good too. Gratefully, we at once began a stalk for them. It proved an arduous undertaking. The alders were terrible. Devil's clubs abounded. The winter-killed grass, knee deep and dried to a crisp, was astonishingly noisy. The wind, blowing in crazy williwaw eddies, came from every direction.

And meanwhile the bears had departed.

We emerged from an interwoven alder tangle, sweating, stuck full of devil's club thorns, ready for action, to stand glumly contemplating the bears' vacated beds. I checked the sign. The wallowed grass still held a trace of body warmth. One of the bears had lingered to deposit a pile of dung, which also was warm. So the pair had been gone only a few minutes, and it wasn't a hasty exit. I mean, they weren't spooked. To our left, a 40-foot-wide snow stringer slashed crookedly down the mountain. We started out onto it for a reconnaissance with our glasses. I figured we would quickly locate the bears. And so we did. Or they located us. Anyway, it was spectacular.

Johnny, always an eager beaver, had taken the lead. The snow crust in the shadow of overhanging alders was cement solid. It would have held up a tractor. But beyond, at the middle of the stringer, the morning sun had got in some good licks. Johnny broke through. Then, as related, he saw the brown bears rocketing down at him and yelled his valedictory to earthly affairs.

Both animals were scrambling to avoid crashing into the kid.

Bill fired again.

The first bear heaved to its feet, naturally went out of control, and came cart-wheeling. It was bottom side up, rump in the air, bawling, when it hurtled past us. Johnny swore afterward that it brushed against him. It spun on down another 50 feet to plow into massed alders where the stringer made a tight bend. That was the last I saw of it. The second bear, the big one, was careening 100 feet behind. Bill had scored on it. I heard him mutter, "Sheezam," whatever that meant, and then his rifle blasted and I saw hair fly. A beautiful shot, everything considered. Hit between the shoulder blades, the bear with its last strength flung itself sideways. It tumbled past Johnny, missing him by inches, and likewise slammed into the barrier thicket, stone dead.

Well, Johnny floundered out of the snow trap. We went down to the carcass. It was a top-bracket trophy, the pelt thick and unblemished, dark chestnut with black and yellow points. It would square 10 feet. I doubted that a better brown bear skin would be taken this season in western Alaska.

"Congratulations," I said to Bill.

And to Johnny, "Boy, don't ever tell me this isn't a capitalist world. You all of a sudden got yourself loaded with dough, and now even the bears respect you."

"Hah. What quaint primitive notions you old-timers have about bears. My old man thinks he's a Bear Boss. Now you come up with the idea that brownies are class conscious and have generous impulses. I sure am glad that I went to school, by gosh, and learned a thing or two."

This Johnny Tyonek was unique.

A husky, university-educated 23-year-old, son of a Bear-Clan Chief, he was very much a junior in the dude-wrangling fraternity but had his sights set high. More and more sportsmen and tourists were coming north. Big-game hunting had become big business. The kid wanted a share of it for his people. He had plans to organize Denna hunters, outfit them, and get them licensed as guides. It would, he was aware, be a considerable task. The Dennas were fine natural woodsmen, and nobody understood the game or knew the country better, but they shied away from competition. The kid declared angrily that Indian guides had been typed as comic characters in so many campfire dialect jokes that they had come to believe that's what they were.

He aimed to change matters. It is important to record, however, that his father thought he was going about it the wrong way. Or had been for the past year. The old man was a grim relic of Denna nobility who held sway at Tyonek Village, 50 miles down the coast from Anchorage. They were both stubborn. They had quarrelled bitterly. This present bit of current history is a consequence of what happened between them. If it gets weird, my defense is that it is all a matter of record.

Johnny was dead broke when I hired him. I had a hunt set up for spring grizzlies in the Wood River country, with a Detroit sporting-goods dealer, name of Walt Bentley. We never got as far as Wood River proper. We were on Cody Creek, a tributary, when bear trouble—an accident—laid the kid low . . .

Walt sharpened the focus of his glasses. He was fascinated. We were crouched in ambush at the rim of a wolf willow thicket watching three Toklat grizzlies—a sow, her yearling cub and an amorous male. They were 600 yards distant, and were having a domestic crisis as old as spring and sex. The male, a trophy bear, was making passes at Mamma. He frisked and curvetted, snorting, in a kind of bruin mambo, and ended up with a front leg draped companionably over her neck. Junior didn't approve. He bounded in with a wail and took a bite out of the trophy male's rump.

That was reckless of him, he was fooling with disaster, but the big male for the moment pretended that nothing had occurred. He figured he had to, I guess, if he was going to get anywhere.

I had told Walt that I wanted him to have a closer shot. Six hundred yards is a far piece, regardless of who is holding the gun. If he missed and the trophy bear made a getaway, he would regret it the rest of his life. You don't get many chances at Toklat grizzlies. Strikingly handsome animals, cream yellow usually, with snub-nosed teddy-bear heads and no shoulder humps, most of them lead a privileged existence inside the boundaries of Mt. McKinley National Park, which in our case was four days' ride westward. I hoped that this trio would move downwind toward us. Otherwise it was going to be tough to shorten the range. They were at the far side of a poppy-starred timberline meadow with no intervening cover.

I got my wish, in an unforeseen manner.

The trophy male nuzzled Mamma affectionately. Clearly he thought he had been accepted, and was so enthusiastic that he neglected to keep a wary eye on Junior. The yearling attacked. Squalling, it set teeth in the big male's flank, where hair is short and hide thin and tender, and yanked with braced paws to tear out a mouthful. Well, it was a mistake. I believe that an adult mountain grizzly, at close quarters, is probably the fastest animal on earth. This one retaliated with such dire speed that I saw only a blur, and I have 20-20 vision and expected the action. One instant the shaggy yellow Romeo had been breathing into Mamma's ear, the next he was facing the other way and had belted Junior a wallop.

Junior was levitated and slung some 15 feet.

"Bravo. Wonderful," Walt applauded. "Exactly what he deserved. Remind me sometime to tell you about a nephew of mine. The little fiend . . ."

I never did get to hear about the nephew. Junior had rolled upright and was fleeing toward us, the trophy male in vengeful pursuit. Mamma sat on her haunches. She was a neutral observer. No doubt she had been through this springtime routine with other suitors and other jealous cubs, and thought what the hell, having been abandoned at such a critical juncture was all in a lifetime.

Walt propped himself on his elbows, cheek snuggled against the ornate stock of the .300 Weatherby he had bought for exactly this opportunity. The trophy male was 250 yards distant when he fired. Heart shot, cleanly killed, the bear skidded amongst the gay Iceland poppies, went over on his side and lay motionless. As for Junior, he was too close to haven in the brush and too scared, I guess, to change course. Anyway, he streaked past us into the thicket. Mamma was loping in the opposite direction.

"That was the most," Walt said. "Anything else that happens on the hunt will be tame anticlimax."

He should have knocked wood. Johnny, as wrangler, was over at the other side of the thicket, on a strip of peavine meadow bordering Cody Creek, holding our string of eight Yakima cayuses. Hardly had Walt finished speaking when a horse bawled, a wild pounding of hoofs resounded and the bad sound of packs being banged together was heard. The kid had a stampede on his hands. This is how he described it later:

"I'm thirsty," he said, "so I slide down this six-foot cutbank to the creek. While I'm lying on my belly drinking I hear a shot, and then the horses spook. I jump up to find out what's wrong. Here comes the pinto lead mare. She's running blind. She sails over the bank and goes to her knees on the gravel. I make a grab for her halter shank, but she lunges up and a corner of her pack spins me backward and I fall into the creek. Before I can get to my feet, the rest of the string piles over the bank. I am hollering at them to take it easy. They are supposed to be friends of mine and have confidence in me. But they pay no attention.

"That dumb sorrel carrying the tents and camp stove runs right over me. He steps on my leg. Another horse, I don't know which one, catches me in the ribs with his heel calks. I'm trying to get up, horses coming at me, water flying, mud in my eyes, when the strawberry roan sideswipes me in the face with a kerosene-case pannier and I go down and out.

"The next thing I know, I am on my back in six inches of water, coughing and gagging. The horses have crossed the creek. They are hightailing through some dwarf cottonwoods, scattering gear, bellering to let one another know how scared they are. I'm hurt. One leg don't work, and it's hard to breathe, but I crawl out of the creek and up the bank onto the grass. When I top the bank I see what has caused the stampede. It is a big yellow yearling grizzly cub. He's galloping across the upstream end of the flat, heading for the mountains. You know, I am beginning to think that my old man, by gosh, has more on the ball than I gave him credit for. He's a Bear Boss, and he told me I was going to have a lot more bear trouble than I could handle."

Well, the kid had no broken bones, but the bruises and contusions he had suffered were remarkable to behold. Walt stayed with him while I rounded up the horses. We got out the medicine kit and rendered rough first aid, then made camp and skinned the grizzly. Next morning Johnny insisted that he could ride. I said to show me. He stayed up there all right, but was weaving and had to hang on. A rugged Injun kid. So we hit the trail for Cap Lathrop's coal mine at Suntrana on the railroad. Traveling slow, we made it across snowpatched Cody Pass and down Healy River in three days. A medic was at the mine. When he had anointed, taped and bandaged the kid, and *hmm hmmed* over the fact that he had been able to ride all those miles, I telephoned for a bush pilot. The plane came upriver from Nenana an hour later.

"I am air-expediting you home to recuperate," I told the kid as we loaded him aboard the single-engined red Waco. "See you next fall."

"Not to Tyonek," he protested. "If you knew my old man as well as I do, you wouldn't send me there. We are feuding. He'll claim that as Bear Boss he sent the bears to make me come home. He's a hardcase primitive from back in the days when sons were property. Anywhere but Tyonek."

"I know him well enough. We hunted together before you were born. Give him my regards."

Johnny's father's Denna name was Gistun. That means "The Spear." I had last talked with him at Anchorage, in January. A fierce-eyed little guy, crowding 80, with the drooping mustaches of a Mongol khan, wearing patched mackinaw pants and an ancient drill parka, muskrat cap pulled down over his ears, he was coming out of a lawyer's office on Fourth Street. Under his arm he carried what I gathered was a rolled blue-linen paper map tracing. He saw me, and halted. A snow-filled wind was whistling off Cook Inlet. Gistun motioned me into the storm entrance of the Diamond Kid's saloon.

"I am glad to see you," he said in Denna. "We are old friends, huh? I mean, well, anyway we have known each other a long time. I hope we are friends because I want you to do something for me. It's this—when Johnny comes home from the university next spring, don't hire him."

"Why not?"

"Because he has got to settle down and live at Tyonek. If he doesn't, I am afraid he will lose his reservation land rights. Also because, damn it, he lacks good sense. I suppose you know that he is trying to organize what he calls Indian Guides, Inc. That is of course a great idea. Our Denna hunters are the best, even if they do sometimes forget that they are. But how will he ever earn the necessary money working for wages? I have given thought to the expenses he would have. To compete with the white guides, the Denna would need many horses. A mountain of rigging, tents and camp gear. A decked launch for use on the inlet, and a good riverboat. An office and somebody to keep books and answer letters and write advertising. At least four permanent hunting camps. To do it right," Gistun clenched a fist and punched the air, "yes, I am sure, they would also have to send a Denna young man to flying school and then buy an airplane."

"To do it right," I agreed. "So?" The old gent had it down pat. I was another who hadn't given him credit.

"So Johnny's only chance, his only possible chance, to get hold of enough money for all that is to come home and stay there long enough to protect his land rights."

Gistun unrolled the map sheet. It was a plat of the Tyonek Indian reservation. With a crack-nailed forefinger he tapped the map's legend, which bore the name of a worldwide oil company.

"They are going to drill," he said. "I just found out. Maybe they will discover oil, and maybe they won't. But tell Johnny to come home. Tell him," he showed square yellowed teeth in a warlock grin, "to remember that if he doesn't come home he is going to have a lot of bear trouble."

Well, the kid was mule-stubborn and unimpressed. The heck with Tyonek. He wanted a job, he said, because not only was he flat broke again but he urgently needed to learn everything he could in a hurry about the dude-wrangling business. So I hired him. Then came the accident on Cody Creek, and he had to go home anyway. He rejoined me in late August. They were drilling at Tyonek, he said, but plenty of the Dennas predicted that they wouldn't find enough oil to grease a pair of boots. I had a backpacking hunt arranged, for sheep and goats in the Chugach Lake country, with a puckish professor of medieval history from Wichita, name of Tom Harrison. It turned out to be a pleasantly ordinary hunt, except for one rather extraordinary experience starring a certain black bear . . .

"That bear is still following us," Tom said, "What's he up to?"

I had first spotted the bear half an hour ago as we were leaving camp. We were making a climb for four bands of goats strung along a mile of mountainside above the east shore of the lake. The bear had plodded out of a wild-rose jungle 300 yards below us. He was nosing our trail as a dog would. I put my glasses on him. He had a nice autumn coat, so jet-glossy that it shone in the sunlight. I figured that probably he had never before encountered humans. This region was seldom hunted, since impassable glaciers bounded it on three sides and the two-mile-wide lake normally was so full of icebergs that pilots hated to risk damaging their floats by landing on it. The bear, I thought, simply didn't know what we were and was following us out of curiosity.

I asked Tom if he wanted the animal. He said no. He was reluctant at this point to alert the goats. Besides, he said, he had a black bear trophy at home.

We went on, the bear following. During the next half hour I saw the strange cuss from time to time, but didn't pay him much heed. I was preoccupied. Twenty-seven goats were in the four bands and at least a third of them were adult billies. Picking the best head was a chore. We stalked all four bands. I stared through 12X glasses until my eyes smarted. Finally I settled on a big, buffalo-humped, hairy-nosed veteran whose horns would go, I thought, 9 1/2 inches. Tom killed the animal. The horns measured 10 inches. While Johnny was taking off the cape, I saw the black bear again. He was 200 yards downwind, peering at us around the corner of a lichen-encrusted grey granite boulder. Just standing there, half hidden, watching us.

It was, I will admit, eerie.

We loaded the goat trophy and the meat onto our packboards and started back to camp. I looked around. The bear was following. Johnny muttered something in Denna. Suddenly, perhaps unreasonably, I was sore.

"You sure you don't want that bear?" I asked Tom.

"How'd you guess?" he said. "I was just going to tell you I had changed my mind. I'm afraid taking this 10-inch goat trophy has gone to my head, made me a reckless spendthrift. How I will ever pay the taxidermist, I don't know. But . . ."

I decided the budget talk was his idea of a joke.

He was carrying a scope-sighted .270 Winchester. The bear, 200 yards above us, came nosing through a fringe of alders. Tom let go a shot, and the bear leaned against the mountainside and then came rolling. It was a steep cloudberry pitch broken by rocky terraces. By the time the animal was a third of the way to us, he was bouncing a couple of yards into the air. He hit a boulder, swapped ends, busted through some low alders, collided with another boulder, rolled again, and piled up against a grassy moraine hump 100 feet distant. Incredibly, after taking all that, he was still alive. He had got his front paws under him and was lurching up when Tom shot him through the head.

"Awesome," Tom said in an awed voice. "I wish I knew why on earth he was following us."

"Ask Johnny. He specializes in offbeat bears."

"Not me," the kid said. "But my old man does. I'll ask him the next time I see him."

That concluded the hunt. We said good-bye to Tom on the depot platform at Matanuska. I noticed as the train pulled out that the conductor and head brakeman were gazing interestedly at Johnny. The kid and I sat on a baggage truck waiting for a northbound extra that was due in a few minutes. I had boarded out the horses at Black Carlson's place in the Broad Pass, and thought we had better go up there and check on the care they were getting. Old Kobuk Jones, a former colleague of mine, came up the grassy street. Spotting us, he hurried across the platform. He grabbed Johnny's hand and, beaming, whacked him on the shoulder.

"Congratulations, boy," he boomed. "We heard the news over the radio." Then, realizing that we didn't know what he was talking about, he said, "An oil company or the gov'ment or somebody has agreed to pay you Tyonek Injuns $7,000,000 fer the oil rights on your land. Not many Injuns qualified. You are one that did. How's it feel to be rich, huh?"

"I don't know yet. Give me time," the kid said, trying to get used to the idea. "But I can tell you that at last, by gosh, the world is going to hear about Denna hunters—if the bears lay off me, that is."

*••• The roving editor of SPORTS AFIELD in the 1960s and early 1970s, Jack Denton Scott covered a variety of topics in the outdoors, but made his name through his accurate, well-researched nature profiles, including the cobra story that follows.—*SEPTEMBER 1970 *•••*

DEADLIEST CREATURE ON EARTH

by Jack Denton Scott

The natives were walking slowly abreast, hoping to drive a tiger before them. But today there was no cat. Suddenly one of the men screamed and flew backward three feet as if pushed by a giant hand. The others fled from him in terror.

The man was silent now; we could hear labored breathing as if he were fighting suffocation. The shikari beside me went tense. He was an Indian friend, a professional hunter, helping me research tigers for my novel, *Elephant Grass*, in which a tiger is the hero. We had rifles and came down the tree fast. As we neared the felled native, the ground before us began to wiggle. Mottled green, twisting. Then it rose to face us. A huge snake, its head swollen into an angry hood. It came for us in a lunging movement, head still high. It menaced, striking viciously. Although it was still 50 feet from us, its size and obvious intent sent me backward, making me forget that I had a rifle. I was ready to turn and establish a new track record when the shikari shot. He had an old .30-06 Winchester, almost as much a part of him as an arm. He shot four times into the lifted hood of the creature. Head shredded, it went to the ground, tremors shooting from head to tail. Life remained in the great snake for 20 minutes.

That was my first meeting with the king cobra or hamadryad (also *Naja hannah* in India), the world's largest venomous snake. The record is 18 feet 4 inches; the one before us measured just over 11 feet. It hadn't the thick body of the python, was an olive color crossbanded with black; the throat and chin were light orange. Herpetologists consider it the most beautiful snake—and the deadliest.

The action had taken just under a half hour. The native was dead. The wound on his leg wasn't deep, and the shikari explained that the large amount of neurotoxic poison injected by the giant didn't require a deep piercing. Cobras strike, bite, chew briefly and the victim has had it. The venom has an immediate effect on the nerve centers, producing death by paralysis of the muscles that control the breathing mechanism.

The shikari was a university graduate who had become a hunter because he loved the jungle and hated the filth and noise of civilization. He had vast respect for the king cobra and, using his knife, showed me that the snake had fangs just over a half-inch long. He explained that what really made it deadly was its personality, plus the size and tremendous amount of venom it possessed.

"It is an insolent snake," he said. "The most aggressive of all. All snakes would rather slither off and hide when they see a man. The king cobra too. But if you happen on him, often he will attack immediately. And when they are nesting their eggs, both male and female will attack anyone approaching. Besides, they are moody creatures. Unpredictable. You never know what to expect."

He told of a 10-foot king cobra attacking a woman picking tea in Assam, holding the woman's leg for eight minutes. The snake released the woman and slithered off when five men came to her rescue. Chased by the men, it whirled and attacked. Now the pursuers were the pursued. They reported later that the snake, despite its size, was supple and very fast, and if one man hadn't had a shotgun and some courage, the king cobra might have performed a mass killing. The woman it had originally attacked, apparently without provocation, died in 20 minutes.

He gave me a classic example of the power of this venom. Last year he had been working with hunting elephants in the north of India, using them to drive a tiger before them in a beat, just as we today were using men. It was a photographic hunt, and not the right season to be moving about the jungle, but Indians declare no right and wrong seasons for themselves and they were trying to locate tigers before the clients arrived. Money is a powerful mover, the shikari said with a sad smile. They were beating through elephant grass and a scattering of trees near a hill pocked with rocky ledges. Suddenly a king cobra rose out of the grass before the lead elephant my shikari was riding.

"There was no provocation," the shikari said. "We didn't just happen on him and nearly step on him. He could have avoided us and escaped into the rock ledges where he probably lived. But no. He was obviously annoyed, as his hood was expanded. He struck quickly, biting my elephant on the tip of the trunk, one of the very few areas where the skin could be penetrated."

The shiraki shook his head. "That was Kalu, one of our best hunting elephants, 25 years old, took five years to train."

The world's largest land mammal, weighing six tons, 70 times the size of a man, was dead from the incredible venom in less than three hours. The king cobra's venom is five times stronger than that of the Russell's viper, famed for its deadliness, and responsible for many of the 20,000 deaths by snake bite in India yearly.

Later, when traveling in Thailand and watching the training of the skilled tuskers in the teak forests, I saw an elephant in Chieng Mai that had been killed by a king cobra. This one had been bitten on the foot, at the juncture of the nail and the foot where the skin was soft. In this case, the big bull had killed the snake, crushing it with his feet. But usually they don't; king cobras frighten elephants. Everything else too. In Thailand several elephants are killed by them every year. This is an expensive loss. It takes several years to train an elephant to work skillfully in the teak forests, and they are valued at $5000 each.

Here he is, a giant with a temper, often attacking man on sight, quick, agile, fearless, with venom that can kill our largest animal in 180 minutes. What else does this creature have that sets him apart? Probably the most important attribute: Intelligence.

The king cobra is smart, a thinking animal. One example: Rodolphe Meyer de Schauense was returning from Asia to the Academy of Natural Sciences in Philadelphia with live zoo specimens. Among them was a 12-foot king cobra. Mr. de Schauense had observed the snakes in the Far East and had a marked respect for them. There was no receptacle for water in the cobra's box, and no one would open it to give it water. Not even de Schauense, who was an expert in transporting wild creatures. He tried giving the snake water from a pitcher. In minutes, the cobra learned to raise its head against the wire of the box and drink from the spout of the pitcher. More: The cobra even recognized the water pitcher and came to the wire when he saw anyone approaching with it.

Raymond L. Ditmars, former curator of Mammals and Reptiles at the New York Zoological Park, claims that he has observed many demonstrations of this singular intelligence of the king cobra. "I use the word 'singular,'" he says, "because other snakes do not act this way." He told of a newly arrived cobra discovering that the material covering the front of its zoo cage was glass. For a day it would strike at visitors pressing against the glass to view him. But that was all the nose-bumping it needed. From then on it stayed away from it, rearing and feinting, but not touching that hard glass. Other snakes would continue to punish themselves against it for weeks. King cobras also recognize the keepers who feed and care for them, and do not bother them, but always react antagonistically toward strangers. At feeding time the cobras come to the rear of their cages, and peer up and down the passageway for the keeper.

Brains, they've got. There is in the London Zoo a king cobra that daintily takes a freshly killed grass snake from her keeper's hands. That, though, is unusual. King cobras are cannibals, eating their own kind alive, both nonpoisonous and poisonous, sometimes even lizards, although lively snakes are their preference.

Again, intelligence is a force in the matter of food selection. They eat heartily once a week: one 14-foot male consuming in recorded test, from July to March, 145 feet of live snakes. If they are extremely hungry, they will eat the venomous snakes, agilely darting in and injecting their own brand of killer fluid before they can be bitten by their victim. But zoo king cobras seem to know they have a choice, and don't have to forage and take what they can get as they do in the wild.

In one test, a zoologist waited until the end of the week when his pair of king cobras would be very hungry, and then gave them a large water snake, and a poisonous water moccasin that looked very much like the harmless snake. The water moccasin was thrown into the cobra cage first. The hungry cobras rushed, then slammed to a stop a few feet from the hissing moccasin. This was the first time in years that the cobras had not pounced and demolished their wiggling meal immediately. They retreated to the other side of the cage and reared, regarding the moccasin cautiously. Were they really hungry? The moccasin was retrieved and they were each given a common grass snake. Gobbled. Again the moccasin was slipped into their cage. The cobras approached hungrily, recognized what it was, halted. Now the moccasin was angry, striking and hissing. The cobras raised straight up four feet and spread their hoods.

Now the real test: The moccasin was again removed and the harmless "double" placed in the cage without the cobras' seeing it accomplished. This large snake was also annoyed, and looked more dangerous than the water moccasin, hissing and striking. The cobras quieted and slithered in to examine the new snake. They attacked instantly, killed and ate it. Conclusion of the test: King cobras will not fight another venomous snake and risk getting bitten themselves unless hunger and circumstances drive them to it.

What about the hood we keep talking about, that swells when the king cobra is angry, and vanishes when he is not? Long movable ribs lie close to the backbone when the snake is not annoyed. When aroused, the king cobra (and his cousins, the smaller cobras) spreads this series of ribs laterally, and lo, the horrid hood. It is like a weird magician's trick designed to frighten.

Inhabiting India, Burma, Southeast Asia and the Philippines, there is nothing usual about the king cobra. They even protect their young, which is unheard of for the snake family. Like all snakes, though, they do hibernate. Mating can take place in spring or fall, before or after hibernation. Fertilization also can occur in the fall. However, due to the largely reduced metabolic activity during the low temperature of the hibernation, development is slowed to the point that the young are often born at the same time as those from the spring mating.

The king cobra lays eggs and hatches its young. Eggs are laid (anywhere from a couple dozen to a record clutch of 56) four to eight weeks after mating. The young, 18 inches long, black, with white and yellow-green crossband, complete with venom, are hatched in 12 to 18 weeks. Temperature influences the time; if it is warm it is speeded up; cool, retarded.

This astonishing snake is also the only one that carefully builds a large nest of vegetable matter or forest debris. In 1955, a female was observed and photographed building such a nest at the New York Zoological Park. It took the 13 1/2-foot cobra two days to construct a nest 18 inches high and 36 inches in overall diameter. She pushed bamboo litter into a neat pile by looping the forward section of her body part way around it, then bringing her body gracefully back in an open loop.

She bulldozed sand into a foundation around the nest, moving her head at a 45-degree angle, then pushing. Leaves she grasped with a body loop, and carried to the nest. As the nest rose in height, she went inside, twisting around and around, probing and pushing and forming the nest, like a plasterer troweling a wall. A fantastic performance. She laid her eggs two days later, covered them with leaves, then coiled atop.

Most snakes lay their eggs, or give birth to their living young, then off they go; the kids are on their own. I can testify that both male and female cobras guard the nest and patrol the territory for a good distance around, attacking anyone on sight.

James A. Oliver, curator of reptiles, New York Zoological Society, in *Snakes in Fact and Fiction*, in a study of the world's most fearful snakes, narrows it to three: the black mamba of Africa, the taipan of Australia, and the king cobra of Asia. He bases this claim on several factors, among them large size, long fangs, powerful nerve-affecting venoms, and excitability and unpredictability. Also, the manner of striking. These snakes do not strike in short jabs as the vipers and pit vipers do, but in what Doctor Oliver calls a "gliding lunge" from which the snake can strike many times in close quarters. This ability, he believes, is what really makes them the top villains in the reptile world. Also, all three species defend themselves in a threateningly mobile manner (even chasing their foes), which makes them much more deadly than the feared varieties such as the rattler that rises from a stationary coiled position to strike.

Dr. Oliver says that a choice to name the deadliest of the three is difficult. "However," he says, "I have more respect for the king cobra, and whether it's just that I like the name, or whether it's based on something more subtle, I personally think he's 'king of snakes'—the most dangerous of all."

••• Gene Hill, whom former editor Lamar Underwood once called "our finest outdoor writer," dominated the back page of the magazine with his monthly "Tail Feathers" column throughout most of the 1970s. The following is an example of how Hill could examine all aspects of the sporting life and put them in their proper, important places. —MAY 1972 •••

TAIL FEATHERS by Gene Hill

A lot of things in my life strike a lot of people as foolish—if not downright shameful—such as being seen in the company of known skeet shooters, dry-fly fishermen and Ed Zern, who is, I insist, really Howard Hughes. But in the last year I have managed to achieve a new low, according to many of my social acquaintances, or more exactly, ex-social acquaintances. Oh hell, I might as well come right out with it: I chew tobacco.

I chew tobacco where nobody else chews tobacco—at fancy dinner parties, during cocktail hours, at business meetings and on airplanes. I chew because I like it, and I expect to continue to chew where I please and when I please. In fact the only problem I have with the whole business is chewing what I please.

When I was a younger fellow I could walk into the general store and stand enthralled before an almost-infinite selection of multicolored packages of snuff—both the kind you tucked under your lip and the kind you pinched between your thumb and forefinger or put on the back of your hand, then snuffed up your nose. There were plugs of chewing tobacco, small, brick-like and efficient-looking.

Day's Work, Apple and *Honey Cut* are the few I remember. The regular chewing tobacco was offered in a multitude of cuts and flavors. I believe the most-popular choices were *Mechanic's Delight, Mail Pouch, Beechnut* and *Red Man.* The last three I can still find if I do a lot of hunting around.

But as a kid, I was a pipesmoker. The nickel corncob was within economic possibilities for me, and since my mother and father, of course, had forbidden me to smoke, I had them hidden all over: in the hen house and in the barn; in hollow trees along my trapline; and a couple down by the lake where we kept the rowboat. Cigarettes were expensive—about two packs for 15 cents, although I seem to remember that I could buy them for a penny apiece. I would once in a great while spring for a pack of *Twenty Grand's* or *Sunshine's,* but for day-in and day-out I stuck with the pipe and a nickel paper of *No. 1* or *George Washington.* I still recall that the nickel papers were strong as a green brush fire, but I must have considered myself a pretty tough fellow, because I stuck with it. But when I struck it pretty good on the trapline or put in a day or so of paid work splitting wood for my grandfather, I temporarily moved up to *Edgeworth* or *Model,* which were twice as expensive.

I know I tried chewing because a lot of the men I admired chewed, but I just couldn't make a go of it. There was a romance about chewing and spitting in the coal scuttle while yarning around the stove. I wished I could have pulled it off, but I had to be content with whatever small dash I could exhibit by lighting kitchen matches under my thumbnail or on the bottom of my front teeth and by firing-up my pipe without showing that I had burned my thumb and that the inside of my mouth tasted of sulphur. All the while I kept an eye peeled for my mother or father or my kid brother, who was forever squealing on me at home about smoking.

You know how things like that stick with you. And the picture of an old bird-shooter pausing for emphasis while he dipped into his pack of *Red Man* and filled his cheek, and worked it down to the spot where it felt just right, has over the years taken on an aura that could not be denied.

About a year ago I began sneaking a little *Copenhagen* snuff when I was out in the field or out fishing or up on the tractor. I liked it allright. I still will dip a little when the mood comes on me, but that still wasn't chewing. Things came to some sort of head when my wife found out that my daughter, who was then attending kindergarten, was sneaking a little snuff in her lunch box. I knew she took a little grain or two when she was with me on the tractor, and I thought it was cute and let it go at that, but my household is not a democracy—I wasn't allowed to vote. Neither was Jennifer.

Anyway, there comes a time in a man's life when he's got to have the courage to stand up to his wife and daughters, however awesome that confrontation can become, and however mightily he would wish it were otherwise, so I got hold of some *Pay Car* and started in. Now it's one thing to want to chew, and it's another thing to do it. You have to learn how—and I went at it solo. You learn first off that chewing is a misnomer. You don't *chew;* you just take an amount, which you determine by your personal physical make-up, tuck it in your face between the gum and the cheek and more or less leave it alone.

Right off, let me tell you that you don't ever need a spittoon, if you calculate the amount right. If you're in a duck blind and want to test yourself against an incoming wind, you can enjoy the skills of expectoration, but you don't absolutely have to spend your day watering the area around you.

Time passed, and the more I chewed, the more I liked it, but I knew something was amiss: there was a void in this new sport, and that was variety. It's hard enough where I live to get chewing tobacco at all, and to have the freedom of choice among flavors, cuts and strengths that the men of my youth enjoyed was no longer possible. Or so I thought, until a friend of mine, as a joke, brought back for me, from a trip down South, a package filled with exotic stuff: several plugs like *Bloodhound, Brown Mule, Black Maria* and *Bull of the Woods;* and a few papers of a chewing tobacco called *Red Fox*. The package itself was a work of art, and as I tucked away a modest amount, I felt delight that must have been near to what Pierre Pérignon felt when he first tasted champagne. You've heard that every man deserves to have one good gun and one good dog. I add to that one perfect chewing tobacco.

It didn't take too long until I'd gone through what he'd brought me, and it took less time to discover that no one, absolutely no one, for what appeared to be a 100 miles around, sold it. It seemed that I had but just discovered the *ne plus ultra* of chews only to realize that I might as well have only dreamed it.

I happened to wistfully mention my lost love to a close neighbor, Tom Young, whom I knew hailed from South Carolina, and whom I knew for a fact was returning there to visit his family. Before too long, Tom had promised to strip the state of *Red Fox* and that after his return I would never want again. Tom left on his trip, and after a week or so I began to scan his driveway, hoping to see his car. Then I'd think that maybe he'd forgotten anyway, and I'd console myself with something else.

I'd about given up on Tom when late one night, he knocked on my door and handed me a paper bag with a note on it. He left saying he'd just that minute gotten home and had to go back and help his wife get the luggage out of the car. I shook open the bag and a dozen packages of *Red Fox* fell on the kitchen table. I couldn't get a handful quick enough! When I was contentedly rolling an ounce or so from one jaw to the other, I picked up Tom's note and read it: "My grandfather, who has been in the business, told me that the secret of good tobacco was not altogether in the leaf. He said that one had to take a mind to how it's cured. Some folk stoke up their fires too fast and they burn it right up. And others are so afraid of burning it that they let their barn get too cold, and it cures green. Good tobacco has to be properly dried, then cured and finally fixed at successively higher temperatures.

"Nowadays, when one is forced to cross the country in a few hours and drink three-day-old beer, ain't it a pleasure to know, as I'm sure you do, that good friends, good bourbon and good tobacco are slowly made."

EYELIDS OF MORNING
by Peter Beard & Alistair Graham

The ancient Greeks called them *kroko-drilos*, "pebble-worms"—scaly things that shuffle and lurk around low places.

For the most part man gets on with crocodiles about as well as he did with dragons; he will banish them from all but the remotest parts of the earth.

At Lake Rudolf we found one of those distant lands where dragons still roam at will, but this does not mean that it will always be so, that mankind is content to let it be. In the face of man's inexorable expansion, Lake Rudolf will one day fall and its dragons be subdued, for civilized man will not tolerate wild beasts that eat his children, his cattle, or even the fish he deems to be his. That would be regression into barbarism.

But there are people who care about crocodiles. They care because these beasts are a part of nature, part of the fast disappearing wilderness whose uniqueness can never be reconstituted. Such people are loath to see that wilderness go before man has established beyond all doubt that it is in his best interests to dispose of it. Just because wild animals are a relic and a symbol of the savagery we mean to rise above does not mean that they have nothing else to offer the hungry, lonely soul of civilized man. Those who bemoan "the rape of the wilderness," who feel we are losing something irreplaceable, may have something real to tell us. We cannot dismiss their ideas as selfish fantasies until we know they are nothing else.

So it seemed to us on Lake Rudolf that rather than abandon the world's last great crocodile population to the whim of man, to be exterminated in the name of inevitability, we might first inquire a little into their lives. By doing so we believed that their fate, already in the clumsy hands of man (to whom even his own fate remains a mystery), might be cast with deliberation and care, in whatever way seemed most reasonable in the light of the facts.

◆　◆　◆

It turned out that in our limited time getting 40 crocs a month was the major problem. So, whether we liked it or not, hunting became for us the dominant activity in the day's work; we had to *be* hunters. We had to learn all the tricks of a croc hunter's trade and naturally adopted many of their ways. Though I needed a random sample and therefore shot any adult available, the bigger ones—being older and smarter—were relatively scarce and therefore more interesting. While hunting we got the habit of referring to our quarry by the names used by croc hunters, who also prize the bigger ones for their bigger hides. Any less than six feet long (the length at which most females mature), being relatively worthless, were given derogatory names. Five- and six-footers were "lizards"; four- and five-footers, "watchstraps"; and any smaller "geckos." Crocs six to eight feet long were "good muggers," and the majority of our specimens were of this size. Those in the range of eight to 10 feet were "bonus gators"; 10- to 13-footers were "magnums," while anything bigger than that, a rare beast, was a "monster pebbleworm."

This classification, of course, bore no relation to a crocodile's status from a biological point of view. Nevertheless it relieved us of the need to be objective, as did another evergreen pastime of all croc hunters—speculations on how big crocs get. There is something intriguing about the dimensions of large animals, particularly mysterious, highly symbolic ones like crocodiles. The temptation to exaggerate is apparently very strong and many a fabulous monster lurks—unmeasured—in the jungles of Africa. "At any rate I have seen several longer than the little A.I.A. and she measures 42 feet . . . 25 yards away lay the biggest crocodile I had yet seen. Comparing him with the A.I.A. . . . . I reckoned him to be quite 50 feet long." This bit of bushwhack, from *A Visit to Stanley's Rearguard*, by a Mr. Werner, is typical of "big croc" stories.

◆　◆　◆

The biggest croc is a mythical beast, but it should be possible to determine at least the "record" croc, the biggest ever convincingly measured. But even this will always be doubtful, for between reading the tape and recording the result the odd foot or two has a sly way of creeping in. Anderson, in his *Zoology of Egypt* (1898), reports that despite a meticulous search of the literature he could find no authentic measurement of a croc as long as 17 feet, though 14- to 15-footers were common. The biggest we shot on Rudolf, which was as big as any we saw, was 15 feet 9 inches long. Of 30,000 crocs the Bousfields claim to have shot on Lake Rukwa, the longest was 17 feet 4 1/2 inches. During Charles Pitman's 17-year campaign to exterminate crocs in Uganda, the biggest he measured was 18 feet. (That this was the only one exceeding 15 feet emphasizes their rarity.) Hugh Cott in 1961 made a search of the published records of big crocs. The biggest he turned up were one 17 feet 5 inches killed by the naturalist Hubbard on the Kafue River in 1927, and one 18 feet 4 inches claimed by the croc hunter Eric von Hippel on the Semliki River in 1954. But the record Nile croc is one shot by an unknown hunter on the Semliki in 1952; the skin was bought by the Marketing Corporation of Uganda (which handled tens of thousands of croc skins in its time) and measured 19 feet 6 inches long.

While a 20-foot Nile croc is probably a fabulous beast, the world-record croc is actually bigger than that. It was an estuarine crocodile, *Crocodylus porosus*, reckoned to yield the biggest individuals of any living species. The trophy belonged to a Frenchman, Paul de la Gironière, who lived near Luzon in the Philippines. In 1825 he was greatly annoyed by a crocodile that killed and ate one of his horses. Assembling a posse of spearmen, he led a chaotic tallyho after the croc which, because of its bulk and the smallness of the river, was unable to escape. Nevertheless, six hours and uncounted spear thrusts later it was still alive. La Gironière had fired several musket shots from close range, once into the reptile's mouth, seemingly without effect. In fact he later found that his musket caused scarcely any injury. Then a resourceful hunter drove a lance into the animal's back with a hammer and by a fluke found the spinal cord and killed the croc.

The beast was so heavy it took all 40 hunters to roll it ashore. "When at last we had got him completely out of the water we stood stupefied with astonishment. From the extremity of his nostrils to the tip of his tail, he was found to be 27 feet long, and his circumference was 11 feet, measured under the armpits. His belly was much more voluminous, but we thought it unnecessary to measure him there, judging that the horse which he had breakfasted must considerably have increased his bulk . . ." Since it was impossible to shoot all the crocs we needed during the day, we had to hunt them at night as well. We (including Peter Beard who shared work at the lake) had hoped to do this from a boat, but the wind ruled that out. Then we found that because the lake was shallow a long way out, most of the crocs were out of range of a hunter walking along the water's edge. So we had to go in after them. Our technique was for one of us to walk in front with a torch, followed closely by a rifleman. Behind him came one of the men to tow our kills along.

This was necessary because if we left them on shore they were quickly stolen by the lions or hyenas that followed us when we were hunting at night.

The torch bearer would cast around for crocs, whose eyes shine red in torch-light. Finding a suitable one, we would try to approach without alarming the wary animal, which more often than not would silently submerge and disappear. Once down, a croc can last up to an hour without breathing. Although the light dazzled the crocs, many things worked against us to warn them of danger. It was essential to keep downwind, for their sense of smell is extremely good. Their hearing is keen too, and this was our greatest problem, for the ground underfoot was seldom easy to traverse soundlessly. Mostly it was a vile ooze studded with sharp chunks of lava and rocks ("sharp stones are under him: he spreadeth sharp pointed things upon the mire"). Every now and then someone would plunge into a soft patch, for it was a constant struggle to keep upright. Many were the crocs lost at the last moment as somebody subsided noisily into the lake. Scattered about were hippo footprints, deep holes in which the lava chunks clutched at you like gin traps. A shoe torn off deep beneath the mud was almost impossible to retrieve without alarming a croc floating a few feet away.

The extensive weed beds the crocs liked were worse than the open water, for the weed contained sharp spicules that lacerated your legs. And in it dwelt a fiendish beast in the form of a small water bug with a bite like a beesting. It was strange how often their attacks coincided with the critical moment when the gunman was about to squeeze the trigger, causing him to give an involuntary, disastrous twitch.

Early evening before the wind got up was the worst time, for one had to be particularly quiet in the still air. But the major problem was lake flies. These tiny insects swarmed in thousands around the light, constantly flying into our eyes and under our clothing. Sometimes the swarms were so dense that they reflected enough light back from the torch to expose us to the crocs. Or they would collect in the pool of light reflected off the water where the croc was, bothering it as they did us, so that it would submerge to avoid them. When the wind got up, hunting was easier for it masked our noise and dispersed the lake flies. But then the waves jostled us, making shooting more difficult, and late at night, after one had fallen over or waded into deep water, it was bitterly cold. Often we would startle six-foot nile perch that swam off with vigor enough to knock us off our feet. Their heads were hard as iron when they collided with your shins.

Floating crocs presented small targets, for only their eyes and the tops of their heads were above water. To guarantee a hit each time we found we had to get within 15 yards. To shoot at greater distance meant occasional misses, and we found that in the long run we got better results by patiently getting really close.

Having fired at a croc it would invariably disappear beneath the muddy water, whether it was wounded, dead or alive. If hit it was often not far under, and a foot would break the surface as it slowly rolled over and over. Usually, though, the bullet caused a sudden wriggle of its tail that drove it rapidly several yards even if it was dead. Thus by the time we stumbled to the spot where the croc had been shot there was seldom any sign of it, nor any means of telling whether it was dead or alive. So we would search for it by treading about until our toes bumped into it, at which point the success or otherwise of the shot would become apparent. As the dead ones give reflex movements long after death, the process of recovery was always full of scaly surprises.

The water was usually two or three feet deep, so once we located the croc we had to raise it to the surface, still unsure if it was alive. A stunned croc tends to lie motionless until disturbed, whereupon it abruptly regains consciousness. Once after "treading up" an eight-footer we took for dead, Peter began to tie a rope around its neck. Without warning the beast reared up with a violent thrashing. Its head struck Peter square in the middle of his chest with a noise like mallet driving in a tent peg. The heavy bone of a croc's skull is covered only by a pear-thin layer of skin and apparently it felt like being hit by a car. Luckily it did not crack his sternum, but the bruise lasted for weeks.

Of all the distasteful tasks we expected the Turkana to perform, night hunting was the most hated. To go into the water in the dark and deliberately provoke crocodiles was to them ridiculous. It was only by appealing to their pride that I got them to do it at all. When Peter was not there I had to rely on one of the men to wield the torch, which meant standing in front of me, i.e., between me and the croc, while I shot. It was all I could do to aim, so hard did they shiver; and our respective ideas of what constituted close range differed widely.

My biggest difficulty was persuading them to hold their ground whenever the situation looked menacing. Once, while hunting with Tukoi in very shallow water, a magnum croc surfaced about six feet away. We had not known it was there and the abruptness of its appearance was alarming. Although a large croc so close looks fearsome, it is easy to kill at that range, and whipping round, I raised the gun to fire. But Tukoi took off like a reedbuck, his feet in the shallow water sounding like the skittering of a duck as it flies off water. The light went with him, of course, and just then the croc lunged past for deeper water, actually brushing my legs as it did so. There is at such times an awful moment of apprehension as one waits in the dark to find out whether the animal is attacking or fleeing.

On another occasion I was hunting in a patch of swamp where a lot of *msuaki* bushes had been drowned by the lake. Going along the water's edge on dry land, we approached a croc near the shore. I fired, but it was a bad shot, and the croc, wounded, made straight for us. Just as I was about to fire again, having let the croc get really close, my torch bearer fled. I never discovered if the croc was simply confused by its wound or attacking me, but in this case I think the latter. As the light disappeared I leapt aside and the croc stormed past me in the dark. Moments later a violent commotion began in the bush behind me, where the croc was thrashing around and roaring. I shouted, not very politely, for the torch, and then saw what had happened. The croc's momentum had driven it firmly beneath the twisted stem of a fallen *msuaki* bush, where it wriggled helplessly, pinned to the ground.

Holding the torch was bad enough, but what the Turkana flatly refused to do was "tread up" the dead bodies. We did not blame them and accepted that as our duty. It was a lot easier on the nerves with a pistol in one hand. But in this as in other matters the Wildman was an exception, and far from having to encourage him, we had to restrain him.

The Wildman's night shooting debut was typical. He had been told by the others what to do and followed quietly behind us as we approached a croc. I shot at it, and we started looking for the body. After several minutes of fruitless search I realized it was probably only wounded. The Wildman meanwhile had been searching with us, and suddenly with a triumphant whoop he reached down into the water and came up clutching an enraged and wriggling croc. Scorning the beast's snapping jaws and whipping tail he staggered towards us to show his find. I gestured to him to let go of it, a command he found rather puzzling, and very reluctantly he dropped it into the lake where I could finish it off.

We got the others to explain to him about wounded crocs and he agreed to be more circumspect in the future, though it in no way dampened his spirits. It seemed that he looked upon night shooting simply as a very fine way to spend an evening.

We got a taste of what could happen with a wounded croc midway through the survey, and the scare of that night was a sharp reminder to shoot accurately. Peter and I were hunting in Moite Bay, along a rocky shore with deep water only a few yards out. The slippery stones under foot made the going extremely difficult. The air was still and cold, with everything around us black as Egypt's night. Behind loomed the mountain, brooding over the bay, the haunt of many large crocs. Altogether it was an eerie place that we seldom hunted. That night we saw a good croc about nine feet long, and approaching successfully, I fired. It seemed a perfectly good shot, and wading up we were surprised when the croc, still very much alive, started thrashing about on the surface, snapping its jaws viciously. I saw that the wound was too far forward, leaving the brain undamaged.

I tried to kill it with my pistol but succeeded only in exciting it further. It began to attack us every time it surfaced, though the wound had dazed it enough for us to dodge each time. Suddenly it disappeared, and thinking that one of my pistol shots had taken effect, we looked for the carcass. The ferocity it had just displayed made us somewhat reluctant, though.

I soon found it. Stumbling around, I bumped into a scaly flank, felt it whip around, and the next moment its jaws closed on my leg. I let out a great howl and wrenched my leg clear. Luckily it could not bite with more than a fraction of its normal strength or I would have been unable to free myself so easily; a croc that size is quite capable of killing a man.

Making a last feeble attempt to find the croc, we easily convinced ourselves that it had gone, and went ashore, glad to leave the place. Examining my leg, we found that I had escaped literally from the dragon's mouth, with nothing worse than deep gashes. They bled a lot but eventually healed without trouble.

The Turkana were aghast at our story. Why, they demanded, did I leave the croc alive after it had bitten me? How could I be so incompetent? Was it not a blatant messenger from God bent on mischief? The fact that I had been bitten and then escaped might mean it was a case of mistaken identity—probably the croc was after them, only realizing its error on tasting the wrong leg. This incident upset them much more than it did us and they never forgot to remind me of my blunder at the start of each new trip to Moite. Somewhere out there in Moite Bay a vengeful crocodile was waiting for someone with a bad conscience.

On our last three trips to Alia, with only 120 crocs to go to reach the quota of 500, we found it increasingly difficult to collect specimens within walking distance of camp. Three schemes got us round the problem. Firstly, as we had done at Moite, we made short flights in the plane north to a big sandspit called Kubi Fora, landing on a dry mudpan just behind the beach. The need to get our kills back to camp for processing before the sun spoiled them tempted us to make unusual demands of our flying machine. I think the most we ever carried—an almost incredible load— was 12 good crocs, plus Peter, the Wildman, myself, and sundry gear—all in the tiny cabin designed for a maximum of three passengers. In this way we got many good muggers, including our all-night record, a monster pebbleworm 15 feet 4 inches long. "Treading" this beast up was something even the Wildman hesitated to do. The water was about five feet deep where it was shot, and it sank immediately. Wading out up to our chests, frankly shivering with fear, we saw a foot slowly break the surface. Clammy as that foot was, it was no more so than the reluctant hand that grasped it. There was no way of telling whether the croc was dead or only stunned; grabbing its foot could very well have unleashed half a ton of carnivorous vengeance.

Our second scheme was a kamikaze invention of Peter's that arose from two observations of crocodile behavior. We noticed that crocs are much warier of disturbances on the land than in the water; and further, that they are easily fooled by strange objects in the water. This is logical, really, because their enemies are mostly terrestrial. It led Peter to experiment with an adaptation of the old croc hunter's trick of crawling towards a "basking" croc very, very slowly, concealed behind a bush which he pushes in front. In his variation, Peter swam towards sleeping crocs pushing an inflated inner tube along in front. The gun lay across the tube, wrapped in kikoys and a broken gun case against the spray. When in range he inched himself up onto a patch of beach and fired. The method was highly successful, with the crocs astonishingly unsuspecting. Peter's greatest triumph came one afternoon when he actually nudged a "watchstrap" out of the way with the rifle barrel to get a shot at a big one beyond. Another time he stopped a nine-footer through the open mouth of a smaller one next door. But it was tedious, cold and dangerous work; several crocs, far from being afraid, were hostile, and came for him aggressively. On three occasions Peter was driven ashore by such challenges.

◆　◆　◆

Of all the characteristics that cause men to fear croc attacks, such as the animal's stealth (or boldness), ferocity or strength, one in particular stands out—the unexpectedness. The concealment of water, the beast's cryptic looks and its hunting skill combine to make croc attacks sudden and therefore more terrifying.

◆　◆　◆

Crocodiles . . . hide under willows and greene hollow bankes, till some people come to the waters side to draw and fetch water, and then suddenly, or ever they be aware, they are taken, and drawne into the water. And also for this purpose, because he knoweth that he is not able to overtake a man in his course or chase, he taketh a great deale of water in his mouth, and casteth it in the pathwaies, so that when they endeavour to run from the crocodile, they fall downe in the slippery path, and are overtaken and destroyed by him.

◆　◆　◆

Crocodile victims fall into three broad categories; the resigned (which includes the majority), that is, those who for one reason or another consider the risk unavoidable. Secondly, the unaware, those who suffer real accidents of chance. Thirdly, the tantalized, men lured by some compelling aspect of a situation into exposing themselves to attack.

It was in the middle of our survey that we learned of a fatal croc attack that took place not far from Lake Rudolf, in southwest Ethiopia. It was typical of countless croc attacks, and its circumstances emphasize the stark reality of such accidents to those who, ignorant of the ways of the bush, do not believe or appreciate that such things actually do take place. As it happened, a professional hunter, Karl Luthy, was there to witness the incident. Luthy also took the trouble to record what took place, thus providing an unusually authentic and vivid description of the circumstances:

◆　◆　◆

Shortly after noon on April 13, 1966, the DC 3 from Addis Ababa landed at Gambela in southwest Ethiopia. The plane brought six Americans of the Peace Corps, two girls and four boys, who had chosen to spend a short vacation visiting Gambela.

Through the village runs a slow, muddy river, the Bara, on the sandy banks of which I was working that day, building a pontoon on which to ferry my equipment across the river so that my client, an American named Dow, and I could resume our safari to the south. Hot and eager for a swim the Peace Corps came down to the river and I heard them discussing the prospect not far away. But their inquiries of the villagers elicited only a strong warning to stay out of the water on account of a large croc, which it was asserted, had only recently killed and eaten a native child, and later a woman in the brazenest manner imaginable—by which I mean right in the middle of town, in plain view of a crowd! I, too, strongly warned them against swimming and for a while they thought better of it.

Not long afterwards I heard a splash and looking up from my work saw one of the Peace Corps in the river striking out for the other bank. At this the others abandoning all caution, also dived into the water and swam to the other side. For a while they splashed and cavorted in the shallows, maybe 150 yards from where I was working. It was naturally alarming, and very annoying to see them completely ignore my warnings and those of so many well-meaning and experienced people; but I did not wish to intervene again, it was no business of mine and in any case out of my control. Yet it was with considerable relief that I saw five of the six swim back to my side and climb out.

Bill Olsen remained behind, why, I never discovered. I recall seeing him on the far side of the river waist high in the water, his feet on a submerged rock. He was leaning into the current to keep his balance, a rippled vee of water trailing behind him; his arms were folded across his chest and he was staring ahead as if lost in thought. I continued working for a while and looked up again a few minutes later. Olsen had gone—vanished without a trace or a sound, and instinctively I glanced around, a prickle of apprehension spreading over me. But he was nowhere to be seen and I never saw him alive again, although we were to meet face to face much later when I fished his head out of the croc's belly.

Give or take half an hour the croc took Olsen at 3:30 P.M. After that events followed in quick succession. Although I knew instinctively what had happened I had, as yet, no definite proof. At this point the other Peace Corps volunteers came back to the river shouting for Olsen to join them, little knowing that he had in fact left them forever. I continued to scan the river and eventually, a short distance downstream, a croc surfaced, with a large, white, partially submerged object in its jaws, whose identity was in no doubt.

About 15 minutes had elapsed since Olsen disappeared. The croc then dived to resurface (still carrying the corpse) 10 minutes later, now some distance downstream and difficult to see. The Peace Corps were at first incredulous at the news, stubbornly unwilling to believe what was obvious. Olsen had wandered off somewhere, they said, he would be back soon; they clutched at the silliest possibilities rather than accept the bitter facts. Eventually my binoculars arrived and they saw for themselves what was obviously the body of their companion in the jaws of a croc. They went to pieces then, crying, full of remorse and self-incrimination, and I confess that one of them received a sharp rebuke when he ran to me pleading for help.

"Help who?" I shouted. "Help him? He's dead! Help you? I should hit you!"

One does not care to see one's fellow men die such needless deaths, however ignorant they may be.

By this time a crowd of excited people had gathered on the river bank and the commotion caused my client, Colonel Dow, to come with his rifle demanding to know what was going on. On learning the story he wanted to try and shoot the croc then and there, but I persuaded him not to, pointing out that killing the animal now, in midstream, would surely result in Olsen's body being lost, possibly for good. I reasoned that the croc would behave like any other croc; that is, he would haul out of the river early next morning, not too far away, to rest in the morning sun for a while, after the activities of the night.

Sure enough, around 7 the next morning, a breathless villager ran up to tell us that a large croc, undoubtedly the croc, was lying ashore across the river not 50 yards from where Olsen had been taken. I got my binoculars and located the beast. That this was our quarry was in no doubt, for hanging from his mouth in some macabre reminder of a recent banquet, was a large piece of pale coloured flesh.

We were determined to destroy this croc, not only because it was a menace to the people on the river but also because an undeniable vengeance was in us. This was no circumstantial accident, but a deliberate and vicious attack in our midst and a certain urge for revenge moved us. Dow wanted to be the one to kill the animal so off he went on a careful route which took him upstream on foot for some distance, then across the Baro in a canoe and back down the other side on a painstaking stalk until eventually he lay directly behind the beast. It was a difficult shot with the croc facing away from him so that its protruding back partially obscured its head. The Colonel shot too high and the bullet struck its neck, temporarily stunning the reptile, but causing only a flesh wound. He then fired four more shots, three of which were well placed, but despite this the croc crawled into the river and disappeared.

I watched all this through binoculars and feared at first that we'd lost the beast. I joined Dow and together we made for a sandbank in midstream, followed by a flotilla of dugouts, carrying the other Peace Corps and as many Amahara and Anuak villagers as could get in the canoes, all very noisy and excited. We stepped out onto the sandbank and began searching the river for some sign of the croc. Quite suddenly it surfaced not 10 yards away and Dow, rather hastily, shot and missed. But the animal, mortally wounded, took no notice and he was able to fire again, this time hitting the head, sending the brute spinning crazily about its own axis. I rushed forward with several other men and we dragged the carcass from the water onto the sand.

There remained only the gruesome business of opening up the croc, and it was not long before Olsen's fate was established beyond all doubt. We found his legs, intact from the knees down, still joined together at the pelvis. We found his head, crushed into small chunks, a barely recognizable mass of hair and flesh and we found other chunks of unidentifiable tissue. The croc had evidently torn him to pieces to feed and abandoned what he could not swallow.

The circumstances of Olsen's killing are of some interest in illuminating the way in which crocodiles set about taking their prey. First of all he disappeared without a sound which suggests that he was not standing on the rock at the final moment—I think he would have had time to scream if he was. It seems to me that he must have started swimming back and was simply pulled under without warning, and held under until he drowned. Secondly , there is the fact that no one saw any sign of the beast before the event although it was flagrantly bold afterwards, illustrating the stealth and cunning with which a crocodile hunts. The croc measured exactly 13 feet and one inch long, by no means a monster but still powerful enough to catch a human like a fish.

• • •

These are the facts of life among crocodiles. So long as one is constantly threatened by savage brutes one is to some extent bound in barbarism; they hold you down. For this reason there is in a man a cultural instinct to separate himself from and destroy wild beasts such as crocodiles. It is only after a period of civilization free of wild animals that man again turns his attention on them seeking in them qualities to cherish.

Conservation is guilt. It springs from fearful introspection, the awful tension between what we *would* do if we obeyed our instincts, and the prohibition of our moral sense. Our urge is to strike out at the people overrunning us, to fight for what we covet, to destroy what we fear and hate—but these aggressive actions and thoughts are culturally taboo. So we invert these dangerous, frightening impulses and counter them with their opposites. Instead of destruction we insist upon preservation. Instead of killing we cry out: Save!

There is a popular expression to describe the vaguely defined sentiments of conservationists—"deeply concerned." Comfortable, affluent, powerful, *well-informed*, racially tolerant, educated, democratic *crowded* people are the kind most susceptible to the affectation of deep concern for wildlife. All over the western world they can be seen squatting hopefully beside their TV's—watching the animals; or driving breathlessly round national parks—watching the animals; snapping hungrily with cameras—watching the animals; squinting earnestly through binoculars—watching animals. All of them feel deeply, deeply concerned about wildlife.

But what are they watching for? Is it some sort of answer? Do they really believe that the poor, dumb, doomed beasts are going to share a revelation with them? ("Will he speak soft words unto thee? Will he make a covenant with thee?") Why is it that between them and the animals there is always a glass shield? Dark glass, plate glass, frosted glass, smoked glass; glass with cross-hairs, glass with *concern* etched into it, glass with despair scratched all over it. They are so near, yet so far. If only they were to insert a mirrored glass, they would find themselves staring at their own earnest, puzzled, *desperate* faces. The riddle would be solved. They would realize that the concern is for *their* fate—not that of the animals. It is so simple really; solve mankind's problems and the predicament of the animals will automatically vanish. But no amount of concern for the animals is going to make any difference to their destiny or ours.

••• *The author of such books as* THE NINEMILE WOLVES *and* THE LOST GRIZZLIES, *Rick Bass has been writing for* SPORTS AFIELD *since 1982 and has been a contributing editor since 1994. The following story was written well before he left Mississippi and moved to the wilderness of the Yaak Valley, which is featured in* THE BOOK OF YAAK (1996). —JULY 1982 •••

THE 4TH OF JULY DASH by Rick Bass

Friday, July 4

I've been waiting a long time for this. Jackson, Mississippi, is the best place for me to make a living, but there's this one small problem. There are no mountains. There aren't even any aspens.

The Pecos Wilderness Area, on the other hand, located 15 beautiful miles up a beautiful winding canyon just west of the sleepy (and beautiful) little mountain town of Las Vegas, New Mexico, has plenty of both. That's why I'm here—to drink in the mountains and the aspens for a brief 4th of July vacation. I left Jackson at noon yesterday because I managed to talk the boss into letting me come into work early (4:00 A.M.) so I could have my eight hours in by noon. I'm due back in the office at 9 o'clock Monday, but could probably get away with 9:15.

By driving straight through (averaging 54 mph and stopping only for gas) it is an 18-hour drive each way, excluding the time change. (I never change my watch back when crossing over because it is too depressing to change it forward again when I come back out. Someday I'll cross that line, pick up an extra hour, and never come back. Someday.) Subtracting this 36-hour round-trip drive from my 93 1/4-

hour vacation gives me 57 hours in the wilderness, in the mountains, in the aspens.

My grandparents live in Fort Worth, a rough midpoint of the journey, and that is where I fritter away the 15 minutes; seven-and-a-half minutes going, seven-and-a-half minutes coming. It is inevitably right around midnight on the return trip, but they don't mind. They are waiting on the porch, waiting with a sack full of out-of-this-world delicacies that grandmothers are famous for—sausage-and-biscuit sandwiches, slabs of angel food cake, pie, fresh peaches, brownies and cookies, barbecued ribs and chicken still warm and wrapped in foil—and we hug, sit on the porch and talk about the weather, baseball, football, the upcoming hunting season, and then I leave. They too used to live in the mountains. They understand.

It is now midafternoon; I got in around dawn this morning, the most beautiful sunrise I've seen since my last three-day weekend. I stopped at the little doughnut store at the foot of the mountains in Las Vegas—they're always fresh and hot at that time of morning—and then headed up the canyon. Reached the Pecos Wilderness Area, turned down a dusty gravel road, headed uphill (my trusty VW bucked and pitched over the stones and cobbles but never faltered), stopped by a stream and a stand of aspens, got out, took a deep breath, then another and another, feeling like a man escaped from prison (surely someone must be chasing me; I half-expected to hear hounds baying in the distance), put my hiking boots on, raised both arms high into the thin crisp mountain morning air and yelled as loud and as long as I could in one breath, and then curled up in a ball on a cold flat rock down by the water's edge and slept for five hours solid, the deepest sleep I've had since, well, since my last three-day weekend.

After I woke up I consulted my topo map, shouldered my pack—and headed up a ridge toward where I hoped the trailhead to Hermit's Peak would be. The forested-yet-rocky mountain loomed in front of me like a barrier, about three miles distant, its sheer cliffs shining bright in the midday sun. The way to get up to the top is to sneak up the backside, up a gruelingly constant 60 pitch of forested switch-backs and loop-arounds. Sometimes it is more of a climb than a hike: Your arms grip rock ledges and pull you up the mountain instead of the more efficient feet-pushing-off-of-solid-ground style. It is an enchantingly torturous trail, through shady woods, past waterfalls and aspens, up and over talus slopes, through stream-fed mountain-green meadows.

On my way up through the aspens, I snack on the last of the sausage-and-biscuits (sweet madeleine!) and suddenly, all is well. I am back home again. The sausage-and-biscuit is the real beginning of the best part of the trip; I always save one for this purpose. Everything before that last Grandmother's-homemade-biscuit is Getting There; everything afterwards is There Itself.

I reach the trailhead a couple hours later, my muscles just now beginning to loosen to the pull of the pack. Because it is the 4th of July, there are a fair (or is it unfair?) number of people here, local people mostly, who have decided to make the all-day four-mile hike up and down the trail to the top of the magnificent, wind-swept Hermit's Peak. Because I want the trail to myself, I try to dislike them for it, but cannot: if I lived in Las Vegas or Trujillo or Sante Fe or Carrizozo it is what I, too, would do.

I've made this trip before, but as I sit at the trailhead watching them come staggering along the trail in groups of twos and threes—staggering like mortally wounded buffalo, tongues dragging and eyes crossing, a new herd every 30 minutes or so—I ask one of them what kind of hike it is.

One of the hikers looks at my pack dubiously. Camera lenses, tripod, tent, sleeping bag, canteens and extra hiking boots (my old ones are threatening to go out any day now) spring out in all directions as if trying to escape.

"How much does your pack weigh?" he asks.

"Sixty pounds," I say. "I plan to stay a while."

He frowns, and I can tell that he is about to tell me that he doesn't think you can get to the top with a 60-pound pack. "It took me six hours up," he says.

"Thank you," I say.

Glancing up at the sun, I figure about five hours left before sundown; just right. I sit by Hermit's Creek and eat chocolate bars and listen to the water, and then, when it is four hours 'til sundown, after the last of the buffalo have filed past with wan and weary smiles, I start up the trail. No one else will be starting up behind me, and there is a good chance most of them will already have come down. I will have Hermit's Peak to myself.

♦ ♦ ♦

Friday, July 4—later in the evening

Up top. The two most delightful words in the world right now, because that is where I am: up top. There is no place else to go. It amazes me that my legs still work, but after a 20-minute layover at Hermit's Spring I was able to make it to the top.

I'm just sitting here, savoring the complete and temporary ownership of the second-highest 200 acres in New Mexico all to myself, watching the alpenglow flush all of eastern New Mexico.

Gads, what's this? *Voices* from behind me, *voices* coming up the trail at sunset! I turn to see two people, a man and a woman, striding eagerly up through the aspens; they are both thin, wiry and tan, and the man has a golden-blond beard. They are both wearing green nylon running shorts and white T-shirts that say "Property of Texas Tech University Track Team." They are not wearing backpacks. I look down at the sun (I am up top, up above it), or rather, where the sun used to be. Ten, maybe 20 minutes of light left; even I can be cordial for that long, I tell myself. I rise and take a step to meet them and offer them a chocolate bar.

"Thanks," says the man, peeling back the wrapper without looking at it, his eyes glued to the dizzying sweep of endless forest far below, never blinking, never looking at anything else, as if he were watching the Second Coming.

"Wow," says the man, still watching the eastern United States as if waiting for something to happen. "I never thought it would be like this."

We all three sit down and watch the wilderness below, just watching and waiting and eating chocolate bars, and then after it is almost too dark to see, they sigh and look wistfully back at the trail behind us.

"We've really got to be going," says the man, like a dinner guest apologizing for leaving so early.

I smile benignly. "That's a shame," I say, almost managing to sound truly sorry. They nod glumly, look back out at the many-miles-distant now-darkened horizon one last time, and turn and start back down the trail. I turn and refocus my attention on the spot where the sun went down—a half-dome of glowing light blue marks the point—and then, remembering my manners, pivot around again to tell them to be careful, but they are already gone, swallowed up. I get up, pitch my tent by the light of a quarter-moon, roll out on top of it, and fall fast asleep immediately, sleeping until 9 o'clock the next morning.

• • •

Saturday, July 5

Right now there is a camp robber watching me from a distance of perhaps four, maybe five feet. If I had the mind to I think I could probably reach out and snatch him up before he even had a chance to think about flying away. He is just watching me, head cocked slightly, looking as if maybe he wants to come still closer. He's the first camp robber I've seen since reaching the summit; I am sitting out on the lip of a 4000-foot (almost a mile!) sheer cliff face and can see Texas and Colorado at the same time. It is too hazy to the south or I bet I could see Mexico too.

The ledge I'm sitting on is sloped so much that if I set a marble on it, it would roll down the ledge a couple of yards before plunging over the edge and falling the 4000 feet into the gorge below, disappearing into the morning haze long before it hit. The ledge is not so steep, however, that I can't sit on it with my feet out in front of me, relaxed, resting perhaps 10 or 12 inches from the edge.

The camp robber has hopped a step closer, not knowing that I do not plan to share my chocolate energy bar with him. Where was he when I was hauling it up the torturous trail? Let him eat pinon nuts.

Despite (or perhaps because of) their lack of glamour, camp robbers are the most ubiquitous wilderness bird I have come across; they are everywhere, like sparrows in the city. I used to be ashamed to find camp robbers waiting for me when I got to the top of high, wild, windy peaks such as this one because camp robbers don't have a lot of romance about them. They make a living (whenever possible) by robbing crumbs from campers' picnic tables. Camp robbers are like the bears at Yellowstone who beg for food, only not as cute.

The reason a lot of experienced and dedicated hikers and climbers choose to look upon camp robbers with no small amount of scorn, or at best, to ignore them, is because camp robbers represent not wild, windy peaks like the ones found in the Pecos Wilderness Area but instead remind them of mobile homes, Winnebagos, picnic tables and 4th of July family reunions down in the campgrounds.

All of which are fine, but not why the experienced and dedicated hikers and climbers came to the wilderness in the first place. They hike and they climb and they hike and they climb and then they get to the top of Hermit's Peak or Wheeler's Peak or Crazy Elk Mountain, and they are disappointed to find that although they have escaped the suburbia of the campgrounds, they have not escaped the camp robbers.

There is merit in their disappointment. After a grueling all-day assault up the steep and rocky trail, after battling altitude sickness, blistered feet, pulled hamstrings and rubbed-raw shoulders and backbones, it would be nice for them to be able to think that they have done something special, something a little gray bird cannot.

I like camp robbers because they have some qualities that I do not have but wish I did. They are extraordinarily friendly to everyone, whether they have to be or not. This is a pretty wild thought, due perhaps to yesterday's bout with altitude sickness; I am convinced that if you could take a camp robber and turn him into a teen-age boy and send him to school for a week, by the end of that week he would not only be elected student body president but would also be named Most Likely to Succeed, Most Representative Senior Boy, Most Handsome and Most Popular. I know of no other creature who shares majestic wilderness so willingly, so completely, with man as the camp robber.

Take, for instance, this rock I am sitting on. The rock swifts who live below it are doing their level best to evict me. They have no hatchlings on their nest, but they don't care: From time to time they fold their wings and dive straight out of the sun at me before suddenly flaring out over the edge of the cliff and rocketing into the haze, their trim, bullet-shaped bodies ripping the air with the sound of tearing cloth, sometimes coming so close that if I had a net and if I were fast enough (fast enough to catch a speeding bullet) I could reach out and net one. They are not amused by my presence. I have not littered, I have not hurled rocks at them as they fly past, I have not even played my harmonica late into the night, and yet they do not like me. They feel toward me the way I felt toward the track couple last night— they will be glad when I leave. But not the camp robbers.

I feel sure there is a lesson in there somewhere but I am getting both sleepy and hungry, so I think I will return to my tent and eat a couple more chocolate bars, drink another can of apple juice, and then stretch out on a warm rock and doze off with only the sound of the wind and nothing else to think about.

• • •

Sunday, July 6

I believe I could tell today is a Sunday morning without even looking at a calendar. There is just something about them, even in the city, but even more so in the mountains, that identifies Sundays. Everything seems slower and more relaxed. This morning my altitude sickness was gone; only the euphoria remained. I slept with my tent flaps open so I could hear the night wind better—it will be Labor Day before I hear it again the way I heard it last night—and so that the first faint light of sunup would wake me, which it did.

It was like a secret meeting, like an elopement. The sky began to lighten in the east around 5:00 A.M., and I got up and began moving around, wearing a light windbreaker and shorts and hiking boots. It was really much cooler than windbreaker-and-shorts weather, but I liked to feel the goose bumps—it would be another two months before I felt them again.

I went out to get wood for a small fire. There is a ton of dried windfall back on the south slope of Hermit's Peak; entire swaths of forest have been hit by lightning (in thunderstorms, the peak acts as the tallest lightning rod for many, many miles) and mowed down by windstorms of up to 100 miles an hour. I spooked two elk on the southwest rim of the peak; they sounded like 10 wild elephants as they crashed through the dead timber in their panic.

I gathered up two handfuls of kindling, came back to my tent, built a small fire on the edge of the face that looked out at the eastern United States, and waited, shivering. Only it was better than a secret meeting, better than an elopement, because I knew for certain that the sun would be coming, that she would show up on time. I could already see her.

It took about an hour from first light until the first tiny flattened arc of orange fire peered up over the horizon, looking much larger than I had expected it would. After the first arc appeared, the rest of the ball was not long in following; it rose as rapidly as if pulled up by a string, like a stage curtain.

My fire dwindled; I poured water on the ashes, stirred them around, folded my tent and broke camp. Headed down the trail, lingering, taking my time. It was still cold and dark on the backside of the peak and would be for another hour or so.

I moved on, feeling both Sunday-morning-calm-and-peaceful and euphoric. I reached bottom in time for lunch. The 4th of July gang was long gone; only my little VW sat waiting patiently for my return, like a horse tied to a hitching post. I loaded my pack into the back seat and took off my hiking boots, wriggled my toes in the cold dust, put on soft old tennis shoes, rubbed my three-days' beard for the first time, and sat on the hood of my car and ate more chocolate bars and looked up a Hermit's Peak for awhile and waited for the euphoria to subside so I could leave. Down low in the campground the mountain air was thin and warm and tasted like Indian summer, like autumn in Mississippi.

I sighed; Mississippi. Mississippi on my mind. It could be postponed no longer; there were papers to be shuffled, reports to be filed, meetings to be attended, a living to be made. Sort of.

I got in my car, turned the engine over, half-hoping it wouldn't start, but it did, and I let the clutch out and drove slowly down the dusty gravel road into Las Vegas. Stopped for doughnuts in Las Vegas, gas in Tucumcari and Abilene, sausage-and-biscuits and barbecued ribs and hugs in Fort Worth, and gasoline again in Shreveport. Made good time, getting into Jackson at 8:30 Monday morning. Swung by the apartment and showered and changed, drove to office (tied my tie, buckled my belt, put my shoes and socks on and field-shaved at red lights), combed my hair in the elevator, stepped out on the 11th floor at 9:08 sharp. Paused at the office doorway before consulting my pocket calendar: 60 more days. I took a deep breath and stepped inside.

••• *A field editor for* SPORTS AFIELD *since 1979, Ted Kerasote specializes in outdoor skills and environmental reporting. As we can see from the following story, he also knows a few things about guns, and fiction.* —DECEMBER 1982 •••

THE ELEPHANT GUN
by Ted Kerasote

One of the largest sporting arms ever built, the elephant gun, was developed in Africa during the last century. It was used in its crude form by the Scots, and then refined by the British. The Scots, coming out to homestead from their gloomy North Sea home, had a history of big weapons behind them. Descended from Norse blood—shields and helmets—they met their southern cousins as well as their own kin with broad axes, halberds and double-edged swords requiring two hands and a savage cry to wield. No wonder that when faced with trumpeting animals that weighed five tons, let alone marauding tribes, they took their blunderbuss—a civilized fowling piece—and closed the bore, strengthened the breech and got it to shoot a projectile that weighed in the neighborhood of a quarter pound. An elephant hit in the head with such a cannon was knocked backwards onto its haunches. The hunter, or more properly the planter protecting his bit of hard-won ground, was knocked backwards as well, about 10 feet if we're to believe the accounts, and usually given a bloody nose and violent headache. But it was all for a good cause, hearth and home, and right in the Scots' line of work.

The British, on the other hand, were sportsmen more than planters and liked to do things with finesse. They had their gunmakers, those suave white-coated fellows around Berkeley Square, slim down the Scots' cannons and give them some rifling and hence accuracy. These double-barreled rifles shot bullets weighing an ounce, but at a high velocity and with great force. When an elephant weighing five tons met a bullet weighing an ounce, but going at something like 1400 miles per hour, the effect was instantaneous. The elephant got knocked back on its haunches while the hunter, posh now in pith and khaki, sauntered over when the dust had settled and had pictures taken. Looking back at their scrapbooks of sepia-toned photographs, one sees these lads resting a nonchalant elbow on the elephant's belly, or sometimes placing a jaunty foot on the elephant's leg. Usually the elephant gun is leaning quietly, job well done, against the elephant's shoulder.

The hunter, of course, went back home to England, where the elephant gun was put up in an honored spot in the gunrack and taken down and oiled on Boxing Day and when the hunter's nephew came down from Yorkshire. That's when the story of the elephant was retold—how the hunter and his guide had trailed the spoor, how they had smelled the elephant, dung and hay, before catching a glimpse of him through the trees, how the beast had charged, ears laid back, and "one-two" was laid low. The nephew looked on in wonder. "Yes, a big gun," said the elephant hunter, still in awe of what the weapon had done—there were the tusks framing the door—and the elephant gun was returned to its rack. No one seemed to mind all this horseplay. No one except the elephants, that is.

● ● ●

A half century later, Gabriel Hunter was born in America of Scotch descent mixed with a touch of English, though family rumor had it that great-grandmother, an independent woman of the West, had brought in a streak of Apache. Gabriel's granddad had come to Colorado from Glasgow in '91 and homesteaded a ranch. In '92 Gabriel's great-uncle Gerad had also decided to seek his fortune. He had set off to the other side of the globe, to Kenya, to plant coffee. In the scrapbook that was passed down to Gabriel, Uncle Gerad leaned a jaunty elbow against a dead elephant twice as tall as he.

Though Gabriel's father grew up on the ranch, his heart was never in stock, and once off to college he took only a passing interest in the spread. He became a banker, married old money, and under the influence of his wife, sent both Gabriel and his sister, Clarissa, to boarding school in the East. But Gabriel soon returned. Disappointing his father a trifle, his mother quite a bit and his sister immensely (she had taken on some eastern airs), he followed his grandfather and great-uncle and grew up loving to shoot.

In the fall he hunted rabbits, partridge, geese and deer. In the winter he shot metallic silhouette targets, a Mexican gambling game in which the marksman shoots at four metallic animal forms—the *gallina*, the chicken; the *guajalote*, the turkey; the *javelina*, the wild pig; and the *borrego*, the ram—and makes the targets ring merrily and fall over when hit squarely. In the spring, when the wind died down, Gabriel shot clay birds, taking off only enough time to stalk a real turkey, which he usually got, and a black bear, which he had never seen. He dressed in chamois shirts and crepe-soled leather boots; he kept a cowardly bird dog, a springer spaniel named

Sam; and collected, in addition to the letters and plantation scrapbook of his great-uncle, the faded accounts of the ivory hunters, the sepia-toned pictures covered with yellow tissue. Someday, more than anything else in the world, Gabriel wanted to shoot not the bear that had eluded him, but an elephant, the largest, wisest and most wonderful of land mammals.

He also knew he never would. There weren't enough elephants left in the world, so everyone said; and as a child he had fed peanuts to enough elephants in the zoo to know that even the most roguish bull was a pushover for a bag of goobers. Far worse, though, a million times worse in fact, was his undeniable, unforgettable experience of actually riding an elephant. It was when his father had take the family to India on an international exchange with a family from the Bank of Delhi. Before settling down in the city, they had toured the country up by the Burmese frontier and there, on a cool evening, with the sun going down, Gabriel had seen an elephant walking through the marketplace. His father saw Gabriel stare; he called the mahout; and Gabriel went bumpty-bumpty-bump, high as a palm tree, out the trunk road and back. Afterwards, while his father paid the Indian, the elephant turned its head around and touched Gabriel on the chest with his trunk. His trunk had been as moist and soft as a hand.

Gabriel wished he had caught the mumps like his sister and arrived in India late. He wished they had lived in a small town without a zoo—or at least a zoo that didn't have elephants. For he still wanted to walk through a green African forest, an elephant gun heavy in his hands, and see a big shadowy form slip through the leaves ahead of him, raise its trunk and charge. Then he wondered what he would do.

Still wondering, he hunted his ducks, his geese and his deer, distributing the freezer-wrapped packages of meat to his parents and his sister, Clarissa, who refused the meat and instead rolled her eyes heavenward and said, "Neanderthal." She made Gabriel feel sad.

One day he went into the gun shop to buy a new set of metallic silhouette targets. He looked down the rack of firearms and saw the old familiar rifles and shotguns he had handled. But there, at the end of the row, was a gun bigger than the rest, its barrel heavy, its sling dark and sweat-stained, its stock dull and businesslike. He picked it up. It was a bolt-action elephant gun, the kind Americans developed after the British had won the war and lost their kingdom, the kind rich oilmen bought in the 50s with no thought to the tradition of elephant hunting and that it might be more cricket to have but two shots instead of five. That way, if you didn't shoot well—"one-two" as they used to say—the elephant stepped on you. The oilmen saw where cricket had gotten the British.

Gabriel raised the gun to his shoulder. Even thought it was a bolt action, it was solid and heavy and had that imposing black hole in its muzzle. It would bellow, not crack as a deer gun. And it would be the only elephant gun he could ever afford. He took it the man behind the counter.

"What do people shoot with one of these?" he asked jokingly, not wanting to admit he was considering buying it.

"Refrigerators," said the cigar-chewing owner. He knocked off an ash that landed on Sam's head. Sam snarled.

Gabriel returned the gun to the rack and bought his metallic silhouette targets. He stepped toward the door. Sam wagged his tail, hopefully. Then Gabriel turned back to the counter, and reached for his credit card.

•   •   •

Elephant cartridges are as big as brass candlesticks and feel similar in the hand. Five of them in your pocket are as heavy as a large rock. When put into an elephant gun, they don't tinkle lightly into the chamber the way deer cartridges do. They insert ponderously, hermetically, smoothly with the sound of restrained omnipotence. When the bolt closes, it closes like a vault or the door to a tomb.

When Gabriel shot the elephant gun for the first time, he was at the public rifle range at the edge of the city dump, aiming at the *gallina,* the metallic chicken. He was lying prone, the chicken was 50 yards away, and when the gun went off Gabriel heard a triple-toned bellow, like a thunderclap on an August afternoon, and simultaneously felt as if he had run full-tilt into a lamp post. The *gallina* disappeared and Sam ran away, howling. Then Gabriel shot the *guajalote* and the *guajalote* disappeared. Then he shot the *javelina* and the *javelina* disappeared. He had five cartridges in the elephant gun, so he also shot the *borrego.* He thought he saw a piece of the *borrego* fly someplace downrange and decided to look. Besides, his shoulder was very sore. He walked past the backstop and in a pile of sand found the ram's horn lying like a crescent moon fallen from the sky. Gabriel shook his head, slung his elephant gun over his shoulder and started toward his car. He whistled for Sam, but Sam wouldn't come. After a few yards he came upon a heap of old rugs and saw, not 30 yards away, resting on some tires, a washing machine. He had one cartridge left in his elephant gun and he crouched, narrowing his eyes. He thought he saw the washing machine move. He whipped the gun off his shoulder, aimed toward the crown, on line between the eyes, and fired. There was a noise like a jet breaking the sound barrier, and the washing machine fell backwards onto its haunches and slid to the bottom of the pile.

That evening Gabriel cleaned and oiled his elephant gun and put it in his gunrack. When Harry Day, Gabriel's skeet-shooting partner, came by to borrow some powder, he saw the elephant gun in the rack.

"What's *that?*" asked Harry, excitement in his voice.

"That's an elephant gun," said Gabriel.

Harry picked it up and opened and closed the bolt. The bolt closed like the door to a tomb.

"What do you shoot with it around here?" Harry asked.

Gabriel was leafing through one of his old books. "Appliances," he said.

•   •   •

Behind Gabriel's house was a mine. It wasn't your run-of-the-mill mine, turning out a little gold and silver from a few old shafts. This mine produced molybdenum from vast caverns under the mountain. Each week there were muffled explosions that shook the earth, and when Gabriel looked out his den window he would see a little more of the mountain sag. It made Gabriel angry.

Once there had been a deer herd on the mountain. Once there had been two golden eagles nesting in the southern crags. At night Gabriel had heard coyotes. Then the construction crews had run slurry lines across the migration route of the deer and put out drugged meat, which sterilized the coyotes. The eagles had left too, hating the helicopters.

Once Gabriel had walked all over the mountain. Once he had hunted partridge in its spruce forests. On its back side was a lake where the first geese used to come. The lake was now a tailings pond and the mine's land, though technically still forest service land, belonging to everyone, had been closed off by a chainlink fence.

At a Labor Day barbecue, when Gabriel's sister, Clarissa, heard him say, "Moly-be-damned," she asked him, "Ever think about what goes into your rifle barrels?"

Gabriel pulled his chin. He wrote letters to several gun companies, and after he received their replies he sold two of his rifles. For good measure he also traded in a favorite knife and junked the bumpers on his car. That satisfied him for awhile but also allowed him, now that his conscience was clear, to hate the mine with a greater passion. And the part of the mine he hated the most was the guardian.

The guardian was gray and looked like a tank. It had caterpillar treads, a blocky conning tower and two oblong ports that shone with an eerie red glow. It hummed and whirred as it made its rounds over the mountain. The guardian was a computerized sentry, and when it spotted a person without a sensex badge it flashed its ports, raised a siren and pursued the trespasser with its radar. A helicopter patrol, linked to the guardian's radar, soon swooped down upon the culprit and took him into custody.

The mine had caught several hikers, one saboteur and a woman who preferred to be called an "eco-raider." Last fall, after crossing the fenceline to hunt partridge with Sam, Gabriel had met the guardian and had his first ride in a helicopter. Sam had run home.

Gabriel didn't sleep well afterwards. At night the guardian's siren would wake him, its light would glare on the ceiling of his bedroom, and he would shiver thinking of it rolling over the nests of partridges, the empty coyote dens and under the crags where the eagles had built their nest. In Gabriel's dreams the guardian came up to his window and pulled him outside. Holding him on the ground, it rolled its treads over his face.

"Join the Sierra Club," said Clarissa when Gabriel complained that he'd been having these dreams for six months.

He eyed the application blank she held out to him.

"Go ahead," she said. ""It won't bite you."

He took the application blank and filled it out. He put on a stamp, kissed his sister good-bye and walked right past her mailbox. When he got home he locked Sam in his kennel and carefully removed his elephant gun from the rack.

He walked around the backside of the mountain until he found a hole under the fence. Gabriel then crawled up through the gama grass and the lodgepole, up through the duff, the pine cones and bracken, the resin smell fading as the sun went down. He had five elephant cartridges in loops on his shirt. He loaded two, like an old elephant hunter, and began to walk through the meadows and stands of fir, looking for the guardian.

He smelled it first—the acrid odor of clustered electronic machinery, like a computer room on the move. He followed, upwind, crossed a streambed and saw a single track in the mud. Gabriel pinched off some blades of grass and tossed them in the air. A crossing breeze; he followed, contouring around the mountain.

Ahead, where a sandy wash came down from the mountaintop, he found the tracks again and knelt by them. On the sand was a dark spatter of greenish fluid, two spots, a third smaller. Gabriel touched the spots with his finger and brought the odor to his nose. The fluid was still warm. He began to walk faster, but quietly, very quietly, placing each foot stealthily down, in control, sensing the duff, the dead twig, the lose rock, his heart racing. His eyes were wide, moving—so wide while his head was still. A jay called once, twice, and cackled. A shadow moved in the trees. It was dusk, half light, and details were blurred. On the drift of the breeze came the acrid smell. Gabriel's hands began to sweat. He walked a half-dozen steps and felt the ground begin to vibrate on his right. He whirled. The guardian's red eyes glared and it bounced, coming fast.

Gabriel raised his elephant gun, aimed between the eyes, and as the guardian reared above him, siren wailing, he fired. There was a triple-toned bellow, like thunder on an August afternoon. Gabriel worked the bolt and took a step back. The guardian stopped, conning tower twisting back and forth while thin gray smoke came from beneath its treads and one eye blinked, the other dark. Gabriel aimed for the blinking eye and fired. The guardian's conning tower stopped and its treads clanked once. With a long-drawn-out fizzle, the guardian sighed.

Gabriel didn't reload. He went up to the sentry; he walked slowly around it; he stood in front of it and reached out and touched its smooth cool skin. Then he gave its tread a thoughtful kick and started out toward home.

• • •

"Aren't you ready yet?" Harry asked impatiently.

It was Sunday, Harry and Gabriel's skeet-shooting day. They were in Gabriel's den.

"Give me another second," replied Gabriel, fetching a cleaning rod.

Harry picked up a magazine from the coffee table and said, "Hey, did you hear about the guy who shot the guardian?"

"No! Really?"

"Yep, put it right out of commission."

Gabriel looked up. "Must have been some eco-nut," he said, running one last patch through his elephant gun.

••• A freelance writer, Jack Kulpa wrote for the magazine throughout the 1980s and early 90s. His powers of observation were always appreciated by readers; he often wrote about inexplicable phenomena. —MAY 1985 •••

THE MIST PEOPLE

by Jack Kulpa

Almost everyone who has traveled the old canoe routes of the North has heard it at one time or another: the sounds and voices of people who weren't there.

It happens most often at night, after the campfire burns to embers and the tent flaps are sealed against the dark. Then, just as the images of dreams begin darting out at you from sleep, a corner of your consciousness catches the low murmur of voices, barely audible above the roar of a rapids or the sound of the wind in the trees. You listen, lying awake and alert, trying to make out the words. But the whispers remain vague and indistinct, as shadowy as the man in the moon.

The old French fur traders who first explored the Lake Superior region credited these incidents to "the mist people"—supernatural beings who haunted wild places. Known also as "the huntsmen" or "the voices of the rapids," the phenomenon usually occurred near places of quick water, and it was here where entire camps were often routed from sleep by the sounds of phantoms passing through the night.

In their search for fur and the fabled Northwest Passage, the voyageurs dared to go where no white man had ever trod. In the 200 years following Etienne Brulé's discovery of Lake Superior in 1623, these intrepid explorers traveled by canoe, braving hostile Indians, unmapped rivers and attacks by rival traders. They chose life in the wilderness over a relatively comfortable existence in the villages along the St. Lawrence River from which many of them came. When asked why, their answer was always the same: "It is the riddles that make life the adventure it was meant to be."

But that was long ago. Today, the voyageurs and much of their beloved wilderness are only a memory, banished to oblivion by a world that has no use for mystery and mirage. Yet, along the old canoe routes of those early explorers, modern-day travelers still hear the mist people murmuring in the dark.

One such place is the Brule River, a tea-colored ribbon of wild and brooding water that lies at the southwest corner of Lake Superior. Presently known as a top-notch whitewater trout stream, the Brule was once a major route of the fur trade.

One night in early May I camped along the river after having spent the day fishing its frigid water. Too tired to pitch the tent, I rolled up in my blankets beside the campfire, shut my eyes and listened to the sounds of the forest—the call of an owl, the sputter of the fire, the sound of the river below. I could feel consciousness slipping away like beads of water rolling down a taut line, when—*thump*—something in the darkness startled me.

I sat up, straining to hear what it was. And then, faint but clearly audible above the sound of a nearby shallow rapids, came the musical murmur of voices.

It was little more than muffled maundering but distinct enough so that there could be no mistaking what it was: a group of men on the river below my camp talking and laughing.

Bump. As I listened to the sound of them dragging their canoes ashore, I was certain it was the group of canoeists I had met earlier in the day. I rolled out of my blankets and put the coffee on the fire, expecting guests at any moment. But when I went down to the river to greet them, there was only the moonlight on the water and the river chinking against the rocks like glass chimes in the wind.

Was it my imagination? Perhaps. And yet, ever since Radisson and Groseilliers first explored the country beyond the Chequamegon Bay in 1659, white travelers to the region have reported hearing the voices. One thing is sure about the existence of the mist people, whether they be the actual whispers of phantoms or the sound of wind and water playing tricks: Nothing in the North is more fantastically unreal to tell about, and yet, when heard, nothing is more astonishingly real.

Curiously enough, veterans of the voyageurs' brigades were seldom alarmed by the mist people. In fact, the mist people rendered impressions of the life voyageurs had left behind: the stony walls of a French town, the bustling marketplace, narrow streets filled with the gay laughter of peasants, the toll of church bells on a sunny Sunday morning. Seldom did the mist people speak of heartache and struggle. As one writer noted, it was as if "The nations of the earth whisper to their exiled sons through the voices of the rapids . . . Perhaps this is the great Mother's compensation in a harsh mode of life."

And yet, eerie adventures can occur whenever the mist people speak. A friend of mine likes to tell of how he heard the ghosts along the Yellow Dog River near Lake Independence, and how, at that instant, a silver-tipped black bear soundlessly walked through his camp, its coat glittering like a constellation of stars in the moonlight. Another time, not far from the old voyageurs' place of rendezvous at Grand Portage, an owl roosted from the ridgepole of our tent. I watched as the horny talons pierced the taut canvas. Even now I can remember how that menacing claw felt cold to the touch, and how, each time I raised a finger to stroke it, the big bird would suddenly bolt away into the dark, always returning to roost the moment I began drifting off to sleep again.

Strangest of all was a night I spent on the remote East Fork of the Chippewa River. We made camp at the rapids below Pelican Lake, and all through the night some large, snarling beast kept circling the tent whenever the campfire dimmed, its guttural sounds unlike anything I had ever heard. In the morning, in a popple copse behind the tent, I found the near-fossilized jawbone of some monstrous animal. It looked as though it had come from a grotesque wolf, the elongated fangs curling back on themselves like tusks. But the bone was huge— twice the size of any wolf's skull I had ever seen—and I was sure that what I was looking at was the remains of some predatory animal that had stalked the mists when mammoths and mastodons still roamed the earth.

Years later I met an Indian at Sand Bay who had had similar experiences. I told him about what I had heard that night and how I had found the strange bone the next morning. The Indian nodded as I talked, but in the end, he too was at a loss to explain things.

"I've heard the ghosts many times," he said, "but I can't tell you what they are. My grandfather probably would have said you were given an omen, but I don't think anybody nowadays knows what such a thing means."

I keep that bone on a shelf where I can always look at it, and each time I do I find myself back on the Chippewa River as phantom creatures snarl at me from the dark. I keep promising myself that someday I'll take the bone to a museum and have it identified, but I know I never will. I'm afraid some paleontologist will look at it and see only a bone, and hear nothing of the strange beasts and beings who called to me from the mists that night.

For some reason, many people never hear the phantoms; this was true even in the voyageurs' time. From all accounts, an experience with the mist people depended on why a man was drawn to the woods and what he hoped to find there.

I learned this during the winter I lived alone in the Iron River country. The cabin had no telephone, no TV, no radio, no link at all to the world of other men, but it was exactly the kind of place I had been seeking.

I wanted the chance to live alone in the woods, to experience the kind of solitude few people ever know today. Most of all, I wanted to find out if I had missed something about life for never having lived it in solitude, and if time spent alone in a wild place could reveal any secrets about myself that I never knew or suspected. But after the first few days, the novelty of living like a recluse began to wear thin, and as the weeks passed I began to actually ache for the sound of another human voice.

"You'll go crazy livin' alone," an old trapper had warned me. "We'll find you at springtime, nutty as a pecan pie." I had laughed at the remark in November, but by the end of March I no longer remembered what I had found so funny.

Luckily, breakup occurred early that year, and by the first of April the woods were roaring with swollen rivers. And then one night, while lying half awake in my bunk with the windows opened, I heard the mist people speak.

At first I was apprehensive. I had heard tales of mad trappers and other backwoods hermits who, in solitude, had heard and then surrendered to the dark side of the voices. I expected to hear the malevolent whispers of demons; yet, when curiosity finally won out, there were only the sunny sounds of human life in motion.

Soon I began looking forward to the time I could spend lying awake in my bunk listening to the murmurs from the river below. I would hear the sound of children playing outdoors on a warm summer evening; at other times it was the bright, nervous laughter of young women discussing men; some nights it was the good-natured banter of close friends on an outing; but always when I went to investigate, I found only the river and the mist.

Another man might have convinced himself that he was going crazy, but I heard only echoes of a life I had left behind. Haunted by the loneliness of my own self-imposed exile, I heard the voices of the rapids as the voyageurs had: "A gift from the great Mother, her compensation in a harsh mode of life."

Since then I have heard the mist people call many times and in many places, each time telling me something about wild places and why I am drawn to them. Like the old adventurers who first explored the North in birchbark canoes, I too am a voyageur, searching for a Northwest Passage of my own. And it's when I'm in the wild places, on those soundless, misty nights, after the tent flaps are sealed and the campfire is only embers, that I sometimes think, I've almost found the way.

But then, in those moments, the mist people always speak.

I know it's an omen, but I can't divine the meaning. As the Indian said, no one nowadays knows what such things mean. Still, I lie awake in my blankets and listen. Like the jawbone I keep on a shelf, it's the riddles—and never the answers—that make life the adventure it was meant to be.

••• Contributing editor Jim Harrison has published eight collections of poetry and six novels, including WOLF, SUNDOG *and* A GOOD DAY TO DIE, *plus three collections of novellas, one of which,* LEGENDS OF THE FALL, *was released as a movie in 1995. His irreverence for convention shows through in this "sermon."*—JUNE 1994 •••

A SPRING SERMON . . . OR SIBERIA

by Jim Harrison

Long before I understood what it meant, the vernal equinox was my most important annual holiday. I think I was 14 when I realized that I tended to go haywire—the current word is "depression"—during the dark winter months in northern Michigan. But around the middle of March and onward, the sap began to rise again. What is now called "seasonal affective disorder" is so widespread in northern climes that only the severest cases are recognizable. Sigurd begins to sob and rams his head through the glass of the jukebox to get closer to the music. That sort of thing.

Survival arrives in the new quality of light, even beneath close cloud cover. I have been reminded countless times that my home area receives less sunlight than any other place in the United States except a specific area in the Pacific Northwest. All of us think our weather is unique; some actually is.

By early April, spring fever is palpable as a barn fire, a kind of interior mange, whose itch is forever out of reach of any salve except physical exhaustion. I have long since stopped sorting my fishing tackle a month before the trout opener, as my father did. It only makes things worse. The ears perk up instinctively for new bird arrivals, and the somewhat pathetic crocuses and skunk cabbage are a welcome sight. It doesn't matter that it snows on trout opener in late April or that the streams are turbid from the runoff. Even the whine of the first mosquito makes the heart glad.

By May it is time to address certain criminal activities, in which I too have been a guilty party. Put aside this magazine. Go to your freezer. How much and what kind of fish and game do you have left in there from the previous summer and fall getting freezer burn? Write it down and subtract it as penance from your bag limit this summer and fall.

If you're not going to prepare the game properly and eat it, don't shoot it. The bird carcasses and fish fillets you take to the dump during spring cleaning represent an unnatural act against the natural world. Pluck your birds, don't skin them. Don't breast ducks, use the whole bird. Otherwise, let it fly on. Our imagined dominion over the natural world, an offshoot of our illusions about manifest destiny, is exhausting our wild lands to the degree that our grandchildren will be stuck with only Nintendo and spectator sports. If you insist on going for numbers, stick to the skeet range or commercial trout ponds, or play the state lottery.

See how much you can do on foot. The sharp reductions of fish and game populations through hunting and fishing are invariably related to mechanization. Unfortunately, our government, when it offers up timber leases, does not demand that log roads be destroyed after cutting. Easy access means diminished quality, even in love.

Don't leave a trace of yourself in the wilds, whether on water or in the forest. The shores of the Great Lakes are lined with detritus on which perch cormorants, whose beaks have been distorted grotesquely by chemical pollution. Strangely, even the fitness-buff sportsmen I know who have cross-trained themselves to a frazzle like to drive the last foot to their destination. I have noticed on my own property that if there's a branch on the road, no one hesitates to expand the road. Traces you shouldn't leave behind also include the piles of bait and garbage that lure mammals into shooting range.

Outdoors writers are fond of prating that "a few bad apples spoil it for the rest of us." Perhaps—if 10 percent comprises "a few"; that is roughly the same percentage of malevolently incompetent doctors and lawyers. We have discovered a principle here. Sadly, we could all do much better. If the writer of the outdoors column in your local newspaper betrays real ignorance of botany, forestry, ornithology, game biology and riverine morphology, holler until the paper hires a better one. It no longer suits our survival as sportsmen to indulge those bumbling sentimentalists and their tales of the old man and the boy and the dog and the 10-point swamp buck that gores the 10-pound brown trout while the American eagle hovered over the $10,000 worth of Japanese equipment the writer got as freebies for touting the stuff.

Another part of your spring coda might be to get involved—no matter your political leanings—in local environmental groups. It is in your interest as an outdoorsman to defend the integrity of your own backyard, your own bioregion, your prized watersheds. And remember that the land rapers of a dozen varieties are always waving their American flags to get themselves off the hook. This sort of patriotism is always the last refuge of scoundrels, as Samuel Johnson pointed out. A couple of thousand wolves roam freely in Minnesota, but to date not a single one has been reintroduced into Yellowstone Park for fear it might nail a cow or two on the surrounding, largely public, grazing lands. You can pay a couple hundred grand in federal taxes, but if you offer a modest suggestion, these entitled freeloaders will call you a tree hugger. The whole notion of "multiuse" public lands will continue to be a scandal as long as the policy is directed by cows and chain saws. I have no objection to grazing on public lands as long as the notorious abuses the government freely permits are corrected. In the end, if sportsmen don't firmly align themselves with centrist environmentalists, we'd better raise a big kitty and buy Siberia.

♦♦♦ *Terry McDonell, the current editor and publisher of* SPORTS
AFIELD, *came to the magazine in 1994 from* ESQUIRE. *Prior to that,
he edited* ROLLING STONE, OUTSIDE, SMART *and* ROCKY MOUNTAIN
*magazines, the last two of which he founded. He speaks of a new
hunting ethos.*—AUGUST 1995 ♦♦♦

WHO WE ARE

by Terry McDonell

Our politicians used to be hunters. Our Presidents wrote books bragging about their exploits. Today, candidates spend brief moments in the field holding shotgun or rod aloft to television cameras, hunting and fishing for votes.

There are still real sportsmen and -women in America, of course, but we are not seen clearly. The media are increasingly cartooned with negative stereotypes of hunters and fishers and this hurts us all. We do not resemble bit players in the film *Deliverance.* We are not mean-spirited "rednecks" or drunken "bubbas" or crazy "hillbillies," and we are tired of offhanded references to Bambi. We spend more time in the woods than anyone, and we live in a food chain we understand. We husband our game.

We also pay the bills. Each day, through license revenues, excise taxes and other income sources like Duck Stamps, sportsmen contribute $3 million to wildlife conservation efforts—over $1.5 billion a year. Through over 10,000 private groups and organizations (such as Ducks Unlimited, Pheasants Forever and the Rocky Mountain Elk Foundation) we contribute an additional $300 million. Shrinking wildlife habitat is our issue and effective game management is our goal. No wonder we bristle when some fashion model or lobbyist accuses us of murder for thinning herds that would otherwise be decimated by winter-kill.

Nothing about hunting is simple, least of all the mind of the predator. Not to recognize this is to miss the point of a new hunting ethos that is as strong in the deer and elk camps of Pennsylvania and Wyoming as it is dimly perceived in the plastic shoe section of Bloomingdale's and the health food bistros of South Beach. The men and women in those hunting camps are after much more than their quarry and they are fed up with not being recognized as the strongest and most dedicated conservationists in the country.

Lately we have all become even more frustrated with talk show patter about how dangerous we are. We do not join militias or blow up government buildings. We look at gun control as an urban/rural issue and do not understand why the shotgun our grandfathers used to teach us to hunt (perhaps the Browning Auto-5 or the Remington 1100) is functionally identical to many on the list of banned assault weapons. Yet many of us agree that waiting periods and personal background checks are good safeguards to attach to firearm purchases.

The wilderness thrills us and gives us life, and while we nurture the traditions of our grandfathers and grandmothers, we are saddened by what we anticipate for our grandchildren. Sometimes, sitting silently in the forest or climbing into the mountains, it occurs to us that we do not want to go home because we have begun to think of ourselves as an endangered species.

The hell with that.